Lecture Notes in Computer Science 5134

Commenced Publication in 1973
Founding and Former Series Editors:
Gerhard Goos, Juris Hartmanis, and Jan van Leeuwen

T0223239

Nikita Borisov   Ian Goldberg (Eds.)

Privacy Enhancing Technologies

8th International Symposium, PETS 2008
Leuven, Belgium, July 23-25, 2008
Proceedings

 Springer

Volume Editors

Nikita Borisov
University of Illinois at Urbana-Champaign
Department of Electrical and Computer Engineering
1308 West Main St., Urbana, IL 61801-2307, USA
E-mail: nikita@uiuc.edu

Ian Goldberg
University of Waterloo
David R. Cheriton School of Computer Science
200 University Avenue West, Waterloo, ON N2L 3G1, Canada
E-mail: iang@cs.uwaterloo.ca

Library of Congress Control Number: 2008930436

CR Subject Classification (1998): H.5, H.4, H.3, I.2, I.3, I.7, J.5

LNCS Sublibrary: SL 4 – Security and Cryptology

ISSN   0302-9743
ISBN-10   3-540-70629-1 Springer Berlin Heidelberg New York
ISBN-13   978-3-540-70629-8 Springer Berlin Heidelberg New York

Typesetting: Camera-ready by author, data conversion by Scientific Publishing Services, Chennai, India
Printed on acid-free paper   SPIN: 12436453   06/3180   5 4 3 2 1 0

Foreword

The 8th Privacy Enhancing Technologies Symposium was held at the Katholieke Universiteit Leuven during July 23–25, 2008. This year completed the transition from workshop to symposium, with a printed proceedings published before the symposium. PETS remains a premier venue for publishing original research on privacy-enhancing technologies. PETS received 48 submissions, each of which was reviewed by at least four members of the Program Committee. Thirteen were accepted into the program, maintaining the selective and competitive nature of the event. The program also included a keynote address by Stuart Shapiro.

A new feature this year was the HotPETs session, designed to balance the desire for rigorous scientific quality of the PETS program and the need for a venue to present work that is not yet fully developed. HotPETs accepted submissions on the hottest, most exciting new ideas and put together an excellent program of presentations.

PETS was once again collocated with the IAVoSS Workshop on Trustworthy Elections (WOTE 2008), with a full day of plenary sessions. In addition, three other privacy-related events were held at K.U. Leuven during the same week, enabling greater exchange of ideas among the respective communities: the closing event of the Privacy and Identity Management for Europe (PRIME) project, a workshop presenting the results from the Advanced Applications for Electronic Identity Cards (ADAPID) project, and a working session of the Future of Identity in the Information Society (FIDIS) Workpackage 13.

The Program Chairs would like to thank, first of all, the authors and speakers for their contribution to the content of the symposium. We would also like to thank the Program Committee for their hard work of a month of reviews and two more weeks of intense discussions, helping to ensure a program of high scientific quality. Moreover, we want to acknowledge the contribution of external reviewers who assisted the Program Committee with the reviews. We want to express a special thanks to the "shepherds," who continued their work after the main review period, working with authors to improve the quality of the final paper versions that appear in the proceedings: Claudia Diaz, Apu Kapadia, Steven J. Murdoch, Carmela Troncoso, Patrick Tsang, and Matthew Wright.

Our General Chair, Claudia Diaz, did an outstanding job taking care of the local arrangements, working with the organizers of the four collocated events, and making sure the symposium ran smoothly. We are also grateful to the Computer Security and Industrial Cryptography (COSIC) group at K.U. Leuven for helping host the symposium. We would also like to thank Jeremy Clark for designing and maintaining the PETS 2008 website. We thank the HotPETs Chairs, Roger Dingledine, Thomas Heydt-Benjamin and Len Sassaman, for organizing that part of the symposium. We are very grateful to the organizers of our collocated events for their parts in coordinating with PETS: Olivier Pereira, Karel

Wouters, Carmela Troncoso, and Vashek Matyas. Finally, we are very grateful for the generous support of Microsoft, who provided student stipends and the cash award for the PET Prize, EU FIDIS Network of Excellence who provided stipends to FIDIS students, and the Office of the Information and Privacy Commissioner of Ontario, who provided the PET Prize statue.

May 2008   Nikita Borisov
                                                              Ian Goldberg

Organization

Organizers

General Chair	Claudia Diaz (K.U. Leuven, Belgium)
Program Chairs	Nikita Borisov (University of Illinois at Urbana–Champaign, USA)
	Ian Goldberg (University of Waterloo, Canada)
PET Prize	Matthew Wright (University of Texas at Arlington, USA)
Stipends	Roger Dingledine (The Tor Project, USA)
HotPETs Chairs	Roger Dingledine (The Tor Project, USA)
	Thomas Heydt-Benjamin (IBM Research Zurich, Switzerland)
	Len Sassaman (K.U. Leuven, Belgium)

Program Committee

Alessandro Acquisti (Carnegie Mellon University, USA)
Mikhail Atallah (Purdue University, USA)
Michael Backes (Saarland University, Germany)
Mira Belenkiy (Brown University and Microsoft, USA)
Alastair Beresford (University of Cambridge, UK)
Lorrie Cranor (Carnegie Mellon University, USA)
George Danezis (Microsoft Research Cambridge, UK)
Claudia Diaz (K.U. Leuven, Belgium)
Roger Dingledine (The Tor Project, USA)
Simson Garfinkel (Naval Postgraduate School, USA)
Philippe Golle (Palo Alto Research Center, USA)
Rachel Greenstadt (Harvard University, USA)
Thomas Heydt-Benjamin (IBM Research Zurich, Switzerland)
Apu Kapadia (Dartmouth College, USA)
Bradley Malin (Vanderbilt University, USA)
David Martin (University of Massachusetts at Lowell, USA)
Nick Mathewson (The Tor Project, USA)
David Molnar (University of California, Berkeley, USA)
Steven J. Murdoch (University of Cambridge, UK)
Andreas Pfitzmann (Dresden University of Technology, Germany)
Andrei Serjantov (The Free Haven Project, UK)
Paul Syverson (Naval Research Laboratory, USA)
Gene Tsudik (University of California, Irvine, USA)
Matthew Wright (University of Texas at Arlington, USA)
Rebecca Wright (Rutgers University, USA)

External Reviewers

Mike Bergmann
Stefan Berthold
Rainer Böhme
Sebastian Clauß
Matt Edman
Karim Eldefrawy
Andrew D. Gordon
Catalin Hritcu
Stanislaw Jarecki
Wei Jiang
Aaron Johnson
Boris Koepf
Stefan Köpsell
Karsten Loesing

Di Ma
Matteo Maffei
Nayantara Mallesh
Sasha Romanosky
Michael Roe
Len Sassaman
John Solis
Claudio Soriente
Sandra Steinbrecher
Carmela Troncoso
Patrick Tsang
Ersin Uzun
Lasse Øverlier

Table of Contents

Analyzing PETs for Enterprise Operations

Stuart Shapiro[1] and Aaron Powell[2]

[1] Principal Information Privacy and Security Engineer
[2] Information Security Engineer
The MITRE Corporation
POC: Stuart Shapiro
+1-781-271-4676
sshapiro@mitre.org

Enterprises (large, often highly distributed organizations) in both the private and public sectors are increasingly recognizing the need to comprehensively address privacy risk. This entails, as it does for information security, a systematic combination of people, processes, and technology. However, while establishing roles and processes governing the management of personally identifiable information (PII) can be done fairly readily (assuming availability of the necessary expertise and experience), finding and deploying appropriate *enterprise* technology—commercial or open source—is proving more problematic. A technological model targeted at enterprises (i.e., data stewards) differs from one targeted at individuals (i.e., data subjects). However, the privacy-enhancing technology research community has tended to focus more on the latter than on the former. Furthermore, various enterprise technologies exist with capabilities that can support privacy, even if not specifically intended to do so. We have adopted the term privacy-*enabling* technologies (PETs) to denote the expansiveness of this field.

This presentation will begin with a discussion of some of the drivers behind enterprise approaches to privacy risk management, with emphasis on developments within the U.S. federal government (MITRE's Privacy Practice supports a variety of government sponsors) and, in particular, within the U.S. Intelligence Community (IC). In addition to the difficulties of implementing in a modern technological environment the privacy protections mandated by the so-called "U.S. Persons Rules," the development of the IC's Information Sharing Environment (ISE) has prompted greater attention to the need for enterprise technologies to address privacy risk. (In the Fall of 2006, the IC held a series of workshops on privacy protection technologies, a report on which has recently been released.) Following discussion of these drivers, we will consider a categorization scheme for commercially-available enterprise PETs, map those categories to generic PII governance processes they can support, and draw out the implications of potential gaps. The presentation will conclude by briefly exploring the notion of a privacy-enabled architecture as an organizing concept for PETs within an enterprise.

N. Borisov and I. Goldberg (Eds.): PETS 2008, LNCS 5134, p. 1, 2008.

Perfect Matching Disclosure Attacks

Carmela Troncoso, Benedikt Gierlichs, Bart Preneel, and Ingrid Verbauwhede

K.U. Leuven, ESAT/SCD-COSIC, IBBT
Kasteelpark Arenberg 10, B-3001 Leuven-Heverlee, Belgium
firstname.lastname@esat.kuleuven.be

Abstract. Traffic analysis is the best known approach to uncover relationships amongst users of anonymous communication systems, such as mix networks. Surprisingly, all previously published techniques require very specific user behavior to break the anonymity provided by mixes. At the same time, it is also well known that none of the considered user models reflects realistic behavior which casts some doubt on previous work with respect to real-life scenarios. We first present a user behavior model that, to the best of our knowledge, is the least restrictive scheme considered so far. Second, we develop the Perfect Matching Disclosure Attack, an efficient attack based on graph theory that operates without any assumption on user behavior. The attack is highly effective when de-anonymizing mixing rounds because it considers all users in a round at once, rather than single users iteratively. Furthermore, the extracted sender-receiver relationships can be used to enhance user profile estimations. We extensively study the effectiveness and efficiency of our attack and previous work when de-anonymizing users communicating through a threshold mix. Empirical results show the advantage of our proposal. We also show how the attack can be refined and adapted to different scenarios including pool mixes, and how precision can be traded in for speed, which might be desirable in certain cases.

1 Introduction

Traffic analysis exploits traffic data to infer information about observed communications. It is the most powerful known attack against anonymous networks. More precisely, Disclosure (or Intersection) attacks use the fact that users' communication patterns are repetitive to uncover communication relationships between them [1,4].

Previous work on Disclosure Attacks [1,4,5] considers a very simplistic model, where users send messages to a fixed set of contacts through a threshold mix. Users choose amongst their communication partners with uniform probability and the effectiveness of these attacks strongly relies on this model. In this paper we present a new attack, the Perfect Matching Disclosure Attack, that requires no assumption on the users' behavior in order to reveal their relationships. Besides its capability to uncover relations amongst users, *i.e.* their sending profiles, in an arbitrary scenario, we demonstrate the strength of our attack in de-anonymizing individual messages, *i.e.* finding the links between messages arriving to the network and messages leaving it. Our method's advantage stems from the fact that it considers all users in a round at once, rather than single users iteratively. This approach is likely to de-anonymize a large fraction of the set correctly in scenarios where a per user approach fails with high probability.

We analyze and compare the Statistical Disclosure Attack (SDA) and the Perfect Matching Disclosure Attack (PMDA) empirically in two scenarios. In both scenarios, we chose a simple threshold mix as communication channel such that we can focus on presenting our techniques. With respect to a simple user behavior model we observe that the SDA and the PMDA perform very similar. In a generic user model the PMDA outperforms the SDA for a limited increase of computational cost. Simulation results show that our method is more accurate when linking senders and receivers of de-anonymized messages and that it allows to derive better estimations of users' profiles. We also propose the Normalized SDA, a trade-off between precision and speed, which yields results nearly as good as the PMDA with a running time slightly higher than the one of the original SDA.

This paper is organized as follows. Section 2 provides an overview of the state-of-the-art of attacks on mix networks. We explain the system model and our models for user behavior in Sect. 3. Section 4 describes the mathematical background for our attack and its application to a threshold mix. In Sect. 5 we show how our attack and the SDA can be applied in practice. An evaluation of both methods is presented in Sect. 6. We explain in Sec. 7 how to construct enhanced user profiles while Sect. 8 deals with further improvements and variants of the PMDA. Finally, we pose some open questions and conclude in Sect. 9.

2   Related Work

Mixes were proposed by David Chaum [3]. Chaum's proposal consists of a router that receives a number of messages of fixed length, performs some cryptographic operations on them changing their appearance and outputs the result in a random order. This ensures that linking inputs and outputs based on timing information is impossible. Mixes can be combined in networks, such that even if a mix is compromised, the user's anonymity is guaranteed. They are widely used in the literature to implement anonymous email [6,17] or e-voting protocols [11,14].

Although mix networks provide good anonymity, they are vulnerable to long-term traffic analysis attacks. An attacker who observes a mix network can collect what is called traffic data: the identities of the messages' senders and receivers, together with the timing of these events. The family of Disclosure Attacks [1,12] aims at identifying users' communication patterns. It is assumed that the participants communicate through a threshold mix. This mix collects a certain number of messages per round, and outputs them in a random order. Applying the Disclosure Attack, an adversary observing the mix, *i.e.* senders and receivers per round, over enough time can uncover the set of Alice's friends. Nevertheless, the Disclosure Attack is very expensive, as it relies on solving an NP-problem and is only feasible for very small systems. A more efficient approach to obtain the exact solution, the Hitting Set Attack was proposed in [13].

Danezis presents a different efficient approach, the Statistical Disclosure Attack [4], which reveals the most likely set of Alice's friends using statistical methods and approximations assuming the same model as in [1]. The attack model was extended to include anonymous replies in [5] and tó consider a pool mix instead of a threshold mix in [7]. More complex models are analyzed and tested by simulation in [16]. Besides discovering a user's set of friends, Danezis proposes in [4] to use Alice's sending profile derived in the attack to individually trace each of the messages she sends to the network.

An approach to measure anonymity has been developed independently by Edman et al. and was recently published in [9]. It is to some extent related to our work as it applies the same fundamental notions of graph theory and optimization problems. However, the goals of their and our work are different. Edman et al. argue that anonymity metrics reflecting the perspective of a single user have certain defects and define a metric that, as they claim, benchmarks the system as a whole. However, they also make clear that their metric is only supposed to complement entropy based metrics and that it can not express the degree of anonymity provided to a single user.

By contrast, we look at mix networks and the anonymity they provide from an adversarial point of view. We derive a robust attack that does not rely on an assumption about the user behavior and focus on pinpointing the success probability of an adversary.

Although the work of Edman et al. is supposed to support system designers while our approach clearly reflects the adversarial side, both works have, to some extent, a common conclusion: whether it is to measure anonymity or to derive strong attack methodologies — considering the perspective of a single user is not good enough. At the same time the works are separate. Their metric is not self-contained and cannot express some necessary aspects of anonymity. Therefore, it can only complement previously derived information-theoretic metrics. We seek to put our proposal into context, empirically rate it against previous work, and show that it is superior in relevant and generic scenarios.

3   System and User Models

In this section we introduce our notation to describe anonymous channels and propose a new generic user model.

Consider a set of users U of cardinality u. We define the sending profile of a user $x \in U$, say x is Alice, as the probability distribution $\mathbb{P}_{Alice}$ of the same size. A given element of the distribution expresses the probability that Alice sends a message to a given user $y \in U$, say y is Bob. So for example, $\mathbb{P}_{Alice}(Bob)$ is the probability that Alice sends a message with Bob. The distribution as a whole describes Alice's sending behavior with respect to the entire population (including herself). For completeness, we note that $\sum_y \mathbb{P}_x(y) = 1$ for all x. As done in previous work [5], we model the sending rate of each individual user

$x \in U$ as a Poisson distribution with parameter λ_x. Further, we use the following notion of friendship: we say y is a friend of x, if x sends a message to y with non-zero probability. That is, if $\mathbb{P}_x(y) > 0$.

We consider two types of populations. The first one, U_0, is a simple and very restrictive user behavior model. Gradually relaxing assumptions on the number of users' friends and the user sending behavior, we construct a series of populations U_1 to U_5. The latter is the most generic model considered in the literature so far to the best of our knowledge and the second population we deal with in this work. We define the models as follows:

U_0: a single user, Alice, has k randomly selected friends; her sending behavior toward her friends is uniform; $\mathbb{P}_{Alice}$ contains k times the value $\frac{1}{k}$ and $u - k$ times the value zero; all other user profiles contain u times $\frac{1}{u}$;

U_5: every user x has an individual number k_x of friends that is chosen at random; the sending probabilities toward the friends are randomly chosen from a uniform distribution and normalized such that $\sum_y \mathbb{P}_x(y) = 1$ for all x;

The anonymous channel, used by both populations, is modeled as a threshold mix. The mix's sole parameter is the threshold t which defines the number of messages in a round.

3.1   Comparison with Previous Models

The original Disclosure Attack and its first sequels [1,4,13] use a model that is almost equivalent to our model with population U_0. The sole difference is that, in their model, Alice sends exactly one message per round in which she participates, contrary to our model where this limitation does not exist.

Mathewson and Dingledine introduce in [16] a more complex model. First, Alice is allowed to send more than one message per round in which she participates and second, all the participants have a set of friends. Nevertheless, their behavior toward them is still uniform. In some of their experiments they go a step further and let Alice, but not the rest of the users, choose with non-uniform probability amongst her friends, thus obtaining a model a bit closer to our U_5. A recently published attack, the Two-Sided Statistical Disclosure Attack [5], is tested under U_0 traffic and in a variant where all users have the same number of friends to which they send with uniform probability. Both models permit several messages of Alice per round in which she participates. The main drawback of the aforementioned models is their narrowness. With the proposed model U_5 we aim at covering a wider range of scenarios, including previous work.

In particular, U_5 requires no assumption about the number of users that have friends, the number of friends they have, and the sending behavior toward their friends.

4   Mathematical Background

In this section we recapitulate the required basic notions of graph theory and introduce our optimization problem. Then we show how we model a threshold mix using these notions and in particular bipartite graphs. Next, we explain how maximum weighted bipartite matchings can be used to efficiently de-anonymize users communicating through a threshold mix. For further reading about graph theory in an anonymity context we refer the interested reader to [10].

A graph $G = (N, E)$ consists of a set of nodes N and a set of edges E. Without loss of generality we assume $N \neq \emptyset$. A bipartite graph $G = (S \cup R, E)$ is a graph whose nodes can be divided into two distinct sets S and R such that every edge in E connects one node in S and one node in R. In other words, there exists no edge between nodes from the same set. In this paper we focus on sets S and R of equal and finite cardinality $t > 1$. A set of edges $M \subseteq E$ is called a matching in the bipartite graph G if no node in G is incident to more than one edge. A perfect matching additionally requires that every node is incident to exactly one edge. In a weighted bipartite graph G each edge $e_i \in E$ is associated with a weight w_i. Figure 1 illustrates the definitions.

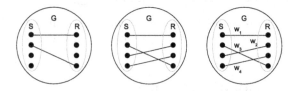

Fig. 1. Bipartite graphs: matching, perfect matching, and perfect matching with weights

A maximum weighted bipartite matching is defined as a perfect matching for which the sum of the weights w_i associated with the edges in the matching has a maximal value, *i.e.* the perfect matching M maximizes $\sum_i w_i | e_i \in M$. If the graph is not complete bipartite, *i.e.* edges which would not violate the requirements of a bipartite graph are missing due to other restrictions, one usually inserts the missing edges with an associated weight of zero. In the rest of this work we focus on maximum weighted bipartite matchings and assume completeness of the graph.

In the literature, finding such matchings is often called the assignment problem. Usually it is assumed that i) the distinct sets of nodes are of equal and finite size and ii) the total weight of the assignment (or matching) is equal to the sum of the weights associated to the edges in the assignment. In this case one deals with a *linear* assignment problem. Algorithms to solve linear assignment problems include the Hungarian algorithm [15] with complexity $\mathcal{O}(N^2 E)$ which can be optimized to $\mathcal{O}(N^2 \log(N) + NE)$, the Bellman-Ford algorithm [2] $\mathcal{O}(N^2 E)$ and the Dijkstra algorithm [8] $\mathcal{O}(N^2 \log(N) + NE)$.

4.1 The Optimization Problem

Let S and R be sets of nodes of cardinality t in a complete bipartite graph $G = (S \cup R, E)$. We define an assignment M as a perfect matching on G. Let

P' be a $t \times t$ matrix containing weights $w_{s,r}$, representing probabilities, for all possible edges $e_{s,r}$ in G. Applying Bayes theorem, the conditional a posteriori probability $p(M|S,R)$ can be computed as

$$p(M|S,R) = \frac{p(S,R|M) \cdot p(M)}{p(S,R)} .$$

Given an assignment M, the sets of nodes S and R are implicitly fixed and thus $p(S,R|M) = 1$. It follows that $p(M|S,R) = p(M)/p(S,R)$. Since the sets S and R are given in the condition, $p(S,R)$ is a constant term and independent of a considered assignment M. Therefore, the assignment M maximizing $p(M)$ also maximizes $p(M|S,R)$.

An assignment M is a perfect matching on G, thus $p(M)$ is the joint probability of the individual edges $e_{s,r} \in M$. Assuming that the edges $e_{s,r} \in M$ are independent, the joint probability $p(M)$ is the product of the individual edge probabilities

$$p(M) = \prod_{e_{s,r} \in M} w_{s,r} .$$

4.2 Mapping to a Threshold Mix

The t messages sent during one round of the mix form the set S. Each node $s \in S$ is labeled with the sender's identity $sen(s)$. That is, two messages from one sender are represented by two different nodes with the same label (note that a node does not represent a specific user, but a message sent by a specific user). Equivalently, the t messages received during one round form the set R where each node r is labeled with the receiver's identity $rec(r)$. An edge $e_{s,r}$ in this graph always connects a sent message s with a received message r, implying that these two messages are the same ($s = r$) and therefore exhibiting the link between sender and receiver. The nodes $S \cup R$ and the edges E form the complete bipartite graph $G = (S \cup R, E)$. A perfect matching M on G links all t sent and received messages.

The weights $w_{s,r}$ associated with the edges $e_{s,r} \in E$ are derived from user profiles $\mathbb{P}_x$. We discuss how to estimate these user profiles and practical issues in a separate section. Recall that for each user x, $\mathbb{P}_x$ describes the sending behavior toward the entire population but, for a given round, only those x and elements of $\mathbb{P}_x$ associated with senders and receivers in the round are of interest. Therefore we derive the $t \times t$ matrix $P'(s,r) := \mathbb{P}_{sen(s)}(rec(r))$, $s \in S, r \in R$.

In the bipartite graph $G = (S \cup R, E)$, an edge $e_{s,r}$ between a message $s \in S$ sent by user $sen(s)$ and a message $r \in R$ received by user $rec(r)$ is associated with $w_{s,r} = P'(s,r)$. Note that a priori the graph is complete bipartite as every sent message can be linked to every received message. If the user profiles exclude certain individuals from the list of possible communication partners due to $\mathbb{P}_{sen(s)}(rec(r)) = 0$, the relation is represented by an edge of weight zero.

In our model, all senders send with the same sending rate such that all combinations of senders $sen(S)$ are equally likely to be observed. Each sender chooses the recipient(s) of her message(s) independently of the choice(s) of all other senders. Further, if a user sends multiple messages, the receivers of these messages are also chosen independently. Therefore, we can model the case that a user sends two (or more) messages by considering her two (or more) distinct senders with identical profiles that each send one message to independently chosen receivers.

Given a round observation, which consists of multisets of senders $sen(S)$ and receivers $rec(R)$, the probability of each assignment M is $\prod_{e_{s,r} \in M} w_{s,r}$. The assignment M maximizing $p(M)$ also maximizes $p(M|S, R)$.

5   Attack Description

In this section we describe the profiling step and the de-anonymization step of the Statistical Disclosure Attack and the improved de-anonymization step of the Perfect Matching Disclosure Attack.

An attacker deploying a Disclosure Attack observes the system during ρ rounds, collecting the identity of the senders and receivers in each of them. We denote $sen(S_i)$ the set of the senders of the t messages arriving to the mix in round i and $rec(R_i)$ the set of the corresponding receivers. We denote the whole set of ρ round observations as the trace $T = (S_i, R_i), 1 \leq i \leq \rho$. We note that both $sen(S_i)$ and $rec(R_i)$ are multisets and may contain repeated elements, meaning that users can send (or receive) more than one message in each round.

5.1   Profiling with the Statistical Disclosure Attack

The SDA, as presented by Danezis in [4], focuses on revealing the *likely* set of friends of a target user, Alice. It was proposed for a scenario very close to our U_0 scenario, where Alice is the only user in the system that has a set of friends ($\mathbb{P}_{Alice}$ contains k positions with value $1/k$ corresponding to her k friends), and the rest of the population choose their recipients uniformly amongst all the users ($\mathbb{P}_{sen(s)}(rec(r)) = \frac{1}{u}$ for all $s \in S, r \in R$, $sen(s) \neq Alice$). The sole difference of Danezis' model with respect to our definition of U_0 is that in his model Alice sends exactly one message per round in which she participates.

In each round where Alice is sending a message, an attacker deploying the SDA considers the probability distribution O of the potential recipients of this message as a combination of the profiles of all the participating senders

$$O = \frac{1}{t}\mathbb{P}_{Alice} + \frac{t-1}{t}\mathbb{P}_x, x \in sen(S_i) \setminus \{Alice\}. \tag{1}$$

For a sufficient number i of observed rounds, the law of large numbers allows to estimate Alice's profile from the empirical mean over the observed rounds:

$$\bar{O} = \frac{1}{t}\sum_i O_i \approx \frac{\mathbb{P}_{Alice} + (t-1)\mathbb{P}_x}{t} \Rightarrow \tilde{\mathbb{P}}_{Alice} \approx t\frac{\sum_i O_i}{t} - (t-1)\mathbb{P}_x. \tag{2}$$

Using the round observations contained in T as input to this method, the attacker estimates the profiles of all the users in the system. We denote the estimated profile of user x obtained in this phase $\tilde{\mathbb{P}}_{x,SDA}$, for each user x in the population, and we denote the whole set of these profiles as $\tilde{\mathbb{P}}_{SDA}$.

5.2   De-anonymization with the Statistical Disclosure Attack

As suggested in [4,5], the estimated profile can be used to rank the potential receivers of a message from Alice according to the likelihood that Alice would send to them. The most likely receiver $rec(r)$ of her message in a round i can thus be easily identified as

$$rec(r) = \text{argmax}_{rec(r)} \ \tilde{\mathbb{P}}_{Alice,SDA}(rec(r)), \ r \in R_i. \tag{3}$$

When de-anonymizing the receivers of several messages in one round, the most obvious, though naïve approach is to repeat this procedure for each individual sent message. Figure 2 depicts the entire de-anonymization process, where the box marked as SDA profiling represents the profiling step described in the previous section, and the output D_{SDA} is the de-anonymization result of the attack.

Fig. 2. De-anonymization with the Statistical Disclosure Attack

5.3   De-anonymization with the Perfect Matching Disclosure Attack

In a nutshell, our idea is to link all messages sent and received during one round such that each message is linked and the joint probability of all links is maximized. Thus, we aim at finding a maximum weighted bipartite matching on the underlying graph, which in terms of algorithmic computer science is an assignment problem. We denote the space of all perfect matchings on the graph G by $\mathcal{M}$ and require that an eligible set of edges belongs to this space, *i.e.* it must be a perfect matching $M \in \mathcal{M}$.

Given the trace T of round observations, the adversary first estimates simple user profiles $\tilde{\mathbb{P}}_{SDA}$ as described in 5.1. Then she uses these profiles to de-anonymize mixing rounds, see Fig. 3. For a round i, she derives the $t \times t$ matrix $P'(s,r) := \tilde{\mathbb{P}}_{sen(s),SDA}(rec(r))$, $s \in S_i, r \in R_i$. The joint probability of all t links in an assignment M is $p_{joint} = \prod_{e_{s,r} \in M} P'(s,r)$.

As derived in Sect. 4.1, the assignment M that maximizes p_{joint} is the adversary's best guess. Note that maximizing p_{joint} does not fit the definition of a linear assignment problem because a maximum weight bipartite matching is achieved by maximizing the *sum* of edge weights in a perfect matching. In order to model our problem as a linear assignment problem one more step has to be taken. To linearize the problem, we replace each element of the matrix $P'(s,r)$ with its logarithmic value $\log_{10}(P'(s,r))$ before associating it to the edge $e_{s,r}$ linking message s to message r.

It is well known that the logarithm is a monotonically ascending function, if the basis is greater than or equal to one. Thus maximizing $\log_{10}(p_{joint})$ is equivalent to maximizing p_{joint}. The advantage is that $\log_{10}(p_{joint})$ can be calculated as a sum

$$\log_{10}(p_{joint}) = log_{10}(\prod_{e_{s,r} \in M} P'(s,r)) = \sum_{e_{s,r} \in M} \log_{10}(P'(s,r)). \qquad (4)$$

Having each edge associated with a log-probability, the assignment problem is linearized and can be solved efficiently. Using as input the matrix P', a suitable algorithm to solve linear assignment problems outputs the most likely sender-receiver combination for all t messages in the round as the perfect matching $M \in \mathcal{M}$. It is a maximum weighted bipartite matching on the graph $G = (S \cup R, E)$ and maximizes p_{joint} for this round. We summarize the approach for one round:

1. sent messages are nodes in S_i and marked with their senders' identities
2. received messages are nodes in R_i and marked with their receivers' identities
3. derive the $t \times t$ matrix: $P'(s,r) := \tilde{\mathbb{P}}_{sen(s),SDA}(rec(r))$, $s \in S_i, r \in R_i$
4. replace $P'(\cdot, \cdot)$ with $\log_{10}(P'(\cdot, \cdot))$
5. solving the linear assignment problem yields the maximum weight bipartite matching M.

Fig. 3. De-anonymization with the Perfect Matching Disclosure Attack

In order to implement the attack, a subtle detail needs to be considered. Taking into account that, before applying the logarithm, $0 \leq P'(\cdot, \cdot) \leq 1$ and that $\log(0)$ is not defined, we need to define $\log(0) = -\infty$ in order for the algorithm to maximize the joint probability. Note however, that i) this case is rarely encountered in practical scenarios unless one has access to very precise user profiles and that ii) replacing 0 with $-\infty$ solely prevents numerical errors and has no influence on the output M of the matching algorithm. Further, some implementations of algorithms for linear assignment problems aim at *minimizing* the sum of the edge weights (*e.g.* costs) in a perfect matching. However, a linear maximization problem can be turned into a linear minimization problem by substituting $P'(\cdot, \cdot) = -P'(\cdot, \cdot)$.

6   Empirical Evaluation of De-anonymization Techniques

In order to evaluate the performance of the Perfect Matching Disclosure Attack, we deploy it in different scenarios and compare it to the original Statistical

Disclosure Attack. Our goal is to study the impact of system parameters on the effectiveness and viability of both attacks.

6.1 Experimental Settings

Our experiments are carried out on populations U of size $u = 1000$ users that send messages through a threshold mix with threshold $t = 100$, ensuring that a considerable fraction of the users participate in each mixing round. Every user $x \in U$ chooses her recipients according to her profile $\mathbb{P}_x$, which depends on the considered user behavior model (see Sect. 3), and initiates communications with the same frequency λ. We note that, given that the attacks need full rounds of mixing, the choice of this parameter's value is arbitrary. As long as all users send messages to the network with equal rate, their frequency of appearance as senders does not depend on the precise sending rate. Although real users are expected to send messages with different frequencies, we chose to fix this parameter in order to create a scenario that allows us to clearly illustrate our techniques.

We study how the number of rounds observed by the attacker affects the performance of the PMDA and the SDA. Both from the adversarial and the designer's points of view, this consists of exploring the effectiveness, efficiency, and scalability of the attacks. For the purpose of our studies we have generated 100 000 mixing rounds. An experiment consists of 1) estimating all user profiles $\tilde{\mathbb{P}}_{SDA}$ from ρ round observations, 2) de-anonymizing 5000 rounds with the SDA, and 3) de-anonymizing the same 5000 rounds with the PMDA (except when $\rho = 1000$, when we only de-anonymized 1000 rounds). Table 1 summarizes the parameters and their values in the experiments.

Table 1. Parameters of the experiments (N=1000, t=100), μ is average number of messages used to profile one user, γ is average number of de-anonymization trials per user

Param \ ρ	1k	5k	10k	25k	50k	100k	Population	N^o of friends k	Profile
μ	100	500	1000	2500	5000	10000	U_0	$\{5, 25, 50\}$	Uniform
γ	100	500	500	500	500	500	U_5	random $[5, 50]$	Non-uniform

6.2 Results

In this section we present the results of our experiments. To measure the effectiveness of the attacks we define two metrics, the *individual success rate* and the *round success rate*. The former expresses the accuracy of the attack when de-anonymizing the receiver of a message from a particular sender, *i.e.* successfully linking a specific sender to a receiver. It is computed by counting how many messages sent by each user in the population have been correctly de-anonymized during the attack, then deriving the success rate per sender by dividing by the number of messages sent by this user. The latter shows the percentage of links correctly de-anonymized per round. We calculate it as the average number of relations successfully identified per round. Both metrics are computed over all 5000 (1000) rounds.

It is important to note that we consider a message as de-anonymized correctly if and only if the attack has identified the receiver of that message correctly. Note that this does not necessarily require to match a sent message to the correct received message. We apply a hard yes/no metric on whether the identity of the matched recipient is correct. This is a more rigorous criterion than the one used in [4,5] where the rank in the sorted probability distribution of potential receivers is taken into account.

Population U_0. We test both attacks in three U_0 populations where Alice has k friends. We look at the influence of the number ρ of rounds used in the profiling step on the success rates of the attacks.

Figure 4 illustrates the individual success rates. As all users except for Alice send uniformly to the entire population, no information can be inferred about them. Therefore the results refer only to Alice's messages and we only consider her individual success rate. We see that the PMDA does not get any advantage in these scenarios, and both attacks score similarly. On the one hand this is due to the lack of information that the rest of senders in the round provide. Since their profile is uniform, they give no hints about who Alice is *not* sending to. On the other hand, Alice chooses uniformly amongst her friends. Therefore, if two or more of her friends appear in the set $rec(R)$, the best the algorithm can do is choose randomly amongst them. This last problem also affects the SDA's effectiveness. One can observe in the graph that, the smaller the number of friends (thus the smaller the probability that this difficulty appears) the higher the success rate of both attacks. The graph shows that in some cases the PMDA performs slightly worse/better than the SDA, but these small differences have no statistical significance.

As expected, increasing the number ρ of rounds to profile users increases the likelihood of successful attacks. It is remarkable, however, that this rate does

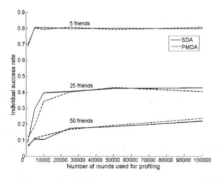
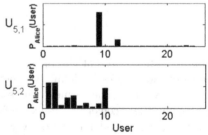

Fig. 4. Individual success rate in a U_0 population

Fig. 5. Alice's profile in a $U_{5,1}$ and $U_{5,2}$ scenario

not increase constantly. When the number of Alice's friends is small ($k = 5$), not much improvement is achieved by increasing the number of profiling rounds above 10 000. Nevertheless, having more rounds helps the attacker when the number of friends increases, as more rounds, in which Alice participates, are needed to observe her sending messages to all of her friends.

Population U_5. For our second set of experiments, we prepared two bench tests, $U_{5,1}$ and $U_{5,2}$, where users had a complex behavior corresponding to U_5 populations. In both cases each user had a random number of friends chosen uniformly from $[5, 50]$. However, the scenarios differ in the way the sending probabilities are distributed amongst these friends. Users corresponding to the $U_{5,1}$ example have a set of contacts where there are one or two very good friends (which they choose as recipients in more than 60% of the cases) and the rest have small probability of being chosen. The users forming the population for the second test, $U_{5,2}$, do not have strong preferences about their contacts, still, their distribution is non-uniform. Figure 5 depicts Alice's profile in the $U_{5,1}$ and $U_{5,2}$ scenarios.

Contrary to the U_0 case, where the SDA and the PMDA performed similarly, the PMDA achieves higher de-anonymization success rates when applied to a U_5 scenario. Figure 6 shows the percentage of users participating in the communication for which the attacks obtain a certain individual success rate in both U_5 scenarios. We represent different values for the number ρ of rounds used for profiling with different line styles.

We see that the PMDA outperforms the SDA in both experiments, but there is a significant difference between them. With respect to the $U_{5,1}$ case (on the left side of the figure) and $\rho = 10\,000$ one can observe that the SDA achieves an average individual success rate of 71.5% while the PMDA scores an average individual success rate of 96.04% and de-anonymizes more than 90% of the messages correctly for 99.6% of the users. With respect to the $U_{5,2}$ case (right side of the figure) and $\rho = 10\,000$ the SDA achieves an average individual success rate of 26% while the PMDA scores 55.35%.

Figure 7 presents the round success rates of the SDA and the PMDA. Like in the individual success rate, our attack outperforms the SDA. In the $U_{5,1}$ case (left), the SDA has a high rate (71.5% in average) of round de-anonymization, whichever is the number of rounds observed. However, the PMDA improves this result de-anonymizing in average 96.05% of the messages in each round when 10 000 rounds have been used for profiling and correctly de-anonymizing the full set of links in 17.22% of the cases. The success of both attacks diminishes when the user's sending patterns tend to be more uniform toward their friends (case $U_{5,2}$, right). For the same number of $\rho = 10\,000$ observed rounds the SDA achieves an average round success rate of 25.6% and the PMDA 55.3%.

It is important to note the influence of the number of rounds observed by the attacker on the success rates of the attacks. Increasing the number of observations makes both attacks more accurate. However, there are notable differences in the effect of this increase depending on the type of population attacked as well as on the attack itself. Analyzing a higher number of rounds provides more

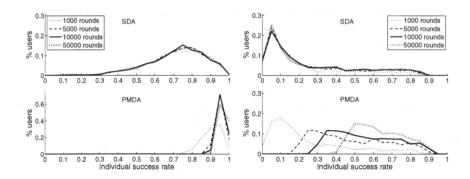

Fig. 6. Individual success rate attacking U_5 populations ($U_{5,1}$ left, $U_{5,2}$ right)

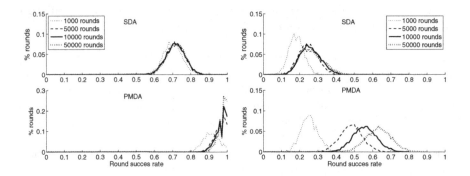

Fig. 7. Round success rate attacking U_5 populations ($U_{5,1}$ left, $U_{5,2}$ right)

information, a fact exploited by the PMDA. On the contrary, the SDA's simple decision algorithm takes little advantage of this extra information and we see that almost no improvement is achieved by observing more than 5000 rounds. Moreover, when the attacks are carried out in a $U_{5,1}$ scenario, the users' profiles have a low entropy, thus the strong friends are early identified and no additional information is extracted from new round observations.

6.3   Scalability of the Attacks

We evaluate the efficiency of both attacks in terms of time. We implemented both attacks in the high-level interpreted language of a commercial numerical computing environment without any optimizations. In our implementation of the PMDA we use the Hungarian algorithm [15] to solve the linear assignment problem of finding the most likely perfect matching between inputs and outputs of the mix. We show in Table 2 the time it takes to carry out all the operations depicted in Fig. 2 for the original SDA and in Fig. 3 for the PMDA in $U_{5,2}$ scenarios with mix thresholds 100, 500 and 1000. In all cases the profiles $\tilde{\mathbb{P}}_{SDA}$

have been derived from $\rho = 50\,000$ rounds and have been used to de-anonymize 5000 rounds (*i.e.*, find the recipients for all s in S_i, $1 \le i \le 5000$). The code for scenarios with threshold 100 and 500 rounds was executed on a machine with a processor running at 2.8 GHz and 512 KB cache and for the threshold 1000 scenario we used a machine with a processor running at 2.2 GHz and 1 MB cache. We include the success rates for $t = 100$ to illustrate the trade off between accuracy and speed.

Table 2. Timings of the attacks: estimation of profiles from 50 000 rounds and de-anonymization of 5000 rounds

Attack	$t = 100$		$t = 500$	$t = 1000$
	Time	Success rate, mean (min)	Time	Time
SDA profiling	3.08m	-	38.33m	66.16m
SDA de-anon	10m	25.6% (0.00%)	3.48h	12.91h
PMDA de-anon	10.2m	62.9% (38.8%)	12.9h	4.69days
NSDA de-anon	13.33m	60.2% (33.5%)	4.28h	15.3h

The PMDA de-anonymization is slower than the SDA de-anonymization and the difference grows as the size of the threshold and thus the underlying bipartite graph increases. Nevertheless, it yields higher success rates. In Sect. 8.2 we propose the Normalized Statistical Disclosure Attack (NSDA), that combines accuracy and speed. Table 2 includes the success rate and timings for the operations shown in Fig. 12 inside the dotted line. Note that all of the attacks' efficiencies would substantially benefit from optimized implementations. Further, the PMDA in particular is suited for parallelization.

7   Enhanced Profiling with the Perfect Matching Disclosure Attack

So far we have focused on the PMDA's de-anonymization capability. In this section, we show how the derived maximum weighted bipartite matchings M_i can be used to better estimate user profiles.

A better estimation of a profile, say $\mathbb{P}_{Alice}$, is built by, instead of considering all possible receivers of her message(s) in a round i as equally likely, considering the receiver(s) indicated by the matching M_i as the most likely. Instead of assigning a probability of $1/t$ to each receiver in $rec(R_i)$, the attacker assigns z to the receiver assigned to Alice's message(s) by M_i and $(1-z)/(t-1)$ to the rest of the elements in $rec(R_i)$. This step is marked with "PMDA profiling" in Fig. 8. The choice of the weight z is not that crucial. It expresses the confidence one has in the perfect matchings M_i. We experimented with different values for this parameter but observed that the effect on the profile estimation is minor. However, there is one hard bound. Choosing the weight z such that $z = (1-z)/(t-1)$ turns the second

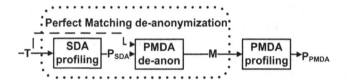

Fig. 8. Obtaining enhanced profiles with the Perfect Matching Disclosure Attack

profiling step useless as this setting reflects the original SDA, and choosing $z <$ $(1-z)/(t-1)$ will effectively hide the actual users' relationships. We chose $z = 0.5$ without a specific motivation. Note that the same ρ round observations used to construct the simple profile $\tilde{\mathbb{P}}_{Alice,SDA}$ are reused to estimate the enhanced profile $\tilde{\mathbb{P}}_{Alice,PMDA}$.

The same procedure can be applied to the decision D_i of the de-anonymization phase of the SDA, yielding a more accurate profile than the one estimated by the original SDA and denoted by $\tilde{\mathbb{P}}_{Alice,eSDA}$.

For a U_0 scenario where Alice has five friends, Fig. 9 shows the profile $\mathbb{P}_{Alice}$ we initially generated for Alice, her profile after the PMDA's profiling step, the approximation of her profile derived with the enhanced SDA, and her profile estimated using the original SDA. Figure 10 shows the corresponding set of profiles for a $U_{5,2}$ scenario. We observe in both cases that the profile estimation $\tilde{\mathbb{P}}_{Alice,eSDA}$ is more precise than $\tilde{\mathbb{P}}_{Alice,SDA}$ but not as good as $\tilde{\mathbb{P}}_{Alice,PMDA}$.

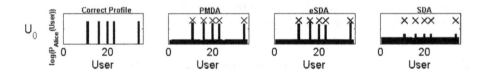

Fig. 9. Alice's profile and estimations (logscale) for U_0, $\rho = 100\,000$. From left to right: $\mathbb{P}_{Alice}$, $\tilde{\mathbb{P}}_{Alice,PMDA}$, $\tilde{\mathbb{P}}_{Alice,eSDA}$, and $\tilde{\mathbb{P}}_{Alice,SDA}$.

In the U_0 scenario, all three estimations allow the adversary to easily identify the set of Alice's friends, even if the exact number k of friends is unknown. However, the enhanced methods increase the contrast between friends and non-friends. In the $U_{5,2}$ scenario, $\tilde{\mathbb{P}}_{Alice,SDA}$ does not allow to identify friends, and even worse, there exist non-friends of Alice that have higher probability than some of her friends. $\tilde{\mathbb{P}}_{Alice,eSDA}$ improves the estimation and allows to identify Alice's best friends (those with high probability in $\mathbb{P}_{Alice}$), but it fails to show more unlikely receivers as for example user 19. In $\tilde{\mathbb{P}}_{Alice,PMDA}$ the estimation is further improved and all of her friends have higher probabilities than her non-friends.

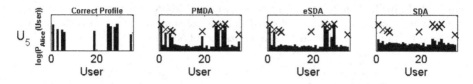

Fig. 10. Alice's profile and estimations (logscale) for $U_{5,2}$, $\rho = 100\,000$. From left to right: $\mathbb{P}_{Alice}$, $\tilde{\mathbb{P}}_{Alice,PMDA}$, $\tilde{\mathbb{P}}_{Alice,eSDA}$, and $\tilde{\mathbb{P}}_{Alice,SDA}$.

8   Extending the Perfect Matching Disclosure Attack

In this section we present variants and extensions of the Perfect Matching Disclosure Attack. The iterated PMDA and the normalized SDA are alternatives with different trade-offs between precision and computational load. We also outline how the PMDA, and any of its variants can be applied to the more realistic scenario of a pool mix.

8.1   Iterated PMDA

The profiles $\tilde{\mathbb{P}}_{PMDA}$ can be used as input to a subsequent PMDA de-anonymization step, yielding the perfect matchings M_i^* as output, which uncover the actual relations between senders and receivers for each round with an even higher rate of success than the PMDA, particularly in U_5 scenarios. Further, the M_i^* can be used for a subsequent PMDA profiling step, yielding user profiles that are slightly better than the $\tilde{\mathbb{P}}_{PMDA}$. Figure 11 illustrates the chaining for two iterations of the PMDA.

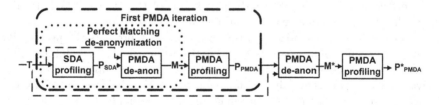

Fig. 11. Iterated Perfect Matching Disclosure Attack

In fact, the PMDA can be chained arbitrarily often, each time yielding a (slight) improvement over the outputs of the previous iteration, and asymptotically approaching the optimal result. The concept of this iterated approach is know as expectation maximization.

Note, however, that each additional instance of the PMDA implies an increase of computational cost. Again, it is possible to trade certainty for speed substituting the PMDA de-anonymization step by the SDA de-anonymization step. Table 3 presents de-anonymization success rates of a two-instances PMDA and a two-instances eSDA when applied to U_0 and U_5 scenarios.

Table 3. Individual success rates of two-instances PMDA and two-instances eSDA de-anonymization; all profiles are derived reusing the same set of $\rho = 10\,000$ rounds, success rates are evaluated from de-anonymization of 5000 rounds

U_0	eSDA	PMDA
k = 5	80.43	78.67
k = 50	10.47	12.15

$U_{5,2}$	eSDA	PMDA
	26.56	60.24

8.2 Normalized Statistical Disclosure Attack

The Normalized Statistical Disclosure Attack, illustrated in Fig. 12, has a similar structure as the SDA but it additionally constructs the matrix P' as in the PMDA and it includes a matrix normalization step.

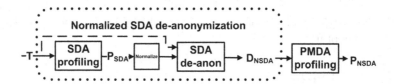

Fig. 12. Normalized Statistical Disclosure Attack

We transform P' into a doubly stochastic transition matrix that, by definition, has the property that each row and each column sums up to one. We use the method proposed by Sinkhorn in [19] in 1964. He showed that an arbitrary positive $N \times N$ matrix, *i.e.* each element is greater than zero, can be transformed into a doubly stochastic matrix by iterative proportional fitting. This means iteratively normalizing the rows and the columns of the matrix. Sinkhorn also proved that the iteration converges and has a unique solution.

An element of the normalized transition matrix P' represents the probability of a link between input messages (row) and output messages (column). This ensures that each sent message is received (all rows sum up to 1) and each received message was sent (all columns sum up to 1). The receiver of a given message s is chosen as the one who maximizes the individual link probability $P'(s, \cdot)$.

The normalization step has two important effects on P' that stem from the fact that the iterative proportional fitting spreads the information contained in each element of P' over the entire matrix. The first effect is best explained in a noise-free toy example. Consider the matrix P' before and after normalization

$$P' = \begin{pmatrix} 0.5 & 0.5 & 0 \\ 1 & 0 & 0 \\ 0 & 0.5 & 0.5 \end{pmatrix} \xrightarrow{normalize} \begin{pmatrix} 0 & 1 & 0 \\ 1 & 0 & 0 \\ 0 & 0 & 1 \end{pmatrix}.$$

The per sender maximum likelihood decision approach of the SDA achieves 66.66% success rate when assigning receivers to senders based on the original version of P'.

The normalization process over the matrix P' implicitly takes interdependencies between the matrix elements in different rows and columns into account and eliminates impossible combinations. In the toy-example, the certainty $P'(2, 1) = 1$ implies $P'(1, 1) = 0$. Hence, $P'(1, 2)$ becomes 1 to fulfill the doubly-stochastic requirement in the first row. This implies that $P(3, 2)$ becomes also 0 and hence $P'(3, 3) = 1$. Therefore, a per sender maximum likelihood decision approach based on the normalized matrix takes more information into account and leads to the only correct assignment with success rate one.

To explain the second effect, we use a noisy version of the same initial matrix P' that contains Gaussian noise with standard deviation 0.1

$$P' = \begin{pmatrix} 0.4006 & 0.4208 & 0.1786 \\ 0.7810 & 0.1432 & 0.0757 \\ 0.0997 & 0.4580 & 0.4424 \end{pmatrix} \xrightarrow{normalize} \begin{pmatrix} 0.2776 & 0.4369 & 0.2856 \\ 0.6673 & 0.1834 & 0.1494 \\ 0.0552 & 0.3798 & 0.5651 \end{pmatrix}.$$

The per sender maximum likelihood decision of the SDA based on the initial P' leads to the correct assignment for the senders 1 and 2 but to a wrong assignment for sender 3. Based on P' after the normalization step, also the third assignment is identified correctly. The estimated profiles obtained by an adversary in a realistic scenario contain noise. The normalization step partially eliminates this noise yielding more reliable data.

The combination of these two effects allow the NSDA to de-anonymize messages with a higher success rate than the original SDA. As we show in Table 2, this attack runs faster than the PMDA for $t = 500$ and $t = 1000$, still it achieves a lower success rate. It is a decision of the adversary which method suits her purposes best.

8.3   Pool Mix

Finally, we outline how our attack can be applied to a pool mix scenario [17]. Figure 13 depicts a simple example with threshold $t = 4$ and internal memory of size $n = 4$. It also shows the link probabilities between incoming and outgoing messages according to the formula given by Serjantov and Danezis in [18] in the upper table, and the relevant part of users' profiles in the lower table. Such profiles can be derived, for example, by applying the SDA [7]. We observe two rounds of the mix. Initially the mix generates two dummy messages p_1 and p_2 and places them in the pool. After the first round two messages stay in the pool participating in the second round. After the second round, two messages, p_5 and p_6, remain in the pool.

Before one can apply the PMDA to a pool mix, the scenario needs to be mapped to a bipartite graph. A simple approach for doing so maps each round individually. The set of sent messages in one round is formed by the messages actually sent in this round and the messages that remained in the pool after the previous round. For the first round of our example that is $S = \{s_1, s_2, p_1, p_2\}$. Equivalently, the set of received messages is composed of messages that left the mix and the messages remaining in the pool, i.e. $R = \{r_1, r_2, p_3, p_4\}$. The initial

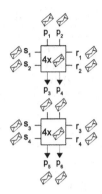

P_{mix}	r_1	r_2	r_3	r_4	p_5	p_6
s_1	0.25	0.25	0.125	0.125	0.125	0.125
s_2	0.25	0.25	0.125	0.125	0.125	0.125
p_1	0.25	0.25	0.125	0.125	0.125	0.125
p_2	0.25	0.25	0.125	0.125	0.125	0.125
s_3	0	0	0.25	0.25	0.25	0.25
s_4	0	0	0.25	0.25	0.25	0.25

	$rec(r_1)$ = Eve	$rec(r_2)$ = Franklin	$rec(r_3)$ = Charlie	$rec(r_4)$ = Bob
$sen(s_1)$ = Alice	0.25	0.25	0.125	0.125
$sen(s_2)$ = Bob	0.25	0.25	0.125	0.125
$sen(s_3)$ = Charlie	0	0	0.25	0.25
$sen(s_4)$ = David	0	0	0.25	0.25

Fig. 13. Left: two rounds of a pool mix scenario; Right: mix probabilities (upper table) and user profiles (lower table)

matrix P' can then be generated from the mix probabilities given in Fig. 13 on the upper right side, *i.e.* $P'(s,r) = P_{mix}(s,r)$ for all $s \in S_i, r \in R_i$, for each round i. However, as observed from the experimental results in Sect. 6.2, the uniformity of the entries in this P' are bad conditions for an attack to operate in.

A better approach is to deal with several observed rounds at once and to compute the probabilities for P' globally from starting point to end point. In our example both rounds can be combined using $S = \{s_1, \ldots, s_4, p_1, p_2\}$ and $R = \{r_1, \ldots, r_4, p_5, p_6\}$. Still we do not expect the attacks to perform well due to the same reasons as given above.

We propose to additionally combine both sources of information, mix probabilities and user profiles, into P'. The senders' choices of their recipients and the choice of the mix on which messages to output are independent. Therefore, one computes the joint probability of two choices as the product of the individual probabilities. We derive P' as

$$P'(s,r) = P_{mix}(s,r) \cdot \tilde{\mathbb{P}}_{sen(s),SDA}(rec(r)), \ s \in S, r \in R.$$

For completeness we note that the senders of messages which are in the pool at the beginning of the observation and receivers of messages which are in the pool at the end of the observation need to be added to the population. The "virtual" senders are best modeled with a uniform profile while the "virtual" receivers need to be inserted into all senders' profiles. Once the initial matrix P' has been generated, the PMDA can be applied to this pool mix scenario.

9   Conclusions

The main drawback of previously published practical Disclosure Attacks is their susceptibility to changes in the user behavior model. Each of them seems to be optimized for a specific and restricted scenario. Our first contribution is a more general user behavior model, where the number of users' friends and the distribution of sending probabilities toward them is not restricted.

Our second contribution is the Perfect Matching Disclosure Attack, that achieves a high rate of success when tracing messages sent through a threshold mix in arbitrary scenarios. Its accuracy arises from the fact that it considers information about all senders participating in a round simultaneously, rather than focusing on individual users iteratively. We empirically compare it with previous work in terms of effectiveness and show that our proposal yields better results when de-anonymizing the sender of a given message in a generic scenario.

The second advantage of the PMDA over previous work is its enhanced ability to estimate user profiles. Concerning a very restrictive user behavior model we empirically confirm that the PMDA yields a better separation of friends and non-friends than previous work. With respect to a generic scenario we show that the PMDA reliably identifies users' friends when previously proposed methods fail.

Although the Perfect Matching Disclosure Attack is computationally more expensive than previously proposed and practical methods, our study of its efficiency shows that it is indeed practical. A particular promising property of our proposal is, that it can be parallelized to a high degree. Further, we show how it can be adapted to different scenarios including pool mixes and how it can be refined to achieve even better results. A significantly sped-up variant, the Normalized Statistical Disclosure Attack, yields slightly worse accuracy than the PMDA but is almost as fast as the original SDA.

Although the new user model presented in this work is more generic than previous proposals, it is not as versatile as one would desire and most probably far from real user behavior. More research needs to be performed on the influence of parameters like the users' sending rate or its variance over time on the effectiveness and efficiency of attacks in order to evaluate their impact on real anonymous communications networks.

Perhaps the most closely related work to ours is the approach toward measuring anonymity proposed in [9]. However, their metric is not self-contained and can only complement entropy based metrics. Our work on the other hand aims at pinpointing an adversary's probability of success though it can also be used as a complement for the evaluation of anonymous systems. Nevertheless, both works allow a common conclusion: whether it is to measure anonymity or to derive strong attack methodologies — considering the perspective of a single user is not good enough.

Acknowledgements

The authors would like to thank Matthew Wright for shepherding this paper and the anonymous Reviewer 1 for his/her insightful comments.

C. Troncoso is funded by a research grant of the Fundacion Barrie de la Maza (Spain). This work was supported in part by the IAP Programme P6/26 BCRYPT of the Belgian State (Belgian Science Policy), by the IWT SBO

ADAPID project, by FWO projects G.0475.05, and G.0300.07, by the Concerted Research Action (GOA) Ambiorics 2005/11 of the Flemish Government, by the European Comission through the IST Programme under Contract IST-2002-507932 ECRYPT NoE, and by the K.U. Leuven-BOF.

The information in this document reflects only the authors' views, is provided as is and no guarantee or warranty is given that the information is fit for any particular purpose. The user thereof uses the information at its sole risk and liability.

References

1. Agrawal, D., Kesdogan, D.: Measuring anonymity: The disclosure attack. IEEE Security & Privacy 1(6), 27–34 (2003)
2. Bellman, R.: On a routing problem. Quarterly of Applied Mathematics 16, 87–90 (1958)
3. Chaum, D.L.: Untraceable electronic mail, return addresses, and digital pseudonyms. Commun. ACM 24(2), 84–90 (1981)
4. Danezis, G.: Statistical disclosure attacks: Traffic confirmation in open environments. In: Gritzalis, Vimercati, Samarati, Katsikas (eds.) Proceedings of Security and Privacy in the Age of Uncertainty (SEC 2003), Athens, May 2003, IFIP TC11 pp. 421–426. Kluwer, Dordrecht (2003)
5. Danezis, G., Diaz, C., Troncoso, C.: Two-sided statistical disclosure attack. In: Borisov, N., Golle, P. (eds.) PET 2007. LNCS, vol. 4776, p. 15. Springer, Heidelberg (2007)
6. Danezis, G., Dingledine, R., Mathewson, N.: Mixminion: Design of a Type III Anonymous Remailer Protocol. In: Proceedings of the 2003 IEEE Symposium on Security and Privacy, pp. 2–15 (May 2003)
7. Danezis, G., Serjantov, A.: Statistical disclosure or intersection attacks on anonymity systems. In: Fridrich, J. (ed.) IH 2004. LNCS, vol. 3200. Springer, Heidelberg (2004)
8. Dijkstra, E.W.: A note on two problems in connexion with graphs. Numerische Mathematik 1, 269–271 (1959)
9. Edman, M., Sivrikaya, F., Yener, B.: A combinatorial approach to measuring anonymity. In: ISI, pp. 356–363. IEEE, Los Alamitos (2007)
10. Hughes, D., Shmatikov, V.: Information hiding, anonymity and privacy: A modular approach. Journal of Computer Security 12(1), 3–36 (2004)
11. Jakobsson, M., Juels, A., Rivest, R.L.: Making mix nets robust for electronic voting by randomized partial checking. In: Proceedings of the 11th USENIX Security Symposium (August 2002)
12. Kesdogan, D., Agrawal, D., Penz, S.: Limits of anonymity in open environments. In: Petitcolas, F.A.P. (ed.) IH 2002. LNCS, vol. 2578, pp. 53–69. Springer, Heidelberg (2003)
13. Kesdogan, D., Pimenidis, L.: The hitting set attack on anonymity protocols. In: Fridrich, J.J. (ed.) IH 2004. LNCS, vol. 3200, pp. 326–339. Springer, Heidelberg (2004)
14. Kilian, J., Sako, K.: Receipt-free MIX-type voting scheme - a practical solution to the implementation of a voting booth. In: EUROCRYPT 1995. Springer, Heidelberg (1995)

15. Kuhn, H.W.: The Hungarian method for the assignment problem. Naval Research Logistic Quarterly 2, 83–97 (1955)
16. Mathewson, N., Dingledine, R.: Practical traffic analysis: Extending and resisting statistical disclosure. In: Martin, D., Serjantov, A. (eds.) PET 2004. LNCS, vol. 3424, pp. 17–34. Springer, Heidelberg (2005)
17. Möller, U., Cottrell, L., Palfrader, P., Sassaman, L.: Mixmaster Protocol — Version 2. IETF Internet Draft (July 2003)
18. Serjantov, A., Danezis, G.: Towards an information theoretic metric for anonymity. In: Dingledine, R., Syverson, P. (eds.) PET 2002. LNCS, vol. 2482. Springer, Heidelberg (2003)
19. Sinkhorn, R.: A relationship between arbitrary positive matrices and doubly stochastic matrices. The Annals of Mathematical Statistics 35(2), 876–879 (1964)

An Indistinguishability-Based Characterization
of Anonymous Channels

Alejandro Hevia[1],* and Daniele Micciancio[2],**

[1] Dept. of Computer Science, University of Chile
ahevia@dcc.uchile.cl
http://www.dcc.uchile.cl/ahevia
[2] Dept. of Computer Science & Engineering, University of California, San Diego
daniele@cs.ucsd.edu
http://www-cse.ucsd.edu/users/daniele

Abstract. We revisit the problem of *anonymous communication*, in which users wish to send messages to each other without revealing their identities. We propose a novel framework to organize and compare anonymity definitions. In this framework, we present simple and practical definitions for anonymous channels in the context of computational indistinguishability. The notions seem to capture the intuitive properties of several types of anonymous channels (Pfitzmann and Köhntopp 2001) (eg. sender anonymity and unlinkability). We justify these notions by showing they naturally capture practical scenarios where information is unavoidably leaked in the system. Then, we compare the notions and we show they form a natural hierarchy for which we exhibit non-trivial implications. In particular, we show how to implement stronger notions from weaker ones using cryptography and dummy traffic – in a provably optimal way. With these tools, we revisit the security of previous anonymous channels protocols, in particular constructions based on broadcast networks (Blaze et al. 2003), anonymous broadcast (Chaum 1981), and mix networks (Groth 2003, Nguyen et al. 2004). Our results give generic, optimal constructions to transform known protocols into new ones that achieve the strongest notions of anonymity.

1 Introduction

Anonymous channels allow users to send and receive messages without revealing their identities. There are many applications for such channels, from protecting "whistle blowers" or guaranteeing source confidentiality in crime tips, to offering access to medical information to potential patients without fear of embarrassment,

---

* Work partially done while the first author was at U. of California San Diego. Supported in part by Conicyt via Fondecyt grant No. 1070332.
** Research supported in part by NSF under grant CNS-0430595. Any opinions, findings, and conclusions or recommendations expressed in this material are those of the author(s) and do not necessarily reflect the views of the National Science Foundation.

or protecting voter privacy in electronic voting [23, 43]. Chaum [14] initiated the modern study of anonymous communication by introducing the concept of mix networks (or *mix-nets*). A mix-net is a protocol in which messages (say, emails) traverse several routers (or mixers) and, in the process, are "mixed" with other messages with the intention that the relation to the original sender be lost. Since Chaum's seminal paper, research in the area has been extensive, from concrete mix-net proposals (see [47, 1, 39, 25, 33, 59] among many others) to very practical protocols based on mix-nets (eg. [29, 34, 40, 17, 51, 19] and references therein). But mix-nets are not the only method to implement anonymous communication. DC-nets (also known as anonymous broadcast networks), also proposed also by Chaum [15] and later improved by many others [10, 57, 58, 32], allow broadcast of messages without disclosing the sender identity. At least initially, most of the effort was put into improving the efficiency and reliability of the constructions, so informal or ad-hoc definitions were common. Indeed, only recently the need for general (and sound) definitions for these types of primitives has drawn some attention. Furukawa [24] and Nguyen et al. [44], in particular, give strong definitions for "proving shuffles" (shuffles are the basic mixing operation) and Wikström [59] presents a formal definition of mix-net in the UC model [13]. These definitions, although helpful in the design and analysis of mix-nets, do not provide a definition of anonymous channels per se. Indeed, the absence of good anonymity definitions that capture realistic concerns motivated this work.

OUR CONTRIBUTIONS: We present a novel framework to organize and compare anonymity definitions. In this framework, we formalize the notions of unlinkability, sender-anonymity, receiver-anonymity, sender-receiver anonymity, and unobservability, giving them new, strong indistinguishability-based formulations without compromising the standard "intuitive" meaning they have in the literature [46]. We also introduce new notions, namely sender unlinkability and receiver unlinkability. These notions, while arguably weak, can be used to implement some of the stronger notions. Then we formally prove some folklore results: we show that sender-receiver anonymity implies both sender anonymity and receiver anonymity, that sender-anonymity and receiver-anonymity (both separately) imply unlinkability, and that unobservability implies all the other properties. In the other direction, we present generic black-box transformations from any "weak" anonymous protocols (eg. sender unlinkability, unlinkability, or sender anonymity) into protocols anonymous under "stronger" notions (like sender-receiver anonymity or unobservability). These transformations are provably optimal in terms of message traffic. We then revisit the anonymity of constructions based on broadcast channels, DC-nets and mix-networks, giving an exact characterization of the anonymity they provide in our framework.

1.1   Coping with Information Leaks

There have been several attempts to characterize the intuitive properties anonymous channels should have. Most proposals so far seem to fall into two categories: (a) they present intuitive but weak definitions (targeted to particular applications with efficiency in mind), or (b) they present strong definitions with often impractical implementations [6, 28, 16]. We seek to bridge this gap by providing strong definitions which can be tailored to specific practical scenarios.

We identify factors or conditions that may realistically *limit* anonymity. These conditions are on specific information that, in principle, may be unrealistic to assume hidden from the adversary. Consider for example,

(a) **Total network flow is usually public:** the total number of messages sent in a system is likely to be known to any party in the system, even external observers.

(b) **Amount of traffic per party is hard to conceal:** the number of messages sent or received by a particular party is often easily inferred by an observer in the party's network vicinity.

(c) **Values sent or received by each party are not necessarily private:** the value of each message[1] sent or received by a particular party could be guessed, known, or even influenced by an adversary.

A proper definition of anonymity should take these "leaks" into account but hide any additional information: *hide everything except what follows from the potentially leaked information.* This idea is already present in security definitions of other cryptographic primitives. For example, if E is a semantically secure encryption function [30], it is standard to assume a ciphertext $E(m)$ hides all partial information about a message m except its length $|m|$. This is because $|m|$ can only be hidden at the cost of unnecessarily increasing the size of $E(m)$. In fact, the definitions in this work are inspired by the indistinguishability-based formalization of semantically secure encryption in [30], which guarantees the hiding of all information on the plaintext other than the plaintext length. Similarly, an anonymous channel should hide all information about the communication except for (some of) the information mentioned above. In this work, we study the possible combinations of the conditions (a),(b), and (c) above, and analyze the resulting notions. There are nine (potentially different) notions. Named following the intuition in [46], they are summarized in Table 1.

Sender Unlinkability and *Receiver Unlinkability* are the weakest notions of anonymity we consider. A protocol is sender unlinkable if it hides any relation between senders and receivers beyond what is implied by the total size of messages sent by each party and the specific values of the messages received by each party. Its dual notion is *Receiver Unlinkability* in which the roles of sender and receiver are reversed. Compared to Receiver Unlinkability, *Sender and Receiver Unlinkability* (or simply *Unlinkability*) strengthens the requirements for the sender, hiding the message values sent and received but not necessaruly the total size of messages exchanged by each party. A stronger notion is *Sender Anonymity* as the number and values of messages for the sender must remain hidden (but not the values of the received messages for each party). Compared to Sender Anonymity, *Receiver Anonymity* simply reverses the roles of sender and

---

[1] We distinguish two properties for each message: its value, that is, the data or *payload* encoded in the message, and its destination.

Table 1. Anonymity variants and their associated mnemonic notation. The notation (X, Y) encodes what information is not assumed to be protected by the definition (ie. the meaning of X and Y), and from whom the information comes: from each sender (X), or each receiver (Y). 'U' stands for "values of the messages sent/received", 'Σ' for "number of messages sent/received", '#' for "total number of messages", and '?' for "nothing".

Anonymity Variant	Mnemonic Notation
Sender Unlinkability	(Σ, U)
Receiver Unlinkability	(U, Σ)
Sender-Receiver Unlinkability	(Σ, Σ)
Sender Anonymity	$(?, \mathsf{U})$
Receiver Anonymity	$(\mathsf{U}, ?)$
Strong Sender Anonymity	$(?, \Sigma)$
Strong Receiver Anonymity	$(\Sigma, ?)$
Sender and Receiver Anonymity	$(\#, \#)$
Unobservability	$(?, ?)$

receiver. Further strengthening of these notions are *Strong Sender Anonymity* (resp. *Strong Receiver Anonymity*) in that protocols can afford to leak at most the amount of traffic per receiver (resp. per sender). The strongest notions are *Sender-Receiver Anonymity*, and *Unobservability*. They differ in that the former may not protect the total network flow (ie. the total number of messages exchanged), while the latter must hide this information.

1.2   Strong, Formal Definitions

We adopt an indistinguishability based formalization under which the adversary produces two message matrices (which encode message senders and receivers in a standard way), is allowed to passively observe the execution of a communication protocol under a random one of these two matrices and then is required to have non-negligible advantage in determining under which of the two matrices the protocol was executed. Within this framework, each different anonymity variant is defined by requiring the adversary to produce two matrices whose "leaked" information is the same. More precisely, if for any message matrix M the anonymity variant assumes a certain information $f(M)$ may not be protected (it may be "leaked"), then the two matrices M, M' produced by the adversary must satisfy $f(M) = f(M')$. Indeed, the notions corresponding to the different anonymity variants mentioned in the previous section follow from instantiating function f with the appropriate function (eg. one that computes the set of message values sent per party, their number, or the total number of messages, for example). Our formalisms build on definitional ideas used for encryption [30, 42, 27] and signatures [31]. Regarding adversaries, an often adopted adversarial type is that of *honest-but-curious* (or passive) adversary, one where the adversary obtains the internal state of the corrupted party, but the party continues to follow the protocol. For simplicity of exposition, we consider passive adversaries with no corruptions (also called *outside* [20] or *global passive adversary* [52]) as it captures most of the subtleties of our model. Extensions to allow (passive) corruptions are discussed in Section 6. We also stress that our results apply to protocols with fixed number of participants.

Since the adversary can freely choose the values and destinations of all messages in the protocol (ie. the message matrix), it follows that a protocol anonymous under this definition must hide all partial information on the message matrix M *except for what is implied by the known information* $f(M)$. In particular, sources and destinations of the messages are hidden up to the extent that they do not follow from the known information. This is a quite strong guarantee.

We stress that we present an unified framework for *all the proposed anonymity variants*. We believe this facilitates the organization and comparison of the notions as well as future extensions.

1.3   Comparing Notions

The indistinguishability-based definitions presented in this paper appear to capture the concerns of most intuitive but informal notions of anonymity proposed in the past [46]. Indeed, in Section 1.4 we argue that previous anonymity formalizations in comparable network models are implied by some of the proposed notions. In addition, we compare the new notions to each other. The comparison is in terms of reductions. We say notion A implies (is stronger than) notion B if any protocol satisfying A can be used to achieve B (via a possibly different protocol).A difficulty arises if we assume point-to-point channels between parties. In this case, protocols for all notions exist because of general secure multiparty computation results [6, 28, 16], which makes the notions trivially equivalent. To avoid this pitfall, we assume that the only communication channel between the parties is an idealized version of a protocol achieving notion A, and then we show how to implement a protocol that achieves notion B in this setting. The communication channel is idealized in the sense that parties only see its input/output behavior. This effectively gives us black-box reductions.

RESULTS: We show three types of reductions between the anonymity definitions: (1) Trivial reductions, in which given a protocol for notion A, the same protocol achieves notion B, (2) Reductions that use cryptography, and (3) Reductions that use "padding" (or "dummy traffic"). Interestingly, in terms of the reductions, cryptography and padding do not appear exchangeable. Our results suggest that in the reductions that require cryptography padding does not help, while in those where padding is necessary, cryptography does not help.

TRIVIAL REDUCTIONS: There exists a partial order of the notions, starting from the weakest ones, sender unlinkability and receiver unlinkability, and ending in the strongest one, unobservability, such that if a protocol achieves a certain notion then the same protocol achieves any weaker notion. These relations give formal justification to previous informal statements such as sender-receiver anonymity implying both sender anonymity and receiver anonymity, or that unobservability implies all the other notions. Interestingly, there is no trivial relation between sender anonymity, unlinkability, and receiver anonymity, which indicates the definitions address incomparable security concerns. In [46], however, it is argued that Unlinkability (called "relationship anonymity" there) is a "weaker property than each of sender anonymity and recipient anonymity". The disagreement disappears when one notices that, under our definitions, such relation is true between *strong* sender (or receiver) anonymity and unlinkability. Our framework allows us then to clarify an implicit assumption in [46], namely that messages in the definitions of sender and receiver anonymity are private.

USING CRYPTOGRAPHY: Under standard computational and setup assumptions, we show that anonymity notions that reveal message values are not intrinsically weaker than those that keep these values private. In particular, we show reductions from unlinkability to sender (or receiver) unlinkability. We also show strong sender (resp. receiver) anonymity is not weaker than sender (resp. receiver) anonymity.[2] The assumptions are standard, namely PKI and key-private secure encryption schemes [4].[3] The reductions are computationally efficient and do not have message overhead – they introduce no new messages – therefore optimal in terms of communication.

USING "PADDING": We conclude showing that our strongest anonymity notions *can* be achieved starting from much weaker anonymity notions, but at a cost of message efficiency. In a nutshell, the reductions show that unobservability, sender-receiver anonymity, strong sender (or receiver) anonymity, and unlinkability are actually equivalent. They also show that neither sender nor receiver unlinkability are stronger than sender or receiver anonymity. These reductions do introduce *dummy traffic* (ie. extra empty messages) but no more than necessary – they have optimal message overhead. These reductions do not require computational or setup assumptions, and are computationally efficient.[4] The results are summarized in Fig. 2.

1.4   Comparison with Previous Anonymity Notions

In this section, we compare the proposed variants with anonymity variants suggested previously in the literature. When necessary, we relax those definitions to match our adversarial model (passive adversaries with no corruptions).

INDISTINGUISHABILITY-BASED DEFINITIONS: Beimel and Dolev [3] define anonymity in terms of computational indistinguishability of the adversary's *view* (i.e. the messages and any extra information obtained by the adversary) in two

---

[2] This proof actually *justifies* the assumption made in [46] mentioned before. We stress that this is not obvious since anonymity does not necessarily implies message privacy, or viceversa.

[3] In fact, based on preliminary results, we conjecture computational or setup assumptions are also necessary.

[4] The reductions *to* Sender Anonymity, Strong Sender Anonymity, and Unobservability require the extra (but rather mild) assumption that a known upper bound on the total network flow exists. See Proposition 4 and remarks at the end of Section 4.2.

cases: when party P_i sends a message to party P_j, and when $P_{i'}$ sends a message to $P_{j'}$, for any i, j, i', j'. Given that [3] does present protocols for multiple senders, we see the definition as somewhat unsatisfactory in the following sense. The definition does not specify how the messages and destinations for parties $P_k \neq P_i$ are selected. If they are chosen either arbitrarily (but the same for both views) or with some probability distribution, then we can show they are strictly *weaker* than sender-receiver anonymity. The alternative, choosing the inputs for parties $P_k \neq P_i$, arbitrarily but different in each view, might work (be equivalent to sender-receiver anonymity) although it is unclear without a formal statement. A similar concern can be raised on the definition proposed by von Ahn et al. in the context of k-anonymity [56]. (Essentially the same definition for the case of a fixed receiver).

Golle and Juels [32] present a definition of anonymity (which they called privacy) in the context of DC-nets [15]. In the definition in [32], a successful adversary must distinguish between an execution where P_1 sends a message to some party P_b, and one in which P_2 sends a message to some party P_{1-b}, where b is a bit chosen uniformly at random and *unknown* to the adversary. The rest of the parties sends messages as instructed by the adversary. Unfortunately, this definition suffers from a problem similar to the one above. The adversary is unable to exploit possible correlations between the destination of P_1's message and the destination of some other party P_3's message. Consequently, this definition can be shown to be strictly weaker than our definition of sender anonymity. Luckily, the DC-net in [32] is strong enough to be proven sender anonymous (see Section 5).

OTHER CLOSELY RELATED DEFINITIONS: Nguyen et al. [44] define privacy of a shuffle by a similar experiment to ours (a notion called indistinguishability under chosen permutation attack or IND-CPA$_S$ under an active adversary). In their definition, the adversary chooses two permutations under which the messages are shuffled and must distinguish which one was used. Translated to our setting, their definition restricts message matrices to be permutations such that each party sends exactly a single message. Also, it does not account for the types of information leaks we consider. The comparison is somewhat unfair, as their concern – privacy of a single shuffle – is different than ours.

Another related definition was suggested (rather implicitly) by Ishai et al. in [38]. There, Ishai et al. describe a functionality for anonymous communication (synchronous setting with rushing). When paired with the appropriate notions of multiparty computation [12] (under our adversarial model), their definition becomes a special case of ours, namely Sender Anonymity (SA). Their work [38], however, does not explore the proposed definition but instead use it to prove the security of other (non-anonymity related) cryptographic protocols.

Recently and independently from our work, Feigenbaum et al. [22] presented a definition of anonymity which, although it was specially tailored to the onion-routing system Tor [19], is closed to ours in spirit. In their work, several variants of anonymity are defined in terms of indistinguishability of configurations, where configurations may include values and destination of messages sent by parties in the system. When considered under our adversarial model, their definition differs from ours as there the indistinguishability property is explicitly expressed in terms of *circuits* (a routing path of a given message sent in any onion-routing system) and messages/actions on them, while our definition does not assume onion-routing-type of operation nor any particular underlying communication system. And, while our definition does seem to capture a wider variety of anonymity variants, the definition in [22] does allow an (arguably) stronger adversarial model. None of the definitions above incorporates provisions to deal with "leaked" information on the granularity done in the present work though.

1.5   Related Work

Dolev and Ostrovsky [20] present "xor-trees" protocols, a generalization of DC-net into a spanning tree, which they prove secure under a notion based on the concept of anonymity set (see below). Similarly, Pfitzmann [45] proposes the notion of k-anonymity – further developped by [56] – which can be seen as an extension of the DC-net model to more practical graph structures (which partition the parties into k-sized autonomous groups). Another approach was proposed by Rackoff and Simon in [49]. They describe a protocol for anonymous communication based on sorting networks, which is shown to satisfy some statistical mixing properties. Relaxations to weaker adversaries were proposed by Reiter and Rubin [50] and Berman et al. [7]. Both works presented alternative notions of anonymity as well as efficient constructions assuming an adversary that does not monitor all communication channels. Camenisch and Lysyanskaya [11] give a formal definition of onion routing [29] (along a provable secure protocol) but they explicitly avoid defining anonymous channels.

An alternative characterization of anonymity has been through the concept of anonymity set [15, 40]. The anonymity set is defined as the set of parties that could have sent a particular message as seen from the adversary [46]. Follow up works [40, 53, 18] have proposed new characterizations of anonymity, mostly in terms of the probability distributions the adversary assigns to each party in order to represent the likelihood such party is the sender of a message. Definitions based on formal methods have also been proposed [55, 37, 52, 41, 26]. Finally, it is worth noticing that Hughes and Shmatikov [36] also present a framework to formalize and compare different notions of anonymity as done here. Using the domain-theoretic primitive of function-view they model different notions of anonymity where information leaks can in principle be factored into the model. Their results, however, are not inmediately comparable to ours, as they focus only on non-probabilistic observers (adversaries) while ours can be probabilistic as long as they are efficiently computable.

ORGANIZATION: The rest of the paper is organized as follows. Section 2, introduces some notation and details on the execution model. Then, in Section 3, we present the formal definition of anonymous channels. Section 4 presents implications between the notions as well as proofs of their optimality in terms of communication. Then, in Section 5, we revisit previously proposed anonymous protocols and examine their security in the current framework. We conclude in

Section 6 mentioning some extensions to the model. Due to space constrains, most proofs are only sketched here. They are provided in the full version [35].

2   Preliminaries

MODEL AND NOTATION: We consider a system of n parties $P_1, \ldots, P_n$, where n is polynomial in the security parameter $k \in \mathbb{N}$, connected to each other by point-to-point communication channels. We distinguish two (possibly overlapping) types of parties: senders and receivers. For any two finite sets A and B, let $A \uplus B$ denote the multiset union (also called sum or join) of A and B, and $|A|$ denote the size of multiset A. By convention, we assume the i, j-th element of any matrix $M = (m_{i,j})_{i,j \in [n]}$ is denoted by $m_{i,j}$. As usual, M^T denotes the transpose of any matrix M, and $m_{i,*} = (m_{i,j})_{j \in [n]}$ a matrix row.

MESSAGES: We let $V = \{0, 1\}^\ell$ denote the message space where $\ell = \ell(k)$. The collection of messages sent by parties as well as their destinations is an $n \times n$ matrix $M = (m_{i,j})_{i,j \in [n]}$, called the *message matrix*. For row index i and column index j, $m_{i,j} \in \mathcal{P}(V)$ is the (multi)set of messages from party P_i to party P_j.[5] The *size* of matrix M, i.e. the total number of messages sent, is denoted by $|M| \stackrel{\text{def}}{=} \sum_{i,j \in [n]} |m_{i,j}|$.

ADVERSARIES AND PROTOCOL EXECUTION: In our setting, adversaries are (possibly external) PPT parties in the system which can passively monitor all the communication between parties. We consider only *passive adversaries* that do not corrupt any party but are able to read (but not alter) all the messages exchanged by the parties. A protocol π is a sequence of instructions that all parties (senders and receivers) must follow. The instructions involve local computations and point-to-point message exchanges between parties. Our execution model is a special case of the model presented by Canetti [12] (since we consider only passive adversaries). Given a message matrix M, we define the execution of protocol π with input M under adversary A, as the process where each party P_i follows the instructions of protocol π using as input the i-th row $m_{i,*}$ of matrix M. In this process, we allow the adversary A to obtain a copy of all messages exchanged in all communication channels. We say protocol π is a *message-transmission protocol* if, for any PPT adversary A and any message matrix M, each receiver P_j's local output y_j after executing π on input M equals the multiset $\uplus_{j \in [n]} m_{i,j}$.

3   Security Notions

Our definition is formalized in an *indistinguishability-type experiment* following similar approaches used in the formalization of semantically secure encryption

---

[5] Actually, we abuse the notation and we see elements of $\mathcal{P}(V)$ as multisets. This extension is needed to consider parties that send duplicated messages to the same receiver (see Section 4.2).

schemes [5]. We define anonymity via an *experiment* or *game*, in which there are two "worlds" (world 0 and world 1). We allow the adversary to choose the messages (values and destinations) sent by each party in each world. These choices are represented by two message matrices $M^{(0)}$ and $M^{(1)}$. Then, world $b \in \{0, 1\}$ is chosen uniformly at random, and message-transmission protocol π is executed by all parties on input $M^{(b)}$. We measure the adversary's success in terms of her ability to distinguish the two worlds.

Our definition is inspired by the standard game used to define semantically secure encryption scheme, namely the *left-or-right* characterization of IND-CPA [5]. There, the adversary arbitrarily chooses two messages of the same length, is returned an encryption of a random one of the two messages and then is required to guess under which message the encryption was generated. The adversary's inability to distinguish the plaintext underlying in the ciphertext effectively means she cannot compute any information on the plaintext except its length [30,5]. Similarly, the definition of our anonymity game guarantees that no information can be efficiently computed on the destinations of the messages sent during the protocol.

As mentioned in the introduction, one important difference between our formulation and the left-or-right game mentioned above is that we restrict the adversary's choices of the values and destinations of the messages to capture what is known to the adversary. These restrictions are captured as follows. Let f_U, f_Σ, and $f_\#$ be functions that map matrices $M = (m_{i,j})_{i,j \in [n]}$ into $\mathcal{P}(V)^n$, $\mathbb{N}^n$, and $\mathbb{N}$ respectively, defined by $f_\mathsf{U}(M) \stackrel{\text{def}}{=} (\uplus_{j \in [n]} m_{i,j})_{i \in [n]}$, $f_\Sigma(M) \stackrel{\text{def}}{=} (\sum_{j \in [n]} |m_{i,j}|)_{i \in [n]}$, and $f_\#(M) \stackrel{\text{def}}{=} |M|$. Also, let $f_\mathsf{U}^T(M) \stackrel{\text{def}}{=} f_\mathsf{U}(M^T)$, and $f_\Sigma^T(M) \stackrel{\text{def}}{=} f_\Sigma(M^T)$. Associated to each function f there is an equivalence relation $R_f \subset \mathcal{M}_{n \times n}(\mathcal{P}(V))^2$ where $(M, M') \in R_f$ if and only if $f(M) = f(M')$. For simplicity, we denote $R_\mathsf{U} = R_{f_\mathsf{U}}$, $R_\mathsf{U}^T = R_{f_\mathsf{U}^T}$, $R_\Sigma = R_{f_\Sigma}$, $R_\Sigma^T = R_{f_\Sigma^T}$, and $R_\# = R_{f_\#}$.

We are now ready to present the main definition. Given an n-party message-transmission protocol π, an adversary A, and label $\mathbf{N} \in \{\mathsf{SUL}, \mathsf{RUL}, \mathsf{UL}, \mathsf{SA}, \mathsf{RA}, \mathsf{SA}^*, \mathsf{RA}^*, \mathsf{SRA}, \mathsf{UO}\}$, consider the experiment $\mathbf{Exp}_{\pi,A}^{\mathbf{N}-anon}(k)$ described below. The experiment is parameterized by label $\mathbf{N}$, which determines the relation $R_\mathbf{N}$ considered. Relation $R_\mathbf{N}$ is defined in terms of $R_\mathsf{U}, R_\mathsf{U}^T, R_\Sigma, R_\Sigma^T$ and $R_\#$ according to the table in Fig. 1. We define the success probability of adversary A attacking protocol π under notion $\mathbf{N}$ as $\mathbf{Adv}_{\pi,A}^{\mathbf{N}-anon}(k) \stackrel{\text{def}}{=} 2 \cdot \Pr\left[\mathbf{Exp}_{\pi,A}^{\mathbf{N}-anon}(k) = 1\right] - 1$ where the experiment is defined as follows:

Experiment $\mathbf{Exp}_{\pi,A}^{\mathbf{N}-anon}(k)$

$\quad b \xleftarrow{R} \{0,1\}$, and $\langle M^{(0)}, M^{(1)} \rangle \leftarrow A(k)$

$\quad$ **if** $\langle M^{(0)}, M^{(1)} \rangle \notin R_\mathbf{N}$ **then return** 0

$\quad$ **else** Execute π on input $M^{(b)}$ under adversary A until A outputs a bit g.

$\quad\quad$ **if** $(b = g)$ **return** 1 **else return** 0

N	Notion	Description of R_N
SUL	Sender Unlinkability	$R_{\mathsf{SUL}} \stackrel{\text{def}}{=} R_\Sigma \cap R_\mathsf{U}^T$
RUL	Receiver Unlinkability	$R_{\mathsf{RUL}} \stackrel{\text{def}}{=} R_\mathsf{U} \cap R_\Sigma^T$
UL	Unlinkability	$R_{\mathsf{UL}} \stackrel{\text{def}}{=} R_\Sigma \cap R_\Sigma^T$
SA	Sender Anonymity	$R_{\mathsf{SA}} \stackrel{\text{def}}{=} R_\mathsf{U}^T$
RA	Receiver Anonymity	$R_{\mathsf{RA}} \stackrel{\text{def}}{=} R_\mathsf{U}$
SA*	Strong Sender Anonymity	$R_{\mathsf{SA}^*} \stackrel{\text{def}}{=} R_\Sigma^T$
RA*	Strong Receiver Anonymity	$R_{\mathsf{RA}^*} \stackrel{\text{def}}{=} R_\Sigma$
SRA	Sender-Receiver Anonymity	$R_{\mathsf{SRA}} \stackrel{\text{def}}{=} R_\#$
UO	Unobservability	$R_{\mathsf{UO}} \stackrel{\text{def}}{=} \mathcal{M}_{n \times n}(\mathcal{P}(V))^2$

Fig. 1. Anonymity variants and their associated relations R_N

Definition 1. (*Anonymous Channels*) *A message-transmission protocol π achieves N-anonymity for $N \in \{\mathsf{SUL}, \mathsf{RUL}, \mathsf{UL}, \mathsf{SA}, \mathsf{RA}, \mathsf{SA}^*, \mathsf{RA}^*, \mathsf{SRA}, \mathsf{UO}\}$, if for all PPT adversaries A, the quantity $\mathbf{Adv}_{\pi,A}^{N-anon}(k)$ is negligible in $k \in \mathbb{N}$.*

4 Relation between the Notions

In this section, we show implications between the notions. We start by formalizing the type of reduction we use.

BLACK-BOX IMPLICATIONS: As mentioned before, we consider a simplified network where the only communication channel between the parties is an idealized implementation of a protocol satisfying a certain anonymity notion N_1. We say notion N_1 *implies* notion N_2 (or alternatively that N_2 *reduces to* N_1), denoted by $N_1 \rightarrow N_2$, if there exists a protocol $\theta^{(\cdot)}$ (with access to the idealized communication channel) such that, for every protocol π, the following holds: if π achieves N_1-anonymity, then θ^π achieves N_2-anonymity.

RESULTS: Our results are summarized in Fig. 2. We first describe some easy implications, most of them folklore results, which until now remained without formal proof. An interesting aspect of the result is that the transformation which enables the reductions is the identity function. Therefore, some definitions are stronger than others in the sense that any protocol achieving one definition also achieves the other one.

Proposition 1. *The following implications hold unconditionally* $\mathsf{UO} \rightarrow \mathsf{SRA} \rightarrow \mathsf{SA}^* \rightarrow \mathsf{SA} \rightarrow \mathsf{SUL}$, $\mathsf{SRA} \rightarrow \mathsf{RA}^* \rightarrow \mathsf{RA} \rightarrow \mathsf{RUL}$, $\mathsf{SA}^* \rightarrow \mathsf{UL} \rightarrow \mathsf{RUL}$ *and* $\mathsf{RA}^* \rightarrow \mathsf{UL} \rightarrow \mathsf{SUL}$.

4.1 Implications under Computational Assumptions

In this section, we show that, under some standard setup and computational assumptions (namely PKI and key-private secure encryption [30,4]), some of the

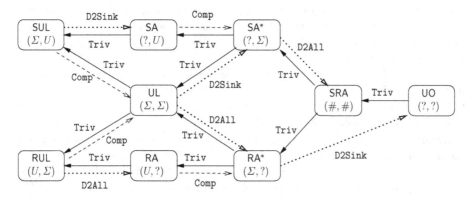

Fig. 2. Relations among notions of anonymity. Arrows labeled `Triv` denote trivial implications (Proposition 1) and those labeled `Comp` denote implications under computational assumptions (Lemma 1). Arrows labeled `D2Sink` and `D2All` denote implications that use the transformation of the same name (Proposition 4 and Proposition 5 respectively). Implications obtained by transitivity are not drawn.

notions are equivalent in the sense that a protocol achieving one definition can be efficiently transformed into a similar protocol achieving the other definition. In particular, RUL, SUL, and UL are all equivalent, as well as SA and SA*, and RA and RA*. Due to space restrictions, the assumptions are formalized in [35].

Lemma 1. *Assume key-private semantically secure public-key encryption schemes and PKI exist. Then* SUL $\to$ UL, RUL $\to$ UL, SA $\to$ SA* *and* RA $\to$ RA*.

For each implication of the lemma, the structure of the proof is the same and is divided into two steps. To prove that notion **N** implies notion **N**′, we first define an intermediate notion, called **I-N**-*anonymity* (or *value oblivious* **N**-*anonymity*, which we prove is implied by **N**, that is, **N** $\to$ **I-N**. Then, we prove that **I-N** $\to$ **N**′. Interestingly, the proof that **N** $\to$ **I-N** is the same for **N** $\in$ {SUL, RUL, SA, RA}, so we present it only once, first. The new notions, although somewhat technical, are the natural extensions of relations R_U and R_U^T to capture indistinguishability of the values instead of equality. Proving that the resulting notion **I-N** is in fact *implied* by the original notion **N** is nonetheless non-trivial.

Let **N** $\in$ {SUL, RUL, SA, RA}. Given **N**-anonymity, we define notion **I-N**-anonymity using an experiment similar to that underlying the definition of **N**-anonymity. In fact, the only difference is that the adversary can specify two PPT *sampling* algorithms $G^{(0)}$ and $G^{(1)}$ from where the elements of the challenge matrices $M^{(0)}, M^{(1)}$ are drawn. The only restriction is that $G^{(0)}$ and $G^{(1)}$ must induce computationally indistinguishable ensembles.[6] Intuitively, this experiment

---

[6] At first look, this type of adversary may seem artificial, as the restrictions on the sampling algorithms cannot be efficiently tested. Nonetheless, this is all we need, as Proposition 3 shows that for each implication **I-N** $\to$ **N**′ any **N**′-adversary can be transformed into this type of **I-N**-adversary, which in turn Proposition 2 shows can be mapped into an "regular" **N**-adversary.

decouples the adversary's control over message values and message destinations. Matrices $M^{(0)}, M^{(1)}$ specify the adversarial choices for sources and destinations of messages, while the sampling pair $(G^{(0)}, G^{(1)})$ specifies distributions for the message values. Details follow.

Let $k \in \mathbb{N}$ be a security parameter. For simplicity, assume that each party only sends a single message to each other party.[7] Two algorithms $G^{(0)}(\cdot, \cdot)$ and $G^{(1)}(\cdot, \cdot)$ form an *indistinguishable sampling pair* if each is PPT on the first input, and the ensembles $\{G^{(0)}(k, a)\}_{k \in \mathbb{N}, a \in V}$ and $\{G^{(1)}(k, a)\}_{k \in \mathbb{N}, a \in V}$ are computational indistinguishable. We say PPT algorithm A is a *legal* adversary if, on input k, A's first output is a tuple $(M^{(0)}, M^{(1)}, \langle G^{(0)} \rangle, \langle G^{(1)} \rangle)$ where $M^{(0)}, M^{(1)}$ are message matrices and $\langle G^{(0)} \rangle, \langle G^{(1)} \rangle$ is the encoding of an indistinguishable sampling pair. Given a legal adversary A, we define the experiment $\mathbf{Exp}_{\pi,A}^{\mathbf{I\text{-}N}-anon}$ as described below. The corresponding success probability $\mathbf{Adv}_{\pi,A}^{\mathbf{I\text{-}N}-anon}(k)$ of adversary A is defined in the usual way.

Experiment $\mathbf{Exp}_{\pi,A}^{\mathbf{I\text{-}N}-anon}(k)$

$b \xleftarrow{R} \{0,1\}$, and $(M^{(0)}, M^{(1)}, \langle G^{(0)} \rangle, \langle G^{(1)} \rangle) \leftarrow A(k)$

if $(M^{(0)}, M^{(1)}) \notin R_{\mathbf{N}}$ **then return** 0

else Parse $M^{(0)}$ as $(m_{i,j}^{(0)})_{i,j \in [n]}$ and $M^{(1)}$ as $(m_{i,j}^{(1)})_{i,j \in [n]}$

For all $i, j \in [n]$, all $d = 0, 1$,

if $m_{i,j}^{(d)} \neq \emptyset$, then set $\bar{m}_{i,j}^{(d)} \xleftarrow{R} G^{(d)}(k, m_{i,j}^{(d)})$, or $\bar{m}_{i,j}^{(d)} \leftarrow \emptyset$ otherwise.

$\bar{M}^{(0)} \leftarrow (\bar{m}_{i,j}^{(0)})_{i,j \in [n]}$ and $\bar{M}^{(1)} \leftarrow (\bar{m}_{i,j}^{(1)})_{i,j \in [n]}$

Execute π on input $\bar{M}^{(b)}$ under adversary A until A outputs a bit g.

if $(b = g)$ **return** 1 **else return** 0

For completeness, the formal definition is presented next.

Definition 2. *Let $\mathbf{N} \in \{\mathsf{SUL}, \mathsf{RUL}, \mathsf{SA}, \mathsf{RA}\}$. A message-transmission protocol π achieves $\mathbf{I\text{-}N}$-anonymity if for all legal PPT adversaries A, the quantity $\mathbf{Adv}_{\pi,A}^{\mathbf{I\text{-}N}-anon}(k)$ is negligible in $k \in \mathbb{N}$.*

We obtain the result of the lemma from the following two propositions. The first one shows that $\mathbf{N} \to \mathbf{I\text{-}N}$ for any notion $\mathbf{N} \in \{\mathsf{SUL}, \mathsf{RUL}, \mathsf{SA}, \mathsf{RA}\}$, and the second one proves the results of the lemma starting from $\mathbf{I\text{-}N}$. Intuitively, this proposition states that the adversary's ability to *choose* the input values for the messages does not weaken the notion of anonymity.

Proposition 2. *Let $\mathbf{N} \in \{\mathsf{SUL}, \mathsf{RUL}, \mathsf{SA}, \mathsf{RA}\}$, and let π be a message-transmission protocol that achieves $\mathbf{N}$-anonymity. Then, π achieves $\mathbf{I\text{-}N}$-anonymity.*

Given any $\mathbf{I\text{-}N}$-anonymous protocol π for $\mathbf{N} \in \{\mathsf{SUL}, \mathsf{RUL}, \mathsf{SA}, \mathsf{RA}\}$, the simple transformation consisting of encrypting (under a key-private encryption scheme [4]) each message under the public key of the recipient produces a protocol that can achieve a stronger anonymity notion. Indeed, next proposition simply shows

---

[7] The implications still hold if more than one message is exchanged between each pair of parties although the proof becomes a little more involved.

that breaking the stronger notion gives raise to a *legal adversary* for the weaker notion **I-N**. The details and proof are in the full version [35].

Proposition 3. *Assume a semantically secure public-key encryption scheme exists [30]. Then I-SUL → UL, and I-SA → SA*. Moreover, if the encryption scheme is key-private [4], then I-RUL → UL, and I-RA → RA*.*

Proof (Lemma 1). It follows directly from combining Proposition 2 and 3.

4.2   Implications That Require "Dummy Traffic"

In this section, we show that notions UL, SA*, RA*, SRA, and UO are equivalent under reductions that involve sending dummy traffic. Notions SUL and SA, as well as RUL and RA are also equivalent.

Let `D2Sink` be the following protocol transformation. Given a message-transmission protocol π, output another protocol that operates like π but where each sender transmits additional empty messages *to a fixed party* (the "sink") until the sender's total number equals a given constant μ_N. The next proposition shows `D2Sink` can be used to achieve stronger notions of anonymity. The reader is referred to the full version [35] for details.

Proposition 4. *Assume the total number of messages in any protocol for the notions SA, SA*, and UO is upper bounded by a publicly known value μ_N. Then, SUL→SA, UL→SA*, and RA*→UO.*

Similarly, let `D2All` be the transformation that instructs senders to transmit one dummy message to everyone else per each valid message to be sent. `D2All` is used to prove the following implications.

Proposition 5. RUL→RA, UL→RA*, *and* SA*→SRA.

4.3   Message Overhead and Optimality of the Transformations

The black-box transformations `D2Sink` of Proposition 4 and `D2All` of Proposition 5 output protocols that use "dummy" messages (those whose value is "⊥" which are ultimately discarded). These messages increase the communication complexity of the protocol, so it is interesting to ask if there are better solutions, possibly based on cryptographic tools. Interestingly, we show that the single transformations `D2Sink` and `D2All` described in previous section cannot be substantially improved, even in the presence of PKI.

Thus, we explore the question of whether more *message efficient* transformations exist, in terms of generating protocols where fewer messages (dummy or not) are sent overall.[8] For simplicity, we consider transformations where the

---

[8] Recall that we say a message m is *sent* by a message-transmission protocol Π if m is an element of the message matrix given to the protocol Π as input. This message should not be confused with the *packets* sent over the point-to-point communication channels between the parties as the result of a particular implementation of Π.

input protocol is invoked via a black-box call only once; the general case is discussed at the end of the section.

Let T be a transformation that maps a protocol ω into another protocol δ_T^ω. We measure message overhead by counting the number of extra messages that any protocol $\delta_T^\omega \stackrel{\text{def}}{=} T(\omega)$ adds on the underlying (black-box) protocol π. Concretely, given two transformations T_1, T_2, we say T_1 has less message overhead than T_2 if protocols $\delta_{T_1}^\omega = T_1(\omega)$ and $\delta_{T_2}^\omega = T_2(\omega)$ when executed on the same input matrix M require subprotocol ω to send t_1 (resp. t_2) messages when invoked as part of $\delta_{T_1}^\omega$ (resp. $\delta_{T_2}^\omega$), where $t_1 < t_2$ for any protocol ω. More formally, let $M = (m_{i,j})_{i,j \in [n]}$ be a message matrix, and denote by $\delta_T^{[\cdot]}(M) \in \mathcal{M}_{n \times n}(\mathcal{P}(V))$ the message matrix on which the black-box protocol (say ω) is invoked via a black-box call during the execution of δ_T^ω on input matrix M. We stress that once M is fixed, matrix $\delta_T^{[\cdot]}(M)$ is well-defined, independently of the message-transmission protocol ω, as ω is invoked as black-box by δ_T^ω exactly once.

Definition 3. *Let* $(N', N) \in \{(\mathsf{SUL}, \mathsf{SA}), (\mathsf{RUL}, \mathsf{RA}), (\mathsf{UL}, \mathsf{SA}^*), (\mathsf{UL}, \mathsf{RA}^*),$ $(\mathsf{RA}^*, \mathsf{SRA}), (\mathsf{SA}^*, \mathsf{SRA})\}$, *and* T *be any transformation underlying implication* $N' \to N$. *The* message overhead *of* T *is* $\mathsf{ovh}(T) \stackrel{\text{def}}{=} \max_M \left\{ \left| \delta_T^{[\cdot]}(M) \right| / |M| \right\}$ *where the maximum is taken over all (allowed) non-empty message matrices M for notion* N.

It is easy to see that, under the assumption that the total number of messages sent is at most μ_N, $\mathsf{ovh}(\mathsf{D2Sink}) = n \cdot \mu_N$. Similarly, but under no assumptions, $\mathsf{ovh}(\mathsf{D2All}) = n$. The next two propositions show that we cannot do better. The proof is by contradiction which is derived from the fact that if there are "too few" messages sent by a party, the underlying black-box protocol may no longer be invoked in a secure way. For Proposition 7, the construction and analysis are similar but considering the number of messages *received* by any party.

Proposition 6. D2Sink *is optimal for* SUL→SA, UL→SA*, *and* RA*→UO.

Proposition 7. D2All *is optimal for* RUL→RA, UL→RA*, *and* SA*→SRA.

UPPER BOUND PER SENDER: A similar analysis holds if a bound $\hat{\mu}_N$ on the number of messages *per sender* is assumed instead, for SA and SA*-anonymity. (We stress that the implication SA → SA* of Lemma 1 is preserved under this restriction). In this case the overhead is $n \cdot \hat{\mu}_N$, which is also optimal. This formulation, although more restrictive, can be more suitable for certain applications.[9] From a theoretical point, however, it is not clear if there is any advantage to this formulation over the one presented above.

SINGLE VS. MULTIPLE BLACK-BOX CALLS: If we consider transformations that output protocols that invoke the input (black-box) protocol more than once, then is it possible to prove that the optimal overhead is n. A protocol δ^π that achieves

---

[9] Upper bounds on the number of messages sent *per party* may help to prevent certain *flooding* attacks against mix nets [34,52].

this is the one that uses a *secure multiparty computation protocol* (eg. [6]) to compute $|M|$ using π as communication channel; then, each party calls ensures it sends $|M|$ messages via π by adding sufficient dummy messages. Even though such a secure multiparty protocol can be computed with constant number of invocations to π [2] (and thus, $\mathcal{O}(n^2)$ messages), it is likely that invoking π more than once will render the resulting protocol impractical.

5   On the Anonymity of Previous Protocols

The ultimate purpose of a definition is to be used to properly characterize the security of concrete protocols. Accordingly, we revisit the security of known constructions based on broadcast channels [8], DC-nets or anonymous networks [15,32,54], and mix-nets [33,44,24]. In Section 5, we examine the basic construction of Blaze et al. [8], which is based on broadcast channels, and we argue it can be shown *strong receiver anonymous*. We also discuss the DC-nets of [32] and sketch how the construction there can be proven *sender anonymous*. Finally, we highlight sufficient conditions to prove the *strong receiver anonymity* of mix-net constructions based on shuffles [33, 44]. (We only sketch these claims due to space constrains. Proofs are provided in the full version.) By combining the constructions that underlie the implications of previous sections, we obtain anonymous protocols provably secure under the strongest notions: *sender-receiver anonymity* and *unobservability*.

BROADCAST NETWORKS: Broadcast channels can be used as a straightforward approach to obtain some form of receiver anonymity [48]. In general, the most obvious protocol of transmitting a message over the broadcast channel is trivially RA-anonymous. Blaze et al. [8] recently suggested a protocol for anonymous routing in the context of wireless networks. Very roughly, their basic protocol is an adaptation of onion routing [29] to broadcast networks. The operation of sending a message is then analogous, and involves computing a path of routers, and a corresponding *onion* (a nested encryption) of the message (see [8] for details). The difference is that each transmission of the "onion" between routers is done via the broadcast channel, so all receivers attempt to decrypt the onion but only the intended recipient succeeds (although not mentioned, some integrity mechanism must be used in the onion). Under passive global adversaries, if the encryption used provides key-privacy [4],[10] the protocol can easily be shown RA*-anonymous. However, due to the shared nature of the wireless medium, transforming it into a UO-secure protocol may not be practical given the message overhead (unavoidable by Proposition 6).

DC-NETS OR ANONYMOUS BROADCAST: DC-nets [15,32] can be seen as particular instances of anonymous broadcast protocols [54]. In these protocols, there is a single message sent which is public. In [32], Golle and Juels proposed very efficient anonymous broadcast protocol based on pairings. Whenever a transmission is to take place, all parties participate in the protocol by transmitting "pads". Each pad contains the (potentially empty) message the party intends

---

[10] This requirement apparently was overlooked in [8].

to transmit. Golle and Juels show how to combine the pads so the transmitted messages are recovered with high probability (and therefore theirs is a message-transmission protocol with high probability). They also show how each party can provide a non-interactive zero-knowledge (NIZK) proof [21] for the correctness of her pad without revealing the underlying message. By the simulatability of the NIZK proof, it then follows that their protocol can be proven SA-anonymous under global passive adversaries as long as the *Bilinear Diffie-Hellman assumption* [9] holds. Notice that this result is not implied by their security proof as the anonymity notion used in [32] is arguably different (see Section 1.4).

MIX NETWORKS: Robust and efficient MIX-net constructions can be built from efficient schemes to *prove a shuffle* [25, 33, 44]. In these constructions, each mixer proves the correctness of the shuffle operation (usually a random permutation and sometimes partial decryption) was done correctly. The resulting mix-net protocol may work as follows: first, all senders send encryptions of their messages to the first mixer (the encryptions are made under a threshold key shared by the mixers). Then, the mixing process starts where each mixer performs (and proves) her shuffle passing the resulting vector to the next mixer. The last mixer broadcast the resulting vector. The shuffles in [33] and [24, Appendix A] can be proven *honest verifier zero-knowledge* (HVZK) arguments. The shuffles in [25, 44] can be shown to satisfy the stronger property IND-CPA$_S$ [44]. Under passive adversaries, both properties suffice to prove the adversary cannot distinguish two executions of the associated mix-nets even under adversarial inputs. Assuming the last mixer broadcasts the output, these constructions can then be proven RA*-secure.

6   Variants and Extensions

k-ANONYMITY: Intuitively, a protocol achieves k-anonymity if any adversary trying to determine the sender (resp. receiver) of a message can only narrow the sender's identity down to no less than k possible senders (resp. receivers). The concept was proposed by Pfitzmann [45] and further developped (along with efficient constructions) by von Ahn et al. [56] as a way to improve the efficiency of DC-nets. We can accommodate the notion of k-anonymity in our framework by further restricting the relation $R_{\mathbf{N}}$. For each of the message matrices output by the adversary we require at least k non-empty rows (resp. columns) to capture the restriction to k senders (resp. receivers).

PASSIVE ADVERSARIES WITH CORRUPTIONS: As mentioned before, it is possible to extend our framework to consider party corruptions. The adversary would be allowed to passively (either statically or dynamically) corrupt senders and receivers, with the obvious restrictions that the local inputs and outputs corresponding to the corrupted parties must be the same in the two message matrices output by the adversary. Note that this conditions immediately hold if the corrupted party that does not send or receive messages and only acts as forwarder (router). The security proofs for the protocols mentioned in previous section carry to this stronger model. Extending our framework beyond passive attacks (active adversaries) is currently part of ongoing research.

References

1. Abe, M.: Universally verifiable mix-net with verification work independent of the number of mix-servers. In: Nyberg, K. (ed.) EUROCRYPT 1998. LNCS, vol. 1403, pp. 437–447. Springer, Heidelberg (1998)
2. Beaver, D., Micali, S., Rogaway, P.: The round complexity of secure protocols. In: Proc. of the 22nd Annual ACM Symposium on the Theory of Computing – STOC 1990, pp. 503–513. ACM Press, New York (1990)
3. Beimel, A., Dolev, S.: Buses for anonymous message delivery. Journal of Cryptology 16 (2003)
4. Bellare, M., Boldyreva, A., Desai, A., Pointcheval, D.: Key-privacy in public-key encryption. In: Boyd, C. (ed.) ASIACRYPT 2001. LNCS, vol. 2248, pp. 566–582. Springer, Heidelberg (2001)
5. Bellare, M., Desai, A., Pointcheval, D., Rogaway, P.: Relations among notions of security for public-key encryption schemes. In: Krawczyk, H. (ed.) CRYPTO 1998. LNCS, vol. 1462, pp. 26–45. Springer, Heidelberg (1998)
6. Ben-Or, M., Goldwasser, S., Wigderson, A.: Completeness theorems for noncryptographic fault-tolerant distributed computations. In: Proc. of the 20th Annual ACM Symposium on Theory of Computing, pp. 1–10. ACM Press, New York (1988)
7. Berman, R., Fiat, A., Ta-Shma, A.: Provable unlinkability against traffic analysis. In: Juels, A. (ed.) FC 2004. LNCS, vol. 3110. Springer, Heidelberg (2004)
8. Blaze, M., Ioannidis, J., Keromytis, A.D., Malkin, T., Rubin, A.: WAR: Wireless anonymous routing. In: Christianson, B., Crispo, B., Malcolm, J.A., Roe, M. (eds.) Security Protocols 2003. LNCS, vol. 3364, pp. 218–232. Springer, Heidelberg (2005)
9. Boneh, D., Franklin, M.K.: Identity-based encryption from the weil pairing. In: Kilian, J. (ed.) CRYPTO 2001. LNCS, vol. 2139, pp. 213–229. Springer, Heidelberg (2001)
10. Bos, J., den Boer, B.: Detection of disrupters in the DC protocol. In: Quisquater, J.-J., Vandewalle, J. (eds.) EUROCRYPT 1989. LNCS, vol. 434, pp. 320–328. Springer, Heidelberg (1990)
11. Camenisch, J., Lysyanskaya, A.: A formal treatment of onion routing. In: Shoup, V. (ed.) CRYPTO 2005. LNCS, vol. 3621, pp. 169–187. Springer, Heidelberg (2005)
12. Canetti, R.: Security and composition of multiparty cryptographic protocols. Journal of Cryptology 13(1), 143–202 (2000)
13. Canetti, R.: Universally composable security: a new paradigm for cryptographic protocols. In: Proc. of the 42nd IEEE Symposium on Foundations of Computer Science, pp. 136–145. IEEE Computer Society Press, Los Alamitos (2001)
14. Chaum, D.: Untraceable electronic mail, return addresses, and digital pseudonyms. Communications of the ACM 24(2), 84–88 (1981)
15. Chaum, D.: The Dining Cryptographers Problem: Unconditional sender and recipient untraceability. Journal of Cryptology 1(1), 65–75 (1988)
16. Chaum, D., Crepeau, C., Damgård, I.: Multiparty unconditional secure protocols. In: Proc. of STOC 1988, pp. 11–19. ACM Press, New York (1988)
17. Danezis, G., Dingledine, R., Mathewson, N.: Mixminion: Design of a Type III Anonymous Remailer Protocol. In: Proc. of IEEE Security and Privacy (2003)
18. Díaz, C., Seys, S., Claessens, J., Preneel, B.: Towards measuring anonymity. In: Dingledine, R., Syverson, P.F. (eds.) PET 2002. LNCS, vol. 2482. Springer, Heidelberg (2003)
19. Dingledine, R., Mathewson, N., Syverson, P.: Tor: The second-generation onion router. In: Proc. of the 13th USENIX Security Symposium (2004)

20. Dolev, S., Ostrobsky, R.: Xor-trees for efficient anonymous multicast and reception. ACM Trans. on Information System Security 3(2), 63–84 (2000)
21. Feige, U., Lapidot, D., Shamir, A.: Multiple noninteractive zero knowledge proofs under general assumptions. SIAM Journal on Computing 29(1) (1999)
22. Feigenbaum, J., Johnson, A., Syverson, P.: A model for onion routing with provable anonymity. In: Financial Cryptography. LNCS, vol. 4886. Springer, Heidelberg (2007)
23. Fujioka, A., Okamoto, T., Ohta, K.: A practical secret voting scheme for large scale elections. In: Proc. of AUSCRYPT 1992. LNCS, vol. 718, pp. 244–251. Springer, Heidelberg (1992)
24. Furukawa, J.: Efficient, verifiable shuffle decryption and its requirement of unlinkability. In: Bao, F., Deng, R., Zhou, J. (eds.) PKC 2004. LNCS, vol. 2947. Springer, Heidelberg (2004)
25. Furukawa, J., Sako, K.: An efficient scheme for proving a shuffle. In: Kilian, J. (ed.) CRYPTO 2001. LNCS, vol. 2139. Springer, Heidelberg (2001)
26. Garcia, F.D., Hasuo, I., Pieters, W., van Rossum, P.: Provable anonymity. In: Proc. of the 3rd ACM Workshop on Formal Methods in Security Engineering – FMSE 2005, pp. 63–72. ACM Press, New York (2005)
27. Goldreich, O.: A uniform complexity treatment of encryption and zero-knowledge. Journal of Cryptology 6(1), 21–53 (1993)
28. Goldreich, O., Micali, S., Wigderson, A.: Proofs that yield nothing but their validity and a methodology of cryptographic protocol design. In: Proc. 27th Symposium on Foundations of Computer Science, pp. 174–187. IEEE Press, Los Alamitos (1986)
29. Goldschlag, D.M., Reed, M.G., Syverson, P.F.: Hiding Routing Information. In: Proc. of Information Hiding. LNCS, vol. 1174, pp. 137–150. Springer, Heidelberg (1996)
30. Goldwasser, S., Micali, S.: Probabilistic encryption. Journal of Computer and System Science 28, 270–299 (1984)
31. Goldwasser, S., Micali, S., Rivest, R.: A digital signature scheme secure against adaptive chosen-message attacks. Siam J. of Computing 17(2), 281–308 (1988)
32. Golle, P., Juels, A.: Dining cryptographers revisited. In: Cachin, C., Camenisch, J.L. (eds.) EUROCRYPT 2004. LNCS, vol. 3027. Springer, Heidelberg (2004)
33. Groth, J.: A verifiable secret shuffle of homomorphic encryptions. In: Desmedt, Y.G. (ed.) PKC 2003. LNCS, vol. 2567. Springer, Heidelberg (2002)
34. Gülcü, C., Tsudik, G.: Mixing E-mail with Babel. In: Proc. of the Network and Distributed Security Symposium – NDSS 1996, pp. 2–16. IEEE Press, Los Alamitos (1996)
35. Hevia, A., Micciancio, D.: Indistinguishability-based Characterization of Anonymous Channels (2008), http://www.dcc.uchile.cl/~ahevia/pubs/
36. Hughes, D., Shmatikov, V.: Information Hiding, Anonymity and Privacy: a Modular Approach. Journal of Computer Security 12(1), 3–36 (2004)
37. Halpern, J.Y., O'Neill, K.R.: Anonymity and information hiding in multiagent systems. Journal of Computer Security (2004)
38. Ishai, Y., Kushilevitz, E., Ostrovsky, R., Sahai, A.: Cryptography from anonymity. In: Proc. of FOCS 2006. IEEE Press, Los Alamitos (2006)
39. Jakobsson, M., Juels, A., Rivest, R.L.: Making mix nets robust for electronic voting by randomized partial checking. In: Proc. of the 11th USENIX Security Symposium (SECURITY 2002), pp. 339–353. USENIX Association (2002)
40. Kesdogan, D., Egner, J., Büschkes, R.: Stop-and-go MIXes: Providing probabilistic anonymity in an open system. In: Aucsmith, D. (ed.) IH 1998. LNCS, vol. 1525. Springer, Heidelberg (1998)

41. Mauw, S., Verschuren, J.H.S., de Vink, E.P.: A formalization of anonymity and onion routing. In: Samarati, P., Ryan, P.Y.A., Gollmann, D., Molva, R. (eds.) ESORICS 2004. LNCS, vol. 3193. Springer, Heidelberg (2004)
42. Micali, S., Rackoff, C., Sloan, B.: The notion of security for probabilistic cryptosystems. Siam Journal of Computing 17(2), 412–426 (1988)
43. Neff, A.: A verifiable secret shuffle and its application to E-voting. In: Proc. 8th ACM Conference on Computer and Communications Security, ACM SIGSAC (2001)
44. Nguyen, L., Safavi-Naini, R., Kurosawa, K.: Verifiable shuffles: A formal model and a paillier-based efficient construction with provable security. In: Proc. of Applied Cryptography and Network Security. LNCS, vol. 3089. Springer, Heidelberg (2004)
45. Pfitzmann, A.: How to Implement ISDNs Without User Observability – some Remarks. Tech. report Fakultät für Informatik, Universität Karlsruhe (1985)
46. Pfitzmann, A., Köhntopp, M.: Anonymity, unobservability, and pseudonymity — A proposal for terminology. LNCS, vol. 2009, pp. 1–9. Springer, Heidelberg (2001)
47. Pfitzmann, A., Pfitzmann, B., Waidner, M.: ISDN-Mixes: Untraceable communication with very small bandwidth overhead. In: Proc. Kommunikation in verteilten Systemen, Informatik-Fachberichte 267, pp. 451–463. Springer, Heidelberg (1991); Slightly extended. In: Information Security, Proc. IFIP/Sec 1991, pp. 245–258 (1991)
48. Pfitzmann, A., Waidner, M.: Networks without user observability. Computers & Security 6(2), 158–166 (1987)
49. Rackoff, C., Simon, D.R.: Cryptographic defense against traffic analysis. In: Proc. of STOC 1993, pp. 672–681. ACM Press, New York (1993)
50. Reiter, M.K., Rubin, A.D.: Crowds: Anonymity for web transactions. ACM Transactions on Information and System Security 1(1), 66–92 (1998)
51. Rennhard, M., Plattner, B.: Practical anonymity for the masses with morphmix. In: Juels, A. (ed.) FC 2004. LNCS, vol. 3110. Springer, Heidelberg (2004)
52. Serjantov, A.: On the Anonymity of Anonymity Systems. PhD thesis, University of Cambridge (2004)
53. Serjantov, A., Danezis, G.: Towards an information theoretic metric for anonymity. In: Dingledine, R., Syverson, P.F. (eds.) PET 2002. LNCS, vol. 2482. Springer, Heidelberg (2003)
54. Stajano, F., Anderson, R.: The cocaine auction protocol: On the power of anonymous broadcast. In: Pfitzmann, A. (ed.) Information Hiding —3rd International Workshop, IH 1999. LNCS, vol. 1768. Springer, Heidelberg (2000)
55. Syverson, P.F., Stubblebine, S.G.: Group principals and the formalization of anonymity. In: Proc. of the World Congress on Formal Methods. LNCS, vol. 1708, pp. 814–833. Springer, Heidelberg (1999)
56. von Ahn, L., Bortz, A., Hopper, N.J.: k-Anonymous message transmission. In: Proc. of the 10th ACM Conference on Computer and Communication Security – CCS 2003, pp. 122–130. ACM Press, New York (2003)
57. Waidner, M.: Unconditional sender and recipient untraceability in spite of active attacks. In: Proc. of EUROCRYPT 1889. LNCS, vol. 434, pp. 302–319. Springer, Heidelberg (1990)
58. Waidner, M., Pfitzmann, B.: The dining cryptographers in the disco: Unconditional sender and recipient untraceability with computationally secure serviceability. In: Proc. of EUROCRYPT 1989. LNCS, vol. 434, p. 690. Springer, Heidelberg (1989)
59. Wikström, D.: A universally composable mix-net. In: Naor, M. (ed.) TCC 2004. LNCS, vol. 2951, pp. 317–335. Springer, Heidelberg (2004)

On the Impact of Social Network Profiling on Anonymity

Claudia Diaz[1], Carmela Troncoso[1], and Andrei Serjantov[2]

[1] K.U. Leuven ESAT-COSIC
Kasteelpark Arenberg 10, Leuven-Heverlee, Belgium
{claudia.diaz,carmela.troncoso}@esat.kuleuven.be
[2] The Free Haven Project
schnur@gmail.com

Abstract. This paper studies anonymity in a setting where individuals who communicate with each other over an anonymous channel are also members of a social network. In this setting the social network graph is known to the attacker. We propose a Bayesian method to combine multiple available sources of information and obtain an overall measure of anonymity. We study the effects of network size and find that in this case anonymity degrades when the network grows. We also consider adversaries with incomplete or erroneous information; characterize their knowledge of the social network by its quantity, quality and depth; and discuss the implications of these properties for anonymity.

1 Introduction

In the last few years defining and quantifying anonymity in the context of communication networks has been a hot research topic. A substantial set of papers focus on the definition of anonymity, others present designs and analysis of new anonymous communication systems or attacks of existing ones. Yet more focus on the theory of mix systems in order to improve our fundamental understanding of anonymity properties which are possible or practically achievable. This paper takes the fine line between theory and practice and attempts to evaluate the anonymity properties of an abstract anonymous communication system within the practical context of a social network.

We consider the anonymity of users belonging to a social network who communicate with each other via anonymous messages. The attacker is the global passive adversary (she observes the inputs and outputs of the anonymous communication network) and also has knowledge of the users' profiles. First we consider the two sources of information available to the adversary separately, then we combine them and examine what happens as the network grows. Interestingly, it turns out that the details of the mixing algorithm employed by the anonymous communication system play a significant role. Next, we briefly show how additional sources of information can be used by the attacker to further reduce anonymity. Finally, we look at how the quantity, quality and depth of knowledge about the users' relationships affects our results.

N. Borisov and I. Goldberg (Eds.): PETS 2008, LNCS 5134, pp. 44–62, 2008.

Our main contribution is evaluating how the uncertainty in the attacker's knowledge of user profiles affects anonymity. Indeed, we show that arbitrarily small errors in the profiles can lead to arbitrarily large errors in the anonymity probability distribution and hence point to the wrong subjects in the anonymity set. We develop the intuition behind this result and evaluate the errors in the anonymity probability distributions in the context of the social network. We conduct our experiments by simulation which helps us examine realistic scenarios.

2   Related Work

This paper belongs to a growing body of work focusing on the anonymity analysis of anonymous communication systems. A substantial part of this literature consists of papers evaluating the effectiveness of mix-based anonymity systems in a theoretical setting; e.g., [6,11,18]. Such work often involves assumptions such as "users pick their communication partners uniformly at random" which help with the mathematics of calculating anonymity, and hence aid our understanding and intuition, but do not necessarily hold in practice. Furthermore, the authors often examine properties of the anonymous communication systems and shy away from incorporating models of users. This paper takes a more practical approach by assuming a social network, deriving the attacker's knowledge about users based on the fact that they belong to such a network and then evaluating the performance of the anonymous communication system in the context of this knowledge. Furthermore, we evaluate how errors in the information gained from the social network influence the correctness of the anonymity (and thus, the attacker's confidence in her result).

In order to evaluate anonymity in a practical setting, it is necessary to incorporate a priori information the attacker might have about communication patterns of users. We briefly mention a number of papers that explore related research problems. Diaz et al. [9] assume that some information on user properties is known, such that the user base can be partitioned in different groups that share a similar profile. Clauß et al. [3, 4] propose a framework and metrics for systems where the adversary has some information on user attributes. In these papers the focus is on user properties or profiles, and little effort is made to combine the knowledge gained through traffic analysis with the profile information available to the attacker. In [3,4], it is mentioned that the communication layer information gained through traffic analysis can be modeled by means of attributes, but no concrete example is given of how this could be realized. Finally, Diaz et al. [13] showed a toy example where the combination of user sending profiles and data gathered through traffic analysis resulted in higher anonymity, contradicting what had been claimed in [4]. However, no general methodology was given in [13] for computing anonymity metrics when several sources of information are available. The most closely related paper which attempts to combine knowledge about profiles with traffic analysis information is [8] where a lot of the Bayesian theory we use is presented, but only a brief demonstration of the technique is given. Here we give a number of practical examples and evaluate the impact of errors in the profiles on anonymity.

Perhaps the most related piece of related work in terms of the spirit of the analysis and in the style of the results obtained is one of Dingledine and Matthewson [16]. They employ simulations in order to evaluate the effectiveness of statistical disclosure attacks on a model of an anonymity system; i.e., they attempt to recover profiles from the communications data while we build assumptions about profiles from the social network and then add the communications data on top.

3   Preliminaries

3.1   System and Attacker Model

We consider a system where a set U of N users send messages to each other through an anonymous communication channel modeled as a mix[1]. Since Chaum [2] first proposed mixes for achieving anonymous communication in 1981, multiple designs have been proposed in the literature both for low-latency communication, e.g. [14] and for high-latency, message-based communication [5,7,15].

The adversary we consider can observe all input messages arriving to the mix (and their respective senders), as well as all output messages leaving the mix (and their recipients), but not the internal operations of the mix. Naturally, the messages are encrypted so the content is hidden. Although the attacker does not know the correspondence between inputs and outputs, she is able to compute the probability distributions linking every input with all possible outputs and vice versa.

In addition to observing the mix inputs and outputs, the adversary has a priori knowledge of the users' sending behavior. We assume users to be linked via a social network, and that users send messages to those who are in their *profile*; i.e., their set of "friends." We have used various methods to generate the user sending profiles, which are described in detail in Appendix A.

3.2   Anonymity with One Source of Information

We draw on the literature, more specifically [12] and [17] for our definition of anonymity. The basic idea of these metrics is to use the Shannon entropy [19] of the probability distribution linking subjects to a message or action (normalized entropy in the case of [12]). The entropy of this probability distribution gives a measure of the uncertainty concerning the identity of the subject who originated/received a message. Entropy-based anonymity metrics take into account both the number of users in the system and their probabilities of being linked to a particular action, and anonymity increases both with the number of users and the uniformity of the probability distribution linking them to messages.

The goal of our adversary is to identify the recipient of messages arriving to the mix (*recipient anonymity*) or the sender of messages leaving it (*sender*

---

[1] Our analysis and experiments apply to any abstract anonymous communication channel for which probabilistic relationships between inputs and outputs can be derived.

anonymity). Therefore, the adversary makes hypotheses of the type "hypothesis h_j is true if u_j is the sender (recipient) of this outgoing (incoming) message," and computes the probability $\Pr(h_j)$ that h_j is true. Given that every message has one sender and one recipient, the probabilities $\Pr(h_j)$ sum to one (i.e., $\sum_{j=1}^{N} \Pr(h_j) = 1$).

In this paper we use the *effective anonymity set size* [17] as the metric for sender and recipient anonymity. For a given message entering (leaving) the mix, the recipient (sender) anonymity A is given by the Shannon entropy of the probability distribution of each of the hypotheses h_j being true; i.e., $A = -\sum_{j=1}^{N} \Pr(h_j) \log_2(\Pr(h_j))$.

Let us first illustrate how anonymity is computed when only one source of information is available to the attacker. If the attacker knows the sending profiles of users, but cannot observe the inputs and outputs of the mix, the recipient anonymity of a message sent by user u belonging to the user population U is given by the entropy of her sending profile. That is, if u chooses user u_j as her recipient with probability $\Pr(u \rightarrow u_j)$, then the recipient anonymity provided by u's profile is $A_p = -\sum_{j=1}^{N} \Pr(u \rightarrow u_j) \log_2(\Pr(u \rightarrow u_j))$. Conversely, when u receives a message, the anonymity of the sender is given by $A_p = -\sum_{j=1}^{N} \Pr(u \leftarrow u_j) \log_2(\Pr(u \leftarrow u_j))$, where $\Pr(u \leftarrow u_j) = \frac{\Pr(u_j \rightarrow u)}{\sum_{k=1}^{N} \Pr(u_k \rightarrow u)}$ is the probability of u_j being the sender of a message received by u. In the remainder, we denote the sending profile of a user u as $P(u \rightarrow U) = \{\Pr(u \rightarrow u_j), \forall u_j \in U\}$ and its recipient profile as $P(u \leftarrow U) = \{\Pr(u \leftarrow u_j), \forall u_j \in U\}$.

Alternatively, we can consider an adversary who can see the inputs/outputs of the mix but does not have a priori knowledge of user profiles. The probability of an input (output) message matching each of the outputs (inputs) depends on the type of mix, overall traffic load and the timing of messages. Let us consider a timed pool mix. Pool mixes work in cycles called *rounds* that comprise three steps (1) **collect**: it collects messages from senders for a period of time T; (2) **store**: upon being received, messages are decrypted with the mix's private key (which allows it to retrieve the destination address), and stored in an internal memory called *pool*; and (3) **flush**: once the timeout T has expired, a fraction of the messages are randomly selected and sent to their destinations, while the rest is kept in the pool for the next round.

The probabilities of matching the mix inputs and outputs are computed as follows [10]. Let m_r be the number of messages contained in the mix in round r (prior to the mix flushing), and s_r be the number of messages sent by the mix in round r. If a message M arrived to the mix in round r, its probability $\Pr(M = O_{r',i})$ of matching each of the $s_{r'}$ outputs $O_{r',i}$ that left the mix in round r' is:

$$\Pr(M = O_{r',i}) = 0 \text{ if } r' < r$$

$$\Pr(M = O_{r',i}) = \frac{1}{m_{r'}} \text{ if } r' = r$$

$$\Pr(M = O_{r',i}) = \frac{1}{m_{r'}} \prod_{k=r}^{r'-1} \left(1 - \frac{s_k}{m_k}\right) \text{ if } r' > r$$

The recipient anonymity A_m provided by the mix to message M is given by the entropy of the probabilities $\Pr(M = O_{r',i})$. The computation of the probabilities $\Pr(I_{r',i} = M)$ linking an output M to all possible inputs $I_{r',i}$ is analogous, and their detailed derivation can be found in [10]. Note that probabilistic relationships between inputs and outputs can also be derived for other types of mixes such as Stop-and-Go [15].

3.3 Anonymity with Several Sources of Information

Bayesian inference is an approach to statistics in which all forms of uncertainty are expressed in terms of probability. It starts with an initial set of beliefs represented by an a priori probability distribution, which is updated as new evidence is collected. The distribution indicates how likely it is for a hypothesis to be true.

Let h_j be the hypothesis that user u_j is the sender (or recipient) of a given message received (or sent) by user u, and $\Pr(h_j)$ the prior probability of this hypothesis being true. Let E be some evidence or observation that gives us additional information on the truthfulness of h_j, and $\Pr(E|h_j)$ be the probability of observing evidence E conditioned to h_j being true. Bayesian inference can be used to compute the posterior probability $\Pr(h_j|E)$ of h_j, given that we have obtained evidence E. We denote this probability distribution by $P(H|E) = \{\Pr(h_j|E), 1 \leq j \leq N\}$:

$$\Pr(h_j|E) = \frac{\Pr(h_j)\Pr(E|h_j)}{\sum_{k=1}^{N}\Pr(h_k)\Pr(E|h_k)}$$

In our setting, we consider that both sender profiles and mix input/output observations are available to the adversary. The prior probability $\Pr(h_j)$ is given by the sending profiles of users, and corresponds to $\Pr(a \rightarrow u_j)$ in the case of recipient anonymity, and to $\Pr(a \leftarrow u_j)$ for sender anonymity (as explained in the previous section). The conditional probability $\Pr(E|h_j)$ is computed as follows. For recipient anonymity (analogous for sender anonymity), let R_j be the set of messages received by user u_j. Given that u sent message M to u_j (i.e., h_j is true), the probability $\Pr(E|h_j)$ of observing the evidence E corresponds to the probability of the mix matching M to one of the messages received by u_j:

$$\Pr(E|h_j) = \sum_{O_{r',i} \in R_j} \Pr(M = O_{r',i})$$

Bayesian inference can be applied recursively if new independent evidence E' becomes available to the adversary. We show results that introduce an additional source of information in Sect. 5.2.

4   Analysis

4.1   Intuition

The attackers' knowledge about the communication partners of users inside the social network comes from two sources—observing the mix and her a priori knowledge of the user profiles. Naturally, if we have a perfectly anonymous communication layer, the anonymity of the system comes only from the attacker's (lack of) information about the profiles. Conversely if the attacker has no information on the profiles of the users, she is restricted to observing the communications layer; i.e., the mix. The more complex setting when the attacker has knowledge of both is examined below.

Consider the case of users belonging to a vast social network and hence knowing a tiny fraction of the overall user population. In our model the attacker can see the inputs and the outputs of the mix and knows the profiles of all the users, so the only mixing that will take place is that between senders who share potential recipients or between recipients who share potential senders. Hence if the network grows and users' connectivity remains constant, anonymity falls. On the other hand, higher traffic load and number of users increase the anonymity provided by the mix. In Sect. 5.1 we show the tradeoff between these two effects.

The increasing popularity of blogs and, more generally, the availability of user-generated content makes it easy to gather a corpus of text linkable to an individual. Different people have different writing styles and patterns (such as word frequency or preferred grammatical constructions), and statistical tests that detect these patterns can be used to help identifying the authors of anonymous text. We study in Sect. 5.2 how the results of such a test can be combined with profiles and traffic analysis information, and its impact on sender anonymity.

The attacker's knowledge of the social network can vary in its quantity, quality and depth. She may know only of existence of links between individuals, the extent of those links, lack knowledge of links in some part of the network and hence have to make do with approximations or, worst of all, assume wrong information. We assess the impact of each of these on anonymity in Sections 5.3, 5.4 and 5.5. Before proceeding to the results of the analysis, we give details of our experimental setup.

4.2   Experimental Setup

We performed the analysis in the setting of a social network with a population of users arranged in a small-world network constructed following the Watts-Strogatz algorithm [21]. We also performed experiments on a scale free network [1] created with preferential attachment and the same number of average users, and the only noticeable difference was a larger variance in the results, which is due to the more uneven distribution of links per node in these networks. Unless indicated otherwise, we consider in our experiments 1000 users with an average of 20 friends each, arranged in a small world network with parameter $p = 0.1$ (i.e., highly clustered).

Users send messages only to their *friends* (i.e., users linked to them in the social network) with the probability specified in their profile. For the purposes of our experiments, we have developed several sets of user profiles with slightly different probability distributions. A detailed summary of the profiles used and the algorithms used to generate them can be found in Appendix A.

We chose a Mixmaster [5, 20] mix, as it is the most widely deployed high-latency network for anonymous email. The time intervals between users sending messages follow an exponential distribution with parameter λ, common to all users. We have chosen $1/\lambda$ to be 25 times greater than the timeout of the mix, so if users send messages on average once a day, the expected delay is between 30 mins and 1 hour. In every experiment we simulate 130 rounds of mixing. We then extract the information which could have been observed by the attacker and compute the sender and receiver anonymity of each message.

5 Results

5.1 Growing the Network

In this section we consider the anonymity of users as the social network is scaled up. To help develop the intuition we show the anonymity calculated from traffic analysis (mix input/output observations) and knowledge of the profiles separately. As the network grows, the anonymity provided by the mix increases as shown in Fig. 1(a)(Mix) simply because more traffic goes through it. As for the anonymity provided by the profiles (corresponding to Uniform profiles in Appendix A), we can see in Fig. 1(a)(Profile) that it remains constant, because we assume that the connectivity does not increase with the network (though in a real network it might increase slightly), which becomes more sparse. Interestingly, Fig. 1(a)(Combined) shows that the combined anonymity decreases with the network size. As we shall see, variations in parameters that have a positive (mix) or no (profiles) effect on anonymity when sources of information are considered separately, can have a negative impact when all information is put together.

In this particular case the decrease in anonymity with network size is due to an interaction between profiles and mix function. Consider a random user Alice. The attacker is aware of her sender profile, so only users who share friends with Alice contribute to her anonymity. Alice and her friends send and receive on average the same number of messages whether the network is large or small. At the same time, the Mixmaster function [5] that determines the fraction f of messages sent per round increases with the traffic load until it reaches its limit[2]—note that in Fig. 1(a)(Combined) anonymity stabilizes beyond that point. Therefore, the larger network induces the mix to flush a higher fraction of messages, which consequently in the mix for fewer rounds. This effect, in fact, decreases the amount of mixing, because friends of Alice who sent or received messages in the rounds before or after her contribute less to her anonymity[3].

---

[2] The maximum fraction of messages sent by Mixmaster is $f = 0.65$. In our setting, this is reached when there are around 2500 users.

[3] Friends who sent messages during the same round as Alice contribute the same amount as in the case of the smaller network.

5.2   Adding Extra Information

In this section we briefly show how Bayesian inference can be used to incorporate additional sources of information. Consider, for instance, a writing pattern recognition test. Let us assume that the attacker can run a test on the messages at the output of the mix and compare the writing to available text from the potential senders. This test outputs a true positive result with probability p_t and a false positive with probability p_f, and therefore produces as result a set of positives U_p and a set of negatives U_n.

Based on the evidence E' produced by the test, the adversary can derive for each user u_j the probability $\Pr(h_j|E')$ that she was the true author of the text. Users testing negative (i.e., $u_j \in U_n$) have probability $\Pr(h_j|E' = 0)$ of being the writer, while those testing positive (i.e., $u_j \in U_p$) are the originator of the message with probability $\Pr(h_j|E' = 1)$.

The posterior probability distribution $P(H|E')$ is computed applying Bayesian inference as explained in Sect. 3.3. The evidence E' is a vector with zeros for users who tested negative and ones for those who tested positive. The prior $P(H)$ corresponds to the (already existing) probability distribution that combines the profile and traffic analysis information. Assuming that E' contains k positives for a population of N users, $P(E'|H)$ is computed as follows:

$$\Pr(E' = 0|h_j) = (1 - p_t)\binom{N-1}{k}p_f^k(1 - p_f)^{N-k-1}$$

$$\Pr(E' = 1|h_j) = p_t\binom{N}{k-1}p_f^{k-1}(1 - p_f)^{N-k}$$

We made experiments where we considered two tests that give correct answers with different degrees of accuracy. The high accuracy test had a true positive rate $p_t = 0.8$ and a false positive rate $p_f = 0.01$, while in the low accuracy one these values were $p_t = 0.5$ and $p_f = 0.1$. The results are shown in Figure 1(b), where we can see how the new information provided by the test reduces (on average) sender anonymity. Note however the outliers: in some instances, the additional information provided by text recognition test does not help reducing anonymity. We further investigate this effect in Sect. 5.6.

5.3   Quantity of Profile Knowledge

In the previous section we compared anonymity in these cases: (i) the adversary knows the profiles of all users, but cannot perform traffic analysis; (ii) the adversary does not know any profiles, but can observe the mix; and (iii) the adversary has access to all profiles and communication data. Here, we look at sender and recipient anonymity towards adversaries who can observe all traffic through the mix but only know a fraction of the user profiles (generated following the Uniform description in Appendix A). We assume that the attacker has perfect knowledge of some profiles, and knows nothing about the rest. Whenever the attacker does not know a profile, she will consider it as uniform.

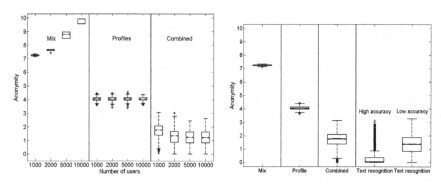

(a) Anonymity vs network growth

(b) Anonymity after combining three sources of information

Fig. 1. Sender anonymity when various sources of information are available

In Figure 2(a) we show the results for recipient anonymity with respect to the percentage of known profiles. On the left hand side of the figure (Mix) we show the anonymity A_m provided by the mix, which is independent from the quantity of profile knowledge and thus invariant for all experiments. The center and right hand side show, respectively, the anonymity A_p of the profiles and the combined A_c. Recipients of users with unknown profiles are unaffected by the percentage of known profiles, and enjoy the maximum anonymity that the mix can offer. For them, the profile anonymity is $A_p = log_2(N)$ and the combined recipient anonymity is $A_c = A_m$. Conversely, recipients of profiled users do not benefit from unknown profiles, and their recipient anonymity is the same regardless of how many other profiles are known. The aggregation of these two sets of recipient anonymity results can be clearly seen in the box plots of Fig. 2(a). Note the sudden jump in the median when half the profiles are known, and the values of the quartiles and outliers.

Unlike in the case of receiver anonymity, the percentage of known profiles affects the sender anonymity of all users, profiled or not, in the same way. This is because recipient profiles $P(u_i \leftarrow U)$ are computed using all sender profiles (see Sect. 3.2), and unpredictability of some users' sending patterns introduces uncertainty for all messages. The results of our experiments are shown in Fig 2(b)—as more profiles become available to the attacker, the sender profile and combined anonymity decrease.

Note that although the behaviour of sender and recipient anonymity is different when the adversary has partial knowledge, the values are the same for the extremes—i.e., sender and recipient anonymity are symmetric (in their distribution of values) both when all profiles are known and when all profiles are unknown, but not when some profiles are and some profiles are not.

Finally, note that in our experiment all users have non-uniform sending profiles (they only send messages to their friends), so the adversary's assumption of uniform behaviour for unknown users introduces errors in her results. We further

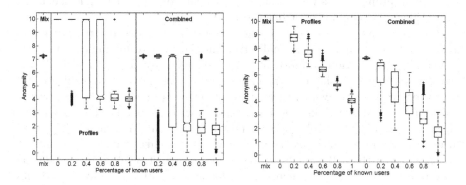

Fig. 2. Receiver (left) and sender (right) anonymity depending on the quantity of profile knowledge

elaborate on the implications of having (or assuming) wrong information in the next section.

5.4   Quality of Profile Knowledge

Human behaviour is hard to model and predict, and even the most sophisticated adversary with access to vast amounts of information can only at best approximate user behavioural profiles. Therefore, we can reasonably assume that in a real world scenario there is going to be some difference between the profiles guessed or predicted by the adversary and the actual user sending patterns. Furthermore, due to the lack of available real-world data, little is known about how user sending profiles might actually look like, or how they evolve in time. For this reason, it is worth looking at the implications for the anonymity adversary of making wrong behavioural assumptions, such as assuming uniform sending profiles. In this section we study how noise in the profiles propagates and find that small errors in the profiles may lead to big errors in the end results.

There are many ways for the adversary to construct her guessed profiles. They can be obtained, to mention some examples, by studying the links between users in online social networks such as Facebook or LiveJournal, by analyzing user sending patterns when messages are sent over a non-anonymous channel (assuming that the user does not always use the mix for sending her messages), or by applying statistical disclosure attacks [8] to previous mix communications of the user. The profile construction method and the quality of data available to the adversary determine not only the accuracy of the profile, but also the nature of the "error" with respect to the real profile. For example, users may be linked in Facebook to acquaintances to whom they rarely or never send messages; they may have friends to whom they only communicate through an anonymous channel (and therefore do not appear in their non-anonymous communications); and the profiles obtained through disclosure attacks are noisy versions of the real sending patterns. Such a wide range of possibilities makes it hard to predict the type of profile errors we can expect in a real world scenario, and has led us to consider various kinds of erroneous profiles.

One important thing to note is the independence between error magnitude and actual anonymity value. Small errors in the final result indicate that the probability distribution obtained by the adversary is roughly similar to the one she would obtain had she used the true profiles; while large errors indicate that the adversary's view on who are the likely senders or receivers of a message is very different from the actual distribution computed with the real profiles—regardless of the entropy of the actual (guessed and true) distributions. Anonymity gives a measure of the adversary's uncertainty on who are the likely senders or recipients messages given that all available information is correct; while errors model the uncertainty of the adversary concerning the accuracy of her anonymity results, assuming that some information may not be correct.

In order to measure and compare the magnitude of the errors in the profile and final result making abstraction of the nature of the error, we use as metric the Euclidean distance $dist(x, y) = \sqrt{\sum_i (x(i) - y(i))^2}$ between true and guessed probability distributions. We have chosen Euclidean distance for its simplicity and well understood meaning, and because it provides clear bounds for the final error—the maximum distance between two probability distributions occurs when they are orthogonal; its value is $\sqrt{2}$ and the minimum distance is 0.

Let us illustrate with a toy example our method for quantifying the impact of errors and the meaning of our results. Consider a simple scenario as the one depicted in Fig. 3, with a population $U = \{A, B, C, ..., Z\}$ and a unique (threshold) mixing round. User A sends with uniform probability $\Pr(A \rightarrow u_j) = 1/4$ to each of her four friends $\{B, C, D, F\}$, and with $\Pr(A \rightarrow u_j) = 0$ to the other users. The attacker, however, has a noisy version of A's profile, and believes that she chooses uniformly from the set $\{B, C, D, Z\}$. The attacker sees a single round of a threshold mix where A sends a message which comes out to either F or Z. Naturally, it was F as Z is not in A's true set of friends. The attacker, however believes it is Z, because he thinks that Z rather than F is in A's set of friends. Hence he wrong profile has led the attacker that Z is the recipient with probability one. We note that in this example, the receiver anonymity computed by the attacker when considering the wrong profile is zero ($A_{attacker} = 0$), as is the one she would obtain if she had precise knowledge of A's sending behavior ($A_{true} = 0$). However, the probability distribution obtained by the attacker is very different from the true result, and consequently her error is large. As the distance between the true and wrong results is much larger than the distance between the true and wrong profiles, this example provides the intuition that small errors in the profile may lead the attacker to completely wrong results.

Given that it is hard to predict the type of error the adversary is most likely to make, we have tested multiple instances of erroneous profiles. These include: (i) adding a *tail* to the profile distribution so that the probability of sending to non-friends appears greater than zero—yet significantly smaller than the one assigned to friends; (ii) introducing *Gaussian* noise; (iii) *eliminating* or (iv) *swapping* friends; and (v) assuming *uniform* behaviour. Appendix B provides a

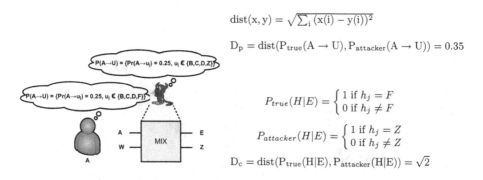

$$dist(x, y) = \sqrt{\sum_i (x(i) - y(i))^2}$$

$$D_p = dist(P_{true}(A \rightarrow U), P_{attacker}(A \rightarrow U)) = 0.35$$

$$P_{true}(H|E) = \begin{cases} 1 \text{ if } h_j = F \\ 0 \text{ if } h_j \neq F \end{cases}$$

$$P_{attacker}(H|E) = \begin{cases} 1 \text{ if } h_j = Z \\ 0 \text{ if } h_j \neq Z \end{cases}$$

$$D_c = dist(P_{true}(H|E), P_{attacker}(H|E)) = \sqrt{2}$$

Fig. 3. Example of how small errors in the profile can induce large errors in the attacker's results

detailed overview of the types of errors we have considered and the algorithms used to generated them.

The results of our experiments are shown in Figures 4(a) and 4(b). In both figures, the X axis represents the distance between the true user profiles (with which the messages were generated) and the erroneous profiles considered by the attacker; i.e., $D_p = dist(P_{true}(A \rightarrow U), P_{attacker}(A \rightarrow U))$. The Y axis expresses the distance between the probability distributions the attacker would obtain with the correct and wrong profiles; i.e., $Dc = dist(P_{true}(H|E), P_{attacker}(H|E))$. The grey dots include results of experiments generated with the five error methods previously mentioned, and we have highlighted in black the results for two types of errors: adding a *tail* to the profile distribution (Fig. 4(a)) and assuming *uniform* profiles (Fig. 4(b)). We can see that the errors induced by adding a *tail* to the profile are relatively benign compared to other types in the background, as they take mostly low values in Y (note that this is the type of error obtained when learning users' profiles with a statistical disclosure attack). On the other hand, whenever the adversary (due to lack of information) assumes users send uniformly, she obtains a distribution that substantially deviates from the correct result—to the extent that she cannot have any confidence on whether or not she is getting a good approximation to the correct anonymity set. This is aggravated when we consider errors coming from swapping or eliminating friends, which cover most of grey area.

5.5   Depth of Profile Knowledge

In some practical scenarios (e.g., Facebook) the adversary may guess the friendship graph but lack enough data to estimate the strength of links between friends. We say that the adversary's guessed profiles lack *depth* when she cannot estimate the frequency with which friends are chosen as recipients, in spite of accurately distinguishing friends from non-friends (to whom users never send messages). In these circumstances, the best the adversary can do is to consider that recipients are picked uniformly at random from the set of friends. This is a special case of

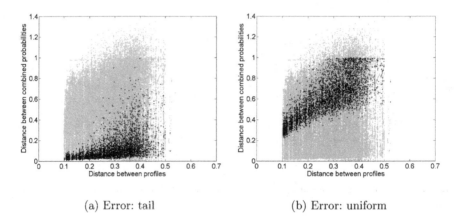

(a) Error: tail   (b) Error: uniform

Fig. 4. Euclidean distance between true and guessed probability distributions vs distance between true and guessed profiles (quality of profile knowledge)

erroneous profiles like those analyzed in the previous section, but we have chosen to present it separately for two reasons: first, because of its practical relevance (such profiles would be reasonably easy to construct); and second, although the profiles are noisy, correctly identifying friends (and non-friends) already provides very valuable information to the attacker.

To better illustrate the impact of the attacker's assumption, we consider that users choose their partners of communication having strong preferences for some of them (Skewed in Appendix A). In Fig 5 we show how the error in the combined probability increases proportionally to the error in the profile. When the true profile of a user is close to uniform[4], the assumption of the attacker is not far from the truth—the distance D_p between both profiles is small, and so the distance D_c between the combined distributions. As D_p increases, so does D_c, but as a rule of thumb we could say that the error D_c is most likely to be smaller than the original error D_p. The contrast with the previous section's results (considering profiles uniform in the whole population) indicates that an adversary who correctly identifies friendship links obtains two advantages: she eliminates non-friends from the anonymity sets, effectively decreasing anonymity; and she has higher confidence in her result, because the true and guessed distributions are comparatively closer to each other.

5.6   How Often Does Additional Information Reduce Uncertainty?

It was pointed out in [13] that in some cases additional information may result in higher anonymity, even if on average anonymity decreases as more information

---

[4] Because of the algorithm used to generate the profiles (see App. A), recipient profiles are on average more uniform than sender profiles, this explains why the values in Fig 5(b) are smaller than in Fig 5(a).

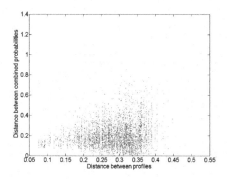 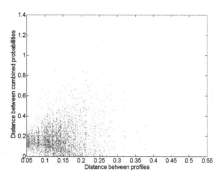

Fig. 5. Receiver (left) and sender (right) anonymity error depending on depth of knowledge

becomes available. In this section we present some results showing under which conditions we can expect these cases to appear. In all experiments we used Mixmaster (i.e., the anonymity A_m provided by the mix is invariant), and a small world network with 1000 users that send to friends with probability Pr_f and to non-friends with Pr_{nf}, such that $0 \leq \text{Pr}_{nf} \leq \text{Pr}_f$. The details of the generation of profiles is available in Appendix A, under the name Step. We study the results according to two variables: the number F of friends per user, and a parameter $0 \leq D \leq \infty$ that tunes the difference between Pr_f and Pr_{nf}, such that $D = 0$ implies $\text{Pr}_{nf} = 0$, and $D = \infty$ implies $\text{Pr}_{nf} = \text{Pr}_f$.

To better understand how sending behaviour affects anonymity, we have studied separately the frequency of cases where the combined anonymity A_c is higher than the anonymity of the mix alone A_m or the profile A_p, and its variation with the parameters F and D. The results in Figs. 6(a) and 6(b) show, respectively, the percentages of messages for which $A_c > A_m$ and $A_c > A_p$, which we denote $f_{c>m}$ and $f_{c>p}$.

To interpret the results, note that increasing F and/or D leaves A_m constant; increases A_p (because it makes the profile more uniform); and A_c increases as well as a result of more uniform profiles. When $D = 0$ users *only* send to friends—i.e., the recipient anonymity set is reduced drastically—and A_c is always lower than A_m and A_p. For $0 < D < 1$ and small F, A_p has increased only slightly, while A_c benefits mostly from messages sent to non-friends—these are "rare[5] events" in which the hints coming from the mix and the profile are "contradictory." Given the profile always points to the highest probability friends, when the mix points to (less probable) non-friends as most likely recipients, the mix and profile distributions compensate instead of reinforcing each other, making the combined distribution more uniform than one or both originals—i.e., $A_c > A_p$ and/or $A_c > A_m$. This also explains the high $f_{c>m}$ for larger values of D. Once F and/or D grow to make $A_p > A_m$, it becomes harder for A_c to catch up with

---

[5] Note that for $D = 1$ half the messages are sent to non-friends, even if the probability of picking a concrete non-friend is small.

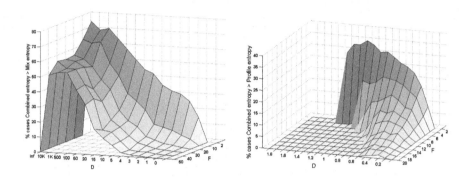

Fig. 6. Percentage of cases where the combined anonymity is higher than the anonymity of the mix only $f_{c>m}$ (a) and profile only $f_{c>p}$(b)

it (we can see in the Fig. 6(b) that $f_{c>p} = 0$ for $F > 15$ and/or $D > 1.25$). When A_p hits its maximum with *perfectly* uniform profiles at $D = \infty$, the profiles stop bringing any additional information and $A_c = A_m$. Thus, $f_{c>m} = 0$ at $D = \infty$ in Fig. 6(a).

6   Conclusions and Future Work

In this paper we examined the anonymity of users in the practical context of a social network. We showed the overall anonymity is low and likely does not increase with the size of the social network—if anything, it decreases as the network becomes more sparse.

The positive result of this paper is that it is necessary to trust the social network entirely to provide high quality information about the sender profiles of the users, otherwise big mistakes can be made in the sender and receiver anonymity of messages. Indeed, unless the profile is perfect, the results may be meaningless as we demonstrated occurrences of huge errors in the anonymity probability distribution even when the profile error is small. We have found however that certain types of errors induce more bounded deviations than others in the overall anonymity.

Many issues remain to be addressed, particularly in the practical setting. Particularly interesting to us is the problem of assessing the anonymity of a real social network such as Facebook and its approximation as mapped by the attacker. Although we believe that we modeled the "friendship" between users to a fair degree of accuracy by using a Watts-Strogatz graph, the extent of the linkage and the resulting sender profiles remain a more difficult issue. Only empirical modeling can gauge how much the real social dynamics differ from the theoretical models employed here.

One extremely promising line of research is to set up and evaluate an attack where the adversary continuously updates the social network graph with new information gained from observing the communication patterns and simultaniously tries to deanonymize the messages. Interestingly, the result of our paper holds in this setting too – whatever the methodology of deriving the social network graph, small errors in the graph may cause large errors in the anonymity of the message. Although complex statistical disclosure attacks may prove efficient at minimizing the errors in the graph, they can never eliminate such inaccuracies which may arise as a result of external factors, for instance changes of user behaviour over time.

References

1. Barabasi, A.-L., Albert, R.: Emergence of scaling in random networks. Science 286, 509–512 (1999)
2. Chaum, D.: Untraceable electronic mail, return addresses, and digital pseudonyms. Communications of the ACM 24(2), 84–88 (1981)
3. Clauß, S.: A framework for quantification of linkability within a privacy-enhancing identity management system. In: Müller, G. (ed.) ETRICS 2006. LNCS, vol. 3995, pp. 191–205. Springer, Heidelberg (2006)
4. Clauß, S., Schiffner, S.: Structuring anonymity metrics. In: Proceedings of the ACM Workshop on Digital Identity Management, pp. 55–62 (2006)
5. Cottrell, L.: Mixmaster & remailer attacks (unpublished manuscript), http://www.obscura.com/~loki/remailer/remailer-essay.html
6. Danezis, G.: The traffic analysis of continuous-time mixes. In: Martin, D., Serjantov, A. (eds.) PET 2004. LNCS, vol. 3424, pp. 35–50. Springer, Heidelberg (2005)
7. Danezis, G., Dingledine, R., Mathewson, N.: Mixminion: Design of a type iii anonymous remailer protocol. In: Proceedings of the 2003 IEEE Symposium on Security and Privacy, pp. 2–15 (2003)
8. Danezis, G., Serjantov, A.: Statistical disclosure or intersection attacks on anonymity systems. In: Fridrich, J. (ed.) IH 2004. LNCS, vol. 3200. Springer, Heidelberg (2004)
9. Diaz, C., Claessens, J., Seys, S., Preneel, B.: Information theory and anonymity. In: Macq, B., Quisquater, J.-J. (eds.) Werkgemeenschap voor Informatie en Communicatietheorie, pp. 179–186 (2002)
10. Diaz, C., Preneel, B.: Reasoning about the anonymity provided by pool mixes that generate dummy traffic. In: Fridrich, J. (ed.) IH 2004. LNCS, vol. 3200, pp. 309–325. Springer, Heidelberg (2004)
11. Díaz, C., Serjantov, A.: Generalising mixes. In: Dingledine, R. (ed.) PET 2003. LNCS, vol. 2760, pp. 18–31. Springer, Heidelberg (2003)
12. Diaz, C., Seys, S., Claessens, J., Preneel, B.: Towards measuring anonymity. In: Dingledine, R., Syverson, P.F. (eds.) PET 2002. LNCS, vol. 2482, pp. 54–68. Springer, Heidelberg (2003)
13. Diaz, C., Troncoso, C., Danezis, G.: Does additional information always reduce anonymity? In: Yu, T. (ed.) Workshop on Privacy in the Electronic Society 2007, pp. 72–75. ACM, New York (2007)
14. Dingledine, R., Mathewson, N., Syverson, P.: Tor: The second-generation onion router. In: Proceedings of the 13th USENIX Security Symposium, pp. 303–320. USENIX (2004)

15. Kesdogan, D., Egner, J., Büschkes, R.: Stop-and-go MIXes: Providing probabilistic anonymity in an open system. In: Aucsmith, D. (ed.) IH 1998. LNCS, vol. 1525, pp. 83–98. Springer, Heidelberg (1998)
16. Mathewson, N., Dingledine, R.: Practical traffic analysis: Extending and resisting statistical disclosure. In: Martin, D., Serjantov, A. (eds.) PET 2004. LNCS, vol. 3424, pp. 17–34. Springer, Heidelberg (2005)
17. Serjantov, A., Danezis, G.: Towards an information theoretic metric for anonymity. In: Dingledine, R., Syverson, P.F. (eds.) PET 2002. LNCS, vol. 2482, pp. 41–53. Springer, Heidelberg (2003)
18. Serjantov, A., Dingledine, R., Syverson, P.: From a trickle to a flood: Active attacks on several mix types. In: Petitcolas, F. (ed.) IH 2002. LNCS, vol. 2578. Springer, Heidelberg (2003)
19. Shannon, C.: A mathematical theory of communication. The Bell System Technical Journal 27, 379–423, 623–656 (1948)
20. Möller, U., Cottrell, L., Palfrader, P., Sassaman, L.: Mixmaster protocol - version 2 (2003), http://www.abditum.com/mixmaster-spec.txt
21. Watts, D., Strogatz, S.: Collective dynamics of small-world networks. Nature 393, 440–442 (1998)

A User Profiles

In order to create a diverse testbed for our experiments, we defined four different kinds of user profiles. We create a profile $P(u \rightarrow U)$ for each user u in the set U of N users connected through a friendship graph, and we say that u_j is a "friend" of u if they share and edge in the graph and a non-friend otherwise. In the following, We denote the set of friends of u as $f_u := \{u_j \in U | Pr(u \rightarrow u_j) \neq 0\}$ (cardinality F), and the set of non-friends as $nf_u := \{u_j \in U | Pr(u \rightarrow u_j) = 0\}$ (cardinality $N - F$). The three first types of profiles (*Uniform*, *Random* and *Skewed*) restrict users to sending only to their friends, while the fourth type (*Step*) allows users to send to non-friends with a smaller probability than to friends.

P_U: **Uniform.** users who send messages according to a P_U profile pick their recipient uniformly at random from their set of friends. $P(u \rightarrow U)$ is defined as:

$$P(u \rightarrow u_j) = \begin{cases} \frac{1}{F} & \text{if } u_j \in f_u \\ 0 & \text{if } u_j \notin f_u \end{cases}$$

P_R: **Random.** in this setting users send non-uniformly to their friends, but they have no particularly strong preferences for any of them. Hence, this profile can be considered a noisy version of P_U. P_R is created by generating a random number between 0 and 1 for each friend, and normalizing the resulting distribution.

P_K: **Skewed.** users whose profile is P_K usually have strong preferences for a small subset of their friends who are chosen as recipients very frequently, while the others only appear sporadically. The algorithm to generate P_K starts defining $\mu = 1$ as the initial probability "budget" available. Then we recursively

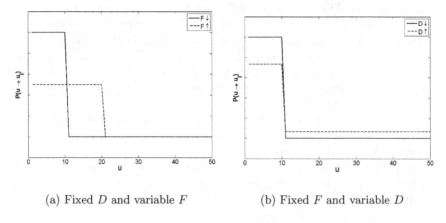

(a) Fixed D and variable F (b) Fixed F and variable D

Fig. 7. Variation of P_T (*Step*) profiles with F and D

assign to each friend a probability p chosen at uniformly at random from the interval $[0, \mu]$, and update the value $\mu = \mu - p$ describing the remaining budget. We repeat the procedure until only one friend is left, to whom we assign the remaining probability μ.

P_T: **Step.** users with these profiles send messages to the whole population. Nevertheless, they choose their friends as recipients more frequently than non-friends. For user u, the probability assigned in her profile to each of her friends u_f is $\Pr_f = \frac{1/F + D/N}{1+D}$, while the probability assigned to each non-friend u_{nf} is $\Pr_{nf} = \frac{D/N}{1+D}$. F is the cardinality of the set of friends, and the influence of its variation in the profile can be seen in Fig. 7(a). The parameter D influences the relation, in terms of probability, between friends and non-friends. As D increases, the sending profile becomes more uniform in all N potential recipients, diminishing the difference between friends and non-friends, as shown in Fig. 7(b). For $D = 0$, users never send to non-friends, and profiles are uniform on the whole population for $D = \infty$.

B   Erroneous Profiles

We simulate the adversary's imprecise information as follows. For each user $u \in U$ we take her true profile $P(u \rightarrow U)$, generated as explained in Appendix A, and we create a set of "erroneous profiles", $P_{attacker,i}(u \rightarrow U)$, by applying one of the following transformations:

Tail: we consider that if the adversary does not have accurate knowledge of u's profile, she will rather not exclude any user as potential contact of u (note that a similar profile shape is obtained after applying statistical disclosure attacks, with friends getting higher probabilities and non friends getting lower—but not zero—probabilities). We model this by distributing 20% of the total probability to the set nf_u, and we subtract this probability uniformly from the set of friends f_u, so that the new profile probabilities add up to one. We use this profile as basis when introducing the following errors.

Gaussian: we create two sets of profiles with this method, where we first add Gaussian noise to each element in the profile and then normalize. The noise samples come from two normal distributions $N(\mu_i, \sigma_i^2)$ with $\mu_1 = 0.01$, $\mu_2 = 0.05$, and $\sigma_1 = \sigma_2 = 0.3$.

Eliminate: this error emulates situations where the attacker misses one or more friends of u in her approximation of the profile, and considers them as non-friends. As explained before, becoming a non-friend does not discard a user as potential receiver of u, but it reduces her probability in u's profile. In our experiments we eliminate an increasing number of friends until only one remains. Each time a friend is eliminated the probabilities of the remaining friends are increased to compensate.

Swap: this error models the case where the attacker not only misses some friends, but wrongly considers non-friends as likely recipients. This effect is modeled by swapping (between one and all) the elements of f_u with elements of nf_u, i.e. when a friend is erased from the set of contacts, a non friend takes his place..

Uniform: this error simulates the case where the attacker has no knowledge about the social network, and thus considers all profiles as uniform over all population.

Shining Light in Dark Places: Understanding the Tor Network

Damon McCoy[1], Kevin Bauer[1], Dirk Grunwald[1],
Tadayoshi Kohno[2], and Douglas Sicker[1]

[1] Department of Computer Science,
University of Colorado, Boulder, CO 80309-0430, USA
{mccoyd,bauerk,grunwald,sicker}@colorado.edu
[2] Department of Computer Science and Engineering,
University of Washington, Seattle, WA 98195-2969, USA
yoshi@cs.washington.edu

Abstract. To date, there has yet to be a study that characterizes the usage of a real deployed anonymity service. We present observations and analysis obtained by participating in the Tor network. Our primary goals are to better understand Tor as it is deployed and through this understanding, propose improvements. In particular, we are interested in answering the following questions: (1) How is Tor being used? (2) How is Tor being *mis*-used? (3) Who is using Tor?

To sample the results, we show that web traffic makes up the majority of the connections and bandwidth, but non-interactive protocols consume a disproportionately large amount of bandwidth when compared to interactive protocols. We provide a survey of how Tor is being misused, both by clients and by Tor router operators. In particular, we develop a method for detecting exit router logging (in certain cases). Finally, we present evidence that Tor is used throughout the world, but router participation is limited to only a few countries.

1 Introduction

Tor is a popular privacy enhancing system that is designed to protect the privacy of Internet users from traffic analysis attacks launched by a non-global adversary [1]. Because Tor provides an anonymity service on top of TCP while maintaining relatively low latency and high throughput, it is ideal for interactive applications such as web browsing, file sharing, and instant messaging. Since its initial development, researchers have analyzed the system's performance [2] and security properties [3,4,5,6,7]. However, there has yet to be a study aimed at understanding how a popular deployed privacy enhancing system is used in practice. In this work, we utilize observations made by running a Tor router to answer the following questions:

How is Tor being used?. We analyze application layer header data relayed through our router to determine the protocol distribution in the anonymous

N. Borisov and I. Goldberg (Eds.): PETS 2008, LNCS 5134, pp. 63–76, 2008.

network. Our results show the types of applications currently used over Tor, a substantial amount of which is non-interactive traffic. We discover that web traffic makes up the vast majority of the connections through Tor, but BitTorrent traffic consumes a disproportionately large amount of the network's bandwidth. Perhaps surprisingly, protocols that transmit passwords in plain-text are fairly common, and we propose simple techniques that attempt to protect users from unknowingly disclosing such sensitive information over Tor.

How is Tor being *mis*-used?. To explore how Tor is currently being misused, we examine both malicious router and client behaviors. Since insecure protocols are common in Tor, there is a potential for a malicious router to gather passwords by logging exit traffic. To understand this threat, we develop a method to detect when exit routers are logging traffic, under certain conditions. Using this method, we did, in fact, catch an exit router capturing POP3 traffic (a popular plain-text e-mail protocol) for the purpose of compromising accounts.

Running a router with the default exit policy provides insight into the variety of malicious activities that are tunneled trough Tor. For instance, hacking attempts, allegations of copyright infringement, and bot network control channels are fairly common forms of malicious traffic that can be observed through Tor.

Who is using Tor?. In order to understand who uses Tor, we present the geopolitical distribution of the clients that were observed. Germany, China, and the United States appear to use Tor the most, but clients from 126 different countries were observed, which demonstrates Tor's global appeal. In addition, we provide a geopolitical breakdown of who participates in Tor as a router. Most Tor routers are from Germany and the United States, but Germany alone contributes nearly half of the network's total bandwidth. This indicates that implementing location diversity in Tor's routing mechanism is not possible with the current distribution of router resources.

Outline. The remainder of this paper is organized as follows: In Section 2, we provide a brief overview of Tor and Section 3 describes our data collection methodology. In Section 4, we explore how Tor is used, and present the observed exit traffic protocol distribution. In Section 5, we discuss how Tor is commonly abused by routers, and describe a new technique for detecting routers that maliciously log exit traffic. Section 6 describes our first-hand experiences with misbehaving clients. Section 7 gives the geopolitical distributions of clients and routers. Finally, concluding remarks are given in Section 8.

2 Tor Network

Tor's system architecture attempts to provide a high degree of anonymity and strict performance standards simultaneously [1]. At present, Tor provides an anonymity layer for TCP by carefully constructing a three-hop path (by default), or *circuit*, through the network of *Tor routers* using a layered encryption strategy similar to *onion routing* [8]. Routing information is distributed by a set of authoritative directory servers. In general, all of a particular client's TCP connections are tunneled through a single circuit, which rotates over time. There are typically three hops in a circuit; the first node in the circuit is known as the *entrance Tor router*, the middle node is called the *middle Tor router*, and the final hop in the circuit is referred to as the *exit Tor router*. It is important to note that only the entrance router can directly observe the originator of a particular request through the Tor network. Also, only the exit node can directly examine the decrypted payload and learn the final destination server. It is infeasible for a single Tor router to infer the identities of both the initiating client and the destination server. To achieve its low-latency objective, Tor does not explicitly re-order or delay packets within the network.

3   Data Collection Methodology

To better understand real world Tor usage, we set up a Tor router on a 1 Gb/s network link.[1] This router joined the currently deployed network during December 2007 and January 2008. This configuration allowed us to record a large amount of Tor traffic in short periods of time. While running, our node was consistently among the top 5% of routers in terms of bandwidth of the roughly 1,500 routers flagged as **Running** by the directory servers at any single point in time.

We understand that there are serious privacy concerns that must be addressed when collecting statistics from an anonymous network [9]. Tor is designed to resist traffic analysis from any single Tor router [1]; thus, the information we log — which includes *at most* 20 bytes of application-level data — cannot be used to link a sender with a receiver, in most cases. We considered the privacy implications carefully when choosing what information to log and what was too sensitive to store. In the end, we chose to log information from two sources: First, we altered the Tor router to log information about circuits that were established though our node and cells routed through our node. Second, we logged only enough data to capture up to the application-level protocol headers from the exit traffic that was relayed through our node.

In order to maximize the number of entry and exit connections that our router observed, it was necessary to run the router *twice*, with two distinct exit policies:[2] (1) Running with an *open exit policy* (the default exit policy[3]) enabled our

---

[1] Our router used **Tor** software version 0.1.2.18.

[2] Due to the relatively limited exit bandwidth that exists within Tor, when we ran the default exit policy, our node was chosen as the exit router most frequently on established circuits. As a result, in order to observe a large number of clients, it became necessary to collect data a second time with a completely restricted exit policy so that we would not be an exit router.

[3] The default exit policy blocks ports commonly associated with SMTP, peer-to-peer file sharing protocols, and ports with a high security risk.

router to observe numerous exit connections, and (2) *Prohibiting all exit traffic*
allowed the router to observe a large number of clients.

Entrance/Middle Traffic Logging. To collect data regarding Tor clients,
we ran our router with a completely restricted exit policy (all exit traffic was
blocked). We ran our Tor router in this configuration for 15 days from January
15–30, 2008. The router was compiled with minor modifications to support additional logging. Specifically, for every cell routed through our node, the time that
it was received, the previous hop's IP address and TCP port number, the next
hop's IP address and TCP port number, and the circuit identifier associated
with the cell is logged.

Exit Traffic Logging. To collect data regarding traffic exiting the Tor network,
we ran the Tor router for four days from December 15–19, 2007 with the default
exit policy. For routers that allow exit traffic, the default policy is the most
common. During this time, our router relayed approximately 709 GB of TCP
traffic exiting the Tor network.

In order to gather statistics about traffic leaving the network, we ran `tcpdump`
on the same physical machine as our Tor router. Tcpdump was configured to
capture only the first 150 bytes of a packet using the "snap length" option (`-s`).
This limit was selected so that we could capture up to the application-level
headers for protocol identification purposes. At most, we captured 96 bytes of
application header data, since an Ethernet frame is 14 bytes long, an IP header
is 20 bytes long, and a TCP header with no options is 20 bytes long. We used
`ethereal` [10], another tool for protocol analysis and stateful packet inspection,
in order to identify application-layer protocols. As a post-processing step, we
filtered out packets with a source or destination IP address of any active router
published during our collection period. This left only exit traffic.

4   Protocol Distribution

As part of this study, we observe and analyze the application-level protocols that
exit our Tor node. We show in Table 1 that interactive protocols like HTTP make
up the majority of the traffic, but non-interactive traffic consumes a dispropor-
tionate amount of the network's bandwidth. Finally, the data indicates that
insecure protocols, such as those that transmit login credentials in plain-text,
are used over Tor.

4.1   Interactive vs. Non-interactive Web Traffic

While HTTP traffic comprises an overwhelming majority of the connections
observed, it is unclear whether this traffic is interactive web browsing or non-
interactive downloading. In order to determine how much of the web traffic is
non-interactive, we counted the number of HTTP connections that transferred
over 1 MB of data. Only 3.5% of the connections observed were bulk transfers.
The vast majority of web traffic is interactive.

Table 1. Exit traffic protocol distribution by number of TCP connections, size, and number of unique destination hosts

Protocol	Connections	Bytes	Destinations
HTTP	12,160,437 (92.45%)	411 GB (57.97%)	173,701 (46.01%)
SSL	534,666 (4.06%)	11 GB (1.55%)	7,247 (1.91%)
BitTorrent	438,395 (3.33%)	285 GB (40.20%)	194,675 (51.58%)
Instant Messaging	10,506 (0.08%)	735 MB (0.10%)	880 (0.23%)
E-Mail	7,611 (0.06%)	291 MB (0.04%)	389 (0.10%)
FTP	1,338 (0.01%)	792 MB (0.11%)	395 (0.10%)
Telnet	1,045 (0.01%)	110 MB (0.02%)	162 (0.04%)
Total	13,154,115	709 GB	377,449

4.2   Is Non-interactive Traffic Hurting Performance?

The designers of the Tor network have placed a great deal of emphasis on achieving low latency and reasonable throughput in order to allow interactive applications, such as web browsing, to take place within the network [1]. However, the most significant difference between viewing the protocol breakdown measured by the number of bytes in contrast to the number of TCP connections is that while HTTP accounted for an overwhelming majority of TCP connections, the BitTorrent protocol uses a disproportionately high amount of bandwidth.[4] This is not shocking, since BitTorrent is a peer-to-peer (P2P) protocol used to download large files.

Since the number of TCP connections shows that the majority of connections are HTTP requests, one might be led to believe that most clients are using the network as an anonymous HTTP proxy. However, the few clients that do use the network for P2P applications such as BitTorrent consume a significant amount of bandwidth. The designers of the network consider P2P traffic harmful, not for ethical or legal reasons, but simply because it makes the network less useful to those for whom it was designed. In an attempt to prevent the use of P2P programs within the network, the default exit policy blocks the standard file sharing TCP ports. But clearly, our observations show that port-based blocking strategies are easy to evade, as these protocols can be run on non-standard ports.

4.3   Insecure Protocols

Another surprising observation from the protocol statistics is that insecure protocols, or those that transmit login credentials in plain-text, are fairly common. While comprising a relatively low percentage of the total exit traffic observed, protocols such as POP, IMAP, Telnet, and FTP are particularly dangerous due

---

[4] Recall that our router's default exit policy does not favor any particular type of traffic. So the likelihood of observing any particular protocol is proportional to the usage of that protocol within the network and the number of other nodes supporting the default or a similar exit policy.

to the ease at which an eavesdropping exit router can capture identifying information (i.e., user names and passwords). For example, during our observations, we saw 389 unique e-mail servers, which indicates that there were at least 389 clients using insecure e-mail protocols. In fact, only 7,247 total destination servers providing SSL/TLS were observed.

The ability to observe a significant number of user names and passwords is potentially devastating, but it gets worse: Tor multiplexes several TCP connections over the same circuit. Having observed identifying information, a malicious exit router can trace all traffic on the same circuit back to the client whose identifying information had been observed on that circuit. For instance, suppose that a client initiates both an SSL connection and an AIM connection at the same time. Since both connections use the same circuit (and consequently exit at the same router), the SSL connection can be easily associated with the client's identity leaked by the AIM protocol. Thus, tunneling insecure protocols over Tor presents a significant risk to the initiating client's anonymity.

To address this threat, a reasonable countermeasure is for Tor to explicitly block protocols such as POP, IMAP, Telnet, and FTP[5] using a simple port-based blocking strategy at the client's local socks proxy.[6] In response to these observations, Tor now supports two configuration options to (1) warn the user about the dangers of using Telnet, POP2/3, and IMAP over Tor, and (2) block these insecure protocols using a port-based strategy [11].

However, this same type of information leakage is certainly possible over HTTP, for instance, so additional effort must also be focused on enhancing Tor's HTTP proxy to mitigate the amount of sensitive information that can be exchanged over insecure HTTP. For instance, a rule-based system could be designed to filter common websites with insecure logins.

Finally, protocols that commonly leak identifying information should not be multiplexed over the same circuit with other non-identifying traffic. For example, HTTP and instant messaging protocols should use separate and dedicated circuits so that any identifying information disclosed through these protocols is not linked with other circuits transporting more secure protocols.

5   Malicious Router Behavior

Given the relatively large amount of insecure traffic that can be observed through Tor, there is great incentive for malicious parties to attempt to log sensitive information as it exits the network. In fact, others have used Tor to collect a large number of user names and passwords, some of which provided access to the computer systems of embassies and large corporations [12].

---

[5] Anonymous FTP may account for a significant portion of FTP exit traffic and does not reveal any information about the initiating client. Therefore, blocking FTP may be unnecessary.

[6] Port-based blocking is easy to evade, but it would protect naive users from mistakenly disclosing their sensitive information.

In addition to capturing sensitive exit traffic, a Tor router can modify the decrypted contents of a message entering or leaving the network. Indeed, in the past, routers have been caught modifying traffic (i.e., injecting advertisements or performing man-in-the-middle attacks) in transit, and techniques have been developed to detect this behavior [13].

We present a simple method for detecting exit router logging under certain conditions. We suspect — and confirm this suspicion using our logging detection technique — that insecure protocols are targeted for the specific purpose of capturing user names and passwords.

5.1 Detection Methodology

At a high level, the malicious exit router logging detection technique relies upon the assumption that the exit router is running a packet sniffer on its local network. Since packet sniffers such as tcpdump are often configured to perform reverse DNS queries on the IP addresses that they observe, if one controls the authoritative DNS server for a specific set of IP addresses, it is possible to trace reverse DNS queries back to the exit node that issued the query.

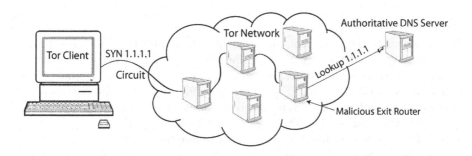

Fig. 1. Malicious exit router logging detection technique

More specifically, the detection method works as follows:

1. We run an authoritative domain name server (DNS) that maps domain names to a vacant block of IP addresses that we control.
2. Using a Tor client, a circuit is established using each individual exit router.
3. Having established a circuit, a SYN ping is sent to one of the IP addresses for which we provide domain name resolution.

This procedure (shown in Figure 1) is repeated for each exit router. Since the IP address does not actually exist, then it is very unlikely that there will be any transient reverse DNS queries. However, if one of the exit routers we used is logging this traffic, they may perform a reverse DNS look-up of the IP address that was contacted. In particular, we made an effort to direct the SYN ping at ports where insecure protocols typically run (ports 21, 23, 110, and 143).

5.2 Results

Using the procedure described above, over the course of only one day, we found one exit router that issued a reverse DNS query immediately after transporting our client's traffic. Upon further inspection, by SYN ping scanning all low ports (1-1024), we found that only port 110 triggered the reverse DNS query. Thus, this router only logged traffic on this port, which is the default port for POP3, a plain-text e-mail protocol. We suspect that this port was targeted for the specific purpose of capturing user names and passwords.

Further improvements on this logging detection could be made by using a honeypot approach and sending unique user name and password pairs through each exit router. The honeypot could detect any login attempts that may occur. This method would find the most malicious variety of exit router logging. In fact, upon detecting the logging exit router (using the method described above), we also used this honeypot technique and observed failed login attempts from the malicious IP address shortly after observing the logging.

These results reinforce the need to mitigate the use of protocols that provide login credentials in plain-text over Tor. Given the ease at which insecure protocols can be captured and the relative ease at which they could be blocked, it is a reasonable solution to block their default ports.

5.3 Discussion

This approach to detecting exit router logging has limitations. First, it can only trace the reverse DNS query back to the exit router's DNS server, not to the router itself. To complicate matters more, there exist free domain name resolution services (such as OpenDNS [14]) that provide somewhat anonymous name resolution for any host on the Internet. If one assumes that the exit router is logging and performing reverse DNS queries in real-time, then it is easy to correlate reverse DNS queries with exit routers using timing information.

If reverse DNS is *not* performed in real-time, then more sophisticated techniques for finding the malicious exit router are required. For instance, if one controls the domain name resolution for several IP addresses, then it is possible to embed a unique pattern in the order of the SYN pings to different IPs through each exit router. This order will be preserved in the exit router's queries and can be used to determine the exit router that logged the traffic. Here we can leverage many of the same principles as explored in [15,16].

The detection method presented makes the key assumption that the logging process will trigger reverse-DNS queries. However, this is not always the case. For example, exit routers that transport traffic at high bandwidth cannot feasibly perform reverse DNS queries in real-time. Also, this technique can be evaded simply by not performing reverse DNS when logging.

6 Misbehaving Clients

While Tor provides an invaluable service to protecting online privacy, over the course of operating a Tor router with the default exit policy, we learned about a wide variety of malicious client behavior. Since we are forwarding traffic on behalf of Tor users, our router's IP address appears to be the source of sometimes malicious traffic. The large amount of exit bandwidth that we provided caused us to receive a large number of complaints ranging from DMCA §512 notices related to allegations of copyright infringement, reported hacking attempts, IRC bot network controls, and web page defacement. However, an enormous amount of malicious client activity was likely unreported.

As a consequence of this malicious client behavior, it becomes more difficult to operate exit routers. For instance, our institution's administration requested that we stop running our node shortly after the data for this paper was collected. Similar accounts of administrative and law enforcement attempts to prevent Tor use are becoming more common as Tor becomes more popular to the masses [17]. The Electronic Frontier Foundation (EFF), a group that works to protect online rights, has provided template letters [18] and offered to provide assistance [19] to Tor router operators that have received DMCA take-down notices.

One solution to our problems could have been to change our router's exit policy to reject all exit traffic, or specific ports (such as port 80) that generate a large portion of the complaints. However, this is not practical, since Tor requires a certain amount of exit bandwidth to function correctly. Another solution is to provide a mechanism for anonymous IP address blocking, such as Nymble [20]. Our first-hand observations with misbehaving clients reinforces the need to further study anonymous IP address blocking mechanisms.

7   Geopolitical Client and Router Distributions

As part of this study, we investigate where Tor clients and routers are located geopolitically. Recall that a client's IP address is visible to a router when that router is used as the entrance node on the client's circuit through the Tor network. In the current Tor implementation, only particular routers, called *entry guards*, may be used for the first hop of a client's circuit. A router is labeled as an entry guard by the authoritative directory servers. All Tor router IP addresses are maintained by the directory servers, and we keep track of the router IP addresses by simply polling the directory servers periodically.

In order to map an IP address to its corresponding country of origin, we query the authoritative bodies responsible for assigning IP blocks to individual countries [21,22,23,24,25]. In order to determine the geopolitical distribution of Tor usage throughout the world, we aggregate IP addresses by country, and present the client and router location distributions observed during the January 2008 data collection period.

7.1   Observations

In this section, we present our observations regarding the client and router location distributions.

Table 2. Geopolitical client distributions, router distributions, and the ratio of Tor users relative to Internet users

Client Distribution		Router Distribution			Relative Tor Usage	
Country	Total	Country	Total		Country	Ratio
Germany	2,304	Germany	374		Germany	7.73
China	988	United States	326		Turkey	2.47
United States	864	France	69		Italy	1.37
Italy	254	China	40		Russia	0.89
Turkey	221	Italy	36		China	0.84
United Kingdom	170	Netherlands	35		France	0.77
Japan	155	Sweden	35		United Kingdom	0.75
France	150	Finland	25		United States	0.62
Russia	146	Austria	24		Brazil	0.56
Brazil	134	United Kingdom	24		Japan	0.32

Client Distribution. During a one day period when our Tor router was marked as an entry guard by the authoritative directory servers, it observed 7,571 unique clients[7] As depicted in Table 2, the vast majority of clients originated in Germany, with China and the United States providing the next largest number of clients. Perhaps the most interesting observation about the client distribution is that Tor has a global user base. While most of the clients are from three countries, during the course of the entire 15 day observation period, clients were observed from 126 countries around the world, many of which have well-known policies of Internet censorship.

To put these raw geopolitical client distributions into perspective, Table 2 includes a ratio of the percentage of Tor users to the percentage of Internet users by country, using data on the distribution of broadband Internet users by country [26]. These percentages were computed by dividing the total number of Tor clients located in each country by the total number of Tor clients we observed, which provides the percentage of Tor users located in each country. For example, the relative Tor usage for Germany is computed as follows: The percentage of the total Internet users who are from Germany is 3.9% and according to our client observations, Germany makes up 2,304 of the 7,571 total Tor clients, which is 30.4%. Thus, the ratio of Tor users to Internet users in Germany is 7.73.

These ratios show that Tor is disproportionately popular in Germany, Turkey, and Italy with respect the the number of broadband Internet users located in these countries. It is unclear why there is such a large scale adoption of Tor in these specific countries, relative to Tor usage in other countries. An investigation of the possible technological, sociological, and political factors in these countries that are causing this might be an enlightening area of research.

Examining the number of clients that utilized our router as their entry router when *it was not marked as an entry guard* provides insight into the approximate

---

[7] We assume that each unique IP address is a unique client. However, dynamic IP addresses or network address translators (NATs) may be used in some places.

number of clients that are using a significantly old version of the Tor client software. Specifically, this indicates that these clients are using a version *before* entry guards were introduced in Tor version 0.1.1.20 (May 2006). Over four days, only 206 clients were observed to be using Tor software that is older than this version.

Incidentally, entry guards were added to prevent routers from profiling clients, and indeed the reliance on entry guards prevented us from profiling a large number of clients beyond what we describe above. Before entry guards were widely adopted, a strong diurnal usage pattern had been observed [27]. Since entry guards are now widely adopted, utilizing multiple entry guard perspectives gives a larger snapshot of the clients' locations and usage patterns. We informally compared our geopolitical client distribution to that which was observed from other high bandwidth entry guard routers. The distribution was consistent across each entry guard. However, we attempted to observe the current client usage patterns, but this required a more global perspective than we were able to obtain.

Tor Router Distribution. During our data collection, we monitored the authoritative directory servers to determine the total number and geopolitical distribution of Tor routers. Over the course of 7 days, we took hourly snapshots of the authoritative directory servers, noting each router's IP address and bandwidth advertisements. During this time, on average 1,188 Tor routers were observed in each snapshot. As shown in Table 2, Germany and the United States together contribute nearly 59% of the running routers. However, in terms of total bandwidth, as depicted in Figure 2, Germany provides 45% of the bandwidth and the United States only provides 23% of the bandwidth.

It has been suggested that location diversity is a desirable characteristic of a privacy enhancing system [28]. However, given the current bandwidth distribution, location diversity while maintaining adequate load balancing of traffic is difficult to guarantee. It is currently possible to build circuits with at least one router from Germany and the remaining routers from other countries. However, if a location-aware routing mechanism mandated that a user's traffic should exit in a specific country, such as the Netherlands, then it is necessary to ensure that there is

Fig. 2. Distribution of Tor router bandwidth around the world

sufficient exit bandwidth in that country. Incentive programs to encourage volunteers to run routers in under-represented countries should be investigated. In addition, mitigating malicious client behavior (as noted in Section 6) can consequently attract more Tor routers.

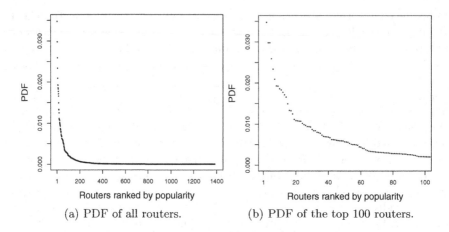

(a) PDF of all routers.   (b) PDF of the top 100 routers.

Fig. 3. PDFs of Tor's traffic distribution over its routers during a one hour snapshot

7.2   Modeling Router Utilization

Understanding the distribution with which different routers are utilized on circuits can provide valuable insights regarding the system's vulnerability to traffic analysis. In addition, a probability distribution can be used to build more realistic analytical models and simulations.

By counting the number of times that each router appears on a circuit with our router, we provide probability density functions (PDFs) to model the probability of each router forwarding a particular packet (shown in Figure 3). In a one hour snapshot during the January data collection period, the top 2% of all routers transported about 50% of traffic from the perspective of our router. Within this top 2%, 14 routers are hosted in Germany, 6 are hosted in the United States, 4 are in France, and Switzerland, the Netherlands, and Finland each host a single router. These numbers are consistent with the bandwidth distributions given in Figure 2, and further highlight the difficulty of providing strict location diversity in Tor's routing mechanism. The PDF curve drops sharply; the bottom 75% of the routers together transported about 2% of the total traffic. The most traffic that any single router transported was 4.1% of the total traffic. This indicates that the vast majority of Tor traffic is handled by a very small set of routers. Consequently, if an adversary is able to control a set of the highest performing routers, then its ability to conduct traffic analysis increases dramatically. Finally, the PDFs calculated from our router's observations are very similar to the router distribution based on routers' bandwidth advertisements, as reported by Tor's directory servers.

8   Conclusion

This study is aimed at understanding Tor usage. In particular, we provided observations that help understand how Tor is being used, how Tor is being mis-used, and who participates in the network as clients and routers. Through our observations, we have made several suggestions to improve Tor's current design and implementation. First, in response to the fairly large amount of insecure protocol traffic, we proposed that Tor provide a mechanism to block the ports associated with protocols such as POP3, IMAP, and Telnet. Given the ease at which an eavesdropping exit router can log sensitive user information (such as user names and passwords), we developed a method for detecting malicious logging exit routers, and provided evidence that there are such routers that specifically log insecure protocol exit traffic. As a final avenue of study, we show the disparity in geopolitical diversity between Tor clients and routers, and argue that location diversity is currently impossible to guarantee unless steps are taken to attract a more diverse set of routers.

Due to its popularity, Tor provides insight into the challenges of deploying a real anonymity service, and our hope is that this work will encourage additional research aimed at (1) providing tools to enforce accountability while preserving strong anonymity properties, (2) protecting users from unknowingly disclosing sensitive/identifying information, and (3) fostering participation from a highly diverse set of routers.

Acknowledgements. We thank Roger Dingledine, Parisa Tabriz, and the anonymous PETS 2008 reviewers whose comments greatly improved the quality of this paper. This research was partially supported by the National Science Foundation under grant ITR-0430593.

References

1. Dingledine, R., Mathewson, N., Syverson, P.: Tor: The second-generation onion router. In: Proceedings of the 13th USENIX Security Symposium (August 2004)
2. Wendolsky, R., Herrmann, D., Federrath, H.: Performance comparison of low-latency anonymisation services from a user perspective. In: Borisov, N., Golle, P. (eds.) PET 2007. Springer, Heidelberg (2007)
3. Goldberg, I.: On the security of the Tor authentication protocol. In: Danezis, G., Golle, P. (eds.) PET 2006. LNCS, vol. 4258. Springer, Heidelberg (2006)
4. Murdoch, S.J.: Hot or not: Revealing hidden services by their clock skew. In: 13th ACM Conference on Computer and Communications Security (CCS 2006), Alexandria, VA (November 2006)
5. Murdoch, S.J., Danezis, G.: Low-cost traffic analysis of Tor. In: Proceedings of the 2005 IEEE Symposium on Security and Privacy. IEEE Computer Society Press, Los Alamitos (2005)
6. Øverlier, L., Syverson, P.: Locating hidden servers. In: Proceedings of the 2006 IEEE Symposium on Security and Privacy. IEEE Computer Society Press, Los Alamitos (2006)
7. Bauer, K., McCoy, D., Grunwald, D., Kohno, T., Sicker, D.: Low-resource routing attacks against Tor. In: Proceedings of the Workshop on Privacy in the Electronic Society (WPES 2007), Washington, DC, USA (October 2007)
8. Goldschlag, D.M., Reed, M.G., Syverson, P.F.: Hiding routing information. In: Anderson, R. (ed.) IH 1996. LNCS, vol. 1174. Springer, Heidelberg (1996)

9. Sicker, D.C., Ohm, P., Grunwald, D.: Legal issues surrounding monitoring during network research. In: IMC 2007: Proceedings of the 7th ACM SIGCOMM conference on Internet measurement. ACM Press, New York (2007)
10. Ethereal: A network protocol analyzer, http://www.ethereal.com
11. Bauer, K., McCoy, D.: Block insecure protocols by default (January 2008), https://tor-svn.freehaven.net/svn/tor/trunk/doc/spec/proposals/129-reject-plaintext-ports.txt
12. Zetter, K.: Tor researcher who exposed embassy e-mail passwords gets raided by Swedish FBI and CIA (November 2007), http://blog.wired.com/27bstroke6/2007/11/swedish-researc.html
13. Perry, M.: Torflow, https://www.torproject.org/svn/torflow/README
14. OpenDNS, http://www.opendns.com
15. Bethencourt, J., Franklin, J., Vernon, M.: Mapping Internet sensors with probe response attacks. In: Proceedings of the 14th conference on USENIX Security Symposium, Baltimore, MD. USENIX Association (2005)
16. Shinoda, Y., Ikai, K., Itoh, M.: Vulnerabilities of passive Internet threat monitors. In: Proceedings of the 14th conference on USENIX Security Symposium, Baltimore, MD. USENIX Association (2005)
17. Cesarini, P.: Caught in the Network. In: The Chronicle of Higher Education, Washington, D.C, vol. 53 (February 2007)
18. Tor: Response template for Tor node maintainer to ISP, http://www.torproject.org/eff/tor-dmca-response.html
19. Dingledine, R.: EFF is looking for Tor DMCA test case volunteers, http://archives.seul.org/or/talk/Oct-2005/msg00208.html
20. Johnson, P.C., Kapadia, A., Tsang, P.P., Smith, S.W.: Nymble: Anonymous IP-address blocking. In: Borisov, N., Golle, P. (eds.) PET 2007. Springer, Heidelberg (2007)
21. American Registry for Internet Numbers, http://www.arin.net/index.shtml
22. Asia Pacific Network Information Centre, http://www.apnic.net
23. Latin American & Caribbean Internet Addresses Registry, http://lacnic.net/en
24. Ripe Network Coordination Centre, http://www.ripe.net
25. African Network Information Centre, http://www.afrinic.net
26. Inernet World Stats, http://www.internetworldstats.com
27. McCoy, D., Bauer, K., Grunwald, D., Tabriz, P., Sicker, D.: Shining light in dark places: A study of anonymous network usage. University of Colorado Technical Report CU-CS-1032-07 (2007)
28. Feamster, N., Dingledine, R.: Location diversity in anonymity networks. In: Proceedings of the Workshop on Privacy in the Electronic Society (WPES 2004), Washington, DC, USA (October 2004)

Formalized Information-Theoretic Proofs of Privacy Using the HOL4 Theorem-Prover

Aaron R. Coble

University of Cambridge Computer Laboratory, 15 JJ Thomson Avenue, Cambridge
CB3 0FD, UK
arc54@cam.ac.uk

Abstract. Below we present an information-theoretic method for proving the amount of information leaked by programs formalized using the HOL4 theorem-prover. The advantages of this approach are that the analysis is quantitative, and therefore capable of expressing partial leakage, and that proofs are performed using the HOL4 theorem-prover, and are therefore guaranteed to be logically and mathematically consistent with the formalization. The applicability of this methodology to proving privacy properties of Privacy Enhancing Technologies is demonstrated by proving the anonymity of the Dining Cryptographers protocol. To the best of the author's knowledge, this is the first machine-verified proof of privacy of the Dining Cryptographers protocol for an unbounded number of participants and a quantitative metric for privacy.

1   Introduction

Gene Spafford once said, "The only truly secure system is one that is powered off, cast in a block of concrete and sealed in a lead-lined room with armed guards – and even then I have my doubts." [11] While some, if not most, of the security community will agree with this sentiment, it does not negate the desire to develop technologies that increase the security of systems and methods to analyze and quantify the relative security of these technologies. As Privacy-Enhancing Technologies (PETs) are developed, the need arises for methods to analyze and quantify the relative privacy guarantees of various PETs. It is important that these methods of analysis are quantitative (rather than a boolean result of "secure" or "insecure") because many deployable PETs must make concessions for the sake of efficiency and do not guarantee absolute privacy. Pioneering work done independently by both Serjantov and Danezis [26] and Díaz [12] proposed the use of entropy as a metric for privacy, thereby linking Shannon's Information Theory [27] to quantitative analysis of privacy and giving rise to a subsequent branch of privacy analysis. Since then most quantitative privacy analysis is rooted in Information Theory. More recent work in this area e.g. Chatzikokolakis' use of Bayes Risk [3], has offered a variety of related metrics for privacy based on Information Theory.

Historically, various products of formal methods research, such as theorem-provers and model-checkers, have been fruitfully applied to security analysis.

N. Borisov and I. Goldberg (Eds.): PETS 2008, LNCS 5134, pp. 77–98, 2008.

Paulson developed the technique of using a theorem-prover to formalize security protocols and perform inductive proofs of security for these protocols [22]. Model-checking has been widely used both for finding bugs in security protocols and for verifying finite instances of security protocols; Lowe's use of FDR to find a bug in the Needham-Schroeder protocol [20] is a well known example. Each of these analysis techniques has its relative advantages and disadvantages. Model-checking requires less human effort because it is fully automatic, once a system and its desired properties are formalized. However, model-checking is limited to (generally) small, finite instances of a system due to a state-explosion which renders larger instances intractable. Clearly verification of a particular instance of the system does not necessarily provide any guarantees about the system generally. This makes model-checking techniques more applicable for bug-finding in security systems than for proving security guarantees. Theorem-proving usually requires a greater amount of human effort than model-checking because proofs are not automatic and must be performed through interaction with the theorem-prover. The advantage of theorem-proving is that proofs can be quantified on the parameters of the system, allowing for a proof of security for the system generally rather than for a particular finite instance. This advantage of theorem proving is exemplified by the proof of privacy of the dining cryptographers protocol discussed in Section 3, which is valid for an *unbounded number* of protocol participants. While theorem-proving is aimed at proof of correctness rather than bug-finding, an unsuccessful proof attempt will provide insight into the reason that the system fails. The further advantage of interactive theorem-proving over pen-and-paper proofs is that proofs are guaranteed to be correct up to the assumptions of the model. (Recent work by Blanchet [2] has focused on bridging the gap between the computational-complexity proofs used by cryptographers and the assumption of perfect cryptographic-primitives commonly used in formal-methods proofs). We do not to claim that a machine-assisted proof is an absolute guarantee of security; Any proof of security is only valid up to the level of abstraction at which the system is modeled – a point widely noted in the literature where security and formal methods research intersect. However, LCF-style theorem provers, such as the HOL4 system used in this work, do guarantee the logical consistency of all proofs they produce [16]. This is achieved by using a small logical core from which all theorems must be derived using basic inferences rules. A substantial amount of mathematical theory, including probability theory, which this work makes use of, has been previously been formalized in HOL4. Since pen-and-paper proofs are often long, complicated, and prone to errors, the guarantee of correctness provided by using a theorem-prover is valuable, particularly for security applications.

Model-checking techniques have been successfully used to analyze various PETs e.g. Shmatikov et al.'s use of PRISM [28] to analyze the Crowds protocol [23]. However, the author is unaware of any prior work applying theorem-proving techniques to quantitative privacy analysis; this paper aims to begin filling that void. In spirit this work belongs both to the branch of PETs research begun by Serjantov, Danezis, and Díaz and to the branch of formal methods work begun by Paulson. Recent work by Malacaria et al. proposed an Information-Theoretic approach to analyzing the information leakage in programs [21] and this work serves as inspiration for the formalized analysis technique presented in this paper. We will now move on to examine a formalization of Shannon's Information Theory in Higher Order Logic (HOL) using the HOL4 theorem-prover and the use of this formalization for quantifying the information leakage of programs. Afterwards, the applicability of this technique to analysis of PETs is demonstrated using the Dining Cryptographers problem [4] as a case study. To the best of the author's knowledge, this is the first machine-verified proof of privacy of the Dining Cryptographers protocol for an *unbounded number* of participants and a *quantitative* metric for privacy. Finally, future directions and applications for this work will be presented.

2   Formal Analysis of Information Leakage Using HOL4

We will now examine a formalization of Shannon's Information Theory in HOL4. Basic concepts from information theory and probability theory will be explained concurrently with their formalization for the benefit of the unfamiliar reader. Hurd's formalization of probability theory in HOL4 [18] serves as a starting point for our formalization. In [18], Hurd formalized measure theory in HOL4 and building on this he formalized a definition for probability spaces and functions on these. (See [14] for an excellent introduction to how probability theory is derived from measure theory). Hurd then used this formalization to verify the correctness of probabilistic algorithms. While the work presented in [18] was a major milestone towards machine-verification of probabilistic algorithms, the scope of that work had its limits. Important results for *independent* functions on probability spaces were developed and theorems about the properties of a probability measure were proved (e.g. the probability of the empty event is 0, the probability of the universe of all measurable events is 1, and a probability measure is countably additive); however, many concepts from probability theory such as definitions for random variables, the expected value of random variables, and conditional probability do not feature in [18]. In [17], Hasan built upon Hurd's work to define the expected value of and prove properties of some common discrete probability distributions including the bernoulli distribution. Unfortunately Hasan's work is not directly applicable for the work presented here, so we must begin where Hurd's formalization ends by defining random variables and their expectation.

2.1   Information Theory Formalized in HOL4

We will now derive a formalization of Information Theory in HOL from basic elements of probability theory. First we recall textbook definitions for a *probability space* and measurable *events* in this space. (The unfamiliar reader is referred to [14,29] or similar introductory texts for further details). The formalization of these two notions is part of the work in [18].

Definition 1. *Let* $\mathcal{P}$(outcomes) *be the powerset of all possible outcomes of some experiment. For a set* $\Omega \subseteq \mathcal{P}$(outcomes) *and function* μ *from elements of* Ω *to* $\mathbb{R}$, (Ω, μ) *defines a* **probability space** *iff (i)* Ω *is closed under countable-unions, -intersections, and -complementations, (ii)* Ω *contains the universe of all outcomes* UNIV *and the empty set* {}, *(iii)* $\forall x \in \Omega$. $0 \leq \mu(x) \leq 1$, *(iv)* μ(UNIV) $= 1$ *and* $\mu(\{\}) = 0$, *and (v)* μ *is countably-additive on* Ω.

Definition 2. *For a probability space* (Ω, μ), *each element of* Ω *is an* **event**. *Each event denotes a set of outcomes for an experiment. For example, let* $\mathcal{E} =$ {*saw 1 red bird, saw 1 blue bird*} *defines an event* $\approx$ *"saw 1 bird". Events can be combined using the usual set operations (Union, Intersection, Complementation, Difference) to define other events.*

We now move on to review a textbook definition of a *random variable* on a probability space and to develop our formalization of this definition in HOL.

Definition 3. *For a measurable space with measurable sets* Ψ *of type* $: ((\beta \text{ set})$ set) *and a probability space* (Ω, μ), *with sample space* Ω *of type* $: ((\alpha \text{ set}) \text{ set})$ *and probability measure* μ *of type* $: (\alpha \text{ set} \to \mathbb{R})$, *a* **random variable** $\mathcal{X}$ *is a map of type* $: (\alpha \to \beta)$ *s.t.* $\forall y. \ y \in \Psi \Rightarrow \{x \mid \mathcal{X}(x) \in y\} \in \Omega$ *i.e. a random variable is* measurable *function from the sample space of a probability space to the measurable sets of a measurable space. The probability of* $\mathcal{X}$ *taking the value* x *is defined as* $P(\mathcal{X} = \text{x}) = \mu \{\text{y} \mid \mathcal{X}(\text{y}) \in \text{x}\}$.

Typically, random variables are real- or natural-valued functions; however we will use the more general definition for our formalization. We can formalize the definition of a random variable and its probability measure in HOL as

```
random_variable (s,mu) X =
    prob_space (s,mu) ∧ measurable X s UNIV
```

and

```
random_variable_prob (s,mu) X = λ x. mu {y | X(y) IN x}.
```

The attentive reader will have noticed that we are requiring a random variable to be measurable on the universe of a type rather than some subset thereof. This is because Ψ from Definition 3 must contain all of the singleton sets in order for the *expected value* of a random variable to be well defined; any Ψ containing all of the singleton sets is necessarily the universe because it must be closed under countable unions in order to be measurable. This condition is clearly satisfied in the typical case where Ψ is defined by the space of the real or natural numbers.

For the present discussion, we are restricting the probability distribution μ to be a *discrete* probability distribution. This does not impose any real restriction on our formalization as we are interested in statements of the form, "What is the probability that the sender of this message was Bob?", P(*sender = Bob*), rather than statements of the form "What is the probability that the Bob's weight is less than 100kg?", P(*weight < 100*). In the interest of brevity, we will also limit the present discussion to *finite* random variables i.e. those X and (s,mu) for which

$$\{x \mid \texttt{random\_variable\_prob (s,mu) X } \{x\} \neq 0\}$$

is *finite*; formalization of *countable* random variables i.e. those for which the above set is *countable* will not be presented here, since finite random variables suffice for the application of interest.

We are often interested in a *vector* of random variables, $\mathcal{X}_1, \ldots, \mathcal{X}_n$, rather than a single random variable; the joint probability measure of such a vector is the natural one $P(\mathcal{X}_1 = x_1, \ldots, \mathcal{X}_n = x_n) = \mu \{y \mid \mathcal{X}_1(y) \in x_1 \wedge \ldots \wedge \mathcal{X}_n(y) \in x_n\}$. A formalization of random vectors and their probability measures can be defined using a list to represent the vector of random variables as follows

$$\texttt{random\_vector (s,mu) [X]} = \texttt{random\_variable (s,mu) X}$$
$$\texttt{random\_vector (s,mu) (X :: XS)} = \texttt{random\_variable (s,mu) X} \wedge$$
$$\texttt{random\_vector (s,mu) XS}$$

and

$$\texttt{random\_vector\_prob (s,mu) XS} =$$
$$\lambda \texttt{ xs. mu } \{y \mid \texttt{FOLDR } \wedge \ \top \ (\texttt{MAP } (\lambda \texttt{ b. (FST b) IN (SND b))}$$
$$(\texttt{ZIP (MAP } (\lambda \texttt{ X. X(y)) XS) xs))}\},$$

where :: is the list construction operation, MAP maps a function over a list, ZIP creates a list of pairs from two lists, FST and SND select the first and second element of a pair respectively, and FOLDR is the fold-right operation on a list. Note: we assume that xs is the same length as XS in order for random_vector_prob to be sensibly defined above. For the sake of brevity, we will not present separate definitions for functions on random variables and random vectors where the extension is obvious.

Having formalized random variables and their probability measures, we now move on to review the definition of the *expected value* of a random variable.

Definition 4. *The* **expected value** *of a real-valued function f and a random variable (or random vector) $\mathcal{X}$ is the average of the values taken by $(f \circ \mathcal{X})$ weighted by the probability measure of $\mathcal{X}$. The expected value is the most likely value for $(f \circ \mathcal{X})$ to take and is defined as*

$$\mathbb{E}(\mathcal{X}) = \sum_x \left(P(\mathcal{X} = x) \right) \left(f(x) \right).$$

In order to formalize a definition for the expected value of finite random variables in HOL, we must first define a function SUM which is the summation of a real-valued function applied to the elements of a finite set. (Expected value for countable random variables is defined using a countably-infinite summation, but this formalization is outside the scope of this discussion). Due to its recursive definition, SUM $(f : \alpha \rightarrow real)$ $(S : \alpha \ set)$ is well defined only when S is finite.

We then define a second HOL function $\mathtt{sum\ f\ S = SUM\ f\ \{s\ |\ f(s)\ \neq\ 0\}}$, which is the summation of f over those elements of S for which f takes a non-zero value. We can now formalize expected value in HOL as

$$\mathtt{expected\_value\ (s, mu)\ X\ f =}$$
$$\mathtt{sum\ \Big(\lambda\ x.\ \big(random\_variable\_prob\ (s, mu)\ X\ \{x\}\big)\big(f(x)\big)\Big)\ UNIV}$$

for random variables, or

$$\mathtt{expected\_value\ (s, mu)\ XS\ f =}$$
$$\mathtt{sum\ \Big(\lambda\ xs.\ \big(random\_vector\_prob\ (s, mu)\ XS\ \big(MAP\ (\lambda\ x.\ \{x\})\ xs\big)\big)\big(f(x)\big)\Big)}$$
$$\mathtt{\{xs\ |\ LENGTH\ xs = LENGTH\ XS\}}$$

for random vectors. (We allow this slight overloading as it is unlikely to cause confusion.)

We are now ready to develop a formalization of information theory in HOL from the formalizations for probability theory developed above. We begin by reviewing the definition of the *entropy* of a random variable and then proceed to formalize this definition in HOL. (Definitions for entropy and the other basic definitions from information theory reviewed below can be found in [27]).

Definition 5. *The **entropy** of a random variable (or random vector) $\mathcal{X}$ captures the uniformity of the probability measure of $\mathcal{X}$ i.e. the degree of uncertainty as to which outcome will occur. If $\mathcal{X}$ takes a particular value with probability 1 then the entropy is 0. If the values of $\mathcal{X}$ with non-zero probability are uniformly distributed (occur with equal probability) then the entropy is maximal.*

$$\mathbb{H}(\mathcal{X}) = -\sum_x P(\mathcal{X} = x) \log(P(\mathcal{X} = x)).$$

Building upon the formalization of expected value above, it is straightforward to formalize the definition of entropy in HOL as

$$\mathtt{entropy\ (s, mu)\ X =}$$
$$\mathtt{expected\_value\ (s, mu)\ X}$$
$$\mathtt{\big(\lambda\ x.\ lg\ (random\_variable\_prob\ (s, mu)\ X\ \{x\})\big)}$$

for random variables, or

$$\mathtt{entropy\ (s, mu)\ XS =}$$
$$\mathtt{expected\_value\ (s, mu)\ XS}$$
$$\mathtt{\big(\lambda\ xs.\ lg\ (random\_vector\_prob\ (s, mu)\ XS\ (MAP\ (\lambda\ x.\ \{x\})\ xs))\big)}$$

for random vectors, using $\mathtt{lg}$ to abbreviate $\log_2$. We choose to use a base of 2 for the logarithm in our formalization of entropy because of its correlation to *bits* of information; this is the typical choice for information-theoretic analysis. The reader is directed to [27] for a detailed explanation of this choice. We now move on to the information-theoretic concept of *conditional entropy*, first reviewing its definition and then developing its formalization in HOL.

Definition 6. *The* **conditional entropy** *of random variable (or random vector)* $\mathcal{X}$ *conditioned on the value of random variable* $\mathcal{Y}$ *measures the uncertainty of* $\mathcal{X}$ *given knowledge of* $\mathcal{Y}$ *and is defined as*

$$\mathbb{H}(\mathcal{X}|\mathcal{Y}) = \sum_y P(\mathcal{Y} = y)\Big(-\sum_x P(\mathcal{X} = x|\mathcal{Y} = y)\log(P(\mathcal{X} = x|\mathcal{Y} = y)\Big).$$

In order to formalize a definition for conditional entropy in HOL, we must first develop a formalization for the conditional probability measure of two random variables (or random vectors). We recall for the reader that the *conditional probability* of two random variables (or random vectors), $\mathcal{X}$ and $\mathcal{Y}$, is $P(\mathcal{X} = x \,|\mathcal{Y} = y) = P(\mathcal{X} = x,\ \mathcal{Y} = y)/P(\mathcal{Y} = y)$, where $P(\mathcal{X} = x,\ \mathcal{Y} = y)$ is the joint probability measure of $\mathcal{X}$ and $\mathcal{Y}$. The formalization of this definition in HOL is straightforward and as follows:

> random_variable_cond_prob (s, mu) X Y =
> $\quad$ λ (x, y).(random_vector_prob (s, mu) [X; Y] [x; y])/
> $\quad\quad$ (random_variable_prob (s, mu) Y y)

and

> random_vector_cond_prob (s, mu) XS YS =
> $\quad$ λ (xs, ys).(random_vector_prob (s, mu) (XS++YS) (xs++ys))/
> $\quad\quad$ (random_vector_prob (s, mu) YS ys),

where ++ is the list-concatenation operation. We now formalize conditional entropy in two steps, first defining something we will call conditioned entropy as

> conditioned_entropy (s, mu) X Y =
> $\quad$ λ y. $-$ sum $\Big(\lambda$ x. (random_variable_cond_prob (s, mu) X Y (x, y))
> $\quad\quad$ lg$\big($random_variable_cond_prob (s, mu) X Y (x, y)$)\Big)$ UNIV

for random variables, or

> conditioned_entropy (s, mu) XS YS =
> $\quad$ λ ys. $-$ sum $\Big(\lambda$ xs. (random_vector_cond_prob (s, mu) XS YS (xs, ys))
> $\quad\quad$ lg$\big($random_vector_cond_prob (s, mu) XS YS (xs, ys)$)\Big)$
> $\quad\quad$ {xs | LENGTH xs = LENGTH XS}

for random vectors, and finally defining conditional entropy as

> conditional_entropy (s, mu) X Y =
> $\quad$ expected_value (s, mu) Y (conditioned_entropy (s, mu) X Y).

Building upon the formalizations developed above, we conclude this section by formalizing the definitions of *mutual information* and *conditional mutual information*; we first review the standard definition of each of these concepts before presenting its formalization in HOL.

Definition 7. *The correlation between two random variables (or random vectors) $\mathcal{X}$ and $\mathcal{Y}$ is captured by their* **mutual information**, $\mathbb{I}(\mathcal{X}; \mathcal{Y})$. *The greater their mutual information the greater the correlation between $\mathcal{X}$ and $\mathcal{Y}$. Thus when $\mathcal{X}$ and $\mathcal{Y}$ are independent $\mathbb{I}(\mathcal{X}; \mathcal{Y}) = 0$. Mutual information measures the amount of information about $\mathcal{X}$ that can be obtained by observing $\mathcal{Y}$ (and vice versa).*

$$\mathbb{I}(\mathcal{X}; \mathcal{Y}) = \mathbb{H}(\mathcal{X}) - \mathbb{H}(\mathcal{X}|\mathcal{Y}) = \mathbb{H}(\mathcal{Y}) - \mathbb{H}(\mathcal{Y}|\mathcal{X}) = \mathbb{I}(\mathcal{Y}; \mathcal{X})$$

We now formalize mutual information in HOL as

```
mutual_information (s, mu) X Y =
    entropy (s, mu) Y - conditional_entropy (s, mu) X Y.
```

Definition 8. *The* **conditional mutual information**, $\mathbb{I}(\mathcal{X}; \mathcal{Y}|\mathcal{Z})$, *of random variables (or random vectors) $\mathcal{X}$ and $\mathcal{Y}$ conditioned on random variable (or random vector) $\mathcal{Z}$ captures the correlation between $\mathcal{X}$ and $\mathcal{Y}$ given $\mathcal{Z}$. Conditional mutual information measures the amount of information about $\mathcal{X}$ that can be learned by observing $\mathcal{Y}$ (and vice versa) given knowledge of $\mathcal{Z}$.*

$$\mathbb{I}(\mathcal{X}; \mathcal{Y}|\mathcal{Z}) = \mathbb{H}(\mathcal{X}|\mathcal{Z}) - \mathbb{H}(\mathcal{X}|\mathcal{Y}, \mathcal{Z}) = \mathbb{H}(\mathcal{Y}|\mathcal{Z}) - \mathbb{H}(\mathcal{Y}|\mathcal{X}, \mathcal{Z}) = \mathbb{I}(\mathcal{Y}; \mathcal{X}|\mathcal{Z})$$

Conditional mutual information is formalized in HOL as

```
conditional_mutual_information (s, mu) X Y Z =
    conditional_entropy (s, mu) X Z -
    conditional_entropy (s, mu) X (Y++Z).
```

2.2   Information Leakage Analysis

Having formalized a sufficient portion of information theory in HOL, we now proceed to develop an information-theoretic approach to analyzing the information leakage of programs using HOL. Intuitively, a program *leaks* information when an observer who knows (or can control) the low-security inputs to the program can learn or infer something about the high-security inputs to the program by observing the program's outputs. We recall from the previous section that conditional mutual-information of $\mathcal{X}$ and $\mathcal{Y}$ given $\mathcal{Z}$, $\mathbb{I}(\mathcal{X}; \mathcal{Y}|\mathcal{Z})$, measures the amount of information that can be learned about $\mathcal{X}$ by observing $\mathcal{Y}$, given knowledge of $\mathcal{Z}$. If $\mathcal{L}$ is a random variable ranging over the low-security inputs to a particular program, $\mathcal{H}$ is a random variable over the high-security inputs, and $\mathcal{O}$ is a random variable over the program's outputs, then $\mathbb{I}(\mathcal{O}; \mathcal{H}|\mathcal{L})$ (or equivalently $\mathbb{I}(\mathcal{H}; \mathcal{O}|\mathcal{L})$) measures the knowledge about the high-security inputs to the program that can be learned by observing the outputs of the program, given knowledge of the low-security inputs. Borrowing from the work of Malacaria [21], Denning [9,10], Clark [5], et al., we define the information leakage of a deterministic program to be $\mathbb{I}(\mathcal{O}; \mathcal{H}|\mathcal{L})$. For privacy (or anonymity) analysis, $\mathbb{I}(\mathcal{O}; \mathcal{H}|\mathcal{L})$ measures how much is learned about private (or identifying) information by an attacker who observes the outputs of a particular program and knows (or controls) any non-private inputs. In [6] Clark, et al. show that, for a deterministic program, the program is non-interfering iff $\mathbb{I}(\mathcal{O}; \mathcal{H}|\mathcal{L}) = 0$.

Programs to be analyzed are modeled in HOL as functions from low and high input states to output states. States are defined to be a polymorphic type, $\beta\ state$, s.t. states are functions $string \to \beta$, namely from variable names to values. Note that this allows us to have infinite state, e.g. $\beta = \mathbb{R}$; the only restriction we make, as noted earlier, is that probability distribution over states is non-zero for a finite number of states. Because HOL functions are deterministic and terminating, the programs we are able to model are also inherently so. We do not consider the termination requirement to be a severe restriction, but many, if not most, PETs involve probabilistic non-determinism in their design which is essential to their privacy guarantees. Fortunately, this restriction is easily overcome. Drawing again from Malacaria et al. [21], we introduce a component of the program input accounting for random behavior. This portion of the input state essentially serves as an oracle determining the resolution of the randomness on a given run of the program, with the distribution over the random behavior simply determined by the distribution over the random input states. For example, the following probabilistic algorithm involving a coin flip and a high and low input variable if heads then l:=h else l:=l+1 becomes a deterministic algorithm involving high, low, and random input variables if r == 1 then l:= h else l:=l+1, assuming the *a priori* distribution on r is s.t. the probability that r == 1 is $1/2$.

Proceeding from above, we define another HOL type $\beta\ prog\_state$, which is the 4-tuple, : $\beta state * \beta state * \beta state * \beta state$, representing a possible program execution: $(high, low, random, output)$.

Definition 9. *A* **program space** *is a pair* $(\texttt{M}, (\texttt{s}, \texttt{mu}))$ *of a HOL function modeling a program,* $\texttt{M}$ (high, low, random) : $(\beta state * \beta state * \beta state) \to \beta state$, *and a probability space,* $(\texttt{s}, \texttt{mu})$, *s.t.* $\texttt{s} = \texttt{UNIV}: \beta\ \texttt{prog\_state}$ *and* $\forall$ h l r o. $(\texttt{o} \neq \texttt{M}(\texttt{h}, \texttt{l}, \texttt{r})) \Rightarrow (\texttt{mu}(\texttt{h}, \texttt{l}, \texttt{r}, \texttt{o}) = 0)$.

The first condition in the definition of a program space, $\texttt{s} \doteq \texttt{UNIV}$, ensures that any program execution (i.e. anything of type : $prog\_state$) is measurable by $\texttt{mu}$; the second condition ensures that only *valid* executions (i.e. those whose output is equal to the program applied to the inputs) have non-zero probability. The probability distribution $\texttt{mu}$ over possible program executions for a particular program $\texttt{M}$ captures the *a priori* distribution of high, low, and random input states and the *a posteriori* distribution on the outputs of $\texttt{M}$ for these inputs. The four random variables

$$\texttt{H} = \lambda\texttt{x}.\{(\texttt{h}, \texttt{l}, \texttt{r}, \texttt{o})|\ \texttt{h} = \texttt{x}\}, \quad \texttt{L} = \lambda\texttt{x}.\{(\texttt{h}, \texttt{l}, \texttt{r}, \texttt{o})|\ \texttt{l} = \texttt{x}\},$$
$$\texttt{R} = \lambda\texttt{x}.\{(\texttt{h}, \texttt{l}, \texttt{r}, \texttt{o})|\ \texttt{r} = \texttt{x}\}, \quad \texttt{O} = \lambda\texttt{x}.\{(\texttt{h}, \texttt{l}, \texttt{r}, \texttt{o})|\ \texttt{o} = \texttt{x}\}$$

define equivalence relations on program executions based on the high input, low input, random input, and output respectively. In our HOL formalization, the random variables H, L, and O correspond to the random variables $\mathcal{H}$, $\mathcal{L}$, and $\mathcal{O}$ in the definition of *leakage* for deterministic programs above. (Note: H, L, and O are random variables from s to s, so random_variable_prob (s, mu) H h reduces to mu(H h) and similarly for L and O and random_vector_prob). Now we can formalize leakage in HOL for a deterministic program M and a program space (M, (s, mu)) as

Definition 10 (Leakage for deterministic programs)

leakage (M, (s, mu)) = conditional_mutual_information (s, mu) O H L.

We have successfully formalized leakage for a deterministic program in HOL, but before defining information leakage for a probabilistic program, we must consider our view of the probabilistic non-determinism in the program. There are two possible views of the non-determinism in the program corresponding to differing capabilities of an observer/attacker. On the one hand, we have the case where an attacker, who is trying to learn about the high input from the output, can observe (but not control) the outcome of the random events (e.g. knows that the coin-flips came up heads) in a particular execution of the program. We shall term this view of the probabilistic behavior as *visible* probabilism, since the resolution of the non-determinism is known to the observer. On the other hand, we have the case where the attacker knows that the resolution of the nondeterminism follows a particular distribution (e.g. knows that a fair coin is flipped), but cannot observe directly how the nondeterminism is resolved in a particular execution of the program (e.g. doesn't know that the coin-flip was heads this time). We shall term this view of the probabilistic behavior as *hidden* probabilism, since the resolution of the non-determinism is hidden from the observer.

If we consider a program to have visible probabilism, then the leakage of the program is the amount of information about the high-security inputs that can be learned from the outputs given knowledge of the low-security inputs *and* the resolution of the non-determinism; however if we consider a program to have hidden probabilism, then the leakage of the program is the amount of information about the high-security inputs that can be learned from the outputs given knowledge of the low-security inputs *only* (i.e. without knowledge of the resolution of the non-determinism). This understanding of leakage is captured by defining leakage to be $\mathbb{I}(\mathcal{O}; \mathcal{H}|(\mathcal{L}, \mathcal{R}))$, for programs with visible probabilism, and $\mathbb{I}(\mathcal{O}; \mathcal{H}|\mathcal{L})$, for programs with hidden probabilism, where $\mathcal{R}$ is a random variable ranging over the *random* inputs to the program that resolve the nondeterminism in a particular run of the program. We can now formalize information leakage of a nondeterministic program M and a program space (M, (s, mu)) as

Definition 11 (Leakage for programs with visible probabilism)

leakage (M, (s, mu)) = conditional_mutual_information (s, mu) O H (L++R),

Definition 12 (Leakage for programs with hidden probabilism)

leakage $(M, (s, mu)) = $ conditional_mutual_information (s, mu) O H L.

Note: we could analyze a program that contains *both* visible and hidden probabilism by splitting the random input into a visible component and hidden component and conditioning the measurement of conditional mutual information on the *visible* component of the random input.

It is important to distinguish these two views of the nondeterminism in our analysis of information leakage in order to be clear what we are measuring. The case study in Section 3 is an excellent example of this as there is no leakage if the probabilism is hidden (i.e. the outcomes of the coin flips are not known to an observer), but the leakage is total if the probabilisim is visible (i.e. the outcomes of the coin flips are known to an observer). In [21], Malacaria et al. do not consider this distinction between the two views of nondeterminism in their analysis. They note that for deterministic programs $\mathbb{H}(\mathcal{O}|(\mathcal{H}, \mathcal{L})) = 0$, so $\mathbb{I}(\mathcal{O}; \mathcal{H}|\mathcal{L}) = \mathbb{H}(\mathcal{O}|\mathcal{L})$. Malacaria et al. recognized this potential computational optimization for deterministic programs, but also noted that it may overestimate leakage for programs with probabilistic non-determinism [21]. Malacaria's example is the program l := random(0, 1), which sets the output to be 0 or 1 with equal probability. For the program above $\mathbb{H}(\mathcal{O}|\mathcal{L}) = 1$, while $\mathbb{I}(\mathcal{O}; \mathcal{H}|\mathcal{L}) = 0$, so there is an overestimation of the leakage of the program. Malacaria proposes that this "extra" leakage can be attributed to uncertainty in the output resulting from the randomness of the program and can be eliminated by conditioning on the random input. Thus they define leakage for nondeterministic programs to be $\mathbb{I}(\mathcal{O}; \mathcal{H}|(\mathcal{L}, \mathcal{R})) = \mathbb{H}(\mathcal{O}|(\mathcal{L}, \mathcal{R}))$, which is our definition of leakage for programs with *visible* nondeterminism only. Therefore, if we were to apply the definition for the leakage of nondeterministic programs adopted in [21] to the case study in Section 3, we would get the unintuitive result that a program which is known to be secure has a total leakage of information. We consider this distinction of visible and hidden probabilism in our definitions for information leakage of nondeterministic programs to be an important contribution of our work.

2.3   Assistance for the Uniformly Distributed Case

In order to prove some property of the information leakage of a program in HOL, we must first model the program and the probability space of possible program executions as HOL terms M and (s, mu). Since our definitions for leakage in HOL are well defined for any M and (s, mu) of the appropriate type, we are obligated to prove that the (s, mu) is in fact a probability space and that (M, (s, mu)) is a program space. Recognizing that some effort is required for these proofs, we have defined a HOL function unif_prog_space which takes as its arguments a program modeled in HOL, M, a set of high input states, high, a set of low input states, low, and a set of random input states, random; unif_prog_space(M, high, low, random) is the program space for M whose probability distribution is uniformly distributed over $\{(h, l, r, M(h, l, r))| \ h$ IN high $\wedge$

l IN low ∧ r IN random}. We have proved that, for any M, high, low, and random which are finite and nonempty, unif_prog_space defines a valid program space. While we will not always be interested in analysis when the inputs are evenly distributed this will often be the case (as it is for the case study), so some initial effort has been eliminated for further applications of our technique. Furthermore, we have developed automation in HOL that proves the leakage of a unif_prog_space for small, finite instances nearly fully-automatically. This automation is only useful for small examples because its memory and computational overheads grow rapidly with the size of the example, but is still of value for automatically proving the base case of a general inductive proof of leakage or as an initial check of our intuitions about the leakage of a program.

3   Case Study: The Dining Cryptographers

Having outlined a method for proving the information leakage of a program in HOL, we now go on to demonstrate the applicability of this technique to proving privacy properties of PETs by proving the total-anonymity of the Dining Cryptographers protocol [4]. We begin below by developing a model for the Dining Cryptographers protocol in HOL using the techniques of the previous section; the protocol is briefly explained for the benefit of the unfamiliar reader. Finally, we discuss the relationship between information-leakage and anonymity for the dining cryptographers protocol. Our information-theoretic proof of anonymity for the dining cryptographers protocol in HOL4 is outlined in Appendix A.

3.1   Modeling the Dining Cryptographers Protocol in HOL

In Chaum's original presentation of the Dining Cryptographers problem [4], a group of cryptographers sit down to dinner and are immediately informed by the Maître d'hôtel that the bill has already been paid. They come to the conclusion that either one of their party has paid, or the bill has been paid by some external agency such as the NSA. They would like to determine which of these has occurred while preserving the anonymity of the payer, in the event that one of the cryptographers has paid. The following solution is suggested. Each cryptographer flips a fair coin under the table and shares the outcome of the coin flip with the cryptographer to his left. All the cryptographers then announce the bitwise exclusive-or (xor) of the two coins they have seen (their own and that of the cryptographer to the right) and whether or not he/she has paid. If the bitwise xor of these announcements is true, then one of the cryptographers has paid, otherwise some outside agency has paid. The anonymity of the Dining Cryptographers protocol relies on the fairness of the coins and properties of xor; Chaum proved the total anonymity guarantee of the Dining Cryptographers protocol in [4]. Note that the nondeterminism inherent in the coin-flipping of the Dining Cryptographers protocol is that which we classified as *hidden* probabilism in the previous section, because the coins are flipped under the table where they cannot be observed.

We begin formalizing the Dining Cryptographers protocol in HOL by defining the sets of valid high-security, low-security, and random input-states. The type of state used is : *string* → *boolean* and since the state is infinite (there are an infinite number of possible variable names) we fix on the convention that any variable names we don't use map to the value $\bot$. The high input identifies which cryptographer has paid when one of them has and we index the cryptographers from 0 to $n - 1$, where there are n cryptographers. If the NSA has paid, the input is that n has paid. We can then define the set of valid high-security inputs as dc_high_states n $\top$ = {(λs. s = "pays n")}, when the NSA has payed, and dc_high_states n $\bot$ = {(λs. s = "pays i") | i < n}, when one of the cryptographers has paid. There are no low-security input variables, so we use dc_low_states = {(λs.$\bot$)} as our null low-input. The random inputs consist of all the possible combinations of coin flips for the n cryptographers, namely those states that map any variable other than "coin 0",..., "coin n − 1″ to $\bot$:

$$\text{dc\_random\_states n} = \{x \mid \forall s.(\forall i.i \nless n \vee s \neq \text{"coin i"}) \Rightarrow \neg \, x \, s\}.$$

We will now define the HOL function formalizing the Dining Cryptographers protocol; this is done in several parts corresponding to the various stages of the protocol. First the cryptographers' high-security coin values are set from the random-input. While this step is not strictly necessary and the coins from the random input could be used in the program directly (without affecting the analysis), this definition seems to reflect more directly the original definition. Note that HOL functions are typically defined recursively.

```
set_coins high random 0 =
    (λs. if s = "coin 0" then random s else high s)
set_coins high random (n + 1) =
    (λs. if s = "coin (n + 1)" then random s
        else set_coins high random n s)
```

The next step of the protocol is to set the announcements of each cryptographer. Since our cryptographers are indexed linearly, $0, \ldots, n - 1$, rather than sitting around a circular table, we adopt the convention that for $0 \le i < n - 1$ cryptographer $i + 1$ looks at coin $i + 1$ and coin i and cryptographer 0 looks at coin 0 and coin $n - 1$.

```
set_announcements low high n 0 =
    (λs. if s = "announces 0" then
        (high "pays 0") xor (high "coin 0") xor (high "coin n")
        else high s)
set_announcements low high n (i + 1) =
    (λs. if s = "announces i + 1" then
        (high "pays i + 1") xor (high "coin i + 1") xor (high "coin i")
        else set_announcements low high n i s)
```

The final step of the protocol is to determine the result (whether one of the cryptographers has paid or not) by xor-ing their announcements. This is done by defining two HOL functions, a helper-function to compute the bitwise xor of the announcements and the function that sets the result to this value.

> xor_announces low 0 = low "announces 0"
>
> xor_announces low (i + 1) =
>
> > (low "announces i + 1") xor (xor_announces low i)

> compute_result low n =
>
> > (λs. if s = "result" then xor_announces low n else low s)

All that is necessary to complete our formalization of the Dining Cryptographers protocol in HOL is the definition of the function that connects the stages we have defined.

> dcprog (n + 3) high low random =
>
> > compute_result(set_announcements low
> >
> > > (set_coins high random (n + 2))
> > >
> > > (n + 2) (n + 2))
> >
> > (n + 2)

Note: the function defining the overall protocol is for the argument $n + 3$, where $0 \leq n$, because the protocol is only valid for three or more cryptographers. The program space modeling the Dining Cryptographers protocol is the one in which the probability distribution is evenly distributed over the valid input-states identified above; this can easily be defined using unif_prog_space described in the previous section as

> dc_prog_space n nsapays =
>
> > unif_prog_space (dc_prog n)
> >
> > > (dc_high_states nsapays n) dc_low_states (dc_random_states n).

3.2   An Information-Theoretic Proof of the Dining Cryptographers

Having formalized a program space modeling the Dining Cryptographers protocol above, we can analyze the information leakage of this protocol using the information-theoretic technique developed in the previous section. We are interested in how much information might be leaked by the protocol about the identity of a cryptographer who has payed the bill, so we focus on the case where one of the cryptographers has payed; the proof of correctness when the NSA has payed is relatively straightforward. We recall from above that leakage measures how many bits of the high-security input can be learned by someone who knows the low-security inputs and observes the outputs; depending on whether or not we deem the probabilism in the protocol to be visible or hidden, the observer may also know the resolution of the probabilistic behavior in the protocol. In the case of the Dining Cryptographers protocol, there are no low-security inputs to be known and we consider the probabilism to be hidden, since the coins are flipped under the table. The outputs of the protocol are the announcements each cryptographer makes and the overall result (i.e. the xor of the announcements). The high-security input states whether or not cryptographer i has payed, for each of the $0 \leq i \leq n - 1$ cryptographers. Exactly one of the cryptographers will have paid, so there are $n - 1$ possible high inputs which are equally likely *a priori*. The high-security input is precisely the identity of the cryptographer who has payed and amounts to $lg(n - 1)$ bits of information. In terms of our anonymity analysis this means that a leakage measure of $lg(n - 1)$ would denote that *all* of the bits of the high-security input can be learned, so an observer can positively identify the payer and anonymity is completely compromised. If we were to obtain a leakage measurement of $(lg(n - 1))/2$, then *half* of the the bits of the high-security input can be learned and an observer can eliminate half of the cryptographers as candidates for being the payer. A leakage measurement of 0 would mean that an observer cannot learn anything about the identity of the payer from the outputs and total anonymity is maintained.

A proof of the total anonymity of the Dining Cryptographers protocol in HOL using the formalizations developed above can be found in Appendix A. The goal we prove is that, for three or more cryptographers ($\mathbf{n} \geq 3$), when one of the cryptographers has paid (**nsapays** $= \bot$), the information leakage of **dc_prog_space** is 0. Due to space constraints, we are only able to outline the HOL proof; the full script for the proof in HOL4 is approximately 1700 lines. When outlining the proof we choose to focus on the more interesting information-leakage aspects of the proof rather than the routine correctness aspects of the proof. Recall that every step of the proof is guaranteed by HOL4 to be logically consistent with our formalization of the protocol, probability theory, and any other mathematical theories used.

4   Summary and Future Work

Above we have developed an information-theoretic technique for proving the information leakage of programs formalized in the HOL4 theorem-prover. The advantage of this method being information-theoretic is that it is quantitative and capable of capturing *partial* information-leakage. Furthermore, by formalizing our analysis in HOL4, any proofs about information-leakage are guaranteed to be logically and mathematically consistent (up to the level of abstraction of the formalization).

After explaining this technique for proving information-leakage in HOL, we demonstrated its applicability to proving privacy properties of PETs by proving the total-anonymity of the Dining Cryptographers protocol [4]. As far as the author is aware, this is the first proof of the anonymity of the Dining Cryptographers protocol, for an *unbounded* number of cryptographers, mechanized in a theorem-prover using a quantitative, information-theoretic metric for anonymity.

Since it was first proposed, Chaum's Dining Cryptographers protocol has frequently been used as an initial case study for many formal methods for analyzing privacy [1, 8, 25]. Now twenty years after it was first proposed, the Dining Cryptographers may be considered a "toy" example when compared to deployed PETs, but it remains useful as an initial proof-of-concept for analysis techniques before applying them to more realistic examples.

As the author considers the case study above as a proof-of-concept for the methodology developed in this paper, future work will include the use of this technique to prove privacy properties of deployed PETs. There are numerous possible applications including anonymous communications systems such as [7, 13,15,19,23,24]. Another interesting use would be to analyze the privacy leakage of algorithms designed to "anonymize" databases e.g. for releasing anonymized versions of government-controlled medical-databases for research purposes.

Another area for future work, is to develop a more robust attacker model for this analysis technique. As presented above, the attacker is a passive observer who cannot inject arbitrary messages into the system, etc. This is sufficient to model many attacks for the dining cryptographers e.g. two cryptographers sitting across from each other can collude and determine which side of the table the payer is on (We model this by making the coins the two cryptographers see part of the *visible* probabilism). However, a passive attacker is insufficient for most attacks on more sophisticated examples, so this remains an important future development for this line of research.

Acknowledgments

The author would like to thank Larry Paulson, Mike Gordon, Joe Hurd, and Magnus Myreen for numerous useful discussions related to this work, the Gates Cambridge Trust for funding this research, and the anonymous reviewers for their many helpful comments.

References

[1] Bhargava, M., Palamidessi, C.: Probabilistic Anonymity, vol. 3653 (2005)
[2] Blanchet, B.: A computationally sound mechanized prover for security protocols. In: IEEE Symposium on Security and Privacy, pp. 140–154 (May 2006)
[3] Chatzikokolakis, K.: Probabilistic and Information-Theoretic Approaches to Anonymity. PhD thesis, Laboratoire d'Informatique (LIX), École Polytechnique, Paris (October 2007)
[4] Chaum, D.: The dining cryptographers problem: Unconditional sender and recipient untraceability. Journal of Cryptology 1(1), 65–75 (1988)
[5] Clark, D., Hunt, S., Malacaria, P.: Quantitative analysis of the leakage of confidential data. Electr. Notes Theor. Comput. Sci. 59(3) (2001)
[6] Clark, D., Hunt, S., Malacaria, P.: Quantitative information flow, relations and polymorphic types. J. Log. Comput. 15(2), 181–199 (2005)
[7] Danezis, G., Dingledine, R., Mathewson, N.: Mixminion: design of a type III anonymous remailer protocol. pp. 2–15 (2003)

[8] Deng, Y., Palamidessi, C., Pang, J.: Weak probabilistic anonymity. In: Proceedings of SECCO 2005. Electronic Notes in Theoretical Computer Science (2005)

[9] Denning, D.E.: A lattice model of secure information flow. Commun. ACM 19(5), 236–243 (1976)

[10] Denning, D.E.: Cryptography and Data Security. Addison-Wesley, Reading (1982)

[11] Dewdney, A.K.: Computer recreations: Of worms, viruses, and core war. Scientific American, 110 (March 1989)

[12] Díaz, C., Seys, S., Claessens, J., Preneel, B.: Towards Measuring Anonymity, vol. 2482 (2003)

[13] Dingledine, R., Mathewson, N., Syverson, P.: Tor: The second-generation onion router. In: Proceedings of the 13th USENIX Security Symposium (August 2004)

[14] Doob, J.L.: Measure Theory. Graduate Texts in Mathematics, vol. 143. Springer, Heidelberg (1991)

[15] Goel, S., Robson, M., Polte, M., Sirer, E.G.: Herbivore: A Scalable and Efficient Protocol for Anonymous Communication. Technical Report 2003-1890, Cornell University, Ithaca, NY (February 2003)

[16] Gordon, M.J.C.: From lcf to hol: a short history. In: Plotkin, G., Stirling, C.P., Tofte, M. (eds.) Proof, Language, and Interaction. MIT Press, Cambridge (2000)

[17] Hasan, O., Tahar, S.: Verification of expectation properties for discrete random variables in hol. In: Schneider, K., Brandt, J. (eds.) TPHOLs 2007. LNCS, vol. 4732, pp. 119–134. Springer, Heidelberg (2007)

[18] Hurd, J.: Formal Verification of Probabilistic Algorithms. PhD thesis, University of Cambridge (2002)

[19] Levine, B.N., Shields, C.: Hordes — A Multicast Based Protocol for Anonymity. Journal of Computer Security 10(3), 213–240 (2002)

[20] Lowe, G.: Breaking and fixing the needham-schroder public-key protocol using fdr. In: Margaria, T., Steffen, B. (eds.) TACAS 1996. LNCS, vol. 1055, pp. 147–166. Springer, Heidelberg (1996)

[21] Malacaria, P.: Assessing security threats of looping constructs. In: POPL, pp. 225–235 (2007)

[22] Paulson, L.C.: The inductive approach to verifying cryptographic protocols. Journal of Computer Security 6(1-2), 85–128 (1998)

[23] Reiter, M.K., Rubin, A.D.: Crowds: Anonymity for web transactions. Technical Report 97-15, DIMACS (1997)

[24] Rennhard, M., Plattner, B.: Introducing MorphMix: Peer-to-Peer based Anonymous Internet Usage with Collusion Detection. In: Proceedings of the Workshop on Privacy in the Electronic Society (WPES 2002), Washington, DC, USA (November 2002)

[25] Schneider, S., Sidiropoulos, A.: CSP and anonymity. In: Martella, G., Kurth, H., Montolivo, E., Bertino, E. (eds.) ESORICS 1996. LNCS, vol. 1146, pp. 198–218. Springer, Heidelberg (1996)

[26] Serjantov, A., Danezis, G.: Towards an information theoretic metric for anonymity. In: Dingledine, R., Syverson, P.F. (eds.) PET 2002. LNCS, vol. 2482. Springer, Heidelberg (2003)

[27] Shannon, C.E.: A mathematical theory of communication. Bell System Technincal Journal (27), 379–423, 623–656 (1948)

[28] Shmatikov, V.: Probabilistic model checking of an anonymity system. Schneider S.(ed.) Journal of Computer Security 12(3/4), 355–377 (2004)

[29] Williams, D.: Probability with Martingales. Cambridge Mathematical Textbooks. Cambridge University Press, Cambridge (1991)

A   Proof of Anonymity for the Dining Cryptographers

We define program, prob, and events s.t. program takes a program space (M,(s,mu)) as its argument and gives the program component M. Similarly, prob and events give the probability measure and the events of a program space respectively. We abbreviate

$$p\,n = \text{prob (dc\_prog\_space } (n{+}3)\ \perp),\ e\,n = \text{events (dc\_prog\_space } (n{+}3)\ \perp),$$

$$\text{prog } n = \text{program (dc\_prog\_space } (n+3)\ \perp),$$

$$\text{valid } n = \{s \mid \text{prob } n\,s \neq 0\},\ \text{high } n = \text{dc\_high\_states } (n+3)\ \perp,$$

(similarly for dc_low_states and dc_random_states), and finally

$$\text{output } n = \text{IMAGE } (\lambda\ x.\ \text{prog } n\ x)\ (\text{high } n\ \text{CROSS low } n\ \text{CROSS random } n).$$

Lemma 1 (There are $(n+3)(2^{n+3})$ valid program-states)

$$\forall\ n.\ \text{CARD (valid } n) = (n+3)(2^{n+3})$$

Proof. Follows directly from basic definitions. Intuitively, there are $n+3$ possible high-inputs, 2^{n+3} possible random-inputs, and 1 low-input.

Lemma 2 (A valid program-state has probability $1/((n+3)(2^{n+3}))$)

$$\forall\ n\ s.\ s\ \text{IN (valid } n) \Rightarrow (p\,n\ \{s\} = 1/((n+3)(2^{n+3})))$$

Proof. Follows directly from basic definitions and Lemma 1. This result is obvious, since the valid program-states are uniformly distributed.

Lemma 3 (There are 2 valid states for a given output and high-input)

$$\forall\ o\ h\ n.\ o\ \text{IN output } n\ \wedge\ h\ \text{IN high } n \Rightarrow$$
$$(\text{CARD}\{r \mid (h, (\lambda\ s.\perp), r, o)\ \text{IN valid } n\} = 2)$$

Proof. We begin by defining a function which determines if a random input r is valid for output o when cryptographer h pays:

```
coins_valid r o h n 0 =
    (r "coin0" = r "coin(n + 2)" xor (XOR o 0) xor (0 ≮ h))
coins_valid r o h n (i + 1) =
    ((r "coin(i + 1)" =
        r "coin(n + 2)" xor (XOR o (i + 1)) xor (i + 1 ≮ h)) ∧
    coins_valid r o h n i),
```

where XOR out i *is the pointwise xor of the announcements 0 through i. It is then straightforward to prove*

$$\forall\ n\ h\ o.\ h \leq (n+2)\ \wedge\ o\ \text{IN output } n \Rightarrow$$
$$(\{r \mid ((\lambda\ s.s = \text{``pays } h\text{''}), (\lambda\ s.\perp), r, o)\ \text{IN valid } n\} = \qquad (1)$$
$$\{r \mid r\ \text{IN random } n\ \wedge\ \text{coins\_valid } r\ o\ h\ n\ (n+2)\})$$

by induction. We then define a function that constructs a valid random-input given o, h, *and our* choice *of whether the first coin is heads or tails*

> make_r o h n choice 0 = $\left(\lambda\right.$ s. if s = "coin0" then
>
> choice xor (XOR out 0) xor (0 $\not<$ h) else $\perp$)
>
> make_r o h n choice (i + 1) = $\left(\lambda\right.$ s. if s = "coin(i + 1)" then
>
> choice xor (XOR out (i + 1)) xor (i + 1 $\not<$ h) else
>
> make_r o h n choice i s)

and prove by induction that

> $\forall$ n h o. h $\leq$ (n + 2) $\wedge$ o IN output n $\Rightarrow$
>
> ({r | r IN random n $\wedge$ coins_valid r o h n (n + 2)} =   (2)
>
> {make_r o h n $\top$ (n + 2); make_r o h n $\perp$ (n + 2)})

from which our goal immediately follows.

Lemma 4 (There are $2(n + 3)$ valid states for a given output)

> $\forall$ n o. o IN output n $\Rightarrow$ (CARD {s | s IN valid n $\wedge$ s IN 0 o} = 2(n + 3))

Proof. By the definition of valid *and set operations, it is sufficient to prove that*

> $\forall$ n o. o IN output n $\Rightarrow$ $\Big($CARD (IMAGE $(\lambda$ (h, r). (h, (λ s.$\perp$), r, o))
>
> {(h, r) | h IN high n $\wedge$ (h, (λ s.$\perp$), r, o) IN valid n})
>
> = 2(n + 3)$\Big)$

and by a property of the cardinality of the image of an injective function

> $\forall$ n o. o IN output n $\Rightarrow$
>
> $\big($CARD {(h, r) | h IN high n $\wedge$ (h, (λ s.$\perp$), r, o) IN valid n} = 2(n + 3)$\big)$.

Our goal follows from Lemma 3, and that there n + 3 *possible high-states.*

Lemma 5 (The probability of a valid output is $1/2^{n+2}$)

> $\forall$ n o. o IN output n $\Rightarrow$ (p n 0 o = $1/2^{n+2}$)

Proof. By Lemma 2 and basic definitions the goal is equivalent to

> $\forall$ n o. o IN output n $\Rightarrow$
>
> $\big($SUM $(\lambda$ s. $1/((n + 3)(2^{n+3})))$\{s | s IN valid n $\wedge$ s IN 0 o} = $1/2^{n+2}$$\big)$.

Since the above is a summation over a constant *function, it is equivalent to*

> $\forall$ n o. o IN output n $\Rightarrow$
>
> $\Big(\big(1/((n + 3)(2^{n+3}))\big)\big($CARD{s | s IN valid n $\wedge$ s IN 0 o}$\big)$ = $1/2^{n+2}$$\Big)$,

which is easily provable by Lemma 4 and basic arithmetic.

Lemma 6 (There are 2^{n+2} valid outputs)

$$\forall\ n.\ \text{CARD}(\text{output } n) = 2^{n+2}$$

Proof. Similarly to Lem. 3, we begin by defining a function that constructs the list of valid outputs,

announces_list $0 = [(\lambda\ \text{s. s} = \text{``announces0''}); (\lambda\ \text{s.}\bot)]$

announces_list $(i + 1) =$

$\left(\text{MAP } (\lambda\ \text{s. } (\lambda\ \text{x. if x} = \text{``announces}(i+1)\text{'' then } \top \text{ else s x}))\right.$

$\left.\text{announces\_list } i\right) + +$

$\left(\text{MAP } (\lambda\ \text{s. } (\lambda\ \text{x. if x} = \text{``announces}(i+1)\text{'' then } \bot \text{ else s x}))\right.$

$\left.\text{announces\_list } i\right)$

outputs_list $(n + 3) = \text{MAP } (\lambda\ \text{l s. } (\text{s} = \text{``result''})\ \vee$

$(\text{if s} = \text{``annouces}(n + 2)\text{'' then} \neg(\text{XOR l } (n + 1)) \text{ else l s}))$

announces_list $(n + 1).$

Building on proofs of the correctness of our model of the d.c. protocol, we can inductively prove that $\forall$ n x. x IN output n $=$ x MEM outputs_list $(n + 3)$. Two relatively straightforward inductive proofs yield that

$$\forall\ n.\ \text{ALL\_DISTINCT}(\text{outputs\_list } n) \tag{3}$$

(all the members of outputs_list are distinct) and that

$$\forall\ n.\ \text{LENGTH}(\text{outputs\_list } (n + 3)) = 2^{n+2} \tag{4}$$

from which our goal follows.

Theorem 1 (Conditional entropy of O given L is $n + 2$)

$$\forall\ n.\ \text{conditional\_entropy } (\text{e } n, \text{p } n)\ [\text{O}]\ [\text{L}] = n + 2$$

Proof. Since there is only one valid low-input, $(\lambda\ \text{s.}\bot)$, the goal reduces to

$$\forall\ n.\ -\text{SUM } (\lambda\ \text{o. } (\text{p } n\ \text{O } \text{o})(\text{lg}(\text{p } n\ \text{O } \text{o}))) \text{ (output } n) = n + 2$$

by Definitions 4 and 6 and basic arithmetic. Using Lemma 5 the goal becomes

$$\forall\ n.\ ((1/2^{n+2})(\text{lg}(1/2^{n+2})))\text{ (CARD (output } n)) = n + 2$$

which follows from Lemma 6, properties of lg, and basic arithmetic.

Lemma 7 (Probability of a high state is $1/(n + 3)$)

$$\forall\ n\ h.\ h\ \text{IN high } n \Rightarrow (\text{p } n\ \text{H } h = 1/(n + 3))$$

Proof. Follows from the fact that there are $n + 3$ evenly distributed high-inputs.

Lemma 8 (There are 2 states with a given output and high-input)

$\forall$ n h o. h IN high n $\wedge$ o IN IMAGE (λ r. prog n (h, (λ s.$\perp$), r)) random n $\Rightarrow$
    $\big($CARD$\{$s $\mid$ s IN H h $\wedge$ s IN O o $\wedge$ s IN valid n$\} = 2\big)$

Proof. By the basic definitions for the protocol, the goal is equivalent to

$\forall$ n h o. h $\leq$ (n + 2) $\wedge$ o IN IMAGE (λ r. prog n ((λ s.s = "pays h"), (λ s.$\perp$), r))
    random n $\Rightarrow$ $\big($CARD$\{$r $\mid$ ((λ s.s = "pays h"), (λ s.$\perp$), r, o) IN valid n$\} = 2\big)$,

which follows from (1) and (2) in Lemma 3.

Lemma 9 (Probability of a valid output & high input is $1/((n+3)2^{n+2})$)

$\forall$ n h o. h IN high n $\wedge$ o IN IMAGE (λ r. prog n (h, (λ s.$\perp$), r)) random n $\Rightarrow$
    $\big($random_vector_prob (e n, p n) [0; H] [o; h] $= 1/((n + 3)2^{n+2})\big)$

Proof. By Lemma 2 and basic definitions, the goal becomes

$\forall$ n h o. h IN high n $\wedge$ o IN IMAGE (λ r. prog n (h, (λ s.$\perp$), r)) random n $\Rightarrow$
    $\big($SUM (λ s. $1/((n + 3)2^{n+3})$)
        $\{$s $\mid$ s IN O o $\wedge$ s IN H h $\wedge$ s IN valid n$\} = 1/((n + 3)2^{n+2})\big)$,

which further reduces to

$\forall$ n h o. h IN high n $\wedge$ o IN IMAGE (λ r. prog n (h, (λ s.$\perp$), r)) random n $\Rightarrow$
    $((1/((n + 3)2^{n+3}))($CARD$\{$s $\mid$ s IN O o $\wedge$ s IN H h $\wedge$ s IN valid n$\}) =$
    $1/((n + 3)2^{n+2}))$

by properties of SUM. The above follows from Lem. 8 and basic arithmetic.

Lemma 10 (There are 2^{n+2} valid outputs for a given high-input)

$\forall$ n h. h IN high n $\Rightarrow$ $\big($CARD(IMAGE (λ r. prog n (h, (λ s.$\perp$), r)) random n)$= 2^{n+2}\big)$

Proof. By (3) and (4) of Lemma 6 it is sufficient to prove that

$\forall$ n h x. h IN high n $\Rightarrow$ $\big($x IN IMAGE (λ r. prog n (h, (λ s.$\perp$), r))
        random n = x MEM outputs_list (n + 3)$\big)$

which can be proved using the correctness *properties of our definition of the protocol. Further details of this proof are omitted due to space constraints.*

Lemma 11 (Conditioned entropy of O given H and L is $-(n + 2)$)

$\forall$ n h. h IN high n $\Rightarrow$
    $\big($conditioned_entropy (e n, p n) [O] [H; L] [h; (λ s.$\perp$)] $= -(n + 2)\big)$

Proof. Since there is only one valid low-input, $(\lambda\ \texttt{s}.\bot)$, the goal reduces to

$\forall$ n h. h IN high n $\Rightarrow$

$$\Big(- \mathtt{SUM}\ (\lambda\ \texttt{o}.\ (\lambda\ \texttt{x}.\ \texttt{x}(\lg\ \texttt{x}))\ (\texttt{random\_vector\_prob}\ (\texttt{e}\ \texttt{n},\texttt{p}\ \texttt{n})\ [0;\texttt{H}]\ [\texttt{o};\texttt{h}])/$$

$$(\texttt{p}\ \texttt{n}\ \texttt{H}\ \{\texttt{h}\}))\ \mathtt{IMAGE}\ (\lambda\ \texttt{r}.\ \texttt{prog}\ \texttt{n}\ (\texttt{h},(\lambda\ \texttt{s}.\bot),\texttt{r}))\ \texttt{random}\ \texttt{n} = -(\texttt{n}+2)\Big)$$

by Def. 6, which then further reduces to

$\forall$ n h. h IN high n $\Rightarrow$

$$\Big(- (1/2^{\texttt{n}+2}(\lg(1/2^{\texttt{n}+2})))$$

$$(\mathtt{CARD}(\mathtt{IMAGE}\ (\lambda\ \texttt{r}.\ \texttt{prog}\ \texttt{n}\ (\texttt{h},(\lambda\ \texttt{s}.\bot),\texttt{r}))\ \texttt{random}\ \texttt{n}) = -(\texttt{n}+2)\Big)$$

by Lems. 7 and 9 and properties of SUM*. The above follows from Lem. 10, a property of the cardinality of the image of an* injective *function, and basic arithmetic.*

Theorem 2 (Conditional entropy of 0 given H and L is n + 2)

$$\forall\ \texttt{n.}\ \texttt{conditional\_entropy}\ (\texttt{e}\ \texttt{n},\texttt{p}\ \texttt{n})\ [0]\ [\texttt{H};\texttt{L}] = \texttt{n}+2$$

Proof. Since there is only one valid low-input, $(\lambda\ \texttt{s}.\bot)$, the goal reduces to

$\forall$ n. $-$ SUM $\big(\lambda$ h. $(\texttt{p}\ \texttt{n}\ \texttt{H}\ \texttt{h})(\texttt{conditioned\_entropy}\ (\texttt{e}\ \texttt{n},\texttt{p}\ \texttt{n})\ [0]\ [\texttt{H};\texttt{L}]\ [\texttt{h};(\lambda\ \texttt{s}.\bot)])\big)$
$\quad\quad\quad$ high n $=$ n $+$ 2

which is equivalent to

$$\forall\ \texttt{n. SUM}\ \big(\lambda\ \texttt{h.}\ (\texttt{n}+2)/(\texttt{n}+3)\big)\ \texttt{high}\ \texttt{n} = \texttt{n}+2$$

by Lemmas 7 and 11 and basic arithmetic. Since the summation above is of a constant *function, the goal reduces to*

$$\forall\ \texttt{n.}\ \big(\mathtt{CARD}(\texttt{high}\ \texttt{n})\big)\big((\texttt{n}+2)/(\texttt{n}+3)\big) = \texttt{n}+2,$$

which follows directly from basic arithmetic and the fact that there are n+3 *valid high-inputs.*

Theorem 3 (The Dining Cryptographer's protocol preserves anonymity)

$$\forall\texttt{n.}\ \texttt{leakage}\ (\texttt{dc\_prog\_space}\ (\texttt{n}+3)\ \bot) = 0$$

Proof. Follows directly from Defs. 8 and 12, Thms. 1 and 2, and basic arithmetic.

Breaking and Provably Fixing Minx

Erik Shimshock, Matt Staats, and Nick Hopper

University of Minnesota
Minneapolis MN, USA
{eshim,staats,hopper}@cs.umn.edu

Abstract. In 2004, Danezis and Laurie proposed *Minx*, an encryption protocol and packet format for relay-based anonymity schemes, such as mix networks and onion routing, with simplicity as a primary design goal. Danezis and Laurie argued informally about the security properties of Minx but left open the problem of proving its security. In this paper, we show that there cannot be such a proof by showing that an active global adversary can decrypt Minx messages in polynomial time. To mitigate this attack, we also prove secure a very simple modification of the Minx protocol.

1 Introduction

In many situations, the ability to communicate anonymously is desirable. Privacy is a valued commodity among internet users, and several cryptographic protocols rely on the existence of anonymous channels. One proposed method of implementing anonymous channels is mix networks. First proposed by Chaum [4], a mix network works by routing messages through a series of mixes. Each mix in the network performs a cryptographic transformation on a received message before resending it, thus making the tracking of messages from mix to mix and sender to receiver very difficult. This process, which is sometimes referred to as onion routing, focuses on routing messages encrypted in a concentric, or layered, fashion, known as *onions* [9]. Each layer of an onion contains routing information for one node, with the goal being that each node in the network can only decrypt enough information to send the encrypted message to the next node in the path [3,5].

Several works have proposed encryption schemes for use in this setting; one scheme of interest is Mixminion, proposed as a successor to the popular Mixmaster scheme [7]. Since the design of Mixminion, several authors [13,3] have proposed schemes with some form of provable security guarantees, although these schemes do not allow for the anonymous replies supported by Mixminion. Additionally, several schemes based on universal reencryption [11] have been proposed; Danezis [6] has shown that several such schemes are not secure when applied to a mixnet.

This paper is concerned primarily with Minx, a packet format and encryption scheme proposed by Danezis and Laurie in 2004 [5]. Minx was designed to provided the same security properties provided by Mixminion but using simplicity

N. Borisov and I. Goldberg (Eds.): PETS 2008, LNCS 5134, pp. 99–114, 2008.

as a key design goal. The authors provide an informal argument for the security of Minx, but leave its formal proof of security as an open question, to be addressed in the future literature.

We resolve this question negatively, by showing that a theoretical algorithm developed by Håstad and Nåslund [12] can be used to exploit a subtle flaw in the Minx design and allow a global active adversary to decrypt messages encrypted under Minx in polynomial time. However, we also present a simple modification to Minx that prevents this attack while preserving its anonymous reply functionality, and prove its security under a security definition derived from the notion proposed by Camenisch and Lysyanskaya [3].

The remainder of this paper is organized as follows: Section 2 gives an overview of the Minx protocol; Section 3 presents our attack; Section 4 proposes a simple modification to mitigate the attack; Section 5 introduces a formal security definition for Minx; using this definition, Section 6 proves the security of our modification; and finally Section 7 provides concluding remarks.

2   Minx

The design of Minx is motivated by the desire to provide simpler operation and lower overhead than Mixminion without sacrificing security. Minx's packet format and associated mix server operation is quite simple, as it removes aspects of Mixminion deemed too complex by Minx's authors. These removed aspects include integrity checks for sent messages and a "swap step" designed to thwart attacks based upon traffic analysis [7,5].

Instead of attempting to detect tagged messages via integrity checks, Minx nodes process and forward all packets they receive. This prevents an attacker from tagging the end of a message in the hopes of noticing a dropped packet when the modification to the packet format is discovered. Furthermore Minx uses error propagating block ciphers so that tagging packets causes unpredictable changes in routing behavior and destroys the message payload[5].

2.1   Encryption and Decryption of Minx Packets

Minx employs three cryptographic primitives to create packets containing messages of fixed length. These are: RSA encryption [14], a symmetric "error propagating" encryption scheme EP, and a symmetric "bidirectional error propagating" encryption scheme $biEP$. The key properties of these schemes is that changing bit i of the ciphertext causes pseudorandom plaintext for bits $j > i$ when decrypting under EP and for all bits when decrypting under $biEP$. Danezis and Laurie suggest using AES in Infinite Garble Extension mode [8] for EP, and setting $biEP(x) = EP(reverse(EP(x)))$. We will let ℓ denote the length of RSA public keys, and κ the length of symmetric keys used in Minx; Danezis and Laurie recommend using $\ell = 1024$ and $\kappa = 80$.

The Minx packet format implements a simple layered encryption scheme. The layer intended for a node N contains three components: a session key k, a field

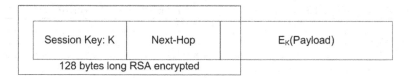

Fig. 1. Minx Packet Format

indicating the packet's next hop, and a payload (the next inner layer) encrypted using EP and session key k. Additionally, the first $\ell/8$ bytes–including the session key, next-hop field, and a portion of the encrypted payload–are RSA encrypted using node N's public key. This is diagrammed in Figure 1. The innermost layer is encoded slightly differently; the next-hop field is set to a special *final* value to indicate that node N is the intended destination, and the payload (the actual message) is encrypted with the $biEP$ block cipher instead of the EP block cipher.

A Minx packet is created as follows. Suppose sender S wishes to send message M anonymously through $n-1$ hops to a receiver at mix node N_n. S chooses $n-1$ intermediate mix nodes $N_1 \ldots N_{n-1}$ in the Minx network and n random session keys, $k_1 \ldots k_n$. Each mix node N_i has an RSA public key associated with it. Let encryption of a data block D using public key of router N_i be represented as $RSA_{N_i}(D)$, and the encryption of a data block D with EP or $biEP$ keyed with k_i be represented as $EP_{k_i}(D)$ and $biEP_{k_i}(D)$ respectively. Similarly, let $RSA_{N_i}^{-1}(D)$, $EP_{k_i}^{-1}(D)$, and $biEP_{k_i}^{-1}(D)$ be the respective decryption operations. Let $|$ represent concatenation of bit strings, and let $M[i,j]$ denote the byte range from byte i to byte j (inclusive) of bit string M. Finally, let $J(l)$ represent a random string of bits of length l. Figure 2 shows the procedure for a sender to encode a Minx packet as well as the procedure for a Minx node to decode and process a Minx packet. Note that P_i and C_i represent the packet intended for node N_i before and after the header is encrypted with node N_i's public key. The sender S thus sends the resulting packet C_1 to node N_1.

When a Minx node receives a packet C_j the decoding process is quite simple. It decodes the first $\ell/8$ bytes of C_j and extracts the session key k_j, the next hop field, and the encrypted payload. To prevent replay attacks the node maintains a table of observed session key hashes, and drops the offending packets. If the next-hop field contains the special *final* value, the packet has reached it's final destination so the node decrypts the payload (with $biEP^{-1}$) and processes the enclosed message accordingly. Otherwise the field indicates the next-hop destination, so it decrypts the payload (with EP^{-1}), pads the resulting packet up to the proper size, and forwards it on to its next stop.

2.2   Reply Packets

A packet sender S can choose to include information allowing receiver R to reply without revealing S's identity. A sender wishing to allow replies creates a special minx packet called a reply block rb_S to allow receiver R to send a message to sender S without knowing the identity of S. The reply block rb_S and the first

Minx Packet Encoding	Minx Packet Decoding
INPUTS:	INPUTS:
message M	packet C_j
node IDs $N_1 \ldots N_n$	node ID N_j
session keys $k_1 \ldots k_n$	PROCEDURE:
PROCEDURE:	$k_j \mid N_{j+1} \mid encC =$
$P_n = k_n \mid final \mid biEP_{k_n}(M)$	$\quad RSA_{N_j}^{-1}(C_j[0, \frac{\ell}{8} - 1]) \mid C_j[\frac{\ell}{8}, -]$
For i from $n - 1$ to 1 :	Check and store $H_{id}(k_j)$.
$\quad P_i = k_i \mid N_{i+1} \mid EP_{k_i}(C_{i+1})$	if N_{j+1} is not $final$:
$\quad C_i = RSA_{N_i}(P_i[0, \frac{\ell}{8} - 1]) \mid P_i[\frac{\ell}{8}, -]$	$\quad C_{j+1} = EP_{k_j}^{-1}(encC)$
Pad C_1 up to a set size: $C_1 = C_1 \mid J_l$	$\quad$ Send padded message $C_{j+1} \mid J_l$ to N_{j+1}
Return C_1	else:
	$\quad$ Process message $biEP_{k_j}^{-1}(encC[0, (l-1)])$

Fig. 2. On the left is the procedure for encode a message M in a Minx packet that will travel the path $N_1 \ldots N_n$. On the right is the procedure for a Minx node N_j to decode and process an incoming packet.

node in the path specified by rb_S are included in the anonymous message sent to the receiver. The receiver can create a reply by encrypting a message M' with a globally fixed key λ and prefixing the encrypted message with the packet rb_S. The ciphertext $rb_S \mid biEP_\lambda(M') \mid J_l$ is then sent to the specified first node.

As the reply block routes the packet through the network back to S, the appended message M' gains layers of encryption. In order for S to recover this appended message, she includes some extra information – the path and session keys – inside of the original reply block rb_S.

2.3   Minx's Claimed Security Properties

The stated goal of Minx is to provide the same security properties as Mixminion. These security goals are:

- Anonymity given the presence of a global passive adversary which controls all but one node on the message path and can perform active attacks against honest mix servers.
- The ability to generate secure anonymous replies.
- Mix servers, given a message, cannot determine either the total length the message will be routed or their position along the message's path.
- Tagging attacks are totally ineffective. Tagging attacks are defined as attacks which modify a correct, encrypted message in an attempt to recognize the result of the modifications at a later point during routing.

Of particular note is the claim that tagging attacks are ineffective. This claim is based on the assumption that the cryptographic transformations above, when used to decrypt tagged ciphertext, decrypt to something unpredictable and thus do not allow useful information to be gained. In the next section, we show how an active attack that carefully submits many modified messages can exploit Minx's use of "vanilla RSA" to recover plaintexts.

3   Attack on Minx

As mentioned previously, Minx does not meet its stated security goals. Specifically, it is vulnerable to a chosen ciphertext attack that allows an active adversary to successively unwrap the layers of encryption from a packet and eventually extract the enclosed message using a bit oracle constructed from the next-hop portion of the packet header.

Our attack relies on recent theoretical work by Håstad and Nåslund [12]. The main theorem from this work is that all individual plaintext bits of an RSA ciphertext are hard core bits: unless RSA can be inverted in probabilistic polynomial time, no single bit of the plaintext can be predicted in polynomial time with non-negligible advantage.

The theorem is proven in the contrapositive, by showing that an adversary can decrypt an RSA ciphertext if they have the ability to predict a single bit of an arbitrary RSA plaintext when given the corresponding RSA ciphertext. More formally, consider an oracle $\mathcal{O}_i$, which when given RSA ciphertext $E(x)$ outputs x_i, the ith bit of x, with probablity $\frac{1}{2} + \frac{1}{p(\ell)}$, for some polynomial p. Håstad and Nåslund describe a probabilistic polynomial time algorithm that uses this oracle $\mathcal{O}$ to decrypt an RSA ciphertext. The description of the algorithm is outside the scope of this paper, but we note that it requires only a polynomial number of queries to $\mathcal{O}$ on randomly sampled ciphertexts, and runs in expected time $O(\ell^{13})$ where ℓ is the bit-length of the RSA modulus.

3.1   Constructing the Bit Oracle

Generally, obtaining an RSA bit oracle is difficult. However, the current design of Minx allows an adversary to construct such an oracle. As described in Section 2.1, when a Minx node receives a packet, it decrypts the first $\frac{\ell}{8}$ bytes using it's RSA private key and then examines the session key and next-hop fields. If the next-hop field specifies another node ID (that is, it doesn't contain the special value *final*), the Minx node uses the session key to decrypt the rest of the packet and forwards it to the specified next-hop destination.

Consider a Minx node that performs no mixing, so that packets are output sequentially in the order they are received. An adversary observing the node's traffic can watch a packet P_j enter and watch the processed packet P_{j+1} leave the node. Since the adversary can observe the destination of P_{j+1}, she knows the corresponding bits of the next-hop field that were in the RSA encrypted header of P_j. This gives a simple construction of a predictor for any bit in the next-hop field of the header. Specifically, given an RSA ciphertext C the adversary implements the oracle $\mathcal{O}$ as follows:

1. Create a packet P with C as the first $\frac{\ell}{8}$ bytes and arbitrary bits for the remainder of the packet (so C is the encrypted header).
2. Send the packet P through the target Minx node.
3. Observe the outgoing packet and record its next-hop destination.
4. Look up the value that corresponds to the next-hop destination.
5. Return the desired bit of the next-hop field.

It is easy to see that with no mixing, the oracle's bit predictions have 100% accuracy. Since the security of Minx is intended to hold regardless of mixing strategy, this will already be sufficient to prove that no asymptotic security proof is possible.

However, even if a Minx node uses a mixing strategy it is still possible to construct a bit oracle, with slightly reduced accuracy. Suppose that for a given mixing strategy, the adversary can determine for any input packet P, a set S of k packets such S contains the decryption of P with probability at least $1 - \rho$. To predict a next-hop bit in this case, the adversary can submit a packet P, and observe the set S of k packets and their next-hop destinations. By uniformly picking a packet from S and predicting the appropriate bit of its next-hop field, the adversary can predict the desired bit with probability at least $\frac{1}{2} + \frac{1}{2k}(1 - \rho)$. Thus this implementation of the bit oracle meets the theorem's requirements.

3.2   Attack Walkthrough

To follow the full attack, consider a target Minx packet P_1 heading towards next-hop Minx node N_1. The adversary is interested in decoding this packet to determine the enclosed message and its intended destination. Recall that the first $\frac{\ell}{8}$ bytes of the packet P_1 consist of the header encrypted with N_1's RSA public key. The adversary proceeds to run Håstad and Nåslund's algorithm to extract the unencrypted header of packet P_1. Whenever the algorithm invokes a call to the bit oracle, the adversary follows the implementation of the bit oracle described above. After successfully running the algorithm, the adversary will have obtained the unencrypted header of packet P_1. From the header the adversary extracts the session key and next-hop value. If the next-hop value indicates that N_1 was the final node in the path, the adversary uses the session key to decrypt the rest of the packet and extracts the original message. Otherwise the next-hop value indicates the next node N_2, and the session key is used to recover the next Minx packet P_2. The adversary then repeats the procedure for packet P_2 with destination N_2. Eventually the adversary will reach the last node in the path and extract the plaintext message and its destination.

In this attack, Minx nodes could occasionally drop packets that contain a previously used session key. Since the oracle queries are chosen from an unbiased pairwise-independent distribution, the probability of this event is negligible in the session key length.

Although this attack is not truly practical, requiring an expected time of $O(\ell^{13})$ for each hop[1], it is sufficient to show that there cannot be a proof of security for Minx in the standard cryptographic security model. Furthermore, it is interesting to note that Minx is somewhat fragile in its security against more practical attacks: if the next-hop portion of the header had been in the most significant bits (before the session key, rather than after it), a simple modification

---

[1] However, it is interesting to note that in some special cases, Håstad and Nåslund's algorithm actually reveals a node's RSA private key, thus allowing the adversary to decrypt *all* messages passing through the node.

of Bleichenbacher's "million message attack" [2] could be used to recover packet plaintexts with only $O(\ell)$ oracle queries for RSA moduli of length ℓ.

3.3 Insecurity of Reply Packets

We note that, in addition to being subject to the same attacks as regular packets, Minx reply packets are subject to an additional attack that distinguishes them from regular packets at the first hop. As outlined in Section 2.2, reply packets are constructed by appending the encryption, under the fixed key λ, of a message M' to a reply packet rb_S, creating $rb_S | E_\lambda(M') | J$. As rb_S is of fixed size and λ is fixed and public, a global passive adversary (or dishonest first-hop mix server) can simply attempt to decrypt the appropriate portion of any packet using key λ. If the result is recognizable as plaintext, the packet corresponds to the first hop of a reply message.

4 Fixing Minx

In this section we propose modifications to Minx. Our attack is possible because routing packets leak information about bits in the packet header plaintext. Our proposed modification is to use a cryptographically secure hash function to obscure the link between the observed behavior and the packet header information, thus removing the bit oracle present in the original Minx specification.

4.1 Details

In our modification, the session key and next-hop field are no longer explicitly encoded in the packet header. When a node processes an incoming packet it computes the hash of the unencrypted header and extracts the session key and next hop from the hash output. The modifications appear in Figure 3. Note that previously only repeated session keys were disallowed, but we now disallow repeated headers. Also note that previously part of the payload was contained in the RSA encrypted portion, but now the payload starts after the $\frac{\ell}{8}$ byte header. The former is done to prevent replay attacks, and the latter to simplify our proof.

The sender is now required to find random headers whose hash indicates the correct next-hop (or *final*). However, this is a minimal burden on the sender as the next-hop field is only 1 byte, and thus the expected number of headers to try before success is only $2^8 = 256$. In an implementation headers could be pulled from a precomputed list, thus reducing the average cost of creating a packet. Furthermore, if the sender does not care about which intermediate nodes are used, they only have to check that the final next-hop value N'_n indicates the correct destination and that none of the intermediate values next-hop values N'_i encode the special *final* value. Also note that the sender no longer explicitly generates session keys, as they are randomly chosen through use of the secure hash function.

Modified Packet Encoding	Modified Packet Decoding
INPUTS:	INPUTS:
message M	packet C_j
node IDs $N_1 \ldots N_n$	node ID N_j
PROCEDURE:	PROCEDURE:
do	$Header = C_j[0, \frac{\ell}{8} - 1]$
$\quad Header_n = \text{random } \frac{\ell}{8} \text{ bytes}$	if $Header$ has been seen before
$\quad (k_n\|N_n') = \text{H}(Header_n)$	$\quad$ drop the packet
until $N_n' = final$	else
$C_n = \text{RSA}_{N_n}(Header_n)\| \text{biEP}_{k_n}(M)$	$\quad$ cache $Header$
For j from $n-1$ to 1 :	$Pay = C_j[\frac{\ell}{8}, -]$
$\quad$ do	$(k_j\|N_{j+1}) = \text{H}(\text{RSA}_{N_j}^{-1}(Header))$
$\qquad Header_j = \text{random } \frac{\ell}{8} \text{ bytes}$	if N_{j+1} is not $final$:
$\qquad (k_j\|N_{j+1}') = \text{H}(Header_j)$	$\quad C_{j+1} = \text{EP}_{k_j}^{-1}(Pay)$
$\quad$ until $N_{j+1}' = N_{j+1}$	$\quad$ Send padded message $C_{j+1}\|J$ to N_{j+1}
$\quad C_j = \text{RSA}_{N_j}(Header_j)\| \text{EP}_{k_j}(C_{j+1})$	else:
Pad C_1 up to a set size: $C_1 = C_1\|J_l$	$\quad$ Process message $\text{biEP}_{k_j}^{-1}(Pay[0, (l-1)])$

Fig. 3. On the left is our modified procedure for encode a message M in a Minx packet that will travel the path $N_1 \ldots N_n$. On the right is our modified procedure for a Minx node N_j to decode and process an incoming packet.

Form Reply Block$(SK, N_1 \ldots N_n, name, IV)$

```
do
    header_n = random
    (k_n|nextHop_n) = H(header_n)
until nextHop = REPLY
for j = n - 1 to 1
    do
        header_j = random
        (k_j|nextHop_j) = H(header_j)
    until nextHop_j = N_j
secretKey = H'(SK|IV)
M = name | IV | EP_{H'(SK|IV)}(name |Nym | n | header_1 |...| header_n)
O_n = RSA_{N_n}(header_n) | biEP_{k_n}(M)
for j = n - 1 to 1
    O_j = RSA_{N_j}(header_j)| EP_{k_j}(O_{j+1})
pad O_1 up to size L' (smaller than normal packet size)
return O_1, secretKey
```

Fig. 4. Reply Block formation

4.2   Reply Packets

As described in Section 3.3, the use of a globally fixed key reduces the security of Minx reply packets. If we have the anonymous sender S send a secret key $secretKey$ along with the reply block rb_S and first node destination, then the receiver can use *secretKey* in place of the fixed key λ. A reply message M' can be created by appending $E_{secretKey}(M')$ to the reply block.

Recall that our modified packet format no longer uses sender specified session keys, and these session keys need to be stored in the reply block so that the sender S can later recover R's reply message. Thus creating the reply block requires precomputing all the headers so that they can be included in the extra information S sends to herself. The creation of a reply block is shown in Figure 4.

5 Formalization of Minx

In order to prove our modification to Minx is secure, we must first formally define what it means for an onion routing encryption protocol to be "secure." Our formal definition of security uses a slightly modified version of the onion routing security framework provided by Camenisch and Lysyanskaya [3]. Note that in both this section and the subsequent proof section our discussion is in terms of "onions" and "routers" as used by Camenisch and Lysyanskaya; these correspond exactly to "packets" and "nodes" when discussing Minx.

Camenisch and Lysyanskaya syntactically define an onion routing scheme to consist of two functions, *ProcOnion* and *FormOnion*. When given a private key SK, an onion O_i and a router N_i, *ProcOnion* decrypts O_i and returns the next router in the path N_{i+1} and onion O_{i+1} to be sent to that router. *FormOnion*$(m, (N_1, \ldots, N_{n+1}), (PK_1, \ldots, PK_{n+1}))$ creates an onion containing message m and path $N_1, \ldots, N_{n+1}$, using the public keys $PK_1, \ldots, PK_{n+1}$.

Camenisch and Lysyanskaya's framework for onion security is defined in the adversary and challenger game format. The challenger picks a challenge router and public key PK and gives it to the adversary A, but keeps the corresponding private key secret. The adversary then picks an path index j, sets $PK_j = PK$, picks n other routers and generates public keys $PK_1, \ldots, PK_{j-1}, PK_{j+1}, \ldots, PK_{n+1}$ (and corresponding private keys). The adversary then submits to the challenger a message m, the index j, the public keys $PK_1, \ldots, PK_{n+1}$. The challenger then forms an onion either containing message m and path $PK_1, \ldots, PK_j$, $\ldots, PK_{n+1}$ as requested by the adversary, or a random message and path $PK_1, \ldots, PK_j$. The resulting outer onion O_1 is then given to A. The adversary can then request to have any number of onions $O' \neq O_j$ decrypted by the challenge router using a procOnion oracle and can observe the results (A knows all the other private keys so it doesn't need an oracle for the other routers). Thus without knowing the private key for PK_j, and not being able to process the critical onion O_j, A's goal is to distinguish which of the two possible onions it was given with nonnegligible advantage over random guessing.

To accommodate Minx in this framework and to simplify our proof of security presented later, we make two simple changes to the framework.

First, in addition to disallowing A from submitting an onion identical to O_j, we add a further restriction and forbid the adversary from submitting any onions with the same header as O_j. This is due to the fact that in Minx modifying the "tail" of a packet doesn't the next-hop information in the current header (though it corrupts the message and the rest of the path). Thus in the context of Minx an adversary could submit to the challenge router an onion $O'_j \neq O_j$ but with the same header and easily determine if the challenge router was the last stop. Also this formal restriction is consistent with Minx's policy of dropping packets with previously used headers.

Second, we drop the requirement in [3] that A cannot "re-wrap" O_j. Consider the specified path of the challenge onion, and let N_{j-1} be the router preceding the challenge router N_j. In Camenisch and Lysyanskaya's framework an adversary instantly "wins" the game (thus proving the protocol insecure) if she can construct a different onion O' that goes through a different router $N' \neq N_{j-1}$ yet when processed yields the onion $O'' = O_j$. This is trivial to perform in the context of Minx - just encrypt O_j with a new header using a different node's public RSA key. Again, since Minx nodes are stateful and drop duplicate headers, this event does not correspond to an attack in the Minx setting.

Our modified definition of security is expressed formally as follows:

1. Adversary A receives a (randomly chosen) challenge public key PK and router name N.
2. A can send any number of onions O_i of her choosing to the challenger and observe the output $(N_{i+1}, O_{i+1}) \leftarrow ProcOnion(SK_i, O_i, N_i)$.
3. A submits a message m, path $N_1...N_{n+1}$, an index j in the path, and public/secret keys for all routers $1 \leq i \leq n+1, i \neq j$. The challenger randomly selects $b \in \{0, 1\}$.

   If $b = 0$, the challenger computes:
   $(O_1, \ldots, O_{n+1}) \leftarrow \text{FormOnion}(m, (N_1, \ldots, N_{n+1}), (PK_1, \ldots, PK_{n+1}))$
   If $b = 1$, the challenger randomly selects $r \leftarrow \{0, 1\}^{|m|}$ and computes:
   $(O_1, \ldots, O_j) \leftarrow \text{FormOnion}(r, (N_1, \ldots, N_j), (PK_1, \ldots, PK_j))$
   O_1 is given to adversary A.

4. A can then send any onion O_i whose header differs from O_j and obtain $\text{ProcOnion}(SK_i, O_i, N_i)$.
5. A outputs a guess $\hat{b}_A$, for the bit b.

We say that an onion routing scheme is secure if for every polynomial time (in the security parameter, e.g. the length of the public key) adversary A, $\Pr[\hat{b}_A = b] - \frac{1}{2}$ is negligible in the security parameter.

Note that as is the case with Minx, Camenisch and Lysyanskaya's framework does not consider the mixing strategy of the onion routers. This allows analysis of the cryptographic aspects of onion routing independently from the mixing strategies used. Under this framework it is easy to see that Minx does not meet this definition of security, since the adversary A can follow the attack described in Section 3 to perfectly distinguish between the $b = 0$ and $b = 1$ cases.

6   Security Proof

In this section we formally prove the security of our modified version of Minx. Recall the game based definition of security in Section 5, in which the adversary is required to try to guess the value of b. If no polynomial time adversary can get a non-negligible advantage over the random guessing strategy, the protocol is considered secure. Our proof is in the random oracle model [1] and relies on two cryptographic assumptions. First, we assume RSA is a trapdoor one-way permutation: given a randomly chosen RSA modulus N, and $E_N(x)$ for a randomly chosen $x \in \{0,1\}^{\lfloor \log_2 N \rfloor}$, no polynomial time algorithm can output x with non-negligible probability. Second, we assume that EP and $biEP$ are implemented using a block cipher (such as AES) in IGE mode, as Danezis and Laurie suggest[5], and that the underlying block cipher is a pseudorandom permutation: given oracle access to a bijection, no polynomial time algorithm can distinguish between an oracle for a uniformly chosen bijection and an oracle for the block cipher with a randomly chosen key. This assumption implies, in particular, that the ciphertexts output by EP and $biEP$, when a key is used only once, are indistinguishable from random bitstrings of the same length [8].

6.1   Outline of Hybrids

Our security proof is similar to standard hybrid arguments, such as appear in [10]. We consider the probability that the adversary outputs 1 in a sequence of four *hybrid* games:

- In Game 0 the challenger always follows the $b = 0$ case from the original game, that is, $O_j = RSA_j(\text{Header}_j)|EP(O_{j+1})$, with the next-hop portion of $H(\text{Header}_j)$ indicating router N_{j+1} as the next hop.
- In Game 1 the challenger acts the same as in Game 0 except when forming O_j. First the challenger forms $O_j = RSA_j(\text{Header}_j)|EP(O_{j+1})$ as he would in Game 0, but then replaces the encrypted header $RSA_j(\text{Header}_j)$ with random bits to yield $O_j = random|EP(O_{j+1})$. The rest of the outer layers are formed as normal.
- In Game 2 the challenger acts the same as in Game 0 except when forming O_j. Instead of forming O_j as he would in Game 0, the challenger sets all the bits of O_j to be random yielding $O_j = random$. The rest of the outer layers are formed as normal.
- In Game 3 the challenger follows the $b = 1$ case, except when forming O_j (note that O_j is the innermost onion in the $b = 1$ case). The challenger first forms O_j as he would in the $b = 1$ case, so $O_j = RSA_j(\text{Header}_j)|BiEP(r)$ where the next-hop field of $H(\text{Header}_j)$ encodes the special *Final* value. The challenger then keeps the same encrypted header, but replaces the payload portion, $BiEP(r)$, with random bits to yield $O_j = RSA_j(\text{Header}_j)|random$.
- In Game 4 the challenger always follows the $b = 1$ case, that is, $O_j = RSA_j(\text{Header}_j)|BiEP(r)$ where the next-hop field of $H(\text{Header}_j)$ indicates *Final*.

We argue that the difference in the probabilities that the adversary outputs 1 in each adjacent pair of games must be negligible. Then by the triangle inequality, we will have that the difference in probabilities between Game 0 and Game 4 must also be negligible.

The adversary, knowing all private keys except the jth private key, can always decrypt O_1 to get O_2, and then decrypt O_2 to get O_3, etc., until obtaining O_j. Additionally, in all of the games $O_1...O_{j-1}$ contain no differences, so in essence the adversary is attempting to distinguish between the two cases for O_j.

6.2   Proof of Indistinguishability

We first provide a lemma that ProcOnion is not useful to an adversary. One might expect calling *ProcOnion* would give the adversary an advantage in distinguishing the games, as *ProcOnion* has access to the jth private key. However, since all information returned by *ProcOnion* is a function of the hash function H, we can simulate the information an adversary would gain from calls to *ProcOnion* by replacing H with a random oracle and appropriately responding to its queries to H.

Lemma 1. *An adversary A cannot distinguish between normal outputs from ProcOnion and a third party T simulating ProcOnion and the Oracle. Thus, A gains no information from ProcOnion.*

Proof. T simulates *ProcOnion* and the Oracle by maintaining a table with three columns: x, y, and h, where x is a header plaintext, $y = E(x)$ is the corresponding header ciphertext, and h is our Oracle output for x. A row will always contain a value in the ciphertext and Oracle output columns, but the plaintext value may be empty/unknown.

When A makes an Oracle query x, T calculates $y = E(x)$ and checks if ciphertext y is in the table. If so he returns the corresponding Oracle output listed in the table. Otherwise T returns a random value r, and places x, y, r in the table. When A queries *ProcOnion* with an onion O consisting of header ciphertext y and encrypted payload d, T checks if ciphertext y is already in the table. If so, T looks at the Oracle output $h = nextHop\|sesKey$. T then decrypts d with $sesKey$ and returns the output along with $nextHop$. Otherwise T picks a random value r and makes a table entry with an empty plaintext, y as the ciphertext, and r as the Oracle output. T then takes $h = nextHop\|sesKey$, decrypts d with $sesKey$ and returns the output along with $nextHop$.

Since A has no information about the value of the hash at the plaintext unless he has already queried the oracle there, and we enforce consistency in these cases, the probability of any outcome with our simulation technique is identical to the probability with a random oracle and a correct *ProcOnion* oracle.

We now show that our steps are indistinguishable, beginning with Games 0 and 1. Let $Pr_i[z]$ equal the probability of event z occurring in game i. Suppose that A can distinguish between Game 0 and Game 1 with advantage $\epsilon = Pr_0[\hat{b}_A = 1] - Pr_1[\hat{b}_A = 1]$. Using A, we construct an algorithm $M(y, PK)$ that decrypts RSA ciphertext $y = E(x)$ for a uniform x given the corresponding public key PK. M will simulate A's calls to ProcOnion and the Random Oracle using a table as explained in the previous lemma. M runs as shown in Figure 5.

$$\mathbf{M}(y, PK)$$

m, path $\leftarrow$ $\mathbf{A}$(PK)
o $\leftarrow$ y $\|$ random payload
b $\leftarrow$ $\mathbf{A}$(o , m, path, public key)
if table contains y in ciphertext column
return corresponding plaintext
else
return random x mod PK

Fig. 5. M distinguishing algorithm

Note that if the ciphertext y shows up in the table, it must be as a result of querying the Random Oracle with a value x such that $y = E(x)$, as A is forbidden from querying *ProcOnion* with an onion that has ciphertext header y. Let Q be the event that A queries the Random Oracle on a value x such that $y = E(x)$. Note that when Q does not occur, there is no difference in A's view of the two games: without querying at x, there is no correlation between the encrypted header and the string $EP(O_{j+1})$. Thus we have $Pr_0[\hat{b}_A = b \mid Q] = Pr_1[\hat{b}_A = b \mid Q]$ for any bit b. Also note that regardless of what A does, $Pr_1[\hat{b}_A = 1|Q] - Pr_0[\hat{b}_A = 1|Q] \leq 1$. Therefore:

$$\epsilon = Pr_1[\hat{b}_A = 1] - Pr_0[\hat{b}_A = 1]$$
$$= Pr_1[\hat{b}_A = 1|Q] \cdot Pr[Q] + Pr_1[\hat{b}_A = 1|\overline{Q}] \cdot Pr[\overline{Q}]$$
$$- \left(Pr_0[\hat{b}_A = 1|Q] \cdot Pr[Q] + Pr_0[\hat{b}_A = 1|\overline{Q}] \cdot Pr[\overline{Q}] \right)$$
$$= Pr[Q] \cdot (Pr_1[\hat{b}_A = 1|Q] - Pr_0[\hat{b}_A = 1|Q])$$
$$\leq Pr[Q] .$$

Since M succeeds with probability exactly that of Q and runs in time proportional to the running time of A, and it is assumed that RSA cannot be broken with non-negligible probability, A's advantage must be negligible, and thus Games 0 and 1 are indistinguishable.

Now we argue that Games 1 and 2 are indistinguishable. Suppose that for some adversary A, $Pr_2[\hat{b}_A = 1] - Pr_1[\hat{b}_A = 1]$ is non-negligible. Then this adversary can be used to create an algorithm M to distinguish between the symmetric encryption of a chosen message (under a random, secret key) and random bits, leading to an attack on the block cipher. M simulates the challenger in games 1 and 2, and invokes the adversary A up until the challenge message is prepared. M prepares onion O_{j+1} as the challenger in games 1 and 2 does, and then requests a symmetric-scheme challenge-string that is either the symmetric encryption of O_{j+1} under an unknown secret key or a string of random bits. In either case, M prepends a random header to this string and gives it to A. In case the symmetric-scheme adversary received random bits, he outputs 1 with probability $Pr_2[\hat{b}_A = 1]$, and otherwise he outputs 1 with probability $Pr_1[\hat{b}_A = 1]$. Since we assumed that the symmetric schemes EP and $biEP$ are implemented in a manner that makes ciphertexts (under a random key) indistinguishable from random bits, Games 1 and 2 are indistinguishable.

The transition between Games 2 and 3 is similar to the transition between Games 0 and 1. The only difference between Game 2 and Game 3 is the header of O_j - Game 2 has a random header and Game 3 has a meaningful header. As in the first transition, an adversary that could distinguish between Games 2 and 3 could decrypt an RSA ciphertext using only the public key. Under the assumption that this is impossible for a polynomially limited adversary, Games 2 and 3 are indistinguishable.

Finally, we argue that Games 3 and 4 are in fact identically distributed. This follows from the fact that with any fixed bijection, $biEP(r)$ for random bits r is uniformly distributed: each block is formed by applying a fixed bijection to a uniformly random string. Thus $\Pr_4[\hat{b}_A = 1] = \Pr_4[\hat{b}_A = 1]$.

Thus we have that for each $i \in \{0, 1, 2, 3\}$, $\epsilon_i = \Pr_{i+1}[\hat{b}_A = 1] - \Pr_i[\hat{b}_A = 1]$ is negligible. Since $\Pr_4[\hat{b}_A = 1] - \Pr_1[\hat{b}_A = 1] = \sum_{i \leq 3} \epsilon_i$, and $\Pr[\hat{b}_A = b] = \frac{1}{2} + \frac{1}{2}(\Pr_4[\hat{b}_A = 1] - \Pr_0[\hat{b}_A = 1])$, we have that any A must have negligible advantage against our modified version of Minx.

6.3   Reply Packets

In order to prove that reply packets are secure, we must first define what security property we want from them. Recall that reply onions under Minx are designed to be indistinguishable from standard onions. A natural question is to ask to whom they should be indistinguishable: the *sender* can clearly differentiate the reply onion until its first hop. And the receiver, if he retains the secret keys, can do so at any hop (e.g. by looking for the encrypted headers). While it is an interesting question whether a reply-onion scheme exists that avoids these issues, we do not address it in this paper. (Nor does the original Minx design)

We define security by a simple game: the challenger picks public keys $PK_1, \ldots, PK_n$ and gives them to the adversary, who then picks a message M that could fit in a reply block. The challenger then flips a coin $b \in \{0, 1\}$; if $b = 0$, he encrypts M in a standard onion, and if $b = 1$, he encrypts M in a reply onion. The resulting onion is given to the adversary, who then outputs a guess $\hat{b}_A$. A reply onion scheme is secure if for every polynomial time adversary, $\Pr[\hat{b}_A = b] - \frac{1}{2}$ is negligible.

Under this definition, it should be clear that our modified reply onions are secure: the only difference between the cases $b = 0$ and $b = 1$ is that for a reply onion, the "ciphertext" after the final header $E(header_n)$ is an encryption under EP of a "short" string followed by an encryption under EP of M using a different key; whereas for a "standard" onion this ciphertext is an encryption under EP of M followed by padding. Since ciphertexts produced by EP are indistinguishable from random bits, the triangle inequality implies the security of our construction.

7   Conclusions and Future Work

Our work here represents two contributions of note. First, we have described a novel attack which demonstrates how leaking one bit in an encrypted message can have significant security ramifications. We hope that our demonstration of this will influence the design of future protocols. Second, we have described a modification to Minx that prevents this attack, and have provided a formal proof that our solution meets the protocol's original security goals.

One shortcoming of our suggested modification is that it wastes message space by appending a full RSA modulus worth of random bits for every layer of encryption; Minx avoids this by encrypting the key, the next hop, and a portion of the next encrypted onion in the RSA header. The design of a scheme that reduces this overhead is an interesting question for future research.

Acknowledgements

We would like to thank Johan Håstad and Mats Nåslund for their correspondences regarding their algorithm. This work has been partially supported by NSF grant CNS-0546162, NASA Ames Research Center Cooperative Agreement NNA06CB21A, NASA IV&V Facility Contract NNG-05CB16C, and the L-3 Titan Group.

References

1. Bellare, M., Rogaway, P.: Random oracles are practical: a paradigm for designing efficient protocols. ACM Press, New York (1993)
2. Bleichenbacher, D.: Chosen ciphertext attacks against protocols based on the rsa encryption standard pkcs #1. In: Krawczyk, H. (ed.) CRYPTO 1998. LNCS, vol. 1462, pp. 1–12. Springer, Heidelberg (1998)
3. Camenisch, J., Lysyanskaya, A.: A Formal Treatment of Onion Routing. In: Shoup, V. (ed.) CRYPTO 2005. LNCS, vol. 3621, pp. 169–187. Springer, Heidelberg (2005)
4. Chaum, D.L.: Untraceable electronic mail, return addresses, and digital pseudonyms. Communications of the ACM 24(2), 84–88 (1981)
5. Danezis, G., Laurie, B.: Minx: a simple and efficient anonymous packet format. In: Proceedings of the 2004 ACM workshop on Privacy in the electronic society, pp. 59–65 (2004)
6. Danezis, G.: Breaking four mix-related schemes based on universal re-encryption. In: Katsikas, S.K., López, J., Backes, M., Gritzalis, S., Preneel, B. (eds.) ISC 2006. LNCS, vol. 4176, pp. 46–59. Springer, Heidelberg (2006)
7. Danezis, G., Dingledine, R., Mathewson, N.: Mixminion: Design of a type iii anonymous remailer protocol. In: SP 2003: Proceedings of the 2003 IEEE Symposium on Security and Privacy, Washington, DC, USA, p. 2. IEEE Computer Society, Los Alamitos (2003)
8. Gligor, V., Donescu, P.: Infinite Garble Extension. Contribution to NIST (2000)
9. Goldschlag, D., Reed, M., Syverson, P.: Onion routing. Commun. ACM 42(2), 39–41 (1999)
10. Goldwasser, S., Bellare, M.: Lecture notes on cryptography. Summer Course Cryptography and Computer Security at MIT 1999, 1999 (1996)
11. Golle, P., Jakobsson, M., Juels, A., Syverson, P.F.: Universal re-encryption for mixnets. In: Okamoto, T. (ed.) CT-RSA 2004. LNCS, vol. 2964, pp. 163–178. Springer, Heidelberg (2004)

Metrics for Security and Performance in Low-Latency Anonymity Systems

Steven J. Murdoch and Robert N.M. Watson

Computer Laboratory, University of Cambridge, UK
http://www.cl.cam.ac.uk/users/{sjm217,rnw24}

Abstract. In this paper we explore the tradeoffs between security and performance in anonymity networks such as Tor. Using probability of path compromise as a measure of security, we explore the behaviour of various path selection algorithms with a Tor path simulator. We demonstrate that assumptions about the relative expense of IP addresses and cheapness of bandwidth break down if attackers are allowed to purchase access to botnets, giving plentiful IP addresses, but each with relatively poor symmetric bandwidth. We further propose that the expected latency of data sent through a network is a useful performance metric, show how it may be calculated, and demonstrate the counter-intuitive result that Tor's current path selection scheme, designed for performance, both performs well and is good for anonymity in the presence of a botnet-based adversary.

1 Introduction

The Tor network [1] is the most widely deployed anonymous communication system, whose estimated 250 000 users include companies, human rights workers and law enforcement. The network's security is therefore critical for the safety and commercial concerns of its users. In common with other deployed low-latency anonymity networks, Tor is vulnerable to an attacker who is able to monitor a user's communication both as it enters and leaves the system. Through traffic analysis, the attacker can use timing characteristics to confirm which incoming connection corresponds to an outgoing one, and so discover the user behaviour Tor seeks to hide. It is thus important to understand how the routing of connections through the Tor network affects the risk of their compromise.

A frequently stated problem with Tor is that it significantly slows down web browsing speed. This is, in part, a consequence of the volunteer-operated nature of servers – many are on slow connections or shared with other activity. It is therefore important to make the best use of the limited capacity available, when selecting the path over which a user's traffic will be routed through the Tor network. In order to prevent an attacker manipulating path selection, the servers on each path are selected by the initiator. For best performance, the path selection algorithm must therefore fairly distribute connections based on server capacity, using only information known to the initiator, while being difficult for an adversary to game.

N. Borisov and I. Goldberg (Eds.): PETS 2008, LNCS 5134, pp. 115–132, 2008.

In this paper we present an analysis of path selection algorithms for Tor, including the currently used ones and proposed improvements. We consider their anonymity and performance consequences, based on simulations and models driven by data collected from the deployed Tor network.

In contrast to previous work, we examine a more realistic threat model, in which attackers are limited not only by number of nodes they control, but also their bandwidth capacity. We find that by introducing this generalisation the relative security of different path selection algorithms is substantially changed.

Previous work has shown that alternative algorithms have improved performance, when only the client tested is modified. We show that, by modelling a network where the new algorithm is fully deployed, performance substantially deviates from previous predictions.

The remainder of the paper is structured as follows: Section 2 introduces the basic operation of Tor, and the threat model we will consider; Section 3 discusses related work on alternative path selection algorithms, metrics for evaluating their anonymity, and attacks which exploit their weaknesses; Section 4 describes, in detail, how the existing Tor path selection algorithm operates; Section 5 introduces our metric for path selection security and presents simulation results; finally, Section 6 evaluates the performance of path selection algorithms, when all clients are assumed to be using the new scheme.

2   Design of Tor

The Tor anonymity network, the latest generation of the Onion Routing project, aims to anonymise TCP traffic while maintaining a low enough latency to be usable for interactive protocols such as web browsing. When the Tor server software on a node (an *onion router*) is first configured, it generates a public/private key pair and sends the public half and other routing details to the *directory authorities*, in the form of a router descriptor. The directory authorities communicate between themselves and establish the subset of onion routers which they are all aware of and sign the resulting *consensus directory*.

Users install the Tor client software on their computer and configure their applications to use Tor as a SOCKS proxy (an *onion proxy*). On receiving a connection, the client establishes the desired destination and selects a path consisting of three Tor nodes listed in the consensus directory (which was downloaded from a directory authority or a mirror). The client then connects to each node on the path (a hop) in turn and builds an encrypted tunnel secured by a session key established through an authenticated Diffie-Hellman exchange. Each connection is made through the previous tunnel, so an external observer can only see the connection to the first hop (the entry node).

The client requests that the last hop (the exit node) connects to the desired destination, then splits data to be sent into 512 byte *cells*, encrypts them under all session keys for the path, and sends them to the entry node. Each node on the path removes one layer of encryption, establishes which is the next hop, and sends the cell on. Once the cell reaches the exit node, the final layer of encryption is removed and the data sent to the destination server. Replies from the server follow the reverse process.

The full details of the procedure are covered in the Tor specification [2], but all that is required to understand for the remainder of the paper is that an encrypted tunnel can be built through the Tor network. Our focus will be on how the onion proxy selects the onion router nodes for each path. Section 4 will describe the path selection algorithms in detail, but we will first discuss what we assume about our attacker's goals and abilities.

2.1   Threat Model

Tor imposes no restrictions on who can join the network, which has led to the rapid growth of network capacity, but increases the risk that some nodes in the network are malicious. We assume that an attacker's goal is to link senders with receivers – that is, to de-anonymise the endpoints of traffic. A *global-passive* adversary, conventionally assumed in the study of high-latency anonymity networks, can break the anonymity properties of currently deployed low-latency systems by correlating traffic patterns; however in many situations such a powerful attacker is unrealistic. Instead, we will consider a weaker attacker who is only capable of monitoring traffic on nodes he has injected into the network.

Tor does not intentionally delay messages, or introduce dummy traffic other than limited message padding, so traffic patterns remain almost unchanged as they pass through the network. For this reason, it was assumed and subsequently demonstrated [3,4] that by observing both ends of a connection, timing patterns are enough to confirm a suspected link between sender and receiver. This attack has also been shown to work even if only a small proportion (e.g. 1 in 2 000) of packets can be observed [5]. We will thus assume that a connection is de-anonymised if both the first and last hop on the path are malicious.

In contrast to Tor, JAP [6] requires that operators promise not to engage in malicious behaviour before being admitted. JAP is also a *cascade* system, in which traffic from all users flow over the same path. If an attacker were able to compromise or monitor the single entry and exit nodes for a given cascade then all of its users could be de-anonymised. Our threat model is only appropriate to a network where data may follow arbitrary paths (a *free route system*), and where nodes may freely join and leave. We will not further discuss JAP-style networks in this paper.

3   Related Work

3.1   Path Selection Algorithms for Tor

At a high level, Tor's path selection algorithm works in two stages. For each hop on the path, Tor first builds a list of nodes which meet requirements (such as reachability and stability) and second, picks a random node according to a weighting scheme. When the design document [1] was written, Tor uniformly weighted random node selection. This was initially adequate, but as heterogeneity of node bandwidth capabilities increased, path selection was changed to take into account bandwidth capacity of nodes. The basic algorithm is described by Bauer *et al.* [3], and our updated description is in Section 4.

Several proposals from the literature, on improving the Tor selection algorithm, have already been applied to the mainline Tor distribution. These include guard nodes [4] and bandwidth/uptime caps [3]. One further notable paper is by Snader and Borisov [7], in which two proposals are made. Firstly, they suggest that bandwidth estimates used for making routing decisions be measured by opportunistically sampling actual throughput, rather than nodes reporting their own capacity. Secondly, they propose a tunable algorithm for selecting nodes, which weights faster nodes more heavily, depending on user preferences for anonymity versus performance. In this paper we will primarily discuss the latter proposal, but will return to the former in Section 5.

While the current Tor path selection algorithm picks nodes with a probability proportional to their contribution to the total network bandwidth, the Snader Borisov (S-B) tunable variant only uses advertised node capacity to produce a rank ordering of nodes. The probability that a particular node will be selected depends solely on its position within this ordering. More precisely, let the family of functions f_s be defined as:

$$f_s(x) = \frac{1 - 2^{sx}}{1 - 2^s} \quad (\text{for} \quad s \neq 0) \tag{1}$$

$$f_0(x) = x \tag{2}$$

To select each node, the n candidates are sorted in descending order of bandwidth and a number x selected uniformly at random from the interval $[0, 1)$. The selected node is at index $\lfloor n \times f_s(x) \rfloor$. This is equivalent to selecting a random number according to the cumulative distribution function (CDF) defined by the inverse of $f_s(x)$.

The value of s is selected by the client according to their preference for faster nodes. For $s = 0$, nodes are selected uniformly (intended for users with high anonymity requirements) but the higher s is, the more will faster nodes be preferred (for users willing to compromise anonymity for better performance). A practical upper limit is suggested to be 10, at which with $n = 1\,000$, the highest ranked node will be selected with probability 6%. By modifying a single client to adopt the new strategy, the authors experimentally confirm that higher values of s leads to better performing connections.

A potential problem with parametrised node selection is that if it is possible to identify a user's selection preference, their actions can be linked. Snader and Borisov used a naïve Bayesian classifier in order to establish how accurately a user's selection preference could be fingerprinted, based on path selection. They found that with a training set of 100 000 paths, the probability of correctly identifying s does not exceed 21%.

3.2   Metrics for Path Selection

The general consensus from the literature is that the further a path selection algorithm deviates from uniform weighting of nodes, the lower the anonymity it provides. Following this intuition, Bauer *et al.* adopt normalised Shannon entropy as their definition of anonymity. i.e. if the probability of selecting node x_i is q_i, for $1 \leq i \leq n$, the entropy is:

$$H = -\sum_{i=1}^{n} q_i \log_2 q_i \qquad (3)$$

H is maximal at $\log_2(n)$ when the selection probability is uniform over all nodes, hence entropy can be normalised, giving a quantity $0 \leq S \leq 1$ representing how skewed the probability distribution is:

$$S = \frac{H}{\log_2(n)} \qquad (4)$$

Entropy and normalised entropy have been used extensively in the study of high-latency remailers, although over users rather than the paths. For example, a traffic analysis attack which attempts to establish the sender of a message will result in a probability distribution over all system users. The users for which the probability is non-zero make up the anonymity set. One simple metric for anonymity system security is the size of the anonymity set, but this does not capture the non-uniformity. For this reason, Danezis and Serjantov [8] proposed entropy of the anonymity set as the effective size, and Diaz *et al.* [9] proposed normalised entropy as the system's degree of anonymity.

Snader and Borisov have adopted a different metric, the Gini coefficient, but it also measures the deviation from uniform path selection. The Gini coefficient G equals the normalised area between the CDF of the probability distribution being measured, and the uniform CDF. Thus $G = 0$ represents uniform distribution over all candidate nodes and $G = 1$ indicates that the same single node will always be chosen.

3.3   Attacks on Path Selection

A number of previous publications have taken advantage of Tor's path selection algorithm in developing attacks. Øverlier and Syverson [4] showed that, by causing a client to repeatedly generate fresh paths, an attacker can quickly gain a high probability of controlling both the first and last hop. This was performed in the context of hidden services, a feature of Tor which permits the pseudonymous operation of a server, but the same concepts apply to normal connections.

In order to de-anonymise connections through Tor, an attacker can simply add enough nodes to maintain a high probability that a connection will start and end with a malicious node – effectively a Sybil attack [10]. However, a much more economical variant, proposed by Øverlier and Syverson [4], is to exploit the fact that load-balancing calculations are based on nodes' self-reported bandwidth.

Bauer *et al.* [3] demonstrated that by artificially inflating bandwidth claims, an attacker could compromise 46% of connections while controlling only 6 out of the 66 nodes on a private Tor network. In this paper we will expand on the results of Bauer *et al.*, simulating this attack while varying path selection algorithm. We also employ node parameters from the real Tor network, rather than a private one, and use a version of the Tor path selection algorithm adapted to respond to Bauer's attack by capping per-node advertised bandwidth.

4   Path Selection in Tor

In this section, we discuss the Tor path selection algorithm and proposed variants. Because the Tor path selection algorithms have changed over time, we have chosen a version from late 2007 based on information from a combination of the Tor path selection specification [11] and the Tor source code.

Tor clients base their path decisions on two types of information: a database of Tor node properties provided by Tor directory authorities in the consensus directory, and the specific requirements of the requested connection. We detail the path selection algorithm in Tor in terms of node properties, path requirements, and node selection weighting.

4.1   Node Properties

Table 1. Node properties used in selecting paths

Network address	The IP address of the node
Node family	Administrator-configured equivalence class
Node bandwidth	Average, burst, and observed capacity; for most purposes, the average bandwidth is used, capped to 10 MB/s in order to limit bandwidth-based attacks
Node uptime	Time since node came online
Node status	Whether the node is *running* or is currently *hibernating* and so unwilling to accept connections
Exit policy	What, if any, types of exit node use is permitted
Publication timestamp	When this information was last received by a directory authority
Tor version	Version of Tor on the node

Table 1 lists the node properties which are reported by nodes to the Tor directory authorities, and to some extent monitored for accuracy. The path selection algorithm takes, as input, the following properties derived from the consensus directory:

– A node is *valid* if the version of Tor running on the node is not one of a number of known-bad versions, which render the node unsuitable for use as an entry or exit node.

- A node is *active* if the publication timestamp in the consensus directory is no more than 20 hours old, the node is valid and is marked as running.
- A node is *stable* if its self-reported uptime is among the top half of Tor network nodes, or whose uptime at least 30 days[1].
- A node is *fast* if its capped advertised bandwidth is among the top 7/8 of Tor network nodes, or whose capped advertised bandwidth is at least 100 kB/s.

4.2   Path Requirements

For any path, no two nodes may be in the same equivalence class, i.e. if their IP addresses have the same most significant 16 bits (in the same /16, following CIDR notation [12]), or if both nodes declares the other to be in the same family. This helps to avoid two nodes on a path being in the same administrative domain, as well as limiting the effectiveness of injecting many nodes using easily attainable /24 address ranges.

A *stable path* is one made solely of stable nodes. Stable paths will be used for connections that are expected to be long-lived, currently determined using a table of port numbers. For example, SSH and IRC connections will use stable paths, with the intent of providing more reliable service.

A *fast path* is one made up solely of fast nodes. Fast paths will be used for almost all connections, except for setting up and connecting to hidden services. The intent here is to provide the latter greater anonymity by allowing more nodes from the network to be used for these security-critical functions.

4.3   Node Selection Weighting

Once the list of acceptable candidate nodes is built, three random selection algorithms may be used to select from them:

- *Simple random selection (SRS)*, in which the node is selected from a set of candidate nodes with uniform probability.
- *Bandwidth-weighted random selection (BWRS)*, in which the node is selected from a set of candidate nodes with probability proportional to their individual capped bandwidth.
- *Adjusted bandwidth-weighted random selection (ABWRS)*, where bandwidth-weighted selection is used, but exit nodes are entirely eliminated from selection if less than one third of overall network bandwidth is advertised by exit nodes, or weighted in order to reduce the chances of selecting an exit node for other points on the resulting path.

Nodes are selected randomly from the set of suitable nodes using one of two path selection algorithms: SRS for paths requiring additional security, and

---

[1] More recent versions of Tor directory authority implement basic validity checking on uptime; as we do not specifically consider time as a resource, this does not change our analysis. However, high-uptime malicious nodes are not difficult for an appropriately resourced attacker to create.

BWRS and ABWRS for fast paths. Entry and middle node selection are adjusted to avoid overload of potential exit nodes. Nodes are selected beginning with the exit node, typically the most constrained in choice due to the need to use a node with a suitable exit-policy, followed by the entry node, and then middle nodes.

5   Measuring the Probability of Path Compromise

Our metric of security is probability, with respect to cost and selection algorithm, that an attacker compromises a connection by controlling the first and last hop. While many factors could be considered in a definition of investment, we address the cost of attack in terms of two elements that act as inputs to the path selection algorithms: the number of nodes available to the attacker, and the bandwidth available for each node.

After one node in a family is selected, other nodes in the same family will be ignored during further path selection so we assume that attackers will invest in nodes only in different families in order to avoid wasting resources. While not traditionally considered, this approach is consistent with an attacker controlling a botnet, because bots are geographically and network topologically diverse. IP addresses and bandwidth could be further mapped into real-world costs, such as the costs of co-location and hardware, if desired.

Our analysis assumes optimal performance by Tor in determining the correct uptime and throughput of nodes; if nodes are able to lead Tor directory authorities to incorrectly publish information on their performance, this may lead to a greater success rate for the attacker, but is beyond the scope of this work. While Tor is currently unable to fully assess whether the advertised bandwidth of a node is accurate, proposals have been made to do so [7]; likewise, Tor increasingly tracks the reputation of nodes in the network in order to evaluate their stability claims.

5.1   Experimental Design

We have created a Tor path simulator, which accepts as input the existing consensus directory tracked by the Tor directory authorities, and a set of artificially introduced malicious nodes with given parameters. The simulator generates paths with specified constraints, such as the requirement for being fast or stable, and evaluates the probability that each path selected is compromised.

We captured a snapshot of the Tor consensus directory on 7 June 2007, which includes 1 484 router descriptors, of which 1 044 are considered active and 521 are considered both active and stable. While the set of nodes available for exit traffic varies by protocol and destination, 325 nodes in the data set are appropriate for general HTTP exit traffic.

We then ran the simulator with various path requirements and attacker node investments in order to evaluate the protection that the path selection algorithms offered. We consider only the overall probability that any given connection will be compromised, not whether any given end-user will have their connection compromised. This requires us to observe the guard requirements for entry nodes, but not to consider the conditional probability of connection compromise given a client's previous path choices.

We compared four path selection algorithms:

B/W: Tor's default bandwidth-weighted algorithm based on a combination of the BWRS and ABWRS algorithms.

Uniform: Tor's uniform selection path algorithm, which uses SRS for more security-sensitive paths, such as with hidden services.

S-B(1): The S-B path algorithm with parameter $s = 1$, reflecting a desire for increased anonymity.

S-B(15): The S-B path algorithm with parameter $s = 15$, reflecting a desire for increased performance.

The simulator selects 1 000 random paths through the network and determines whether the first and last hop are malicious, generating an approximate probability of compromise given the attacker model and path selection algorithm. We implement two attacker investment strategies that reflect possible cost models: one in which each additional node adds a fixed amount of bandwidth, and a second in which the attacker is able to invest a fixed total amount of bandwidth over a variable number of nodes.

The former reflects a world in which many sites contribute malicious nodes with bandwidth, such as a botnet[2], and the latter in which a single site is able to use diverse network addresses over a single link of fixed bandwidth, such as in a co-location centre[3]. These represent extremes in strategy, but allow us to evaluate the effectiveness of different path selection algorithms inside, and outside, of their assumptions.

5.2 Results

In our first experiment, shown in Figure 1, we compare the rate of path compromise when injecting 20 kB/s and 256 kB/s malicious nodes over the four path selection algorithms. The uniform and S-B(1) algorithms are unaffected and relatively unaffected, respectively, by the differing bandwidth of injected nodes. With low bandwidth injected nodes, the compromise rate for the bandwidth-weighted path selection algorithm is similar to S-B(15), but with higher bandwidth injected nodes it is comparable to uniform selection.

In our second experiment, shown in Figure 2, we compare compromise rate, while injecting 20 kB/s nodes for HTTP and SSH connections. Tor requires the use of a stable path for SSH, due to the expectation of longer connection life

---

[2] Dagon [13] has determined that botnets see both high geographic and network topology distribution. One small botnet consists of 1 965 members distributed over 305 unique ASes, 70 unique /8s, 1 084 unique/16s, and 1 872 unique /24s.

[3] Because collocation centres frequently carry network traffic for many different customers and participate fully in BGP, we consider them to also have considerable address space access, able to span multiple /16 networks.

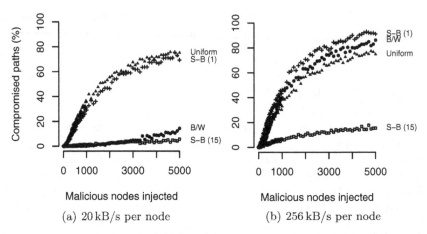

Fig. 1. Percentage of 1 000 generated paths compromised by injecting nodes at 20 kB/s per node or 256 kB/s per node, using the Tor bandwidth-weighted, uniform, S-B(1) and S-B(15) path selection algorithms

spans, unlike HTTP. As a result of the smaller pool of stable nodes, the compromise curve for uniform selection has a significantly steeper slope with SSH than it does for HTTP. It requires one third fewer malicious nodes (and hence two thirds the bandwidth) for an attacker to compromise half of the connections using 20 kB/s malicious nodes.

In our third experiment, shown in Figure 3, we examine the probability of compromise when a fixed investment of bandwidth (100 MB/s) is shared over a varying number of nodes. The Tor uniform path selection algorithm exhibits the expected behaviour that rate of compromise corresponds simply to the number of nodes injected, and not their bandwidth. S-B(1) tracks the Tor uniform path selection algorithm, placing little weight on bandwidth. Because the Tor bandwidth cap is 10 MB/s per node, the full investment of bandwidth is only realised once at least ten injected nodes are present. The Tor bandwidth-weighted path selection algorithm therefore offers essentially a constant compromise rate, once the bandwidth per node drops below the bandwidth cap.

The S-B algorithm with parameter 15 exhibits quite interesting behaviour: as long as the malicious node bandwidth is greater than the bandwidth of almost all Tor nodes, performance grows rapidly to a 50 percent compromise rate at 24 nodes. After that point, the probability of compromise drops rapidly because the bandwidth of malicious nodes drops and the probability of selecting them is greatly reduced.

These results lead to a surprising conclusion: the Tor bandwidth-weighted path selection algorithm and S-B(15), tuned for better performance, have a significantly lower compromise rate for low-bandwidth malicious nodes injected in large numbers, than the Tor uniform and S-B(1) path selection algorithms, which are tuned for better anonymity. Both the Tor uniform and the S-B(1) path selection algorithms resist attack from a small number of malicious high

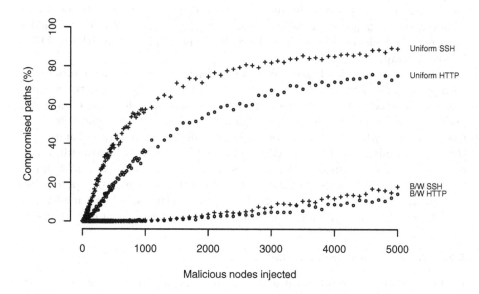

Fig. 2. Comparison of HTTP and SSH compromise probability when injecting 20 kB/s malicious nodes

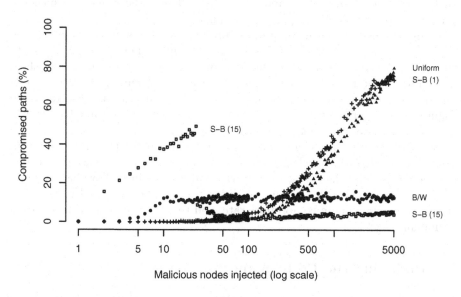

Fig. 3. Compromise rate as a bandwidth budget of 100 MB/s is distributed over a varying number of malicious injected nodes

bandwidth nodes. However, botnets allow attackers to obtain large quantities of low-bandwidth nodes. This is in contrast to the higher bandwidth nodes apparently envisioned by the Tor designers when implementing the 10 MB/s bandwidth cap.

Metrics of anonymity based solely on uniformity of path selection, such as entropy or Gini coefficient do not capture these factors. The link between these metrics and practical security depends on the assumption that cost of injecting nodes is independent of the path selection algorithm and node parameters. In the case of Tor, where path selection probability depends strongly on bandwidth, this is analogous to assuming that an attacker has unlimited bandwidth, but is constrained by IP addresses. Where a more realistic view of the threat model is adopted, in which both bandwidth and IP addresses have a cost, path selection algorithms which are supposedly less secure under the entropy model may actually resist attack, provided bandwidth capacity can be accurately tracked.

5.3   Generalising the Attacker

In this section, we examined attackers with a variable number of nodes, and different constraints on bandwidth. We can generalise this approach by modelling an attacker as having a budget c, and where the cost of buying n nodes each using b bandwidth is $C(n, b)$. Such an attacker can chose to occupy any point (n, b) such that $C(n, b) \leq c$, and rationally will pick the point at which the probability of compromising paths is the highest.

Figure 4 shows the path compromise probability for a series of points in the (n, b) space. Lines overlaid show the bandwidth and node tradeoffs available to the three attackers discussed in this section – previous graphs represent slices in Figure 4. The attacker shown in Figure 1(a) and Figure 2, with a variable number of 20 kB/s nodes can be modelled as $b \leq 20$; the attacker shown in Figure 1(b) is similar, with $b \leq 256$. An attacker with a constant bandwidth, shown in Figure 3, can be modelled as $n \times b \leq 100\,000$.

No one path selection algorithm gives the minimum compromise rate for all points, so no algorithm is clearly the most secure. Instead, the best-performing scheme depends on the threat model, which in turn defines allowable points in the (n, b) space. Once this is done, each strategy can be examined to establish the attacker's maximum compromise rate, and the selection algorithm with the minimum selected.

6   Modelling the Performance of Tor

Our metric for performance is the expected processing time for a cell. One other proposed metric for performance, as measured by Snader and Borisov, is the throughput of a node which adopts the modified selection scheme. This is a good measure for user desires, but it does not take into account system-level effects that would result if all nodes adopted the same strategy. In contrast, this section models the effect of modifying the full network.

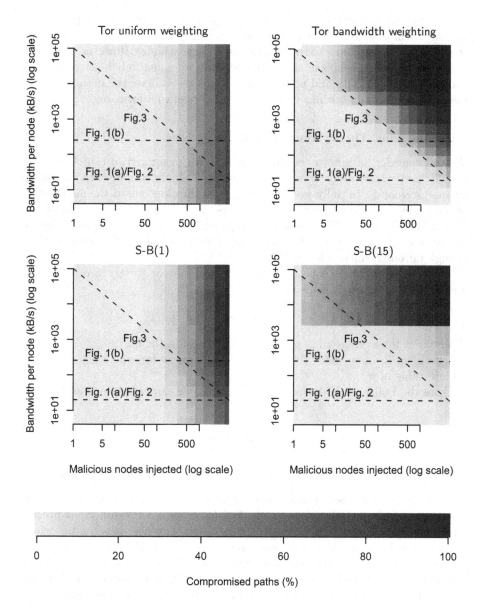

Fig. 4. Compromise rate versus nodes injected and bandwidth per node, for each path selection strategy. Dashed lines indicate the slice of points used for previous figures.

In the previous section, we evaluated the performance of four Tor path selection algorithms with respect to their susceptibility to compromise, concluding that they vary in response to the injection of malicious nodes. However, that analysis is not useful in isolation, as the Tor design is intended to balance competing demands for anonymity and performance. Here, we evaluate the performance of the path selection algorithms with respect to network performance.

6.1   Queueing Theory Background

We will consider an infinite length queue Q, with mean arrival rate λ cells per second, and whose requests are processed by a single server, each taking on average $\bar{x}$ seconds. Initially we will make no assumptions about the distribution of processing duration, but the input process is assumed to be Poisson i.e. we have a M/G/1 queue. The Poisson assumption is known not to perfectly match actual usage, but with a sufficiently large number of users it should be close enough for our results to be useful.

The average time a request will wait in the system (firstly waiting in the queue, then being serviced) is therefore:

$$t = \bar{x} + \bar{w} \tag{5}$$

Where $\bar{w}$ is the average time a request will remain in the queue.

Let the *utilisation factor* for Q be $\rho = \lambda\bar{x}$. A queue for which $0 \leq \rho < 1$ has a finite value of $\bar{w}$.

From the Pollaczek-Khinchin result [14, p16], we can calculate $\bar{w}$ as follows:

$$\bar{w} = \frac{\lambda\overline{x^2}}{2(1-\rho)} \tag{6}$$

6.2   Calculating Waiting Time for a Family of M/D/1 Queues

We will model a single-hop anonymity network as a family of M/D/1 queues, that is an infinite length queue Q_i, for $1 \leq i \leq n$ with a Poisson input process with rate λ_i and constant processing time of x. The user-base of the whole network can be treated as a Poisson process of rate Λ. Each client will select paths according to a path selection algorithm, which results in node i being selected with probability q_i. The traffic at any individual node λ_i will therefore be $q_i\Lambda$. From Equation 5 and Equation 6, the average time t_i a cell will wait in queue Q_i is:

$$t_i = x_i + \frac{q_i\Lambda x_i^2}{2(1 - q_i\Lambda x_i)} \tag{7}$$

The expected waiting time for a cell is t_i weighted by the probability of Q_i being selected, i.e.

$$T = \sum_{i=1}^{n} q_i t_i = \sum_{i=1}^{n} \frac{q_i x_i(2 - q_i x_i\Lambda)}{2(1 - q_i x_i\Lambda)} \tag{8}$$

6.3   Waiting Time for Tor's Bandwidth-Weighted Algorithm

We will first consider the average waiting time for the Tor network, with the bandwidth-weighted algorithm. Here, the probability q_i of selecting a node is the ratio between that node's bandwidth $1/x_i$ and the network total M.

$$q_i = \frac{1}{x_i M} \tag{9}$$

From Equation 8 and Equation 9, the time a cell is expected to wait in the network is:

$$T_{\text{b/w weighted}} = \sum_{i=1}^{n} \frac{2 - \frac{\Lambda}{M}}{2(M - \Lambda)} = n \frac{2 - \frac{\Lambda}{M}}{2(M - \Lambda)} \tag{10}$$

6.4   Waiting Time for Tor's Uniform Path Selection Algorithm

In contrast, when bandwidth is not considered, the probability of selecting a node Q_i is n^{-1}. Hence from Equation 8 the expected waiting time becomes:

$$T_{\text{uniform}} = \sum_{i=1}^{n} \frac{n^{-1} x_i (2 - n^{-1} x_i \Lambda)}{2(1 - n^{-1} x_i \Lambda)} \tag{11}$$

6.5   Waiting Time for the S-B Selection Algorithm

The selection probability q_i for the S-B scheme depends on the position of the node Q_i in the bandwidth ranking. From this, $T_{\text{S-B}}$ can be found by substituting the expression for q_i into Equation 8. The CDF for the probability distribution of q_i is the inverse of Equation 1 and Equation 2. If x_i are sorted in ascending order the selection probability is therefore:

$$q_i = s^{-1} \left(\log_2(1 - \frac{n - i + 1}{n}(1 - 2^s)) - \log_2(1 - \frac{n - i}{n}(1 - 2^s))) \right) \tag{12}$$

6.6   Comparing Path Selection Algorithms

We can calculate the expected latency for the whole network from Equation 8, by establishing the selection probabilities q_i for each of the path selection algorithms. Also, we require x_i which can be obtained from our Tor consensus directory snapshot. Finally, we need the input rate for the network. Each Tor node reports how much traffic it has processed over a number of 900 second periods, so by taking the median for each node, and summing these, we can approximate Λ. We find that the utilisation factor for the network is 49.6%.

When calculating the expected network latency, we face the problem that for the S-B path selection algorithm, some nodes have a utilisation factor greater than 1 (750 nodes for S-B(1) and 53 nodes for S-B(15)). In our model these nodes would have an infinite queue length and hence our expected latency for the

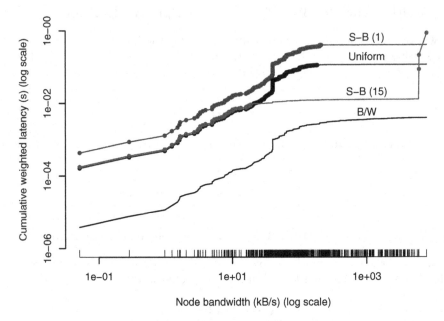

Fig. 5. Cumulative weighted expected waiting time at each node in the network. The rightmost point shows the expected latency for the whole network. Dots are drawn at nodes which will be overloaded.

network would also be infinite. The expected latency, using the Tor bandwidth-weighted algorithm, is 4 ms. In contrast, when only a single node was modified to use S-B(15), its latency approximately halved [7]. The fact that the network cannot sustain the same overall throughput with the S-B algorithm, strongly suggests that the current Tor path selection algorithm is superior.

To quantitatively compare path selection algorithms, we can instead drop the overall throughput and see at which point the expected queue length becomes non-infinite. Even at 1% throughput, the expected waiting time is still infinite, but now because of 4 and 1 low-bandwidth nodes for S-B(1) and S-B(15) respectively. The throughput must be reduced to 0.25% for S-B(15) to generate a well defined expected latency of 13 ms; at the same point Tor's bandwidth-weighted algorithm gives 3 ms. At 0.025% throughput, S-B(1) has an expected latency of 48 ms whereas Tor's bandwidth-weighted algorithm still gives 3 ms.

Alternatively, for nodes which are overloaded, we can clip the expected latency to the maximum value of the rest of the network (analogous to a timeout). The result is shown in Figure 5. Here we can see that the expected network latency is still far higher for the S-B selection algorithms: 401 ms for S-B(1) and 275 ms for S-B(15), compared to 4 ms for Tor's bandwidth-weighted algorithm. Also, the timeout failures are substantial: 65% for S-B(1), because of the 750 nodes which are overloaded (72% of the network) and 44% for S-B(15), because the top three nodes are overloaded, which are used for 43.9% of selections.

7 Conclusion

In this paper, we have analysed the effectiveness of several Tor path selection algorithms with in terms of two metrics: probability of path compromise with respect to attacker investment, and expected latency. This analysis has demonstrated the surprising result that not only does Tor's default bandwidth-weighted path selection algorithm offer improved performance over the supposedly more secure Tor uniform path selection algorithm, but also offers improved anonymity in the presence of node-rich but bandwidth-poor attackers.

The vulnerability of supposedly secure path selection algorithms reflects a historical assumption that bandwidth is a low-cost commodity to acquire, but that large numbers of nodes in different equivalence classes are expensive. We believe that this assumption no longer holds due to the proliferation of botnets, which frequently have poor upstream bandwidth from each individual node, but high network and geographical diversity.

Acknowledgements

The authors gratefully acknowledge the Tor Project and Google, Inc. for supporting this research. We would like to thank Nikita Borisov, Richard Clayton, George Danezis, Roger Dingledine, Markus Kuhn, Nick Mathewson, Andrei Serjantov, and the anonymous reviewers for their feedback, and Claudia Diaz and Carmela Troncoso, who shepherded the paper. We would also like to thank David Dagon for providing the botnet data we used in our analysis.

References

1. Dingledine, R., Mathewson, N., Syverson, P.: Tor: The second-generation onion router. In: Proceedings of the 13th USENIX Security Symposium (August 2004)
2. Dingledine, R., Mathewson, N.: Tor protocol specification. Technical report, The Tor Project (October 2007),
   https://www.torproject.org/svn/trunk/doc/spec/tor-spec.txt
3. Bauer, K., McCoy, D., Grunwald, D., Kohno, T., Sicker, D.: Low-resource routing attacks against anonymous systems. Technical Report CU-CS-1025-07, University of Colorado at Boulder (2007)
4. Øverlier, L., Syverson, P.F.: Locating hidden servers. In: Proceedings of the 2006 IEEE Symposium on Security and Privacy, Oakland, CA, US. IEEE Computer Society Press, Los Alamitos (2006)
5. Murdoch, S.J., Zieliński, P.: Sampled traffic analysis by Internet-exchange-level adversaries. In: Borisov, N., Golle, P. (eds.) PET 2007. LNCS, vol. 4776. Springer, Heidelberg (2007)
6. Berthold, O., Federrath, H., Köpsell, S.: Web MIXes: A system for anonymous and unobservable Internet access. In: Federrath, H. (ed.) Designing Privacy Enhancing Technologies. LNCS, vol. 2009, pp. 115–129. Springer, Heidelberg (2001)
7. Snader, R., Borisov, N.: A tune-up for Tor: Improving security and performance in the Tor network. In: Network & Distributed System Security Symposium. Internet Society (February 2008)

8. Serjantov, A., Danezis, G.: Towards an information theoretic metric for anonymity. In: Dingledine, R., Syverson, P.F. (eds.) PET 2002. LNCS, vol. 2482, pp. 259–263. Springer, Heidelberg (2003)
9. Diaz, C., Seys, S., Claessens, J., Preneel, B.: Towards measuring anonymity. In: Dingledine, R., Syverson, P.F. (eds.) PET 2002. LNCS, vol. 2482, pp. 184–188. Springer, Heidelberg (2003)
10. Douceur, J.: The Sybil Attack. In: Druschel, P., Kaashoek, M.F., Rowstron, A. (eds.) IPTPS 2002. LNCS, vol. 2429. Springer, Heidelberg (2002)
11. Dingledine, R., Mathewson, N.: Tor path specification. Technical report, The Tor Project (October 2007),
    https://www.torproject.org/svn/trunk/doc/spec/path-spec.txt
12. Fuller, V., Li, T.: Classless inter-domain routing (CIDR): The Internet address assignment and aggregation plan. RFC 4632, IETF (August 2006)
13. Dagon, D.: Personal communication
14. Kleinrock, L.: Queueing Systems, vol. 2. John Wiley, Chichester (1976)

Studying Timing Analysis on the Internet with SubRosa

Hatim Daginawala and Matthew Wright

University of Texas at Arlington, Arlington, TX 76019, USA
h_atim@hotmail.com, mwright@cse.uta.edu
http://isec.uta.edu/

Abstract. Timing analysis poses a significant threat to anonymity systems that wish to support low-latency applications like Web browsing, instant messaging, and Voice over IP (VoIP). Research into timing analysis so far has been done through simulations or unrealistic local area networks. We developed SubRosa, an experimental platform for studying timing analysis attacks and defenses in low-latency anonymity systems. We present results of experiments on PlanetLab, a globally distributed network testbed. Our experiments validate the major conclusions, but not the detailed results, obtained by prior simulation studies. We also propose a new lightweight defense based on the principles of mix design called γ-buffering and show the limitations of this approach. Finally, motivated by our experimental results, we introduce spike analysis, a new timing analysis technique that takes advantage of unusual delays in a stream to substantially reduce errors over prior techniques.

1 Introduction

Low-latency anonymity systems provide network-level privacy for interactive applications such as Web browsing and secure shell (ssh). Such applications have timing constraints that prevent the use of techniques such as batching and reordering messages, as found in mixes [5]. Perhaps the most well-known and heavily-used low-latency anonymity system is Tor [10], a highly-distributed network of volunteer-run anonymizing proxies called Tor nodes. Users pass their TCP packets through a *circuit* of three Tor nodes and use a technique called *layered encryption* to ensure that the first Tor and second Tor nodes cannot see the contents and final destinations of the packets. In particular, this prevents the first Tor node from linking the user to her packets, which would compromise the user's privacy.

Ideally, an attacker that seeks to break the user's privacy would have to compromise or control all three Tor nodes on the user's circuit. However, timing analysis is a well-known threat to low-latency anonymity systems like Tor. In essence, an attacker that observes packets on both ends of a path can use the timings of those packets to confirm that the sender and receiver are communicating. Powerful global eavesdroppers can extend this attack to perform traffic analysis on the entire network [6]. More limited attackers, such as an eavesdropper that can see only parts of the network [17] or a malicious subset of the anonymizing proxies [14], can also perform traffic analysis.

In the case of a subset of malicious proxies, the first proxy and the last proxy on the circuit can use timing analysis to confirm that they share the same circuit. This allows

N. Borisov and I. Goldberg (Eds.): PETS 2008, LNCS 5134, pp. 133–150, 2008.

the attacker to link the user with her packets with only two proxies. Although this may not seem much harder than controlling all three proxies on a Tor circuit, prior work shows that it likely means an order of magnitude more effort for the attacker [30].

Several prior studies have shown that timing analysis can be highly effective against low-latency anonymity systems [6,14,31]. In fact, it seems to be effective despite expensive countermeasures such as circuits with more proxies and the use of *traffic shaping*, in which packets are sent only at specified times and *dummy packets* are sent when user packets are not available [14]. These prior studies, however, have either used simulation [6, 14] or small-scale experiments over local area networks [31].

Network timing over the Internet is difficult to model accurately for simulation or emulate correctly with delay generators. For example, one study uses exponentially-distributed delays [6], while another uses normally-distributed delays [28]. One study of Voice over IP (VoIP) network dynamics shows that the delay characteristics varied, such that they would best be modeled as gamma-distributed sometimes and exponentially-distributed other times [12]. Another study of VoIP dynamics suggests that a shifted gamma distribution is the best to model the network delay [15]. Choosing one of these may be sufficient to understand the performance of networks, but may not provide an adequate basis for the precise timings involved in timing analysis. Realistic models are important in understanding anonymity properties; in high-latency mixes, assumptions that the input traffic was Poisson distributed led to a design with poor anonymity properties [9].

To address the issue of realism in timing analysis experiments, we introduce Sub-Rosa[1], an experimental platform for studying timing analysis and low-latency anonymity, designed to run on PlanetLab [1]. PlanetLab is a global overlay network that supports the development of new network services. SubRosa consists of server, client, and sink components that emulate the behavior of a low-latency anonymity system. We used SubRosa to evaluate a single timing analysis method and several defenses. In particular, we apply the *cross-correlation* method of timing analysis introduced by Levine, et al [14], and study *constant-rate cover traffic*, *defensive dropping*, and a new light-weight defense against timing analysis that we call γ-*buffering*. γ-buffering is designed to remove timing correlation from the network stream through limited delays at the proxies.

Our results show that defensive dropping is more effective than shown in simulation, even at lower drop rates than previously studied, and that γ-buffering is surprisingly ineffective unless buffering exceeds any burst of traffic. Deeper investigation into the causes of these results has led us to identify traffic patterns that are present even when defensive dropping makes typical statistical correlation ineffective. In particular, we have developed a new timing analysis technique that we call *spike analysis*, by which the attacker can achieve substantial improvements against all defenses, and defensive dropping in particular.

In Section 2, we discuss prior work in performing and defending against timing analysis in low-latency anonymity systems. Section 3 discusses the γ-buffering algorithm in depth. We then overview the SubRosa experimental platform, the PlanetLab testbed,

---

[1] The name is based on the Latin phrase, meaning "under the rose," which has been used to signify secrecy, and was notably found in the recent novel The Da Vinci Code [4].

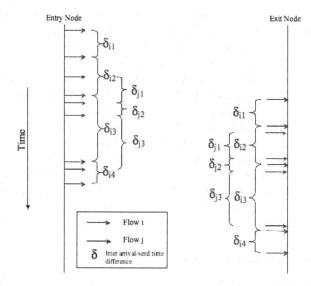

Fig. 1. Timing analysis based on correlating flows

and our experiment setup in Section 4. We present and discuss the results of our experiments, as well as the spike analysis algorithm, in Section 5 and conclude in Section 6.

2 Related Work

Many systems have been proposed and developed for low-latency anonymous communications (e.g., [2, 10, 11, 18, 22, 23]). Various studies have investigated how to break the anonymity provided by these systems and developing further defenses against their attacks. This study focuses on timing analysis attacks: attacks designed to link users with their messages based on the timings of packets in the network. Timing analysis attacks can be classified into two categories: passive and active. A passive adversary attempts to perform timing analysis based only on observations of the timings of packets. An active attack assumes that the adversary not only can observe traffic but can also delay and inject packets. Active attackers certainly are more powerful, as they can overcome limited random perturbations in the packet timings [28, 29]. However, these attacks require the ability to delay packets with very precise timings, and this can be more difficult for large-scale attacks than simply eavesdropping and recording the delays.

Other active attacks, such as the congestion-based attacks of Murdoch and Danezis [16], use a different attacker model and seek a different result. For example, recent work by Hopper et al. combines latency measurements with a congestion attack to see if two Tor paths are the same, thereby linking ongoing connections [13]. We are specifically seeking to de-anonymize the connections, i.e. to identify the IP address of the sender.

We believe that both active and passive approaches to timing analysis should be examined. For this study's threat model we use a passive adversary who controls a subset of the mixes. A nearly equivalent model is that of a passive eavesdropper that can monitor the timings of packets entering and exiting a subset of the mixes. Our results also can be helpful for understanding the capabilities of a global passive eavesdropper. We discuss this distinction in more detail in Section 5.

Figure 1 shows the basis of timing analysis; the relative time difference (δ) between two consecutive packets remains roughly the same as flows traverse the overlay network. In other words, δ between two packets leaving the entry node will be approximately the same as that of the packets entering the exit node of the circuit. This property of the network flow is used for timing analysis. Statistical correlation can be found between various distinct streams to determine the most likely sender and receiver of the stream and compromise the anonymity [14]. A dropped packet in the stream, whether intentional or due to network congestion, will cause the timings of the packets to be off by one. As a result, the correlation will be calculated between packets that do not match. To avoid this effect, the attacker can count of the number of packets received during a time window instead of simply matching the timings of packets [14].

2.1 Defenses against Timing Analysis

Constant rate cover traffic along the entire path is a known defense against timing analysis attacks. When all the participating nodes send data as the same constant rate, cover traffic makes all the streams look the same and makes it difficult to find correlations based on the time difference to isolate the streams. Pipenet [7] and ISDN-Mix [21] use end-to-end cover traffic whereas Tarzan [11] uses hop-by-hop cover traffic. Constant rate cover traffic, however, adds tremendous overhead to the network. For the cover traffic to be foolproof, all the nodes must be synchronized and transmit the packets at the same constant rate. Even with synchronized constant rate cover traffic vulnerability to an active adversary still remains. For these reasons, and under the assumption that the routing infrastructure is uniformly busy, systems like Tor [10] and Crowds [22] do not use any cover traffic.

Based on the idea of cover traffic, to reduce the timing correlations, various defense mechanisms have been proposed. In partial-route padding [26], all the cover traffic is dropped at a designated intermediate mix. Defensive dropping [14] generalizes the idea of partial-route padding, where the initiator creates a dummy packet and marks it to be dropped at any intermediate mix at random. When the packets are dropped at random at a sufficiently large frequency, the timing correlation is reduced [14]. Adaptive padding [25] is designed to reduce timing correlation by inserting dummy packets in the network stream, instead of dropping the packets. It is used to fill statistically unlikely gaps in the packet flow without adding latency. We note that it is highly effective. However, it requires that inserted dummy packets be sent to the responder, which may not be practical in many scenarios. This is especially true when end-to-end traffic is not encrypted, as packets with random or computer-generated content should be easy for the attacker to identify and remove from streams.

3   A New Approach to Buffering for Low-Latency Anonymity

In the original mix design, each user must send one packet in each batching period. This has previously been extended to low-latency mixes by the use of constant rate traffic, in which each user emits packets at a constant rate, using dummy packets when real user traffic is not available. Constant rate traffic reduces the correlation between different flows since all the flows receive constant number of packets with the same time difference. For practical mix designs, various batching approaches have been proposed [8]. Relatively few designs that include buffering, however, have been proposed for low-latency anonymity systems. In this section, we introduce γ-buffering, a new lightweight defense that extends the idea of constant rate traffic to better prevent timing analysis attacks.

3.1 γ-Buffering

γ-Buffering is a technique for buffering traffic that can be used to undermine traffic analysis attacks in low-latency anonymous communications systems. This technique is designed with the aim to maintain low latencies at the cost of some cover traffic and can be adapted for different levels of allowable latency and bandwidth use.

The main insight behind this technique is that, with sufficiently high traffic rates, standard batching techniques from mixes can be used without slowing down traffic excessively. While low-latency mixes setup and utilize paths for streams of packets, packet-level batching can effectively intertwine the streams' timing characteristics and destroy many of the patterns that attackers would seek to use in timing analysis. Furthermore, batching creates a variable intermediate delay that may be able to remove watermarking introduced by an active attacker [27].

One obvious concern with batching in low-latency anonymity systems, however, is that users would have different activity levels and some streams would be greatly delayed while buffers waited for activity on the other streams. If, however, the system uses a high rate of end-to-end cover traffic, there will typically be enough traffic on all streams. The amount of traffic entering a proxy at a given time, however, can still depend on the number of connections entering the proxy and the network conditions for each connection. We could require that each path send a packet, as proposed in Pipenet [7], but that could lead to long delays and denial-of-service (DoS) attacks. An adversary could prevent a proxy from sending messages by preventing an initiator or number of initiators from sending messages to the mix.

In an attempt to remove enough timing patterns without introducing such risks, we have designed γ-buffering to be more flexible. The algorithm is simple: if there are p incoming connections to a proxy, then the proxy buffers at least $\gamma * p$ packets before sending the batch, where γ is a fraction that can vary depending on the system needs. This effectively turns each proxy into a threshold mix, with a threshold of $\gamma * p$ messages [24].

When $\gamma = 1$, each proxy will get an average of one packet from each incoming connection before sending the batch. For $\gamma > 1$, larger batch sizes help ensure security at the cost of higher average latencies. For $\gamma < 1$, we can ensure a low latency when no more than $(1 - \gamma) * p$ connections are blocked or delayed. The buffering parameter γ can be controlled at the system level or by individual proxies. When controlled by proxies, different proxies may offer different γ values, allowing users to select paths with higher or lower amounts of buffering to suit their needs. If the ratio of users to proxies grows, meaning that there are more connections per proxy, then γ may be lowered due to greater cover traffic. This kind of non-uniform path selection, however, may have other consequences for user anonymity [3], and further investigation is beyond the scope of this work.

The other primary benefit of γ-buffering would be its resilience to changing network conditions and DoS attacks. When other users' connections fail or are delayed, this creates delays for the user. Some delay is good; if the user sends traffic too aggressively, then she will be subject to easier traffic analysis. The delay is bounded, however, as long as at least the user's own traffic continues to reach the proxy. End-to-end attacks will become more difficult, even when conducted by a global adversary, as long as some other paths continue to operate.

Another way in which γ-buffering would be resilient to active attacks is that delays introduced along a user's path will multiply to show delay on many other paths in the system. The increased delay, introduced early in the path, will likely delay an entire batch of packets at the next proxy. These delayed packets cause further upstream delays, with an effect that is exponential in the length of the path. An attacker may observe a delay that has propagated along either the original path or one that has been introduced by the buffering, making it difficult to distinguish false positives from correct matches. Unlike the addition of random delays along the path, γ-buffering introduces delays simultaneous with other delays in the system, so that timing effects occur together and are much less useful to the attacker for differentiating between paths.

We note that an attacker-controlled node could choose to not buffer packets properly. However, an attacker controlling the first and last proxies would still need to contend with buffering at intermediate nodes. If the attacker needs to control the intermediate nodes to be successful, then we have made a substantial improvement in the system's defense. If the exit and intermediate nodes are compromised, but the first node in the circuit is not, then the attacker will not only need to eavesdrop on the initiator or the first node, but also contend with buffering at the first node. The attacker has similar problems when the last node is not compromised.

3.2   Partial Buffering

Due to early findings that γ-buffering was not as effective as we had expected, we also developed a slight variation that we call *partial buffering*. Partial buffering implements γ-buffering at the intermediate proxies only, not at the first or last proxies. In particular, buffering at the first proxy creates variation in the traffic patterns that could then be observed at the last proxy. Intermediate buffering may only remove some of this variation. With partial buffering, these variations are not introduced by the first proxy, but we still get the benefits of buffering at the intermediate proxy. We evaluate both γ-buffering and partial buffering in our experiments.

4   Experimental Design

In this section, we describe SubRosa, an experimental platform for investigating timing analysis on the Internet. We also describe our experiments using SubRosa, which were conducted on PlanetLab.

4.1   PlanetLab

PlanetLab (see http://www.planet-lab.org) is a global research network that supports the development of new network services. It is an overlay network consisting of computers distributed over six continents, with the highest concentration of nodes in North America, Europe, and East Asia. Most of the machines are hosted by participating research institutions; all of the machines are connected to the Internet, and some have Internet2 connections. All the computers on PlanetLab run a Linux-based operating system from a read-only media. The key objective of PlanetLab's software is to support distributed virtualization – the ability to allocate a slice of PlanetLab's network-wide hardware resources to an application. This allows an application to run across all (or some) of the machines distributed over the globe, where at any given time, multiple applications may be running in different slices of PlanetLab.

One effect of virtualization is that our testing process may not get access to the system for relatively long periods of time. The advantage of this is that the system does not behave like a set of dedicated servers for individual streams — performance varies depending on the load from other experiments. The disadvantage is that the platform is less consistent than we might expect anonymizing servers with many simultaneous connections to be. Following the guidance of Peterson et al., this does not prevent us from getting accurate latency measurements [20]. To provide consistent expected performance and dedicated resources on a community shared network, PlanetLab allows for reservation of resources through the Sirius Calendar Service. Reservation entitles the slice a dedicated 25% of CPU capacity and 2.0 Mbps of the system's bandwidth. All other active slices share the remaining resources with equal priority. Unfortunately, Sirius is still under development and does not reliably schedule and allocate resources. PlanetLab has over 800 computers located in over 400 locations as of October 2007.

A distributed and geographically dispersed Linux-based network testbed was an ideal platform for collecting data for this research. The global distribution of Planet-Lab nodes allows us to test the effects of real network latency. We created a slice with over 300 nodes for our experiments on PlanetLab. Sites with explicitly identified Internet2 connection were excluded. PlanetLab has various deployment and monitoring tools available, but we developed our own to meet our needs as the existing tools were lacking features needed to manage our experiments.

4.2   SubRosa: An Experimental Platform for Studying Timing Analysis

We developed SubRosa to run on PlanetLab and collect data for this study. We designed SubRosa to emulate the behavior of a Tor-like network over the unreliable UDP transport. It is a simple application for collecting timing data and does not use encryption. Only information visible to an adversary in the presence of encryption has been used to perform timing analysis in our experiments. This means that SubRosa does not capture delays due to encryption and decryption at the proxy. However, we found that the delays due to virtualization on PlanetLab nodes were occasionally quite high (more than one second) and likely suffice to emulate high-load scenarios. SubRosa is written in C and consists of three components: controller, srserver, srclient.

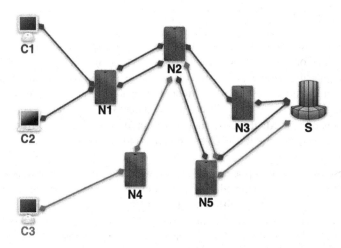

Fig. 2. Data flow in an anonymizing network

- The *controller* component starts, stops and checks the status of the other components. We used it to deploy the rest of SubRosa onto PlanetLab and keep track of the versions of the components while conducting experiments.
- The *srserver* component acts as the Mix. It can act as the first mix, the last mix, or as any intermediary mix on multiple paths simultaneously and it also captures timing information of the packets it sends and receives.
- The *srclient* component represents the client and is responsible for generating data on the network.

SubRosa is designed to collect timing data for various defense algorithms against timing analysis and, hence, it is versatile. Hooks and exits are designed to collect timing data as well as easily implement different algorithms for collecting data. All the variable parameters are read from the configuration file.

Data flow in SubRosa is shown in Figure 2; circuit-building proceeds as in Tor [10]. $N1$ through $N5$ are nodes running srserver, $C1$ through $C3$ are nodes running srclient, and S is the responder, or sink. We did not utilize a sink in this study.

4.3   Methodology

In our experiments, we fixed the path length to three. Since we did not use a sink, the exit node on the path acts as a sink and generates the response. All the traffic generated for the experiments was constant bit rate. Five PlanetLab nodes were selected based on the load and the available bandwidth to act as servers for our experiments. Due to the nature of the test bed, if and when a node was not available or was heavily loaded, that node was replaced by another carefully chosen node. For use as servers, we only selected nodes with uptime of more then 3 days, no bandwidth restrictions, and less than 0.5 seconds response time. Servers were selected by manual use of the CoMon monitoring infrastructure for PlanetLab. All the servers were closely monitored during the experiments using CoTop slice-based top for PlanetLab. Results were not considered in the analysis if the node did not perform consistently for the duration of the experiment.

More than 300 nodes were used as clients. For each experiment, clients were chosen at random from this set nodes. At startup, clients randomly choose three out of the five server nodes. Circuits are then established with those three nodes on the path. The duration of our experiments was approximately 15 minutes each. Logs were collected for analysis after each experiment, and timing data was extracted from the logs using Perl scripts. Timing data was converted to zero base time to avoid time synchronization issues and to accommodate the scripts for analyzing the data which were provided by [14]. Experiments were conducted using 25 clients and packets were generated every 300ms and 100ms. We also collected data with larger numbers of clients, up to 100, but saw no trends in the data as the number of clients grew.

Timing Analysis. For the timing analysis, we use the methodology and programs used for the work of Levine et al. [14]. We describe the basic idea here, but refer the reader to that paper for more details.

The main observation of our timing analysis method is that the timings seen by the first proxy on a given path and the timings seen by the last proxy should be statistically correlated. Thus, standard methods for statistical correlation should be effective in determining whether the two proxies are observing the same path. There is a significant caveat, however, in that a single dropped packet could cause the wrong packet times to be compared. Finding the right match between sent and received packets could be computationally expensive and is likely to only be an approximation. Levine et al. propose to divide time into *windows* and count the number of packets that arrive for each proxy during a given window. They use the timings of early packets to line up the windows. Finally, a statistical *cross-correlation* is taken on the packet counts. A number of these correlations is taken for each pair of first and last proxy, using a reasonable range of alignments for the windows, and the best such correlation for the pair is chosen.

The cross-correlation values provide a statistical diagnostic test that tells the attacker how closely the streams seen by the attacker are correlated. These values can compared for streams that are and are not on the same path. We set a *threshold* correlation value and say that the attacker thinks that all pairs of streams with correlation values above the threshold are indeed on the same path.

We also introduce a new timing analysis technique called spike analysis. This technique is described in Section 5.2.

γ-**Buffering.** γ-Buffering is implemented on the servers. Multiplier γ is configured at the start of the application. γ is multiplied with the number of active circuits on the node to obtain the number of packets to buffer, before queuing it on the send queue. During the buffering period all the packets received are stored in a list in random order. Once the desired number of packets is buffered, the packets from the list are put on the send queue and sent out using a pool of threads. The thread pool is created at the startup and is kept alive for the life of the application to avoid overhead and improve the response time. A pool of five threads was used for γ-buffering. γ-buffering was implemented with a delay of 180 seconds after the server started, to avoid lockups during the circuit building process. The packets sent during the first four minutes were discarded to compensate for the startup delay. γ values of 0.5, 1.0 and 1.5 were used for the experiments.

Defensive Dropping. Defensive dropping is initiated by the client. The client, at random, selects the packets to be dropped and marks it to be dropped at the intermediary node. The drop command is set in the header for the intermediary node and, hence, no other nodes on the path are aware of the dropped packets. The server, upon receiving a packet with a drop command, logs the packet and stops further processing of the packet by discarding it from the receive queue. We used drop rates of 20% and 50%.

Constant-rate Cover. Baseline data using simple constant rate cover traffic, and no other defenses against timing analysis, were also collected for experiments with 25, 50, 75 and 100 nodes. Packets were generated at every 100 milliseconds and 300 milliseconds; other parameters were kept in line with other experiments.

5   Results and Discussion

In this section, we present the results of our experiments on timing analysis of a Tor-like network. We begin by showing how effective each defense is against statistical analysis. We then then examine timing results in more depth, describe a new timing analysis technique called *spike analysis*, and show the effectiveness of this technique.

5.1   Effectiveness of Defenses

We now show relative effectiveness of various defenses against statistical cross-correlation analysis. The attacker's correlation-based diagnostic test is subject to two types of errors: *false negatives*, in which the attacker fails to identify two streams as belonging to the same path and *false positives*, in which the attacker incorrectly identifies two streams from different paths as being from the same path. False negatives occur when the threshold value is too high, i.e. the attacker expects the correlation to be higher than it is. Similarly, false positives occur when the threshold value is too low. Thus, as the threshold rises, the false positives drop off at the expense of a rise in false negatives.

A Receiver Operator Characteristic (ROC) curve is a graphical representation of the trade off between the false negative and false positive rates for every possible threshold. Conventionally, ROC curves show the false positive rate on the x-axis and the *detection rate*, the attacker's chance of correctly linking the two streams, on the y-axis. Note that the detection rate is one minus the false negative rate. We plot different ROC curves on the same graph to visualize the relative comparison. Curves that are closer to the upper left-hand corner are better, in our case, better for the adversary. The worst case for an adversary would be a 45 degree diagonal, i.e. $x = y$, which is the same as random guessing.

We also estimate the area under the curve (AUC) for each ROC curve. The AUC gives us a single numeric value for each test that can be used for quantitative comparisons. The maximum AUC is 1.0, representing error-free detection, and the practical minimum is 0.5, which is given by the ROC curve $x = y$. We calculate our estimate of the AUC using a trapezoidal Riemann sum with the ROC points in our curves, i.e., the area under the curve between two points (x_1, y_1) and (x_2, y_2) is estimated as

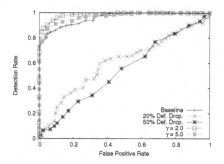

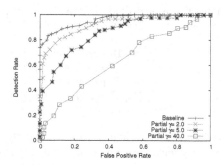

Fig. 3. ROC curves for detection against defensive dropping and γ-buffering

Fig. 4. ROC curves for detection against partial buffering with varying values for gamma

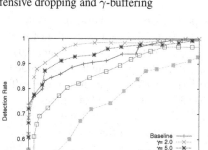

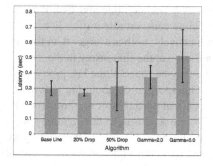

Fig. 5. Comparison of detection against partial buffering and γ-buffering

Fig. 6. Latency (RTT) for each defense. Error bars show the average standard deviation.

$A = \frac{1}{2}(y_1 + y_2) \times (x_2 - x_1)$, where $x_1 < x_2$. We have approximately five times as many points in our AUC calculation than shown in our graphs. For each set of results, we also calculate the *equal error rates* (EERs) — the point in the ROC curve where the false positive and false negative rates are equal. Table 1 shows the AUC, EER, and latency values for several settings.

We present a comparison of our baseline traffic (constant rate cover traffic), defensive dropping, and γ-buffering in Figure 3. First, we see that the attacker does quite well when only constant rate cover traffic is used. The ROC curve approaches the upper left hand corner, depicting a high success rate with relatively few errors. Table 1 shows that the attacker gets an AUC of 0.959. This appears to validate the simulation results of Levine et al. [14]. In particular, when the latency averages 50 ms and there are 1% drop rates on each application layer hop in their simulations, they report equal error rate of 8.1%. We show a higher rate of 12%, still validating the main point that statistical correlation-based traffic analysis is effective.

We see that defensive dropping is very effective against our timing analysis — both 20% and 50% dropping rates result in ROC curves close to a straight line $x = y$. Against defensive dropping of 20% and 50%, the attacker achieves AUCs of only 0.602

Table 1. Area under the curve (AUC), equal error rate (EER), and latency values for defensive dropping (DD) and partial buffering (PB)

Defense	Baseline	DD 20%	DD 50%	PB $\gamma = 2$	PB $\gamma = 5$
AUC	0.959	0.602	0.539	0.926	0.856
EER	12%	38%	48%	17%	24%
Latency (sec.)	0.300	0.271	0.314	0.375	0.515

and 0.539, respectively. This is a significant improvement for defensive dropping in contrast with the simulation results of [14]. The equal error rates of 38% and 48% for defensive dropping rates of 20% and 50%, respectively, both greatly exceed any equal error rates achieved in their study. We explore the reasons for this difference in Section 5.2.

Perhaps more surprising is the relatively poor performance of γ-buffering. With values of γ between one and five, the attacker is as successful, if not more, than for the baseline constant rate traffic. For $\gamma = 2$ and $\gamma = 5$, we get AUCs of 0.983 and 0.970, respectively; both are larger than for the baseline traffic. We speculate that this is due to buffering at the first proxy in the circuit. This buffering can cause patterns in the traffic that may be found at the last proxy, despite further delays at intermediate nodes.

Our speculation about the failure of γ-buffering appears to be validated by relative success of partial buffering, in which the first proxy does not buffer packets. We show ROC curves for detection against partial buffering in Figure 4 and in comparison with γ-buffering in Figure 5. The latter figure only show the upper left hand quadrant of the curve for better viewing. As the curves show, partial buffering provides a better defense than the baseline constant rate traffic and much better than γ-buffering. Table 1 shows that for $\gamma = 2$ and $\gamma = 5$, we get AUCs of 0.926 and 0.856, respectively. For $\gamma = 5$, the equal error rate is 24%, which is a significant improvement over the baseline. For $\gamma = 2$, the equal error rate is 17%. Nevertheless, defensive dropping is much more effective than either setting. To get higher error rates, we set $\gamma = 40$ for a set of experiments. Even at this setting, which is impractical due to substantial delays for every packet, we only get an AUC of 0.635 and an equal error rate of 41% — approximately equivalent to 20% defensive dropping.

We note that the difference between γ-buffering and partial buffering depends on the attacker model in an important way that we have ignored to this point. If the attacker controls the first and last proxies on the path, then our analysis holds. If the attacker can eavesdrop on all of the traffic going into and exiting these same two nodes, but doesn't control the first proxy, it is somewhat more difficult for the attacker. In this case, γ-buffering may be better than partial buffering to help hide the link between the user and the traffic exiting the first proxy. Exploring the implications of this attacker model in greater depth is beyond the scope of this work.

We also examine the latency from each of our schemes. As we see in Figure 6, the latency is roughly the same for the baseline and defensive dropping cases, between 271 ms and 314 ms round trip time (RTT). We see an increase in RTT as we introduce partial buffering. For $\gamma = 2$, we get a 25% increase in the average RTT over the baseline data. For $\gamma = 5$, this rises to 72%. This suggests that small values of γ are likely to be practical, while values over $\gamma = 5$ would increase latencies too much for general use.

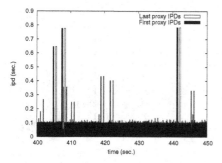
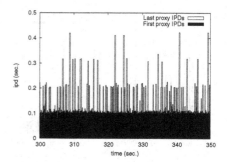

Fig. 7. Partial view of IPDs for a Baseline flow

Fig. 8. Partial view of IPDs for a flow with 20% defensive dropping

The error bars show the average of the standard deviations of the RTTs within each run. The large standard deviation values for 50% defensive dropping and $\gamma = 5$ appear to reflect experimental variation. The maximum RTT was over seven seconds.

5.2 Taking Advantage of Bursty Traffic

We now take a deeper look at the traffic patterns that lead to the results described above. To more carefully study the variability of the timings, we present representative graphs showing inter-packet delays (IPDs), which are the gaps between packets. In Figures 7, 8, 11, 12, 9, 10, we show the IPDs as sent by the first proxy in the circuit (dark bars) and as received by the last proxy in circuit (light bars). In other words, they represent the two timings used in our timing analysis techniques. We show 50 second intervals and the two sets of times have been offset slightly to make patterns visually recognizable. We say that *spikes* in these graphs represent high IPDs.

We see in Figure 7 a good match between the first proxy and last proxy IPDs for our baseline constant rate streams with no other defense. In particular, we see that every spike in the first proxy IPDs is matched with a nearly identical spike in the last proxy IPDs. Some additional spikes are present in the last proxy's IPDs, as would be expected due to additional delays and possible variability between the two measurement points. Given the similarity in the patterns, the success of statistical methods is not surprising. In contrast, we can look at a sample of IPDs from experiments with 20% defensive dropping in Figure 8. We see that there is relatively little connection between the two streams' timings. The two largest spikes in the first proxy's measurement may or may not be represented among the other spikes in the last proxy's measurement; matching the timings with confidence is difficult. Essentially, the spikes due to defensive dropping are larger than the spikes due to normal variations between the client and the first proxy.

An interesting question to consider is why we get higher error rates for the attacker than were reported in simulations by Levine et al. [14]. We speculate that perhaps in simulation, one can get better and more consistent matches in timings between the first and last proxy. If there is, e.g., clock skew, this could cause problems for the attacker. Such an effect would be less problematic for attacking constant rate streams, in which

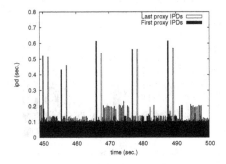

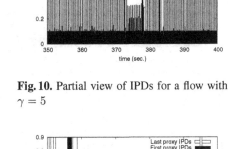

Fig. 9. Partial view of IPDs for a flow with $\gamma = 2$

Fig. 10. Partial view of IPDs for a flow with $\gamma = 5$

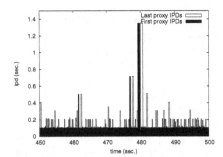

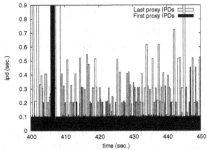

Fig. 11. Partial view of IPDs for a flow with 20% defensive dropping

Fig. 12. Partial view of IPDs for a flow with 50% defensive dropping

there may be enough matching data early in the stream. Compensating for clock skew is possible [19], but is beyond the scope of this work.

Spikes are quite prominent when γ-buffering is used. For $\gamma = 2$, shown in Figure 9, we see that large spikes transfer easily from the first proxy to the last proxy. In Figure 10, we see that a few spikes carry through despite the larger variation in IPD. These results help to illustrate how statistical correlation can still find timing correlations despite buffering.

Although much of the information in a stream is lost when defensive dropping is used, defensive dropping can still leave spikes in traffic, especially larger spikes. In Figures 11 and 12, we see a number of large spikes that have apparently transferred from the first proxy through to the last proxy despite defensive dropping. This motivated the development of a simple timing analysis technique called spike analysis that is designed specifically for when there are spikes in the IPDs, e.g. due to slow response time on the proxies or by the user node.

The spike analysis algorithm is given as tested in Algorithm 1. The essential idea is to match the top f largest spikes (we use $f = 5$) in the first proxy's IPDs with f out of the top l largest spikes (we use $l = 25$) in the last proxy's IPDs. We use $l > f$, as we expect additional spikes in the last proxy's IPDs. We try a range of offsets, up to

---

Algorithm 1. Spike Analysis

TopFirstIPDs = GetTop5(FirstProxyIPDs)
TopLastIPDs = GetTop25(LastProxyIPDs)
MinError = ∞
for Offset = -100.0 sec. to 100.0 sec. by 0.01 sec. **do**
  Error = 0;
  for all fIPD in TopFirstIPDs **do**
    Match = GetClosestInTime(fIPD, TopLastIPDs)
    if TimeDifference(fIPD, Match) $>= 1$ sec. **then**
      Error += 1 sec.
    else
      Error += $(|fIPD - Match|)^2$
    end if
  end for
  Error = SquareRoot(Error / 5)
  if Error $<$ MinError **then**
    MinError = Error
  end if
end for

---

100 seconds on either side of our best time synchronization estimate. The IPD values in Algorithm 1 include both the time of occurrence and the IPD. Matching an IPD from the first proxy's data with an IPD from the last proxy's data means finding an IPD that is close in the time of occurrence. We choose the closest matches given the offset and calculate the error as the standard deviation. If no match is within 1.0 seconds, we add an error of 1.0 s econd (prior to dividing by the number of matches sought and taking the square root). These are arbitrary values that worked well in our tests. Finally, we select the offset that gives the lowest error.

In Figure 13, we see the effectiveness of spike analysis on our data in the form of ROC curves. Table 2 provides AUC and equal error rates. The main result is that defensive dropping can be attacked much more successfully with spike analysis than with statistical correlation. In particular, the AUC for 20% defensive dropping is 0.913 and the equal error rate is 17% when using spike analysis, as compared with 0.602 AUC and 38% equal error rate for statistical correlation. Note that the figure shows only the upper left hand quadrant and that the axes have been shifted slightly to show the lines with zero error rate. In particular, the attacker gets zero error for baseline traffic — he can get 100% detection with no false positives as shown by the line touching the point $(0, 1)$ in the graph. The AUC for baseline traffic is the maximum of 1.0.

We also see that partial buffering with $\gamma = 2$ is much less effective against spike analysis than statistical analysis, with an AUC of 0.989 and an equal error rate of only 4%. Perhaps more interestingly, we see that partial buffering with $\gamma = 5$ is only a little bit less effective against spike analysis. The AUC is slightly higher at 0.864 and the equal error rate of 24% is the same as with statistical analysis. In fact, this is the most effective defense of the settings we tried against spike analysis. As we see with Figure 10, the IPD graphs when $\gamma = 5$ have many spikes at the last proxy. From this observation, we speculate that spike analysis with two mismatched streams is finding

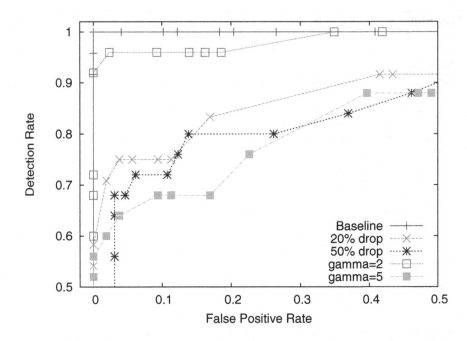

Fig. 13. Spike Analysis: ROC curves for different defenses

Table 2. Spike Analysis: Area under the curve (AUC), equal error rate (EER), and latency values for defensive dropping (DD) and partial buffering (PB)

Defense	Baseline	DD 20%	DD 50%	PB $\gamma = 2$	PB $\gamma = 5$
AUC	1.0	0.913	0.871	0.989	0.864
EER	0%	17%	20%	4%	24%
Latency (sec.)	0.300	0.271	0.314	0.375	0.515

spikes in the last proxy's IPDs that fit the profile of the first proxy's IPDs. This leads to false positives. We have observed that tightening the time requirements for more precise matches can lead to more false negatives. Thus, with enough buffering, we seem to able to maintain a defense against these passive timing analysis techniques.

6   Conclusion

To facilitate the research of low-latency anonymous systems in general and timing analysis on low latency systems in particular, we developed the SubRosa experimental platform. We modeled SubRosa on Tor-like systems but choose UDP as the transport protocol to best study systems in which packet timing can be dictated by design choices rather than TCP behavior. We ran experiments on the PlanetLab overlay network and collected network timing data. Using this data, we performed successful timing analysis and evaluated several known defenses to avoid the attack. We introduced a light-weight defense against timing analysis attack, γ-buffering, based on threshold mixes. Our results show that defensive dropping provides the best defense among those we tested against statistical correlation-based timing analysis attacks by a passive adversary.

We also introduced spike analysis, a new timing analysis approach motivated by our observations of inter-packet delays. Spike analysis takes advantage of the presence of large spikes in the IPD traffic pattern. If the largest spikes are smaller than the changes in IPD caused by perturbations like defensive dropping and γ-buffering, the attack will not work well. However, an attacker who controls the first proxy in the circuit could induce the necessary spikes by delaying packets. This active attack requires much lower timing precision than the watermarking methods of [28] and we have shown here that delaying only five packets can be enough to get good results. A reputation system or other mechanism to ensure that attackers do not manipulate traffic in this way would have to be very sensitive to relatively small changes in the traffic pattern. The adaptive padding approach of [25] may be a useful supplement to the defenses we have tested here, as it actively seeks to remove the spikes that form the basis of spike analysis. The practical issues involved in using this technique, however, would need to be further refined.

Acknowledgments

The work of Daginawala and Wright was supported in part by National Science Foundation award CNS-0549998. Thanks to George Danezis for valuable discussions during early phases of the work and Cyrus Bavarian for insight and suggestions into the design of SubRosa. Thanks also to the anonymous reviewers for their valuable comments and to Jaideep Padhye for a useful way to visualize our data.

References

1. Planetlab, http://www.planetlab.org
2. Back, A., Goldberg, I., Shostack, A.: Freedom 2.0 security issues and analysis. Zero-Knowledge Systems, Inc. white paper (November 2000)
3. Bauer, K., McCoy, D., Grunwald, D., Kohno, T., Sicker, D.: Low-resource routing attacks against TOR. In: ACM WPES (2007)
4. Brown, D.: The Da Vinci Code. Doubleday Press (2003)
5. Chaum, D.: Untraceable electronic mail, return addresses, and digital pseudonyms. Communications of the ACM 24(2), 84–88 (1981)
6. Danezis, G.: The traffic analysis of continuous-time mixes. In: Martin, D., Serjantov, A. (eds.) PET 2004. LNCS, vol. 3424. Springer, Heidelberg (May 2005)
7. Dei, W.: Pipenet 1.1 (August 1996),
   http://www.eskimo.com/~weidai/pipenet.txt
8. Diaz, C., Preneel, B.: Taxonomy of mixes and dummy traffic. In: Proc. Intl. Information Security Management, Education and Privacy (I-NetSec 2004) (August 2004)
9. Diaz, C., Sassaman, L., Dewitte, E.: Comparison between two practical mix designs. In: Samarati, P., Ryan, P.Y.A., Gollmann, D., Molva, R. (eds.) ESORICS 2004. LNCS, vol. 3193. Springer, Heidelberg (2004)
10. Dingledine, R., Mathewson, N., Syverson, P.: Tor: The next-generation Onion Router. In: Proc. USENIX Security Symposium (August 2004)

11. Freedman, M., Morris, R.: Tarzan: A peer-to-peer anonymizing network layer. In: Proc. ACM CCS (November 2002)
12. Ganesh, R., Kaushik, B., Sadhu, R.: Modelling Delay Jitter in Voice over IP. ArXiv Computer Science e-prints (January 2003)
13. Hopper, N., Vasserman, E.Y., Chan-Tin, E.: How much anonymity does network latency leak. In: Proceedings of CCS 2007 (October 2007)
14. Levine, B.N., Reiter, M., Wang, C., Wright, M.: Timing analysis in low-latency mix systems. In: Proc. Financial Cryptography (February 2004)
15. Li, H., Mason, L.: Estimation and simulation of network delay traces for voip in service overlay network. In: Proc. Intl. Symposium on Signals, Systems and Electronics (ISSSE 2007) (July 2007)
16. Murdoch, S.J., Danezis, G.: Low-cost traffic analysis of Tor. In: Proc. IEEE Symposium on Security and Privacy (May 2005)
17. Murdoch, S.J., Zieliński, P.: Sampled traffic analysis by internet-exchange-level adversaries. In: Proceedings of the Seventh Workshop on Privacy Enhancing Technologies (PET 2007) (June 2007)
18. Nambiar, A., Wright, M.: Salsa: a structured approach to large-scale anonymity. In: Proc. ACM Conference on Computer and Communications Security (CCS 2006) (October 2006)
19. Paxson, V.: Measurement and Analysis of End-to-End Internet Dynamics. Berkeley, California. Ph.D Dissertation (1997)
20. Peterson, L., Pai, V., Spring, N., Bavier, A.: Using PlanetLab for Network Research: Myths, Realities, and Best Practices. Technical Report PDN–05–028, PlanetLab Consortium (June 2005)
21. Pfitzmann, A., Pfitzmann, B., Waidner, M.: ISDNMixes: Untraceable communication with very small bandwidth overhead. In: Proc. GI/ITG Communication in Distributed Systems (February 1991)
22. Reiter, M.K., Rubin, A.D.: Crowds: Anonymity for Web Transactions. ACM TISSEC 1(1), 66–92 (1998)
23. Rennhard, M., Plattner, B.: Practical anonymity for the masses with MorphMix. In: Juels, A. (ed.) FC 2004. LNCS, vol. 3110. Springer, Heidelberg (2004)
24. Serjantov, A., Dingledine, R., Syverson, P.: From a trickle to a flood: Active attacks on several mix types. In: Proc. Information Hiding Workshop (IH) (October 2002)
25. Shmatikov, V., Wang, M.H.: Timing analysis in low latency mix networks: Attacks and defenses. In: Gollmann, D., Meier, J., Sabelfeld, A. (eds.) ESORICS 2006. LNCS, vol. 4189. Springer, Heidelberg (2006)
26. Syverson, P., Tsudik, G., Reed, M., Landwehr, C.: Towards an analysis of Onion Routing security. In: Workshop on Design Issues in Anonymity and Unobservability (July 2000)
27. Venkateshaiah, M., Wright, M.: Evading stepping stone detection under the cloak of streaming media. Technical Report CSE-2007-6, Dept. of Computer Science and Engineering, U. Texas at Arlington (2007)
28. Wang, X., Chen, S., Jajodia, S.: Tracking anonymous peer-to-peer VoIP calls on the Internet. In: Proceedings of the ACM Conference on Computer Communications Security (CCS) (November 2005)
29. Wang, X., Chen, S., Jajodia, S.: Network flow watermarking attack on low-latency anonymous communication systems. In: Proceedings of the IEEE Symposium on Security and Privacy (S&P 2007) (May 2007)
30. Wright, M., Adler, M., Levine, B.N., Shields, C.: The predecessor attack: An analysis of a threat to anonymous communications systems. ACM Transactions on Information and Systems Security (TISSEC) 7(4) (2004)
31. Zhu, Y., Fu, X., Graham, B., Bettati, R., Zhao, W.: On flow correlation attacks and countermeasures in mix networks. In: Martin, D., Serjantov, A. (eds.) PET 2004. LNCS, vol. 3424. Springer, Heidelberg (2005)

Bridging and Fingerprinting: Epistemic Attacks on Route Selection

George Danezis[1] and Paul Syverson[2]

[1] Microsoft Research, Cambridge, UK
[2] Naval Research Laboratory, USA

Abstract. Users building routes through an anonymization network must discover the nodes comprising the network. Yet, it is potentially costly, or even infeasible, for everyone to know the entire network. We introduce a novel attack, the *route bridging attack*, which makes use of what route creators do *not* know of the network. We also present new discussion and results concerning route fingerprinting attacks, which make use of what route creators do know of the network. We prove analytic bounds for both route fingerprinting and route bridging and describe the impact of these attacks on published anonymity-network designs. We also discuss implications for network scaling and client-server vs. peer-to-peer systems.

1 Introduction

Anonymous communications were first introduced for electronic mail with the mix network [3] and then extended to internet streams by onion routing [10, 21, 2, 6]. Since then, attempts have been made to totally decentralize the provision of anonymity services. First Tarzan [9, 8], then other systems [15, 26, 12] have applied the peer-to-peer paradigm to ensure that all protocol participants are both clients and routers that anonymize streams.

Besides the differences in the type of traffic carried or division of tasks within the network, all those systems share a common architecture. Initiators of communications relay their messages or streams through third parties to evade identification. The communication contents are encrypted to foil trivial passive linkage, and in some cases countermeasures are applied against traffic analysis, such as making messages uniform size or delaying them or injecting cover traffic.

Despite their common architecture, mix-based, onion-routing, or peer-to-peer anonymizing networks protect against radically different threat models. Mix networks should be secure when under full surveillance, and when a large fraction of routers used are corrupt [1]. Traditional onion routing and stream-based peer-to-peer anonymizers, like Tarzan, are unable to resist even a passive attack and cannot guarantee anonymity if both the initiator and responder of the communication are under surveillance [24]. Similarly, even an entirely passive adversary controlling the first and last node in the path can trace the anonymized stream, unless large amounts of cover traffic are used [23].

N. Borisov and I. Goldberg (Eds.): PETS 2008, LNCS 5134, pp. 151–166, 2008.

A key contribution of this paper is to present a novel class of traffic analysis attacks against relay-based anonymizers, called *bridging* attacks. Bridging uses some a priori information about the route selection of initiators to effectively bridge over honest stages of mixing, making tracing a full path easier for the adversary. As a technique bridging is closely related to *route fingerprinting* [4]. We present an analytic bound on route fingerprinting, using the Tarzan design as an example, and discuss the impact of route fingerprinting against other classes of anonymity systems. In particular, we compare route-fingerprinting resistance for client-server designs vs. peer-to-peer designs and discuss the (encouraging) implications for network partitioning.

2 Fingerprinting

2.1 Young Tarzan Leaves Telltale Fingerprints on the Vine

The early Tarzan design [9] aims to provide strong anonymity against a global eavesdropper using a fully peer-to-peer architecture. The core design is based on ideas from onion routing, with some modifications to distribute services that are otherwise centralized in standard onion routing. The most important distributed service in Tarzan is the directory server providing a list of nodes with their associated keys. Furthermore, Tarzan designers recognized that large scale networks make low-latency traffic more susceptible to tracing, and to alleviate the problem attempt to route multiple streams together by forcing them through restricted routes, called *mimics*—a facet of Tarzan we do not discuss here.

Distributing the directory server functionality over a peer-to-peer network is not straightforward and has deep repercussions on security. Tarzan relies on the use of a Distributed Hash Table (DHT) [20] to store mappings of nodes and keys. A DHT is a peer-to-peer protocol that allows nodes to construct a distributed database mapping keys to values. Nodes are assigned a particular section of the key space for which they store values, and there are efficient $\mathcal{O}(\log N)$ algorithms for finding the node corresponding to a particular key. Tarzan nodes store their directory descriptors as values, and the key of the descriptor is simply its hash.

A Tarzan node joining the network has, as in traditional onion routing, to 'discover' a set of peers along with their directory descriptors containing their cryptographic keys, to be able to construct paths and anonymize streams of traffic. The original Tarzan design required nodes to discover at random only a small subset of other nodes, and used a small subset of those to build anonymous routes. Sampling was performed by selecting a random nonce and finding the closest DHT key and associated directory entry, an operation that is efficient in DHTs.

This approach introduces two problems. First, the sampling procedure is not guaranteed to be uniform in the presence of adversaries prepared to subvert the Distributed Hash Table. For any random key K the client choses, the adversary can simulate a node with a directory descriptor mapping to a close-by key K' that is closer than the closest genuine key K_g. Hence the adversary can easily populate the client's entries with corrupt nodes, making any routing over them ineffective.

This attack is active, and requires the adversary to corrupt the underlying DHT protocols (which is easy, since few DHT designs protect against such attacks effectively). Attacking and defending DHTs is not the focus of this paper and we will not concern ourselves any further with this line of attack.

Second, the client only chooses routes from a small subspace of all nodes, and this subspace is known to the adversary. This in turn can help the adversary identify which routes belong to each client. This family of attacks was briefly introduced in route fingerprinting [4], and in this paper we present a novel attack in this family we call route bridging.

To avoid fingerprinting attacks the final Tarzan design [8] requires each node to know all other nodes—something hardly practical due to the large size and churn of peer-to-peer networks. Our analysis and discussion of these attacks concludes that for weaker threat models this approach may be over-conservative.

2.2 Bounding Route Fingerprinting

We assume that there are $N + 1$ peers in the system, and each of them samples $n < N$ others to create routes. (We assume nodes do not create routes through themselves.) Assume an adversary determines $k < n$ nodes on a particular route. How many peers on average will know all k nodes, and therefore are possible initiators of this route?

Each node can build up to $\binom{n}{k}$ k-tuples out of a maximum of $\binom{N}{k}$ that could exist in the system. Therefore any peer knows those k nodes with probability $p = \binom{n}{k}/\binom{N}{k}$.[1] We define an indicator random variable I_i for each node i that takes the value one when this is the case, and zero otherwise. The expected number of nodes that could be initiators is $A_k = E[\sum_{i=0}^{N} I_i]$ which is at most:

$$A_k = E[\sum_{i=0}^{N} I_i] \le (N+1) \frac{n^k}{N^k} \left(\frac{N}{N - (k-1)} \right)^k \approx \frac{n^k}{N^{k-1}}, \text{ when } \frac{k-1}{N} \to 0 \quad (1)$$

Proof. We start by the definition and apply linearity of expectations.

$$A_k = E[\sum_{i=0}^{N} I_i] = \sum_{i=0}^{N} E[I_i] \quad (2)$$

$$= (N+1) \cdot p = (N+1) \cdot \frac{\binom{n}{k}}{\binom{N}{k}} = \frac{(N+1)n!(N-k)!}{N!(n-k)!} \quad (3)$$

$$\le \frac{n^k(N+1)}{(N-k+1)^k} \quad \text{(keep max. and min. values.)} \quad (4)$$

$$= (N+1) \frac{n^k}{N^k} \left(\frac{N}{N-(k-1)} \right)^k \quad (5)$$

Take the limit $\lim_{\frac{k-1}{N} \to 0} \left(\frac{N}{N-(k-1)} \right)^k = 1$ to conclude the proof.

---

[1] An equivalent combinatorial formulation is $p = \binom{N-k}{n-k}/\binom{N}{n}$.

2.3   Anonymity Loves Company, But Hates a Big Crowd

What does this attack mean in practice? As expected, if the adversary cannot observe any nodes on a path ($k = 0$), anonymity is perfect and $A_0 = N + 1$. This assumption imposes an unacceptably weak threat model.

The first realistic threat model is for the attacker to be the receiver of the communication, and thus to observe just one node in a path, the final one. We expect that given this information ($k = 1$) there are on average $A_1 \approx n$ nodes in the network that could have been the initiators. This is of some interest since it is equal to the number of candidates if the network were split into $\frac{N}{n}$ smaller networks of equal size n, in which all nodes knew all other nodes. In case the adversary controls, and does not merely see a connection originating from the last node, they can associate $A_2 \approx n^2/N$ initiators (the final node and the penultimate node on the path) with each incoming link (since $k = 2$).

Next assuming that the adversary controls the two last nodes on a path (but not the first few). What is the expected number of nodes that could have been the initiator? The two corrupt nodes know that the initiator must have sampled them, as well as the previous node, and therefore $k = 3$. The number of possible initiators is $A_3 \approx \left(\frac{n}{N}\right)^2 n$, and in general for $k > 1$ we have that $A_k < n$, which means that the security of the system will always be worse than if the networks were simply partitioned into smaller cliques.

This attack, and its associated analysis, prove two key intuitions. First it illustrates again, that for some threats the larger the network the less security we get. As N grows the fraction $\frac{n}{N}$ becomes smaller, and in turn the number of candidate nodes that could have created any particular route becomes smaller. Similarly to the predecessor attack against crowds[2] we see that increasing the number of potential senders does not automatically increase anonymity if the system does not ensure that the anonymity sets are constituted using all of them—the route fingerprinting attack illustrates that anonymity may in fact decrease.

Second, one may take a step back and ask "does this attack really matter for onion-routing-based systems?" Onion routing only preserves anonymity against a partial adversary, as long as the first and last node are not compromised [22]. This means that with probability c^2 the system provides no anonymity at all, where c is the fraction of compromised nodes in the network. On the other hand a route fingerprinting attack requires $k \geq 2$ to be truly effective, i.e., to reduce anonymity below the effect of simply splitting the network. The most obvious way for the adversary to achieve this is to compromise at least the final node. If

---

[2] The predecessor attack was first described and analyzed in the original crowds paper [14], and that design provably prevented predecessor attacks on persistent crowds. However, it was later shown that a predecessor attack was possible when crowds reformed, i.e., every time someone joined a crowd. The same work that uncovered this attack also first observed that anonymity vs. this attack decreases as the crowd size increases [19]. Further analysis of predecessor attacks on crowds and other systems was done by Wright et al. [25].

the final node is corrupt, there is still some anonymity left if $n^2 >> N$, even if the sets of known nodes for each participant are available to the adversary.

To make attacks more effective, more nodes on the path need to be compromised. For short paths ($l = 3$), this attack is no more likely than attack through the normal running of the system. For longer paths, fingerprinting can be used in conjunction with timing analysis, to break the security of paths that start with an honest node. As an example consider an adversary that controls the second and last node on a long path. They are able, using timing analysis, to infer that the two corrupt nodes belong to the same path, and apply fingerprinting to reduce the number of candidate initiators to A_5 (they can identify five nodes known by the initiator: the two dishonest ones, and the three honest nodes surrounding them.) Even for paths of length 3, fingerprinting combined with ordinary correlation attack is slightly more effective than correlation alone.

The probability of two or more corrupt nodes being on the path, including a last corrupt node is $c(1 - (1 - c)^{l-1})$. This is always higher than the probability of compromise (c^2) through controlling the first and last node. In such cases the initiator set can be narrowed down to A_3 or fewer nodes, depending on the positions of the corrupt nodes on the path. This demonstrates that fingerprinting does lead to weaker security for onion-routing networks.

2.4 Better to Have Nothing to Do with Each Other Than to Stay Together in Ignorance

Tor [6] is the current widely-deployed-and-used onion-routing network. Concern about knowledge-based partitioning has deferred any deployment within Tor of a system that gives clients only a partial list of nodes in the network despite the usability, network load, and other issues that have come with maintaining and distributing the increasingly large list to every Tor client. As we have seen, to avoid such knowledge-based attacks the design of Tarzan actually moved in the other direction, towards requiring clients to know the full list.

Our results apply to peer-to-peer versions of onion routing such as Tarzan. In the client-server setting of Tor, the number of clients C is a few orders of magnitude larger than the number of servers N. In that case the number of candidates given k servers on the path is $A_k \approx (n/N)^k \cdot C$. This further increases anonymity when only the last server is compromised (making $k = 2$), hence architectures that allow such systems to scale should not be discarded solely because of the route fingerprinting attack.

To be concrete, at the time of writing, Tor has an estimated 200000-500000 clients and around 2000 routers (server nodes). Suppose we would like to maintain as a security parameter with respect to exit-node route fingerprinting an anonymity set size of 50000. Then, using a conservative number of clients, each one should know about half of the routers. However, note that one could partition both the client set and the network in four such that all clients in a partition know all 500 nodes in one clique and still produce the same resistance to route-fingerprinting by the exit node. This analysis is too simple and overlooks the fact that nodes are not all the same in Tor: they carry widely differing numbers of circuits (paths) and amounts of traffic; some serve as persistent entry nodes for clients; only about a third are exit nodes, etc. Our analysis illustrates that while scaling such systems can maintain adequate anonymity in the face of route fingerprinting, splitting the network outright may be more desirable.

However, there remain too many concerns for this to be a recommendation in practice: one must securely split the network and clients so that no single authority can take advantage of the splits, and the basic c^2 probability of end-to-end compromise is still affected by network size, etc. To underscore this last limitation let us revisit the analysis of the current Tor network with an anonymity-set security parameter of 50000 clients. Note that the same result as above applies if the client set is partitioned into four even sets of 50000 and, instead of being partitioned evenly, the node set is partitioned into three sets of 10 nodes each and one set of of 1970 nodes. There is no epistemic attack because each client in each set of 50000 knows all the nodes in its assigned partition, but it is much easier for an adversary to monitor all the network connections of ten nodes than the five hundred that would result from an even partition.

Relatedly, onion routing would appear to benefit from a move to a more peer-to-peer design for all of the reasons that make such designs desirable. However, the above shows that a client-server design has some inherent anonymity advantages over a peer-to-peer design, and the assumption that a peer-to-peer architecture would facilitate further scaling up and therefore improve anonymity cannot be justified in general. Specific proposals for P2P designs and deployment strategies thus need to be examined closely to determine if there are indeed anonymity benefits, or at least acceptable anonymity costs.

When fingerprinting is deployed on mix systems instead of onion routing, which are secure with probability $1 - c^l$, it often allows an adversary to de-anonymize users much faster than before, and this should be considered a threat. So, in practice, one is not advised to use a Tarzan-like selection strategy for high security mix-based anonymous communications. In case high levels of security are sought, a second attack that leverages the limited knowledge of nodes, *route bridging*, becomes of interest.

3   Route Bridging

> *"We also know there are 'known unknowns'; that is to say we know there are some things we do not know."*
>
> *Donald Rumsfeld* — U.S. Secretary of Defense

Route bridging assumes that a passive adversary can put some nodes in a mix network under surveillance. It is also relevant to strengthened onion routing schemes that provide protection against correlation attacks, since it provides an alternative method to link incoming and outgoing streams of traffic.

The key intuition behind bridging attacks is that the nodes constructing the routes only know a fraction of all potential routers, as it was the case for the early

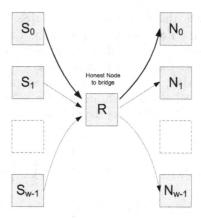

Fig. 1. The setting of the bridging attack when R is the first node

versions of Tarzan. As a result not all combinations of incoming and outgoing links to/from a router form valid paths—some of those are simply not possible, i.e. no node knows all routers necessary to construct them. In the extreme case some paths do not benefit from any anonymization at all, since for one input link there is a unique possible output link. The key question regarding the route bridging attack is to determine the probability of such a total compromise. It is essentially an epistemic version of the $n-1$ attack [17].

3.1 Bridging a First Node

We illustrate the attack first in the simplest setting, where an adversary tries to bridge the first, presumably honest, node. In this case we consider w initiators $S_0, \ldots, S_{w-1}$ that concurrently use the honest node R as the very first node in their paths—and the adversary tries to infer the outgoing node $N_0, \ldots, N_{w-1}$ to which each incoming stream corresponds. In the subsequent sections we generalize our results to other settings.

Consider w incoming messages or streams, from $S_0, \ldots, S_{w-1}$ leading to w outgoing messages to $N_0, \ldots, N_{w-1}$, passing through a mix R. (For convenience, we will use 'message' generically below, but observations we make generally carry over to streams as well.) Without loss of generality we assume that the first sender S_0 routes through the mix a message that is destined to node N_0. What is the probability this message is compromised by a route-bridging attack? The link from S_0 to N_0 can be uniquely recovered, if one of two conditions is true (and these are not exhaustive). Either the node S_0 does not know any of the other destination nodes $N_1, \ldots, N_{w-1}$, which we denote as $\Pr[S_0 \not\to N_1, \ldots, N_{w-1}]$; or none of the other senders $S_1, \ldots, S_{w-1}$ know the destination node N_0, which we denote as $\Pr[S_1, \ldots, S_{w-1} \not\to N_0]$. We bound the probability of a successful attack, P_{bridge}, by:

$$\left(1 - \frac{n-2}{N-2}\right)^{w-1} \leq P_{bridge} \leq 2\left(1 - \frac{n-2}{N-2}\right)^{w-1} \qquad (6)$$

Proof. First we calculate the two probabilities $\Pr[S_0 \not\rightarrow N_1, \ldots, N_{w-1}]$ and $\Pr[S_1, \ldots, S_{w-1} \not\rightarrow N_0]$. $\Pr[S_0 \not\rightarrow N_1, \ldots, N_{w-1}]$ is the probability each distinct $N_1, \ldots, N_{w-1}$ is not in the set of $n-2$ nodes that S_0 knows and would route through in this way (assuming that the nodes R, N_0, and S_0 itself are excluded). Probability $\Pr[S_1, \ldots, S_{w-1} \not\rightarrow N_0]$ represents how likely it is that no other node from $S_1, \ldots, S_{w-1}$ has N_0 in its set of $n-2$ remaining nodes, after excluding the router node R, as well as their actual outgoing link and the node S_i itself.

$$\Pr[S_0 \not\rightarrow N_1, \ldots, N_{w-1}] = \frac{\binom{(N-2)-(w-1)}{n-2}}{\binom{N-2}{n-2}} = \prod_{i=0}^{w-2} \left(1 - \frac{n-2}{N-i-2}\right) \quad (7)$$

$$\Pr[S_1, \ldots, S_{w-1} \not\rightarrow N_0] = \left(1 - \frac{n-2}{N-2}\right)^{w-1} \quad (8)$$

First we note that if $i > 0$ then $\left(1 - \frac{n-2}{N-i-2}\right) \leq \left(1 - \frac{n-2}{N-2}\right)$ which in turn means that:

$$\Pr[S_0 \not\rightarrow N_1, \ldots, N_{w-1}] \leq \Pr[S_1, \ldots, S_{w-1} \not\rightarrow N_0] \quad (9)$$

The sought probability P_{bridge} is in fact equal to the union of the events described by the probabilities above. Trivially applying the union bound to $P_{bridge} = \Pr[S_0 \not\rightarrow N_1, \ldots, N_{w-1} \cup S_1, \ldots, S_{w-1} \not\rightarrow N_0]$, as well as the fact that one of the probabilities is always larger than the other, we have that:

$$\Pr[S_1, \ldots, S_{w-1} \not\rightarrow N_0] < P_{bridge} < 2\Pr[S_1, \ldots, S_{w-1} \not\rightarrow N_0] \quad (10)$$

The proof can be concluded by substituting for $\Pr[S_1, \ldots, S_{w-1} \not\rightarrow N_0]$.

This attack assumes that the adversary's only information, besides which nodes are known to which system participants, is the router concerned and the nodes providing input and receiving output for a given mix batch. This makes the attack applicable to bridging the first node in the path. The adversary need only know the knowledge set of the target S_0 for the lower bound we have stated to hold; she need not be aware of which nodes are known to the other S_i. Alternatively, she may only be aware of the knowledge sets of the other S_i and not that of S_0. Note that the nodes $N_j \neq N_0$ need not be distinct for these results to hold. In fact they could all be the same node.

Looking at this simple scenario it is clear that as the number of streams or messages crossing a router increases, the probability that any of them is compromised through this route bridging attack decreases. But what order of magnitude should the batch size w be to neutralize the attack? We note that the probability of security is $1 - P_{bridge} < \frac{(w-1)(n-2)}{N-2}$ (by Bernoulli's inequality), so if the system has to have a chance of providing full security that is close to optimal we should require $1 - \epsilon < \frac{(w-1)(n-2)}{N-2}$, which provides a lower limit on w:

$$w > \frac{(1-\epsilon)(N-2)}{n-2} + 1 \quad (11)$$

So to even start contemplating the possibility of full security the number of mixed messages or streams should be $\mathcal{O}(\frac{N-2}{n-2})$. In a fully peer-to-peer system the number of streams multiplexed is only $\mathcal{O}(l)$, where l is the length of paths in the system. This is usually a small number, way too small to guarantee maximal security.

In low-latency systems like Tarzan or Tor, the threat of route bridging is likely to be dominated by the ability to correlate streams in two locations through simple timing and packet counting for the foreseeable future [13, 18]. In proper mix systems, however, it could prove to be a near-term practical threat. The batch size w provides some guidance on how to set the parameters of each mix to mitigate against the route bridging attack.

3.2   Building Bridges Further Down the Road

> *"Confusion will be my epitaph, as I crawl a cracked and broken path."*
>
> *King Crimson* — Lyrics to "Epitaph"

Bridging could also be applied to the final router in a path. One would, however, need to assume that the adversary knows which ultimate destinations are known to whom. For the anonymity systems we have been considering, these destinations are not assumed to be part of the network; so this information would not be available by the means we described above. Feigenbaum et al. [7] present such an analysis of what a partial network adversary who knows the a priori distribution of ultimate destinations for every client of an onion-routing network can learn by observing the (fully-discovered) network.

What if messages entering router R were from initiators known to the adversary? Note that here the chooser of routes are not the intermediary nodes S_i. Thus it's not the nodes N_{i_j} unknown to S_i that we are considering; it's the nodes unknown to the initiating peer that routed from S_i to R to N_{i_j}. If all paths have been compromised for at least k nodes prior to R, then the bound becomes even tighter in this combination of fingerprinting and bridging.

$$\left(1 - \frac{n-k-1}{N-k-1}\right)^{w-1} \le P_{bridge} \le 2\left(1 - \frac{n-k-1}{N-k-1}\right)^{w-1} \qquad (12)$$

This situation of so many paths being fully known for more than one hop in their routes is perhaps unlikely; however, we can also determine lower bounds in case just the path of the message entering R from router S_0 and exiting to router N_0 is known to the adversary. Again assuming that the k nodes prior to R in this path are compromised, we can determine $\Pr[S_0 \not\to N_1, \ldots, N_{w-1}]$. We cannot say anything about $\Pr[S_1, \ldots, S_{w-1} \not\to N_0]$ in this case because we do not know about the path nodes chosen prior to the S_i for $i \neq 0$ and cannot trace each back to a unique initiator. For this reason, we cannot give an upper bound. But we can give a lower bound.

$$P_{bridge} = \prod_{i=0}^{w-2} \left(1 - \frac{n-k-2}{N-k-i-2}\right) \geq \left(1 - \frac{n-k-2}{N-k-2}\right)^{w-1} \quad (13)$$

Bridges without compromise anywhere you like. If the path up to R is not compromised the attack becomes less likely to succeed but is still possible in some cases. As before we assume that a node R receives messages from nodes $S_{0...w-1}$ and outputs those messages to nodes $N_{0...w-1}$. Without loss of generality we assume that the message from S_0 is routed through R to N_0 and try to calculate the probability the adversary can infer this without any doubt.

Unlike our assumption so far, the adversary does not a-priori know which set of w initiators are responsible for the w streams going through node R. Our first observation is that the number of potential initiators, N', for each incoming link is much smaller than the total $N+1$ nodes, since they are assumed to know at least nodes S_i and R. According to our results on the fingerprinting attack we expect about $A_2 = E[N'] = (n/N)^2 \cdot N$ potential initiators for each link.

As before we try to calculate the probability an adversary can bridge over node R and uncover the path $S_0 \rightarrow R \rightarrow N_0$. This is possible if *either*:

- there is no initiator that knows nodes S_0 and R and other destinations $N_{1...w-1}$. We denote this as
  $\Pr[(S_0 \rightarrow R) \nrightarrow N_1, \ldots, N_{w-1} | S_0 \rightarrow R \rightarrow N_0, N']$
  or,
- there are no initiators that know nodes R and N_0 as well as any of the nodes $S_{1...w-1}$. We denote this as
  $\Pr[(N_0 \leftarrow R) \nleftarrow S_1, \ldots, S_{w-1} | S_0 \rightarrow R \rightarrow N_0, N']$.

The probability of a successful bridging attack in this context is:

$$\left(1 - \frac{n-2}{N-2-(w-2)}\right)^{(w-1)(N'-1)} \leq P_{\text{bridge}} \leq 2\left(1 - \frac{n-2}{N-2}\right)^{(w-1)(N'-1)} \quad (14)$$

Proof. We first calculate the probability
$p_1 = \Pr[S_0 \rightarrow R \nrightarrow N_1, \ldots, N_{w-1} | S_0 \rightarrow R \rightarrow N_0, N']$ that no other node knows S_0, R and any of the other destinations $N_1, \ldots, N_{w-1}$. This means that the other $N'-1$ nodes have not chosen any of $N_1, \ldots, N_{w-1}$ as part of their remaining $n-2$ nodes. The probability of this happening for any of them is $\binom{N-2-(w-1)}{n-2}/\binom{N-2}{n-2}$ and there are $N'-1$ independent nodes for which this must hold. Hence,

$$p_1 = [\Pr[S_0 \nrightarrow N_1, \ldots, N_{w-1}]]^{N'-1} = \left[\frac{\binom{N-2-(w-1)}{n-2}}{\binom{N-2}{n-2}}\right]^{N'-1} \quad (15)$$

Now note that $p_2 = \Pr[N_0 \leftarrow R \nleftarrow S_1, \ldots, S_{w-1} | S_0 \rightarrow R \rightarrow N_0, N']$ is in fact equal by symmetry to p_1. Since bridging is successful if either of those holds, by the union bound we get:

$$\left[\frac{\binom{N-2-(w-1)}{n-2}}{\binom{N-2}{n-2}}\right]^{N'-1} \leq P_{\text{bridge}} \leq 2\left[\frac{\binom{N-2-(w-1)}{n-2}}{\binom{N-2}{n-2}}\right]^{N'-1} \quad (16)$$

The lower bound is simply derived by assuming that only one of the two events takes place.

We can loosen a bit the bounds in order to get some intuitions about how the different quantities influence the probability of successful bridging. We note that:

$$\frac{\binom{N-2-(w-1)}{n-2}}{\binom{N-2}{n-2}} = \prod_{j=0}^{w-2} \left(1 - \frac{n-2}{(N-2)-j}\right) = \alpha \qquad (17)$$

By assigning to the fraction in α the maximum and the minimum values j assumes we get:

$$\left(1 - \frac{n-2}{N-2-(w-2)}\right)^{w-1} \leq \alpha \leq \left(1 - \frac{n-2}{N-2}\right)^{w-1} \qquad (18)$$

We substitute the derived inequalities for α into eq. 16 to derive our final bound on the probability of successful bridging in eq. 14. Intuitions about its behaviour are present in the next section.

3.3 But Can the Army Walk Across It? Building Bridges in the Real World

In the previous sections we described bridging and derived analytic bounds when the first node is compromised, when paths from all or from just a specific source to an honest mix are compromised, and even for the more general case where an adversary tries to bridge an arbitrary honest node in the network. Let us now examine the relevance of this attack to real world systems.

The first difficulty in applying the attack relates to the threat model it assumes. A local passive adversary is required to observe all incoming and outgoing messages or streams around the node to be bridged. Mix systems usually try to protect against such adversaries, but stream-based anonymization systems, which are already susceptible to timing attacks, do not. Yet even in the case of stream-based systems, such as onion routing (including Tor), an adversary might find it advantageous to use bridging if possible: it only requires connection information, rather than the exact timing of packets traveling in the network. If applicable, bridging requires several orders of magnitude less information about each link and node than timing attacks—and this information can be inferred through sampling network packets [11] or observing short windows of traffic.

A global passive adversary may be required to discover the sets of nodes known by each initiator in the system, depending on the exact network discovery protocol employed. Tarzan proposed the use of a DHT that can easily be infiltrated by a few nodes to observe all other nodes' activity. Current widely-used distributed anonymizing systems (Tor, mixmaster, mixminion) use a distributed but more centralized directory architecture to provide routing information. If any of these were to move away from assuming that every client in the network knows all servers, it could be subject to epistemic attack if just one of the directory servers is dishonest. It may be possible to bootstrap off using a core anonymizing network known to all clients that could be used to obtain node information from directories or to use private retrieval or other techniques to counter these. However, more research is needed to determine if there are scalable, efficient, and secure techniques for partial network discovery in any directory system from centralized to diffusely distributed. In case node discovery is unobservable by the adversary, the attacker would have to resort to monitoring the network to infer the sets of nodes know by each initiator. Distributing such unobservable sets for each client is an open research problem.

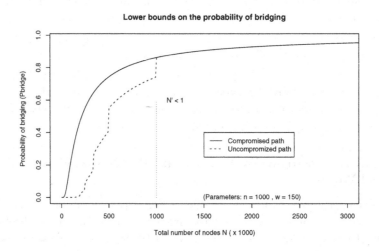

Fig. 2. The effectiveness of bridging given a compromised or uncompromised path.

The analytic bounds provided can be of great help to attackers or to system designers wishing to evaluate security, but they offer little intuition into the effectiveness of the attack in a realistic setting. To illustrate we assess the probability of success of bridging in a network where each node knows $n = 1000$ others and the batch size of relays is $w = 150$. Figure 2 plots this probability as the total number of nodes in the network N grows. As expected, the lower bound for the probability of success if the initiator of the connection is known (the compromised path case) is always greater or equal to the case where the initiator is not known. If the path has not been linked unambiguously to an initiator (uncompromised path case), then the probability is lower according to the expected number of nodes that could be initiators of an observed link. Since $N > n^2$, we expect the number of such initiators to be at most one, and the probabilities of success for the two cases are equal for average N'.

Figure 2 illustrates clearly that the probability of bridging is not negligible: if nodes know only 1-in-500 other nodes, it is already higher than 1/2 even if the initiator is unknown. When the initiator is known the probability of compromise rises above 3/4. Furthermore those are lower bounds, and the adversary is very likely to be able to do better in practice.

The analysis of bridging we present is centered around the probability of successful attack P_{bridge}. This represents the probability that an adversary using the techniques describe is able to infer *with absolute certainty* the link between an incoming and outgoing message or stream. Even when this is not possible, bridging will lead to a severe reduction in anonymity. Despite the theoretical number of output streams being w, an adversary is very likely able to reduce the candidate output streams, even if they never manage to isolate a single one. This can be used to reduce anonymity and to skew the probability distributions describing who might be the sender or receiver of a message.

Similarly, an adversary with some incomplete information about which nodes are known to which users might still perform some variant of bridging to reduce anonymity. The adversary could also perform more sophisticated variants on bridging. For example there may be relations between the sets of nodes known to the other originators of streams that affect what patterns are possible amongst the observed streams that are not attacked and what can thus be inferred about the attacked stream. In that sense, our P_{bridge} actually represents only the simplest form of bridging attack. Bridging can also be performed alongside other attacks, integrating different constraints of anonymous paths like length, or the lack of cycles. This will increase the probability of successful bridging. Measures of anonymity [16, 5] taking into account those effects could be used to quantify any reduction in anonymity, but deriving analytic results in this setting might be hard. This is a promising avenue for future research.

4 Conclusion

In this paper we have examined effects of partial network knowledge on anonymity, based on both what is known and what is not known by those building routes through an anonymity network.

We presented a simple analytic bound on route fingerprinting, which is based on what route builders know about the network, and introduced a new attack, route bridging, which adds consideration of what clients do not know about the network. We also proved analytic bounds for different cases of route bridging. We illustrated our results on the initially published Tarzan design, which we found to be vulnerable to our attacks.

Successful attacks on Enigma in WWII were based on a property of the device that it would never produce an output letter that was the same as its input. Using this "nonoccurrence" statistical analysis made it possible to break encrypted messages. With the introduction of route-bridging attacks we show again that in security one must pay attention not only to what can happen but also to what cannot happen.

Our results also suggest that any attempt at scaling anonymity networks by limiting node discovery to a level below full network discovery should be carefully compared to simple partitioning as a first test. While it may be possible to maintain anonymity by such limitation, one may obtain better results, at least in this regard, simply by partitioning. On the other hand, our results also showed that the threat of epistemic attack is substantially mitigated in a client-server architecture such as that of Tor, and there is reason for cautious optimism that this threat will not preclude scaling of the design.

Wright et al. [24] suggested that to protect against passive logging attacks one might be better off choosing both entry guards and exit guards. For Tor and other three-hop anonymity systems, however, random middle nodes could do route fingerprinting with $k = 3$ and in fact a very small n as well. That is, the middle node will see both ends; so $k = 3$. And, because guards are used at both ends, any client will be choosing entry and exit nodes from a small persistent set. Current entry guards for Tor start with a default of three nodes. Which entry and exit guards are chosen by a client would not be directly apparent to the adversary from node discovery or from observation of a single route selection but would instead have to be discovered by observing repeated connections. An adversary owning a single node was able to quickly uncover entry guards by watching repeated connections (at least for circuits used by hidden services) on the live Tor network of several hundred nodes that existed in early 2006 [13]. Clearly this requires further examination. As we have noted, having orders of magnitude more clients than servers substantially diminishes such threats for Tor itself. But, vulnerability would grow if the ratio of clients to servers were to drop and the size of the network to persist or grow. This seems to be a basic difficulty for pure peer-to-peer anonymity designs unless we can anonymize network discovery without having the anonymization that the network can provide once discovered.

Acknowledgments. We would like to thank Richard Clayton, with whom the first versions or route fingerprinting were developed, and Roger Dingledine of the Tor project, for his keen interest in what happens, security-wise, when nodes only have a partial view of the network. Aaron Johnson and Emilia Käsper each read a draft of this paper and offered many helpful suggestions, for which we are grateful to them. Work by Paul Syverson supported by ONR.

References

1. Borisov, N., Danezis, G., Mittal, P., Tabriz, P.: Denial of service or denial of security? How attacks on reliability can compromise anonymity. In: De Capitani di Vimercati, S., Syverson, P., Evans, D. (eds.) CCS 2007: Proceedings of the 14th ACM Conference on Computer and Communications Security, pp. 92–102. ACM Press, New York (2007)
2. Boucher, P., Shostack, A., Goldberg, I.: Freedom systems 2.0 architecture. White paper, Zero Knowledge Systems, Inc. (December 2000)
3. Chaum, D.: Untraceable electronic mail, return addresses, and digital pseudonyms. Communications of the ACM 4(2), 84–88 (1981)
4. Danezis, G., Clayton, R.: Route fingerprinting in anonymous communications. In: Sixth IEEE International Conference on Peer-to-Peer Computing, P2P 2006, pp. 69–72. IEEE Computer Society Press, Los Alamitos (2006)

5. Díaz, C., Seys, S., Claessens, J., Preneel, B.: Towards measuring anonymity. In: Dingledine, R., Syverson, P.F. (eds.) PET 2002. LNCS, vol. 2482, pp. 54–68. Springer, Heidelberg (2003)

6. Dingledine, R., Mathewson, N., Syverson, P.: Tor: The second-generation onion router. In: Proceedings of the 13th USENIX Security Symposium, August 2004, pp. 303–319. USENIX Association (2004)

7. Feigenbaum, J., Johnson, A., Syverson, P.: A probabilistic analysis of onion routing in a black-box model. In: Yu, T. (ed.) WPES 2007: Proceedings of the 2007 ACM Workshop on Privacy in the Electronic Society, pp. 1–10. ACM Press, New York (2007)

8. Freedman, M.J., Morris, R.: Tarzan: A peer-to-peer anonymizing network layer. In: Atluri, V. (ed.) Proceedings of the 9th ACM Conference on Computer and Communications Security, CCS 2002, November 2002, pp. 193–206. ACM Press, New York (2002)

9. Freedman, M.J., Sit, E., Cates, J., Morris, R.: Introducing Tarzan, a peer-to-peer anonymizing network layer. In: Druschel, P., Kaashoek, M.F., Rowstron, A. (eds.) IPTPS 2002. LNCS, vol. 2429, pp. 121–129. Springer, Heidelberg (2002)

10. Goldschlag, D.M., Reed, M.G., Syverson, P.F.: Hiding routing information. In: Anderson, R. (ed.) IH 1996. LNCS, vol. 1174, pp. 137–150. Springer, Heidelberg (1996)

11. Murdoch, S.J., Zieliński, P.: Sampled traffic analysis by internet-exchange-level adversaries. In: Borisov, N., Golle, P. (eds.) PET 2007, vol. 4776, pp. 167–183. Springer, Heidelberg (2007)

12. Nambiar, A., Wright, M.: Salsa: A structured approach to large-scale anonymity. In: Wright, R.N., De Capitani di Vimercati, S., Shmatikov, V. (eds.) CCS 2006: Proceedings of the 13th ACM Conference on Computer and Communications Security, October 2006, pp. 17–26. ACM Press, New York (2006)

13. Øverlier, L., Syverson, P.: Locating hidden servers. In: IEEE Symposium on Security and Privacy (S&P 2006), May 2006, pp. 100–114. IEEE Computer Society Press, Los Alamitos (2006)

14. Reiter, M., Rubin, A.: Crowds: Anonymity for web transactions. ACM Transactions on Information and System Security 1(1), 66–92 (1998)

15. Rennhard, M., Plattner, B.: Practical anonymity for the masses with morphmix. In: Juels, A. (ed.) FC 2004. LNCS, vol. 3110, pp. 233–250. Springer, Heidelberg (2004)

16. Serjantov, A., Danezis, G.: Towards an information theoretic metric for anonymity. In: Dingledine, R., Syverson, P.F. (eds.) PET 2002. LNCS, vol. 2482, pp. 41–53. Springer, Heidelberg (2003)

17. Serjantov, A., Dingledine, R., Syverson, P.: From a trickle to a flood: Active attacks on several mix types. In: Petitcolas, F.A.P. (ed.) IH 2002. LNCS, vol. 2578, pp. 36–52. Springer, Heidelberg (2003)

18. Serjantov, A., Sewell, P.: Passive attack analysis for connection-based anonymity systems. In: Snekkenes, E., Gollmann, D. (eds.) ESORICS 2003. LNCS, vol. 2808, pp. 116–131. Springer, Heidelberg (2003)

19. Shmatikov, V.: Probabilistic model checking of an anonymity system. Journal of Computer Security 12(3-4), 355–377 (2004)

20. Stoica, I., Morris, R., Liben-Nowell, D., Karger, D.R., Kaashoek, M.F., Dabek, F., Balakrishnan, H.: Chord: a scalable peer-to-peer lookup protocol for internet applications. IEEE/ACM Trans. Netw. 11(1), 17–32 (2003)

21. Syverson, P., Reed, M., Goldschlag, D.: Onion Routing access configurations. In: Proceedings of the DARPA Information Survivability Conference & Exposition, DISCEX 2000, vol. 1, pp. 34–40. IEEE Computer Society Press, Los Alamitos (1999)
22. Syverson, P., Tsudik, G., Reed, M., Landwehr, C.: Towards an analysis of onion routing security. In: Federrath, H. (ed.) Designing Privacy Enhancing Technologies. LNCS, vol. 2009, pp. 96–114. Springer, Heidelberg (2001)
23. Venkitasubramaniam, P., He, T., Tong, L.: Anonymous networking amidst eavesdroppers (October 2007) arXiv:0710.4903v1 at arxiv.org
24. Wright, M., Adler, M., Levine, B.N., Shields, C.: Defending anonymous communication against passive logging attacks. In: 2003 IEEE Symposium on Security and Privacy, May 2003, pp. 28–43. IEEE Computer Society Press, Los Alamitos (2003)
25. Wright, M., Adler, M., Levine, B.N., Shields, C.: The Predecessor Attack: An Analysis of a Threat to Anonymous Communications Systems. ACM Transactions on Information and System Security (TISSEC) 4(7), 489–522 (2004)
26. Zhuang, L., Zhou, F., Zhao, B.Y., Rowstron, A.I.T.: Cashmere: Resilient anonymous routing. In: 2nd USENIX Symposium on Networked Systems Design and Implementation (NSDI 2005), pp. 301–314. USENIX Association (2005)

Chattering Laptops

Tuomas Aura[1], Janne Lindqvist[2], Michael Roe[1], and Anish Mohammed[3]

[1] Microsoft Research, Cambridge, UK
[2] Helsinki University of Technology, Finland
[3] Royal Holloway, University of London, UK

Abstract. Mobile computer users often have a false sense of anonymity when they connect to the Internet at cafes, hotels, airports or other public places. In this paper, we analyze information leaked by mobile computers to the local access link when they are outside their home domain. While most application data can be encrypted, there is no similar protection for signaling messages in the lower layers of the protocol stack. We found that all layers of the protocol stack leak various plaintext identifiers of the user, the computer and their affiliations to the local link, which a casual attacker can observe. This violates the user's sense of privacy and may make the user or computer vulnerable to further attacks. It is, however, not possible to disable the offending protocols because many of them are critical to the mobile user experience. We argue that the most promising solutions to the information leaks are to filter outbound data, in particular name resolution requests, and to disable unnecessary service discovery depending on the network location. This is because most information leaks result from failed attempts by roaming computers to connect to services that are not available in the current access network.

Keywords: Privacy, anonymity, mobile computing, wireless networks, network location awareness.

1 Introduction

When mobile computer users connect to the Internet at wireless hotspots, cafes, hotel rooms, airport lounges and other public places, they tend to think that nobody can recognize them. Some are aware that sophisticated techniques, such as correlating the appearances of the network interface card's MAC address or other statistically unique information, could be used to trace them. Few know that their computer is openly broadcasting information about them to the local network, including usernames, computer names, and identifiers linkable to their employer, school or home. In this paper we explore the identifiers leaked by mobile computers to the access network.

Our attacker is a passive observer at the same local link, who has no resources for making global observations or skills for sophisticated analysis of the data but who is curious enough to capture network traffic and to see what other network users explicitly tell about themselves. The attacker may be operating the local network or access point, or he may be just another user in the same network.

N. Borisov and I. Goldberg (Eds.): PETS 2008, LNCS 5134, pp. 167–186, 2008.

The user's own computer is not malicious but leaks information accidentally or because of conflicting design goals. We focus on business users whose computers are members of a managed domain.

There is no great drama in being identified in a public place. Most people, however, prefer not to wear a name tag after leaving the office and enjoy the privacy and protection afforded by the relative anonymity. Sometimes, announcing a person's name or affiliation could expose them to further attacks. This vulnerability also applies to computers: a random computer at a cafe is not particularly interesting to a hacker but one belonging to a well-known organization might invite attacks.

Computers perform many tasks automatically without the user's knowing; things just work. The automatic tasks often involve the discovery of network services, which means sending packets to the network. These packets usually identify the service and often also the user. It should be noted that the automatic actions happen by design: most users would probably not want to see any additional dialog windows asking for their permission to go ahead, and disabling the automatic services would destroy the seamless mobility experience that software vendors are hard trying to create.

In this paper, we are mainly interested in identifiers in signaling protocols, packet headers and communication metadata, that is, data that cannot be easily encrypted at the application level. It is often falsely assumed that end-to-end encryption solves all privacy issues apart from traffic analysis. In real networks, not all communication is end-to-end. There are many protocols that are executed with the access network and with global network infrastructure. For example, the DHCP and DNS protocols cannot be protected by encryption. Yet, these protocols reveal all kinds of information about the mobile host. Much work has been done on randomizing the most obvious permanent identifiers (MAC and IP addresses), and, on the attack side, on fingerprinting mobile hosts based on statistical characteristics. In this paper, we consider more explicit user, computer and organization identifiers such as usernames. Clearly, randomized addresses only help privacy if the higher-layer identifier leaks are also controlled, and the statistical attacks matter only if there is no easier way to identify the target.

We use domain-joined Windows XP and Vista laptops as examples throughout the paper because they are common in business use and perform many tasks automatically. Domain members have more identifiers and credentials than typical standalone computers and they tend to access more services. Thus, there is more information that could potentially be leaked.

This paper makes the following contributions: we identify network chatter by mobile computers as a major threat to mobile user privacy, develop a tool for detecting identifier leaks, and use it to examine network traces captured from business laptops. We analyze the causes of the leaks and describe a solution based on network-location awareness. The lessons of this paper could be summarized by saying that using a laptop computer is akin to wearing a name badge that reveals the person's identity and affiliation, and that not telling everyone who you are turns out to be surprisingly hard because there are so many name badges in places that you never knew about. We argue that most of the leaks are caused by unnecessary network chatter, mainly failed attempts at name resolution and server connections, which could be avoided by designing software to be aware of the network locations.

The rest of the paper is organized as follows. We overview related work in Section 2. Section 3 introduces the analysis tools. Section 4 details the sources of identifier leaks. In Section 5, we analyze the findings. Section 6 suggests solutions to the problem and Section 7 concludes the paper.

2 Related Work

Information leaks from mobile computers

Information leaks caused by unencrypted network traffic have been noted many times in the literature. There are few systematic studies, however. Kowitz and Cranor [KC05] study how user attitudes change when they are explicitly shown plaintext strings from the network traffic. The strings are mostly application data such as email, instant messages and web searches, but the paper also mentions NetBIOS as one source of information. We see the information leaks as a technical problem rather than as a question of user awareness.

Saponas et al. [SLH07] bring attention to ubiquitous computing devices which can be traced by their unique identifiers or reveal which content the user is downloading. Akritidis et al. [ACL+07] mention RSS subscriptions, plaintext instant messaging, web-browser cookies, and the hostname in the DHCP request (see Section 4.3) as means for identifying mobile users. Pang et al. [PGM+07] suggest confidential discovery of wireless access points.

DNS was originally designed for fixed networks but is increasingly used as a reachability mechanism for roaming hosts. Guha and Francis [GF07] point out that dynamic DNS can be used to query and map a mobile host's location. Broido et al. [BSF06] discuss unnecessary DNS updates for private address ranges, which may also leak information about the host to the foreign access network. In this paper, we discuss more basic operations of DNS and observe that most privacy-compromising data is revealed unnecessarily.

Anonymity and routing

Anonymity in communications networks has many meanings. Traditionally, the main goal has been end-to-end anonymity, i.e., to hide the client's identity from the servers or peers to which it connects over the Internet. Anonymous routing systems, such as the mix networks introduced by Chaum [Cha81], hide the connection between senders and recipients of messages also from third parties who are assumed to monitor network traffic globally. Onion routing, as described by Syverson et al. [SGR97] extends the idea to hidden servers, i.e., to hiding the recipient from the sender. These mechanisms assume a very strong attacker model and are expensive to implement, yet tend to be fragile against analysis methods that take advantage of the non-ideal characteristics of the underlying technologies. The most common applications for anonymous routing are in content distribution (e.g., Freenet by Clarke et al. [CSWH00]) and anonymous web browsing and censorship resistance (e.g., Tor by Dingledine et al. [DMS04]), where there is a strong incentive for hiding the identities of the communicating parties. Application-specific anonymity systems include remailers and anonymizing web proxies (e.g., Mixmaster by Möller et al. [MCPS03] and Crowds by Reiter and Rubin [RR98]). Simple HTTP proxies and native address translation (NAT) also provide some privacy benefits. The same routing mechanisms can be used for location privacy, i.e., to hide a mobile computer's location from its peers. Mobility protocols, like Mobile IPv6 [JP02], achieve some level of location privacy by routing all packets to and from the mobile via a fixed proxy.

Despite the number and diversity of end-to-end anonymity mechanisms, they share the common goal of hiding the mobile's identity or location from peer nodes over the Internet. Our work differs from this in that we want to protect against observers at the mobile's local link. Our attacker model is also different in the sense that the attacker is assumed to be present only at the access network.

Randomized identifiers

Communications protocols use various kinds of identifiers and addresses that can act as identifiers. For example, the MAC address of a network interface is a globally unique identifier. IPv6 addresses often have the MAC address embedded in their bits in order to guarantee uniqueness [TN98]. A common solution to the issues caused by unique identifiers is to replace them with random, periodically changing values. There is a standard way of generating IPv6 addresses with a pseudo-random number generator [ND01]. Similar randomization has been suggested for the MAC address by Gruteser and Grunwald [GG03b] and many others. The identifier changes have to be carefully timed, with possible silent periods, to maximize anonymity protection and to minimize disruption to communications, which is also noted by Beresford and Stajano [BS03] and Jiang et al. [JWH07]. Clearly, unencrypted higher-level identifiers such as IP addresses have to be changed at the same time as the MAC address. Mobility protocols can be used to guarantee continuity of end-to-end communications over the identifier changes, e.g., as suggested by Lindqvist and Takkinen [LT06]. Since the issues with IP and MAC addresses have already been extensively covered in the literature, we will focus on other identifiers.

The level of anonymity provided by such mechanisms can be measured as the size of the anonymity set or as entropy (see Sweeney [Swe02], Serjantov and Danezis [SD02] or Díaz et al. [DSCP02]), both of which measure the level of uncertainly about the identity of a node. Given the number of users and mobile devices on the Internet, the hope is that the uncertainly will be very large. The academic literature has concentrated on theoretically strong or at least measurable guarantees of anonymity and location privacy. The work presented in this paper differs from the literature in that we consider a rather more elementary goal: not explicitly telling everyone who you are, which turns out to be surprisingly hard.

Host fingerprinting

Fingerprinting of mobile radios based on their non-ideal characteristics is an old military intelligence technique which enables tracing the movements of individual stations. The same kind of analysis has been applied to wireless LAN cards, e.g., by Gerdes et al. [GDMR06]. The analysis of radio signals requires sophisticated hardware and skilled operators, however. A more practical approach is to fingerprint hosts based on their higher-level characteristics such as the MAC-layer capabilities and configuration, which can be combined with network-layer traffic-analysis data for better accuracy (Franklin et al. [FMT06], Greenstein et al. [GGP+07] and Pang et al. [PGG+07]). Some hardware characteristics, such as clock skew and temperature variations (Kohno et al. [KBC05] and Murdoch [Mur06]) can be used to fingerprint hardware remotely. The same techniques could be used to identify devices on the local link. In effect, the hardware and communications fingerprint becomes a unique identifier for the device and user.

Our work differs from the device fingerprinting in that we concentrate on explicit identifiers instead of implicit ones. For example Kohno at al. use the set of peer IP addresses as an implicit identifier that is treated as a set of numbers. We, instead, record the DNS names to which the host connects and look for ones that reveal the client identity or affiliation.

Information flow

One approach to preventing information leaks is to analyze information flow in the system. In the terminology of multi-level security, the user identifiers are high input data, from which information should not leak to the low output, i.e., messages sent to the network. By proving information-flow properties, such as non-interference [GM82], we could be certain that the system does not leak the high data. While such models remain theoretical, there has been progress, e.g., in the language-based proof techniques of Sabelfeld and Myers [SM03].

On the more practical side, we can trace the information flow dynamically in a running system. Most such mechanisms aim to protect system integrity, rather than confidentiality of data. In the Perl programming language, untrusted inputs can be marked as tainted and the tainting is propagated to any values derived from them. Chow et al. [CPG04] use data tainting in a simulated system to analyze the lifetime of confidential data, such as passwords, in the system memory while Zhao et al. [ZCYH05] show evidence that taint propagation can be traced in real time in a production system. Yumerefendi et al. [YMC07] suggest a clever way of detecting data leaks by executing a parallel copy of the process with random bits replacing the confidential data; if the outputs differ, some information is leaking. The same techniques could be used to flag identifiers and other anonymity-compromising data and to detect whether they are being sent to the network. We consider data tainting a potentially useful approach; however, the solutions suggested in this paper are even more practical in nature.

Privacy policy and preferences

Another approach to privacy is not to discuss the technology but the policies. In addition to legal frameworks, there are several technical policy frameworks for

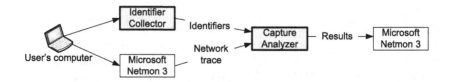

Fig. 1. Data flow between the analysis tool components

location privacy [Zug03][CJBMM04][GG03a][Pet02] and languages for expressing preferences on the disclosure of personally identifiable information [Cra02] [AHK03]. We do not explicitly discuss privacy policies or user preferences in this paper. In Section 6, however, we suggest an implicit privacy preference mechanism that interprets any networking functionally explicitly enabled by the user as a policy decision.

3 Tool for Analyzing Network Chatter

We initially became concerned over information leaks to the access network when looking at network traces. As we started to comb through them for previously unknown issues, it soon became apparent that a more systematic approach was needed. For this reason, we developed a tool for detecting leaked identifiers in network traces. The tool is defensive in the sense that it can only be used to analyze leaks from one's own computer. This limitation allows us to find offending user, machine and organization identifiers in places that have not been previously catalogued. We have previously used a similar tool to detect user identifiers in electronic documents [AKR06].

The general structure of the tool is shown in Figure 1. It consists of two modules: Identifier Collector and Capture Analyzer. The Netmon network monitor is used for recording network traffic and for viewing the discovered information leaks in their context.

3.1 Collecting Personal Identifiers

The Identifier Collector gathers the user's personal identifiers, which will then be used as search strings in the capture file analysis. It finds identifiers from the local computer and from the active directory (AD), which is a directory service for Windows computers. The identifiers include the username, machine name, NetBIOS group, domain name, globally unique identifiers (GUIDs), names of various domain-specific services, as well as less obvious identifiers such as postal address and telephone number. An alternative would be to let the user type in the sensitive identifiers but we wanted the tool to be as automatic as possible. In addition to improving usability for non-expert users, automation makes the results reproducible.

3.2   Capture-File Analysis

The Capture Analyzer module searches for the identifiers in a network capture file. We use two different search algorithms for this purpose. The main difficulties were that the format of the captured packets is complex, variable and sometimes unknown, and that we would like to detect information leaks in any protocol layer or data field.

Data formats

One approach to the search would be to parse the packets in the same way as in network monitoring software such as Ethereal, Wireshark or Netmon and then search each data field separately, taking into account its data format, for the offending identifiers. A limitation of this approach is that we might miss some data fields that are not correctly identified by the parser. For this reason, we decided to search through the raw packet data using algorithms that can handle a large number of data and text encodings. We parse the packets and pinpoint any suspicious protocol fields only after detecting identifiers in the raw packet data. The tool offers two different tradeoffs between speed and completeness of the search.

Simple string search

The Aho-Corasick algorithm [Aho75] performs a fast text search for multiple search strings. We encode textual search strings, such as a username, with a number of common string encodings: ASCII, Unicode UTF8, UTF16 in big- and little-endian byte order, and UTF32. The search is case-insensitive and ignores accents and common character variations. Thus, for example, the character values aàáâãäåAÀÁÂÃÄÅ are all considered matches for each other. Short strings are also encoded as NetBIOS identifiers, which have their own peculiar format. Additionally, we look for copies of the MAC address outside the Ethernet header and for Windows GUIDs of the user, computer and domain. Binary identifiers are treated as special cases based on their specific characteristics. The number of encodings has been tuned to keep the tool speed acceptable for fast interactive use.

Regular expression search

The second string search algorithm aims to perform a more complete search than the simple string search above, which was optimized for speed and not assurance. With a slower search algorithm we wanted to detect any identifiers that may be missed by the simple string search. Regular expressions provide flexibility to support multiple layers of data encoding. We start with a simple tree-shaped expression constructed from the original search strings and expand this by replacing each character in the expression with its different encodings. This is done recursively for multiple layers of encodings: upper and cases; accents and other character variations; URL, XML and C escapes and numeric representations; and, finally, Unicode and other character encodings. The resulting regular expression is large but represents an even larger number of multi-layer encodings of the search strings. Figure 2 shows a simplified example of how the

original character: N
upper and lower case, accents: (n|ñ|N|Ñ)
various escape notations:
(n|(((\x?)|%|(&#?)| |-)0*((156)|(110)|(6e));?)|ñ|(((\x?)|%|(&#?)| |-)0*((361)|(241)|(f1));?)|N|(((\x?)|%|(&#?)| |-)0*((116)|(78)|(4e));?)|Ñ|(((\x?)|%|(&#?)| |-)0*((321)|(209)|(d1));?))
ASCII, UTF-8, little and big-Endian UTF-16:
((00*6e)|((((00*78)?00*5c)|(00*25)|((00*23)?00*26)|(00*20)|(00*2d))(00*30)*((00*3100*3500*36)|(00*3100*3100*30)|(00*3600*65))(00*3b)?)|(00*(3f|(c3b1)|f1))|((((00*78)?00*5c)|(00*25)|((00*23)?00*26)|(00*20)|(00*2d))(00*30)*((00*3300*3600*31)|(00*3200*3400*31))(00*6600*31))(00*3b)?)|(00*4e)|((((00*78)?00*5c)|(00*25)|((00*23)?00*26)|(00*20)|(00*2d))(00*30)*((00*3100*3100*36)|(00*3700*38)|(00*3400*65))(00*3b)?)|(00*(3f|(c391)|d1))|((((00*78)?00*5c)|(00*25)|((00*23)?00*26)|(00*20)|(00*2d))(00*30)*((00*3300*3200*31)|(00*3200*3000*39)|(00*6400*31))(00*3b)?))

Fig. 2. Regular expressions for encodings of 'N'

regular expression for one character of a search string is constructed. Because of the expression size, the search is done with a non-deterministic automaton, which means it consumes a lot of memory. We tuned the number of encoding layers and their complexity to keep the memory consumption for even a large set of identifiers below 1GB. The aim was to keep the search time under an hour for large datasets.

3.3 Integration with Netmon 3

The Capture Analyzer works together with the Microsoft Netmon 3 network-monitoring software. It takes as input a network capture file and a list of identifiers and produces a Netmon filter that lists the matching packets. This is loaded into Netmon for detailed manual analysis of the information leaks in the capture. Currently, the tool can only be used for offline analysis.

3.4 Discussion of Completeness

It is rather difficult to assess the completeness of the search. We have enhanced the tool to detect all classes of identifier leaks that we initially knew about, suspected, or found by manual methods. The tool has some specific limitations, however. It cannot find intentionally obfuscated information, which falls outside our attacker model, and it cannot search encrypted data. Currently, we do not search through compressed data or other encodings that do not respect byte boundaries (e.g., Base64 and uuencode). Fortunately, such encodings are rarely used in signaling messages below the application layer.

Since we look at the capture files as raw bytes and do not parse the packets, we cannot detect data that spans across multiple packets. The most likely reason for this to occur is when an identifier has been split into two TCP segments and, thus, is non-contiguous in the packet capture data. In the future, we may enhance the tool to support TCP segmentation. Fragmented IP datagrams could pose a similar problem. We initially planned to implement defragmentation at the IP layer but failed to do this because the sample data did not contain any fragmented packets.

Some false positives are produced by the case- and accent-insensitive search, which means that 3- or 4-character names have some accidental matches in binary files (e.g., "tĭÑå" would match "Tina". The number of false positives was acceptably small for the purposes of research. If the same algorithm is used for routine monitoring, it would be easy filter recurring false positives. Another class of false positives arises if the user is affiliated with an organization whose name occurs frequently in network traffic (e.g., Google) or is a common word (e.g., Time).

Active attacks are entirely beyond the scope of this paper. They are, however, not as difficult to implement as one might first believe. In fact, it may be easier for the attacker to induce the mobile computer into executing a specific protocol, such as IKE or DHCP, than to sit passively on the network and wait for events to occur spontaneously. We plan to continue this work in the direction of active-attack analysis.

4   Information Leaks to Local Link

This section reports findings from the analysis of network traces collected at various locations using domain-joined computers running Windows XP and Vista and a range of client software that is commonly found on business laptops. The analysis was done with the search tools described in the previous section.

4.1   DNS

The domain name system (DNS) is a directory service that resolves human-readable host names into IP addresses. The literature (see Section 2) already considers the privacy issues created by dynamic updates to the DNS. We look at a more basic operation: name resolution.

DNS queries

Connecting to online services may reveal information about the client. We will discuss examples of such services in the following sections. However, before connecting to almost any service, the client will resolve the DNS name of the server using the local DNS in the access network. Consequently, the easiest way to track the activities of a mobile computer is to record its DNS requests. For example, if the computer connects to a VPN gateway of its organization (e.g., vpn-gw.contoso.com), a look at a DNS log is sufficient to identify the company. The user may not be aware that many such queries happen automatically, without an explicit user action.

Resolving private names

Many organizations use a private IP address range (e.g., 10.0.0.0/8) for their internal network and a private DNS zone (e.g., *.private.contoso.com or *.contoso.local) to name the computers on the private network. The private names can only be resolved by the local DNS server at the intranet and are not visible from outside. DNS resolvers on client computers do not, however, know when they are in the intranet. Thus, a mobile computer may try to resolve a private name when it is roaming outside the private network. The name resolution will fail but the DNS request reveals the name of a server and organization.

Default suffixes

Since human users prefer to type short computer names (e.g., hobbit) rather than fully qualified domain names (FQDN) (e.g., hobbit.sales. contoso.com.), the resolver automatically appends default suffixes to the name. For example, when resolving hobbit, the computer typically queries for hobbit.sales.contoso.com and hobbit.contoso.com, in that order. Originally, there was a security reason for trying the longer name and, thus, the more local name space first: it prevented users from accidentally entering their password to a prompt presented by a more remote host than the one they intended to access.

The default DNS suffix for stationary computers used to be configured either manually or by DHCP. Mobile computers may have two possible suffixes: a primary suffix from their home domain and a connection-specific suffix obtained from DHCP at the access network. We are concerned about the primary suffix because it reveals the mobile host's affiliation. When the computer tries to resolve any DNS name, such as google.com, it will start by querying for google.com.sales.contoso.com. This means that any DNS query will leak the mobile's default domain suffix to the access link and to the local DNS server.

4.2   Other Name Resolution Protocols

NetBIOS over TCP (NBT) provides another name service, which is mainly used in closed Windows domains (or workgroups) at workplaces and homes. Computers broadcast name queries to the local network and answer them directly or via WINS proxy.

NetBIOS lookup

Similar to DNS, NetBIOS name lookups reveal to the access network the names of the services to which the user or computer is connecting. The names are broadcast to the local link and, thus, can be heard by any computer on the same access link, even on a switched wire network. Unlike the hierarchical DNS names, NetBIOS names are not globally unique. For this reason, the protocol is rarely needed when roaming outside the user's workplace or home, yet it is typically enabled everywhere.

WINS registration

When a computer connects to a network, it may also try to register its NetBIOS name and group in the WINS server. Since it does not know whether a server exists in this network, the registration is attempted regardless of the location. The registration attempt reveals the computer name (e.g., hobbit), which is typically the same as the first part of the FQDN, and the computer's Windows domain or workgroup (e.g., sales or contoso). Again, this information is broadcast to the access link.

LLMNR

The link-local multicast name resolution (LLMNR) protocol is also intended for the local link. Unlike NetBIOS, it also works over IPv6. The queries are sent as link-scope multicast. Although we have not observed this protocol in actual use, Windows Vista laptops sometimes send spontaneous LLMNR requests for their own name in order to detect possible name conflicts.

4.3 DHCP

The dynamic host configuration protocol (DHCP) is used to configure a host with network-specific parameters such as an IP address and the local DNS suffix. It is often the first protocol executed when a computer attaches to a network. A typical execution consists of two request-response pairs: the client broadcasts a DISCOVER message and receives one or more OFFERs from servers. It then sends a REQUEST for one of the offers and the chosen server responds with an ACK. The main purpose of the protocol is to transfer configuration information from the server to the client, i.e., to the mobile host. Thus, the client does not necessarily need to reveal anything about itself. In practice, however, clients do tell quite a lot.

Host identification

The DHCP protocol allows the client to identify itself by sending its hostname in the DISCOVER message. This enables the network to select host-specific parameters such as a permanently assigned IP address. Hostnames are unique only to a specific domain and, thus, have little significance to a DHCP server at a foreign network. In principle, the identifier could be simply left out while roaming. Unfortunately, when the client sends the DISCOVER message, it may not yet know whether it is connected to the domain network or roaming elsewhere.

DNS registration

The DHCP client may want to register its new address in the DNS. The client itself can connect to the a dynamic DNS server at its home organization to update the forward record, i.e., the mapping from name to IP address. The DHCP server, on the other hand, is responsible for updating the backward record from the newly allocated IP address to the DNS name. Within a Windows domain, the DHCP server may also update the forward record on the client's behalf. Either way, the DHCP server needs to know the client DNS name. For this reason, a Windows client sends its FQDN to the DHCP server in the REQUEST message. It does this regardless of the network location and, thus, reveals the host name and domain suffix to the access network.

4.4 Domain Controller

The domain controller (DC) is the authentication and directory server for a particular Windows domain. It implements a version of the LDAP directory-access protocol. When a client is configured to be a member of a domain, it always tries to find the domain controller of the network. It performs a DNS query for a service resource to find the domain controller, e.g., LDAP._TCP.dc._msdcs.sales. contoso.com. If the DC is found, the client knows it is on the intranet and starts sending LDAP queries to the controller. On the other hand, if the DC is not found, the client (Netlogon service) may try to use a cached IP address to send the queries. For stationary computers and ones that move in the intranet, this improves reliability in case of DNS failures. For roaming computers, however, the attempts to connect to the DC will fail anyway.

Both the domain name and the cached IP address will reveal the mobile's affiliation. The IP address will be cached only for 15 minutes. We found, however, that if the computer was put into a sleep-saving mode at the intranet and resumed later in a foreign network, the cached addresses were still used for several minutes.

4.5   File Shares and Printers

Operating systems such as Windows try to improve the user's roaming experience by discovering previously used network services and setting them up for quick access. This can, however, result in unnecessary network chatter and failed connection attempts.

Mounted network drives

The user in Windows can assign a drive letter to a network share so that it appears as a local disk (e.g., map \\contoso-srv-2\alice\ as the Z: drive). These shares are automatically mounted when the user logs in or connects to a network. In order to find out whether the share is available, the client needs to probe the server. The attempt to resolve the server's DNS or NetBIOS name can be seen by anyone observing network traffic at the access link. Although we tested only Windows shares, automounted NFS volumes would presumably cause similar privacy issues.

Shortcuts to network shares

Shortcuts to network file shares on other machines may cause similar attempts at name resolution. These are usually accessed only after a user action but it is not always obvious to the user which actions trigger the network access. For example, right-clicking a shortcut may cause an attempt to connect to the server.

Printers

Windows saves information on all printers that have ever been configured for use, unless they are explicitly deleted. A roaming user may sometimes use a local network printer at the access network. These printers accumulate into the printer list on the client computer, which many users never clean. When the user views the list of printers, the computer automatically tries to connect to the printers and shows which ones are online. These connection attempts may reveal not only the user's organization but where the user has been roaming. For example, one of our test laptops readily revealed to the network that it had been printing in three cities on different continents.

4.6   IKE and Kerberos

IKE with GSSAPI authentication

One of the most surprising sources of information leaks is the Internet key exchange (IKE) protocol. IKE is designed to protect the participants' identities against sniffing (in the main mode, which is implemented by Windows). This protection is achieved by first performing an unauthenticated Diffie-Hellman key exchange and by encrypting the following authentication with the session key. The identity protection is considered one of the main security features of IKE.

The standard IKE authentication methods are based on shared keys and public-key certificates. Windows extends this with Kerberos authentication using the GSSAPI [PS01]. The client requests Kerberos authentication in the first message it sends to the server. The client then obtains a Kerberos ticket from the authentication center (AC) and uses this ticket for authentication in IKE.

The most obvious information leak happens because the GSSAPI authentication method sends the client computer name and domain to the server in the first IKE message (in the SA payload). This may not appear to be a privacy issue because Kerberos authentication is used only in the intranet and, thus, the data should never be sent when the computer is roaming in a foreign access network. In reality, the leak does sometimes occur when the client has just moved from the intranet to a foreign access network (usually via sleep mode) and applications still attempt connections to intranet servers based on previously resolved IP addresses.

Kerberos ticket request and ticket

Windows clients also sometimes attempt to connect the Kerberos server while roaming. The ticket request contains the client computer name in plaintext. Since this is a rare occurrence, we were not able to establish the exact cause of the request. Since the Kerberos server is usually not reachable from outside the intranet, the client will not receive a ticket. If it did, the ticket would further reveal the name of the server for which the ticket is intended.

4.7   TLS/SSL

Plaintext certificates

The TLS handshake protocol sends the certificates unencrypted over the network. Usually, only the server is authenticated and only the server certificate is sent. This means that if the client connects to a secure web server of its own organization, the name of the organization will appear on the wire. Sometimes, TLS is used also for client authentication. This may happen, for example, when the client application is not a web browser but a web-service client, an email client or a TLS-VPN client. In that case, the plaintext client certificate and name are seen on the network, which allows easy and reliable identification of the client.

EAP-TLS

Secure 802.11 wireless LANs do not leak much information to those who are not authorized to join the network. However, wireless networks in managed domains may use certificates and the EAP-TLS protocol for client authentication. The TLS handshake in EAP-TLS reveals the client identity to anyone listening, even to those who themselves are not authorized to access the network. This problem has been addressed by a recent privacy enhancement to the EAP-TLS protocol [SAH08].

4.8   Application Metadata

It is clear that plaintext access to email, web pages, search engines and other online services leaks confidential data. For example, we found unencrypted instant messaging (IM) clients sending not only the messages themselves but also the username, real name, gender, birth date, post code, buddy list and block list over the network. Unencrypted SIP signaling for IM or VoIP also reveals the user name and possibly who his contacts are. All this information could, however, be protected from sniffing by encrypting the messages between the client and the server.

A particularly interesting case is the iTunes music-player software, which discovers other iTunes users nearby. It does this by broadcasting advertisements to the local link, which contain the username and computer name. (The protocol is Apple Bonjour, which is based a proposal for multicast DNS [CK06]). This allows the users to listen and purchase the same music. There is no obvious way to encrypt this communication as the aim is to communicate with new people without configuring a security association.

5   Discussion of the Leaks

In the information leaks discovered above, essentially the same data is revealed again and again:

- user identifiers (username, GUID, email address, real name),
- computer name, and
- user affiliation (DNS suffix, domain or workgroup, servers accessed).

One way to understand the consequences of such data leaks is to compare carrying a mobile computer to wearing a name badge or an RFID tag that broadcasts the name and affiliation of the person carrying it. Although the user's real name is not sent to the network as frequently as other identifiers, an email address or username and domain are usually sufficient to discover the user's personal web page or other information about the user. Although being identified is not very dangerous in itself, it may expose the user to unwanted attention from other people, and it may put the computer to a higher risk of attacks by hackers on the same access link.

Broadcast links, such as wireless access points, are the most opportune places for the casual observer. Most public-access wireless links are unencrypted or use the same shared key between all stations. On a switched wire Ethernet, a casual observer can only see broadcast packets. These comprise mainly DHCP DISCOVER and REQUEST messages and NetBIOS name lookups and registrations. Together, these packets may reveal the computer name and the user's organization but usually not the username. A typical situation where one can see many such broadcast packets is a wire network at a hotel or airport lounge.

Few public wireless access points currently use link-layer encryption. Those that do will block out unauthorized users but only for the purpose of charging. They will still let in mutually distrusting users who have paid paid for the access. Most access points now support per-client encryption keys between the AP and the client. The resulting level of privacy is similar to switched wire Ethernet.

It may seem that preventing a computer from sending a name or an identifier to the network is a simple task. If it were a question of one identifier sent by one piece of software, this would indeed be the case. What makes the problem difficult is that there so many protocols, at all layers of the network stack, and so many applications are sending so many different identifiers at different times. Naturally, all these protocols serve some purpose and cannot be simply disabled without causing inconvenience to the user.

The current practice in software engineering is to build the protocols, applications and services to be independent of each other and let each one perform its own discovery procedure. As a result, there is no single product or manufacturer in control of all the data that is sent to the network by a mobile computer. In this sense, Internet-enabled appliances are in a more reasonable position to protect the user privacy while it is almost impossible to know or control what data is sent to the network from a fully-fledged computer.

Most of the information leaks occur because of failed service discovery attempts. That is, the roaming computer is trying to find and access network services that are not accessible on the foreign network or it is trying to execute protocols that are only used between computers that belong to the same domain. The computer does this because it doesn't know which network it is on or which services are available there. In most cases, the client receives a "non-existent domain" response to the DNS requests, no response to the NetBIOS lookups, or finds that the server IP address is unreachable. These failed queries and connection attempts constitute unnecessary network chatter. If the client had some way of knowing whether the service can be accessed from the current location, it would not need to send out any of those packets. That is the reasoning behind the solution we introduce in Section 6.

Some of the identifier leaks are caused by public Internet services such as instant messaging, VoIP and various toolbars. The obvious solution is to encrypt the data between the client and server in a way that protects the client identity; for example, authenticate the client inside an TLS/SSL tunnel or deploy IPsec in identity-protecting mode. The technology exists and its deployment is simply a business issue.

A slightly more subtle problem is created by services that are operated by the mobile computer's home organization and are accessible from the Internet. These

include email servers, web-mail interfaces, and VPN gateways. Encryption hides
the identity of the user and computer but cannot mask their affiliation with the
server. The identity of the organization could be obscured a little by hard-wiring
the server IP addresses to the client or by using nondescript DNS names. A more
robust solution is an anonymous routing mechanism such as Tor (see Section 2)
at the cost of relatively poor real-time performance.

6   Preventing Unnecessary Chatter

In this section, we describe a strategy for preventing the unnecessary network
chatter. The basic idea is to identify the access networks and to attempt connection to a service only on the networks where the service exists.

Some laptops (e.g., those with Mac OS X) have for some time allowed the
user to configure network profiles and select them manually. Windows Vista
implements a network-location-awareness (NLA) service that identifies the access
network automatically, without user interaction. Since this mechanism is not yet
widely known, we explain it in some detail. NLA creates a fingerprint of the
access network, which is a set of parameters associated with the network. NLA
then computes a network identifier as a cryptographic hash of the fingerprint.
Applications and operating-system components can query NLA for the network
identifier and use it as a database key to store and retrieve any information
related to networks. On the first visit to the network, the network identifier is
just a random-looking number. On the following visits, it can be used to recognize
the network. Windows Vista currently uses NLA to remember the choice of a
firewall profile for each access network, so that the user is asked only once at
each network (and not asked at all for the intranet).

The choice of parameters in the NLA fingerprint varies by network type;
for the purposes of this paper, it suffices to think of the security profile for
authenticated networks and the gateway MAC address for others. Although the
gateway MAC address can be spoofed, the casual attackers considered in this
paper would not know the address value. For this purpose, we have proposed an
enhancement to the NLA mechanism would authenticate the DHCP server on the
network and use the server public key as the network fingerprint [ARM07]. This
kind of authentication would enable us to authenticate any previously visited
network without a PKI, which is exactly what is needed for the chatter-limiting
mechanisms explained below.

Given the NLA mechanism, the next step is to disable and enable service
discovery protocols depending on the network location. For this purpose, we
propose the following policy: *When client software stores information about an
online service for the purpose of connecting to it later, it must also store the NLA
network identifiers of the access links where the service is known to be accessible.
Automatic connection attempts to the service are only allowed on those networks.*

In a sense, when the user or administrator decides to access a service on
a network, he is making a policy decision to enable the same service always on

the same network. The rule applies both to applications and operating-system components that act as service clients. Some default policies should also apply:

- The active directory and Kerberos server should only be accessed on the intranet.
- NetBIOS should disabled by default and enabled separately for each network if needed.
- The default DNS suffix should be disabled outside the domain network.
- Network file shares may be accessed automatically and printers probed for availability only in the network where they were originally configured, or if the user explicitly request connection on another network.
- IKE with GSSAPI authentication should only take place in the intranet.

As a result, there should be no failed attempts at name resolution or failed connections to servers when the computer is on the wrong access network. While we believe this is the right approach in the long term, it requires changes to all the different service clients and applications that send data to the network. It can be argued that this requires a culture change to the way network client software is designed, which we see as necessary.

Another way to control network chatter is to filter outbound traffic from the computer at a host firewall. This would enable us to implement immediately some of the policies mentioned above, such as disabling specific DNS or NetBIOS queries. Packet filtering is a temporary emergency measure, however, because it is typically done at very coarse granularity, such as disabling access to all files shares instead of access to specific ones. The practicality of deep packet inspection for this purpose remains to be tested as there are potential issues with the firewall performance. Another problem with using firewalls is that dropping packets may cause unpredictable failure of applications.

Finally, some of the information leaks described in section 4 are transitory in the sense that they occur only when the mobile computer has just moved from the intranet or home to a public access point. This happens because software caches state data, such as IP addresses, and uses them even after moving to a new network. These problems can be solved by detecting when the mobile computer has disconnected from a network and by discarding any state data that may be stale after the event. The same should be done after the computer has been in a sleep mode and possibly moved to a new location.

7 Conclusion

In this paper, we analyzed identifier leaks from mobile computers to the access link. We discovered that the username, computer name and organizational iden-tifiers such as the domain suffix are sent unencrypted to the network by a large number of different protocols and applications. This is a breach of privacy and may expose users and their computers to unnecessary risks or embarrassment. The privacy concerns could discourage people from using new communications technology to its full potential. We suggest a solution based on network location awareness (NLA). Client software should remember the networks on which it has been configured to access each service. It should not try to automatically discover the service at other locations. This solution requires changes both to application clients and to many parts of the network stack; in effect, we are proposing a change of culture in the way service discovery in network network-enabled software is implemented.

References

[ACL+07]   Akritidis, P., Chin, W.Y., Lam, V.T., Sidiroglou, S., Anagnostakis, K.G.:
            Proximity breeds danger: Emerging threats in metro-area wireless net-
            works. In: Proceedings of 16th USENIX Security Symposium, Boston,
            MA, USA, August 2007. USENIX Association (2007)
[Aho75]   Aho, A.V., Corasick, M.J.: Efficient string matching: an aid to biblio-
            graphic search. Communications of the ACM 18(6), 333–340 (1975)
[AHK03]   Ashley, P., Hada, S., Karjoth, G., Powers, C., Schunter, M.: Enterprise
            privacy authorization language (EPAL 1.2). Research Report RZ 3485,
            IBM (March 2003)
[AKR06]   Aura, T., Kuhn, T.A., Roe, M.: Scanning electronic documents for per-
            sonally identifiable information. In: Proceedings of 5th ACM Workshop
            on Privacy in the Electronic Society (WPES 2006), Alexandria, VA, USA,
            October 2006. ACM Press, New York (2006)
[ARM07]   Aura, T., Roe, M., Murdoch, S.J.: Securing network location awareness
            with authenticated DHCP. In: Proceedings of 3rd International Confer-
            ence on Security and Privacy in Communication Networks (SecureComm
            2007), Nice, France, September 2007. IEEE Press, Los Alamitos (2007)
[BS03]   Beresford, A.R., Stajano, F.: Location privacy in pervasive computing.
            IEEE Pervasive Computing 2(1), 46–55 (2003)
[BSF06]   Broido, A., Shang, H., Fomenkov, M., Hyun, Y., Claffy, K.: The Win-
            dows of private DNS updates. Computer Communication Review (ACM
            SIGCOMM) 36(3), 93–98 (2006)
[Cha81]   Chaum, D.L.: Untraceable electronic mail, return addresses, and digital
            pseudonyms. Communications of the ACM 24(2), 84–88 (1981)
[CK06]   Cheshire, S., Krochmal, M.: Multicast DNS. Internet-Draft draft-
            cheshire-dnsext-multicastdns-06, IETF, Expired (August 2006)
[CPG04]   Chow, J., Pfaff, B., Garfinkel, T., Christopher, K., Rosenblum, M.: Un-
            derstanding data lifetime via whole system simulation. In: Proceedings
            of 13th Usenix Security Symposium, San Diego, CA, USA, August 2004,
            pp. 321–336. USENIX (2004)
[CSWH00]   Clarke, I., Sandberg, O., Wiley, B., Hong, T.W.: Freenet: A distributed
            anonymous information storage and retrieval system. In: Federrath, H.
            (ed.) Designing Privacy Enhancing Technologies. LNCS, vol. 2009, pp.
            46–66. Springer, Heidelberg (2001)
[Cra02]   Cranor, L.F.: Web Privacy with P3P. O'Reilly, Sebastopol (2002)
[CJBMM04]   Cuellar, J.R., Morris Jr., J.B., Mulligan, D.K., Peterson, J., Polk, J.M.:
            Geopriv requirements. RFC 3693, IETF (February 2004)
[DSCP02]   Díaz, C., Seys, S., Claessens, J., Preneel, B.: Towards measuring
            anonymity. In: Dingledine, R., Syverson, P.F. (eds.) PET 2002. LNCS,
            vol. 2482. Springer, Heidelberg (2003)

[DMS04]   Dingledine, R., Mathewson, N., Syverson, P.: Tor: The second-generation
           onion router. In: Proceedings of the 13th USENIX Security Symposium,
           San Diego, CA, USA. USENIX Association (August 2004)
[FMT06]   Franklin, J., McCoy, D., Tabriz, P., Neagoe, V., Randwyk, J.V., Sicker,
           D.: Passive data link layer 802.11 wireless device driver fingerprinting. In:
           Vancouver, B.C. (ed.) 15th Proceedings of USENIX Security Symposium,
           Canada, July 2006, pp. 167–178. USENIX Association (2006)
[GDMR06]   Gerdes, R., Daniels, T., Mina, M., Russell, S.: Device identification via
           analog signal fingerprinting: A matched filter approach. In: Proceedings of
           13th Annual Network and Distributed System Security Symposium (NDSS
           2006), San Diego, CA, USA, February 2006. Internet Society (2006)
[GM82]   Goguen, J.A., Meseguer, J.: Security policies and security models. In:
           Proceedings of IEEE Symposium on Research in Security and Privacy,
           Los Alamitos, CA, USA, April 1982, pp. 11–20. IEEE Computer Society
           Press, Los Alamitos (1982)
[GG03a]   Gruteser, M., Grunwald, D.: Anonymous usage of location-based services
           through spatial and temporal cloaking. In: Proceedings of MobiSys 2003:
           The First International Conference on Mobile Systems, Applications, and
           Services, San Francisco, CA, USA, May 2003, pp. 31–42. USENIX Asso-
           ciation (2003)
[GG03b]   Gruteser, M., Grunwald, D.: Enhancing location privacy in wireless LAN
           through disposable interface identifiers: a quantitative analysis. In: Pro-
           ceedings of 1st ACM International Workshop on Wireless Mobile Appli-
           cations and Services on WLAN Hotspots (WMASH), pp. 46–55 (2003)
[GF07]   Guha, S., Francis, P.: Identity trail: Covert surveillance using DNS. In:
           Borisov, N., Golle, P. (eds.) PET 2007. LNCS, vol. 4776. Springer, Hei-
           delberg (2007)
[GGP+07]   Greenstein, B., Gummadi, R., Pang, J., Chen, M.Y., Kohno, T., Seshan,
           S., Wetherall, D.: Can Ferris Bueller still have his day off? Protecting
           privacy in the wireless era. In: Proceedings of 11th Workshop on Hot
           Topics in Operating Systems (HotOS XI), San Diego, CA, USA, May
           2007. USENIX Association (2007)
[JWH07]   Jiang, T., Wang, H.J., Hu, Y.-C.: Preserving location privacy in wire-
           less LANs. In: Proceedings of 5th International Conference on Mobile
           Systems, Applications, and Services (MobiSys 2007), San Juan, Puerto
           Rico, USA, June 2007, pp. 246–257. ACM Press, New York (2007)
[JP02]   Johnson, D.B., Perkins, C.: Mobility support in IPv6. RFC 3775, IETF
           (June 2004)
[KBC05]   Kohno, T., Broido, A., Claffy, K.: Remote physical device fingerprinting.
           In: Proceedings of IEEE Symposium on Security and Privacy, Oakland,
           CA, USA, May 2005. IEEE Computer Society Press, Los Alamitos (2005)
[KC05]   Kowitz, B., Cranor, L.: Peripheral privacy notifications for wireless net-
           works. In: Proceedings of Workshop on Privacy in Electronic Society
           (WPES 2005), Alexandria, VA, USA, November 2005, pp. 90–96. ACM
           Press, New York (2005)
[Law03]   Lawton, G.: Instant messaging puts on a business suit. Computer 36(3),
           14–16 (2003)
[LT06]   Lindqvist, J., Takkinen, L.: Privacy management for secure mobility. In:
           Proceedings of Workshop on Privacy in Electronic Society (WPES 2006),
           Alexandria, VA, USA, October 2006, pp. 63–66. ACM Press, New York
           (2006)

[MCPS03]   Möller, U., Cottrell, L., Palfrader, P., Sassaman, L.: Mixmaster Protocol —
            Version 2. Internet-Draft draft-moeller-v2-01, IETF, Expired (July 2003)
[Mur06]   Murdoch, S.J.: Hot or not: Revealing hidden services by their clock skew.
            In: Proceedings of ACM Conference on Computer and Communications
            Security (CCS 2006), Alexandria, VA, USA, November 2006, pp. 27–36.
            ACM Press, New York (2006)
[ND01]   Narten, T., Draves, R.: Privacy extensions for stateless address autocon-
            figuration in IPv6. RFC 3041, IETF (January 2001)
[PGM+07]   Pang, J., Greenstein, B., McCoy, D., Seshan, S., Wetherall, D.: Tryst:
            The case for confidential service discovery. In: Proceedings of the 6th
            Workshop on Hot Topics in Networks (HotNets-VI), Atlanta, CA, USA,
            November 2007. ACM Press, New York (2007)
[PGG+07]   Pang, J., Greenstein, B., Gummadi, R., Seshan, S., Wetherall, D.: 802.11
            user fingerprinting. In: Proceedings of 13th Annual International Confer-
            ence on Mobile Computing and Networking (MobiCom 2007), Montreal,
            QC, Canada, September 2007. ACM Press, New York (2007)
[Pet02]   Peterson, J.: A privacy mechanism for the session initiation protocol
            (SIP). RFC 3323, IETF (November 2002)
[PS01]   Piper, D., Swander, B.: A GSS-API authentication method for IKE. Internet-
            Draft draft-ietf-ipsec-isakmp-gss-auth-07, IETF, Expired (July 2001)
[RR98]   Reiter, M.K., Rubin, A.D.: Crowds: Anonymity for web transactions. ACM
            Transactions on Information and System Security 1(1), 66–92 (1998)
[SM03]   Sabelfeld, A., Myers, A.C.: Language-based information-flow security.
            IEEE Journal on Selected Areas in Communications 21(1), 5–19 (2003)
[SLH07]   Saponas, T.S., Lester, J., Hartung, C., Agarwal, S., Kohno, T.: Devices
            that tell on you: Privacy trends in consumer ubiquitous computing. In:
            Proceedings of 16th USENIX Security Symposium, Boston, MA, USA,
            August 2007. USENIX Association (2007)
[SD02]   Serjantov, A., Danezis, G.: Towards an information theoretic metric for
            anonymity. In: Dingledine, R., Syverson, P.F. (eds.) PET 2002. LNCS,
            vol. 2482. Springer, Heidelberg (2003)
[SAH08]   Simon, D., Aboba, B., Hurst, R.: The EAP-TLS authentication protocol.
            RFC 5216, IETF (March 2008)
[SGR97]   Syverson, P.F., Goldschlag, D.M., Reed, M.G.: Anonymous connections
            and onion routing. In: Proc. 1997 IEEE Symposium on Security and Pri-
            vacy, Oakland, CA, USA, May 1997, pp. 44–54. IEEE Computer Society
            Press, Los Alamitos (1997)
[Swe02]   Sweeney, L.: k-Anonymity: a model for protecting privacy. International
            Journal on Uncertainty. Fuzziness and Knowledge-based Systems 10(5),
            557–570 (2002)
[TN98]   Thomson, S., Narten, T.: IPv6 stateless address autoconfiguration. RFC
            2462, IETF (December 1998)
[YMC07]   Yumerefendi, A.R., Mickle, B., Cox, L.P.: TightLip: Keeping applications
            from spilling the beans. In: Proceedings of 4th USENIX Symposium on
            Networked Systems Design & Implementation, Cambridge, MA, USA,
            April 2007, pp. 159–172. USENIX Association (2007)
[ZCYH05]   Zhao, Q., Cheng, W.W., Yu, B., Hiroshige, S.: DOG: Efficient informa-
            tion flow tracing and program monitoring with dynamic binary rewriting.
            Technical report, MIT (2005)
[Zug03]   Zugenmaier, A.: Anonymity for Users of Mobile Devices through Location
            Addressing. PhD thesis, University of Freiburg, Freiburg, Germany (2003)

How to Bypass Two Anonymity Revocation Schemes

George Danezis[1] and Len Sassaman[2]

[1] Microsoft Research,
Cambridge, UK
gdane@microsoft.com
[2] K.U. Leuven, ESAT/COSIC,
Kasteelpark Arenberg 10,
B-3001 Leuven-Heverlee, Belgium
Len.Sassaman@esat.kuleuven.be

Abstract. In recent years, there have been several proposals for anonymous communication systems that provide intentional weaknesses to allow anonymity to be circumvented in special cases. These anonymity revocation schemes attempt to retain the properties of strong anonymity systems while granting a special class of people the ability to selectively break through their protections. We evaluate the two dominant classes of anonymity revocation systems, and identify fundamental flaws in their architecture, leading to a failure to ensure proper anonymity revocation, as well as introducing additional weaknesses for users not targeted for anonymity revocation.

1   Introduction

Anonymous communication systems have been studied extensively since David Chaum introduced the mix in 1981 [5]. Their principal aim is to hide the fact that Alice is communicating with Bob from network adversaries or corrupt nodes in the anonymity-providing system. Practical anonymous communication systems have been proposed and fielded for email [13,25] and web-browsing [2,32]. They are based on intermediate nodes relaying the communication and hiding the correspondences between their inputs and outputs to obscure who is talking with whom. An extensive survey of anonymous communication channels and their properties is provided in [12].

Many approaches have also been proposed to mitigate the potential for abuse of anonymous communications. These approaches fall into two main classes. The first one, based on blacklisting [21], is respectful of users' anonymity and empowers service providers to block abusive users without ever finding their true identity. This approach is similar to the blacklisting of anonymous credentials [33,4]. Another form of blacklisting is used by Mixmaster; as senders of abusive content cannot be identified, recipients of abusive content who do not wish to receive mail from the anonymous remailer network can submit their email addresses to be blocked, so that they will not receive unwanted communication in the future.

N. Borisov and I. Goldberg (Eds.): PETS 2008, LNCS 5134, pp. 187–201, 2008.

This technique has been implemented in Mixmaster on a per-remailer basis with support for the network-wide "Remailer Abuse Blacklist" (RAB), which ensures the silencing of abusive messages regardless of the remailer used (as long as it is a participant in the RAB.)

The second approach is based on anonymity revocation or anonymity escrow, and allows a collection of authorities to revoke the anonymity of a user associated with a particular communication. Revocation has fundamentally different aims from blacklisting, and can be applied to tracing arbitrary messages between (even consenting) users to prevent covert communication.

Two lines of research have been developing in engineering revocation mechanisms into anonymity systems. The first family of systems is by Díaz and Preneel [16, 8, 9] (DP), and the second and latest by Köpsell, Wendolsky and Federrath [23] (KWF). Given the similarity in their approach, we will examine in detail the latest KWF system [23], and show in the discussion how our results are applicable to the first set of systems.

The key feature of the DP and KWF anonymity revocation mechanisms is that they "wrap-around" any anonymity system without modifying its internal functioning. Decoupling revocation from the anonymity channel is a wise design choice. It recognizes that building anonymous communication systems requires a careful balance between engineering and security, and adding more requirements into the core of the designs may lead to unsafe systems. This approach also adds generality, since, in theory at least, it would allow any secure anonymity system to be easily modified to include a revocation mechanism. A secondary design aim of the revocation mechanisms is to retain the same set of trust assumptions and security properties as the underlying anonymity systems.

In this work, we demonstrate that both revocation mechanisms are not as effective as believed, and some forms of anonymous communication are always possible despite them. The scheme's independence from any particular anonymous channel turns into a weakness: as we show, there exists no concrete practical channel to instantiate it securely. Even a single party within the anonymization infrastructure, adverse to the revocation protocol, is sufficient to help senders bypass it to achieve anonymity without revocation, and without a significant reduction in the quality of anonymity.

Furthermore, for onion-routing systems, the proposed architectures could lead to a reduction in security even when the revocation mechanism is not exercised. In most cases, the grafting of the revocation mechanism opens systems to Denial of Service attacks and heightens the risk of censorship.

This paper is organized as follows: the basic architecture of the KWF system is outlined in Section 2, and the key techniques necessary to bypass it in Section 3. Section 4 enumerates specific instances of KWF with concrete anonymous channels and describes how to bypass revocation in each case. Concerns about weakening the security of the anonymous channels by adding KWF to them are presented in Section 5, and questions about the desirability of revocation systems are discussed in Section 6. KWF and DP are contrasted in Section 7, and conclusions on our work are offered in Section 8.

2   The Internals of the KWF Scheme

The KWF [23] mechanism is a generic construction adding revocation capabilities to any anonymous communication channel. The aim of the KWF scheme is to not interfere with any of the security properties provided by the anonymous channel unless the anonymity of the communication is to be revoked. In such cases, the revocation authorities should reliably learn the identity of the sender or initiator of the revoked anonymous communication. This property should hold under the same security assumptions guaranteeing anonymity made by the underlying channel.

The KWF scheme implements mechanisms for revocation by requiring users to perform special steps before sending an anonymous message, as well as examining all messages output from the anonymous channel to the world. It relies on threshold group signatures for its security; using those, a member of a group can sign a message identifying himself as a member of the group without leaking any additional information about his identity. However, a quorum of group managers can invoke a revocation procedure to uncover a user's identity if some abuse is detected.

The KWF scheme also includes special features that allow operators not to learn any information about the identity of the traced user. These are, to a large extent, irrelevant to our attacks. Therefore, we shall not examine them in detail. We refer the reader to the full scheme [23] for further details.

Aside from the parties taking part in the anonymous communications, as well as the parties facilitating anonymization, the KWF scheme relies on some additional entities. Since the scheme uses group signatures, an entity is designated to be the *group manager*, that has the power to trace a group signature to a specific pseudonym. A *third party* is trusted to check senders' real identities and correctly package cryptographic tokens based on them. A *verifier* is entrusted with verifying signatures and censoring invalid messages. Finally, some abstract *authorities* are authorized to learn the senders of revoked messages – these parties possess by design (as opposed to being due to an accidental weakness in the system) the ability to remove any user's anonymity, as well as ensure that node operators comply with the protocol.

The skeleton of the KWF protocol proceeds as follows:

1. *Login.* A user wishing to send an anonymous message first logs in to a third party and acquires a signed 'revocation token'. This token is a ciphertext of his real identity (this may be a strong identity, derived from a public-key certificate, or simply the IP address of the user) encrypted using a threshold crypto-system. The user becomes a member of the group that is allowed to send messages through the channel. The third party gives the user the secret key to prove membership to the group, using a (revocable) group signature scheme.

2. *Sending.* The user signs his message using his group signature key and packages it cryptographically, as appropriate for the specific anonymous channel. He then sends the message, or performs whatever action is necessary to execute the anonymous communication channel protocol.

3. *Checking.* Once the message is output from the anonymous channel, it is given to a verifier. The verifier checks the group signature on the message; if it is not valid, the message is discarded. If the signature is valid, the message is forwarded to the intended recipient of the message.

4. *Revocation.* In case the message offends some policy, the revocation procedure is set in motion. The group signature associated with the message is provided to the group manager that traces it to a particular pseudonym. The pseudonym is used to retrieve the 'revocation token', and the real identity of the sender is retrieved by threshold decryption, performed by some third parties, and given to the authorities.

An important objective of the KWF scheme is to not modify the trust model of the anonymous channel. For this reason, the third parties necessary to perform the threshold decryption and provide the identity of the user to the authorities are chosen to be the same third parties that facilitate the anonymization of messages, i.e., the anonymization infrastructure itself. The stated aim is for the revocation protocol to be secure under the same conditions as anonymity is secured: when a threshold of honest servers exists in the network.

Our attacks against the KWF scheme, and the closely-related DP scheme, show that the protocols do not meet this objective. It is possible to bypass the revocation mechanisms and achieve strong anonymity if even a single participant in the anonymity infrastructure is unwilling to follow the revocation protocol. For some common choices of anonymous channels, it is even possible to bypass the revocation mechanisms without the help of any insider.

3   Outline of the Bypass Attacks

The key assumption on which the KWF and DP schemes base their security is that there can be no leakage of information from inside the channel to the world unless it passes through the verification step. In the KWF design, the anonymous channel is presented as a pipe with a clear entry and exit point, while in the DP design, the mixes are assumed to be unable to misbehave.

In practice, anonymous channels are complex multi-party protocols involving many often-untrusted participants who are in a position to learn a lot of information about the messages in transit. Engineering anonymous channels devoid of covert channels has never been a core objective of designers. The idea that the verifier is able to 'catch' all message flows from the network to the outside world is particularly hard to implement when the sender is *intentionally* trying to leak information through an accomplice that is part of the infrastructure.

Our attack only modifies the *Sending* step of the KWF protocol. A user correctly logs into the third party and acquires the appropriate credentials to use the anonymity system. However, he does not sign the message that he wishes to send. Instead, he packages it in such a way as to take advantage of a single accomplice in the infrastructure that will leak the message to the world (or to co-conspirators) without first presenting it to the verifier. We shall examine in detail, in the next section, how this can be done in the most common anonymizing channels.

Why does the attack work in general? Anonymous channels have been designed to be *incentives compatible*. They rely on the parties that will benefit from the anonymity properties, the senders in our case, to package their messages in such a way as to leak no information about their content or destinations. With the exception of anonymous channels designed for elections,[1] there is no mechanism preventing users from packaging their messages in a way that reveals their contents to arbitrary third parties.

The KWF design provides incentives for users to bypass the verifier. It is trivial in almost all anonymity designs to make use of a corrupt insider (and often even an observer) to leak their messages out of the channel without being subject to the verifier's scrutiny.

It is important to understand the role of the insider that enables non-revocable anonymous communications: the only service they provide is leaking the message to the outside world without vetting it through the verifier. As such, insiders only facilitate a covert channel, but are not required to provide any anonymity: the use of the anonymous channel, and the otherwise honest participants, already provides this. Therefore, the insiders do not need to act as anonymizing relays, but merely as exits from the channel.

It is not necessary for the corrupt insider to have any details about the real identity of the sending user, and it is impossible to obtain any additional information by observing any of its internal state. Therefore, a compromise of the insider nodes does not lead to a compromise of the senders' identities.

4   Bypassing Specific KWF-* Mechanisms

To illustrate our attacks, we will show how a sender can use unintended covert channels in most anonymity systems to leak messages to others without being subject to the verifier's censorship.

We will have to show in all cases that (1) the message benefits from the anonymity properties of the channel (without the corrupt insiders contributing to the anonymity); (2) that a single corrupt insider is sufficient to bypass the system; (3) that the message can be leaked in a way that does not arouse suspicion. We shall denote the instances of the KWF systems as KWF-*, where the "*" denotes the specific anonymous channel used by the system.

KWF-cascades. The KWF is first presented in terms of mix cascades [2, 18], so we should start by demonstrating that a single dishonest member of the mix cascade can bypass the verifier.

Mix cascades anonymize messages by relaying them through a predetermined and fixed set of intermediary nodes. The messages are encoded in

---

[1] It is important that election systems provide a method for the voter to verify that her vote is counted, but prevent the voter from proving how she voted to a third party, to achieve coercion resistance.

multiple layers of encryption, and each intermediary strips a layer before passing the message along to the next mix. With n mixes in the cascade, the message leaving the sender should be encrypted under the public keys of all mixes and look like:

$$\mathrm{M}' = E_{K_1} E_{K_2} \dots E_{K_n}(A, M) \tag{1}$$

Where $E_k(\cdot)$ denotes encryption under the key k, A the final address of the message and M the message itself. M' is sent to the first node N_1, where it is decrypted and forwarded to the next node.

Assume that the single node N_j and the sender are collaborating to bypass the revocation mechanism. The sender simply packages the message as:

$$\mathrm{M}' = E_{K_1} E_{K_2} \dots E_{K_j} E_{K_{\mathrm{secret}}}(A, M) \tag{2}$$

The key K_{secret} can be a shared key between the sender and node N_j. The message will be correctly relayed until node N_j. At this point, it will appear in the clear to node N_j, which can leak it to any third party.[2] The node N_j should then forward the ciphertext $E_{K_{\mathrm{secret}}}(A, M)$ along, to make its observable operation indistinguishable from an honest node. The message arriving at the final node will be indistinguishable from a random plaintext, and will be discarded by the verifier as not having a valid signature.

The double encryption of the message received by N_j provides compulsion resistance. The mix is able to follow the protocol unaltered and decrypt the message first with its public key K_j. Then it can covertly check whether the message is to be leaked, by checking on whether it decrypts correctly with the key K_{secret}. Yet if an adversary captures the node, and compels it to reveal its secrets, there is no way to prove that any key exists beyond the first one. To achieve this, messages encrypted under K_{secret} should be indistinguishable from those destined to the next stage of mixing – a property that is simple to implement.

Compulsion resistance protects the collaborating mix from reprisal, but is not necessary to maintain anonymity. In case both keys N_j and K_{secret} are leaked, the message still benefits from the anonymity provided by the mixes $N_1, \dots, N_{j-1}$.

Since the message contains no signature to revoke, it is not possible to trace it back when the verifier receives it. Furthermore, if the message has gone through at least a single honest node before reaching the node N_j, it has benefited from the anonymity of the channel without being traceable. It is also clear that a single N_j is sufficient to leak the messages, and that that sender has a high bandwidth channel to leak and anonymize messages. (The bandwidth is at least as high as if it were using the legitimate system.)

We conclude that for the KWF-cascades system, the security goal that the revocation mechanisms should work if there is a threshold of honest users does not hold.

---

[2] Of course, node N_j may very well be the intended recipient, with no further dissemination of the message necessary.

KWF-mix. Mix systems [5] are sets of routers that decrypt and forward messages to a designated address. Multiple mixes are chained together to form paths, over which messages are relayed. As with cascades, the cryptographic format of messages upon injection into the mix network is:

$$M = E_{K_1}(N_2, E_{K_2}(\dots(N_n, E_{K_n}(A, M))))$$ (3)

Messages are encrypted using multiple layers with the public keys of intermediate mix nodes. Unlike the formatting of messages for mix cascades, the address of the next node is included in the encrypted envelope to facilitate routing.

Mix systems can trivially be used to implement the bypass attack by including in the path a single corrupt mix that will leak a message to its final destination. A message can be formatted as:

$$M = E_{K_1}(N_2, E_{K_2}(\dots(N_j, E_{K_j} E_{K_{\text{secret}}}(A, M))))$$ (4)

Node N_j is dishonest, decrypts the message and forwards it to its final destination without checking its signature or mediating the communication through the verifier. Indistinguishability from honest behaviour can still be achieved. If node N_j comes under compulsion, it can reveal its private key, but without revealing K_{secret}, it is impossible to distinguish its operation from the honest nodes. Messages can still contain valid routing information for a subsequent path [11], making it impossible for an adversary to distinguish the node that leaks messages.

As with cascades, a single dishonest node is able to bypass the revocation mechanism and allow anonymous communication to take place. Even if node N_j is under passive surveillance, the message has benefited from the anonymity offered by nodes $N_1 \dots N_{j-1}$. Therefore, for general mix systems, the KWF revocation mechanism does not meet its security goals.

Other considerations. Other covert channels are available in some mix systems, allowing for covert communication even without the need for a corrupt party. Proposals to make mix networks robust assume that inputs and outputs of relayed messages are published on a public bulletin board [20, 26]. In such designs, Alice and Bob can communicate covertly by sharing a key and encoding the message so that it exits some mix "in the clear".

Requiring mix systems not to publish any information would make universal verifiability of delivery impossible to implement using efficient techniques, and would make such networks insecure against denial-of-service attacks [3].

KFW-or/tor. Onion routing architectures [32, 17] employ layered encryption and paths over networks of routers, and are architecturally very similar to mix networks. As a result, the same techniques can be used to route the stream through a dishonest node that leaks information to the outside world without checking signatures or presenting them to the verifier.

While architecturally related to mixing, onion routing defends against a very different threat model, and it is likely that the verifier will be able to mount de-anonymization attacks if it relays and checks all streams of traffic.

This is due to the onion routing being susceptible to passive attacks, while mix networks should be secure against a global passive adversary. We discuss this further in section 5.

KFW-buses. Buses [1] is a broadcast anonymization protocol. Nodes arrange themselves in one or multiple paths, over which "buses" travel. Buses are bit-strings containing multiple messages that are encrypted and re-encrypted as the 'bus' is relayed by each node, making it impossible to tell at what node they were introduced or removed. Messages are encrypted under the secret key of the final recipient, which detects them by trial decryption.

The peer-to-peer nature of buses makes it difficult to implement the KWF scheme, since only the final recipient gets to see and decrypt the message, not any other intermediary. Therefore, the KWF architecture cannot be applied to buses, since covert channels to the final recipients are intrinsic to the security of the scheme.

The obvious modification to accommodate KWF would be to address all messages to the verifier, who would then forward them to their respective receivers. This architecture would be equivalent to using the verifier as a single-hop proxy, since all the messages would simply be encrypted under its public key. This falls short of the original security properties of buses, which offer perfect receiver anonymity.

KWF-pir. Recently, proposals for the use of Information Theoretic Private Information Retrieval [7] in anonymous communications have been made [30, 19]. In Information Theoretic PIR, a set of databases (all containing an identical data set) are queried such that it is impossible for an adversary to determine what information is being requested by the user making the query unless some threshold of databases being queried are in collusion. In the proposed anonymity systems built on this form of PIR, the PIR database is used to store messages for pseudonyms.

Information-theoretic distributed-trust PIR systems derive, in part, their security from the fact that a user sends a set of queries to ℓ databases which he chooses from all of the databases in the system. Each query in the set is constructed such that the union of some number of elements of the query set reveals the location in the database of the message which the user wishes to retrieve; if another entity can observe the entire query set, it can determine which message the user is retrieving. Routing all requests through the verifier, as the KWF scheme requires, would thus expose the full query set to the verifier, thereby automatically linking each user to the messages he retrieves and compromising receiver anonymity by default.

Furthermore, anonymous covert channels exist in systems where large amounts of random data are passed between different entities [28], and an identity-revocation solution would not be likely to prevent anonymous communications if a communicating party operated part of the infrastructure.

There are two protocols in the literature, Crowds [29] and Dining Cryptographers' networks (DC-nets) [6], for which the KWF scheme would be applicable.

DC-nets are information-theoretically secure and devoid of covert channels. It is therefore possible to imagine all users contributing their inputs to the centralized verifier server that combines, shares, and outputs the final message only if it is valid. This centralized architecture would be secure, but would scale poorly. Scaling problems, as well as sensitivity to denial of service, are so prevalent in DC-nets that they are not used in practice.

Crowds [29] is a simple pass-the-parcel mechanism, in which nodes probabilistically relay messages in the clear before forwarding them to their final destination. A naive implementation of the KWF mechanism could be bypassed: the sender simply does not include a ring signature into the sent messages. Given the limited control the sender has over the routing of messages, delivery is only possible if the message reaches a collaborating node. Therefore, the attack has to rely on a large fraction of collaborating nodes being part of the Crowds network — a much stronger assumption than those made so far.

The KWF mechanism could also be easily modified to be robust even against those attacks. The KWF protocol would have to be augmented to ensure that all honest Crowds nodes check the validity of the signature of all messages they relay and report those nodes that forward messages without valid signatures. This is possible in Crowds since relayed messages are visible to nodes in clear. In practice, Crowds is not in use because of the weak anonymity properties it provides, which also enable checking the KWF signatures at each step.

5   Unintentionally Introduced Weaknesses in the KWF Scheme

The KWF scheme aims to "allow for deanonymisation without weakening the general trust model of an anonymity service." Yet through the introduction of a new infrastructure component, "the verifier", users of the system become more susceptible to attacks by an adversary not in collusion with the operators of the revocation system.

End-to-end traffic analysis. The verifier greatly reduces the difficulty of performing *end-to-end traffic analysis attacks*, by serving as a convenient single end-point in a fixed location. The fact that all traffic leaving the anonymity system can be observed, and timed, at the verifier facilitates multiple attacks described in the literature.

Many of the statistical disclosure attacks are made easier in this architecture [14, 24], since the message recipients are readily available to the verifier. Onion-routing security is greatly affected, since the verifier can collaborate with any entry node to correlate the low-latency streams of traffic to trace them [34, 10]. In general, the KWF architecture interacts poorly with anonymity systems providing security against a partial adversary only, since it requires the verifier to act as a centralized global observer. Classic active attacks such as the $(n-1)$ attack [31], in which an adversary injects a single message in a mix along with many of their own messages, are much easier to perform against the whole network by the verifier.

Furthermore, the effectiveness of dummy traffic is greatly reduced. Network-generated cover traffic cannot contain valid ring signatures to get past the verifier and reach the final recipients. Therefore such dummy messages, injected by mixes to thwart traffic analysis, are easily distinguishable from user-generated messages exiting the network, rendering them useless.

Denial of service. The verifier acts as a computational and communication bottleneck, since it has to inspect every message. That further exposes the system to denial-of-service attacks. Even a single rogue node, or client, can create a near-limitless number of messages with syntactically-correct, semantically-invalid signatures, to force the verifier to perform a verification of the signature – an expensive public-key operation. The anonymity of this node would be protected by the operation of the network, and it would be difficult to uncover and stop it.

Censorship. The verifier can easily be turned into a censor. Instead of attempting to trace messages violating an arbitrary policy, it can simply silently drop them. This feature of the revocation protocol goes against the latest attempts to make anonymous communications more robust against censorship [22]. The login servers could also act as censors by not providing signature keys to selected individuals.

This form of denial-of-service in anonymity systems does not simply impact availability, but can also be used as a tool to decrease anonymity. Therefore, the ability of the verifier to drop messages allows an adversary to increase its chance of tracing a message [3].

Anonymity-set reduction. Multiple anonymity revocation orders may be issued against the same anonymity set, thus weakening the anonymity provided to "legitimate" users. This is a concern that any user of such a system could justifiably hold, for they have no control over the identity or actions of the other members of their anonymity set (which in most systems is a random set of users highly correlated to the time in which the system is used.) If a significant portion of the traffic is deanonymized by the revocation mechanisms, the legitimate users will be put at risk of identification as well.

6   Additional Concerns

The KWF scheme takes great pains to ensure that multiple parties (the anonymization node operators) are involved in revoking anonymity. The intent is to demonstrate that the individual node operators all cooperate in providing the revocation of the anonymity their services provide; however, since participation in such a system is presumed to be compulsory, the nodes participating in such a system must be considered "in collusion", or at best "under compulsion", from the standpoint of the existing anonymity threat models. This is especially true in the KWF system, where a mechanism is employed to hide the identity of the traced user from the operators, making it impossible to judge the legitimacy of any revocation order before complying.

The discussion of jurisdiction issues with regard to the system presented in the KWF and DP papers is also missing. Backdoored anonymity systems are unlikely to be preferred in jurisdictions where they are not mandatory, thus resulting in separate networks for different jurisdictions, eliminating many of the benefits of jurisdictional arbitrage. This leaves many unanswered questions regarding which law enforcement agencies and judges are empowered to order the revocation of a user's anonymity, and presents difficult problems with regard to maintaining a single cohesive anonymity-set.

A system which has a known weakness as part of its design is likely to reduce the overall trust of the system—and for good reasons, as we have demonstrated. From a deployment point of view, it is unclear why users would use a revocable anonymity system instead of the easily accessible global anonymity solutions that are free of backdoors. An attempt could be made to impose such restrictions on the Internet as a whole, or put up country-level censorship systems (such as those used in China and Iran [15]) to prevent the use of true anonymity systems, but both of those approaches present their own problems beyond the scope of this paper.

The designers of the KWF scheme indicate that the system is to be used to revoke the identities of users sending to "suspicious addresses" or visiting "suspicious websites." Besides the obvious question of "what makes a recipient suspicious?" there can be legitimate concerns that "suspicious" websites may be created for the purpose of entrapment, to learn the identity of a user because of legitimate past communications. An attack whereby a user is tricked into visiting a given "suspicious website" could easily be implemented through the use of hidden frames in an unrelated site. E.g., if an attacker knows that website A is "suspicious", the attacker could embed an element of website A in an innocuous website B or in an HTML email, causing the user to unwittingly visit the "suspicious" website. This could lead to the targeted deanonymization of honest users for reasons other than those stated in an official warrant, and even allows for corruption of this process by non-governmental agents.

7   Discussion of the DP Design

The DP class of revocable anonymity solutions has its origins in the APES European Union project. Part of the project is intended to further develop anonymous communications, and also includes methods for the "control" of anonymous communications [9].

We refer to the DP solutions as a "class" of revocation technologies, because there are subtle differences between proposals. We focus on the most recent proposal published by Díaz and Preneel [16]. The DP scheme is harder to evaluate than the KWF scheme, because only a high-level design is proposed. Many difficult questions of security emerge when the gaps in the design are filled in.

The DP scheme shares some elements in common with the KWF scheme: a *certification authority* that holds users' identities in escrow, *judges* who are empowered to revoke the system, and a *credential* that is associated with any communication sent through the network. There are some basic problems with the DP approach not found in the KWF-* system, following from the fact that the identity credential is not cryptographically bound to the data being communicated. Hence, a mix can "frame" a user by associating the credential of a "suspicious" user with a legitimate user's traffic. This may be done specifically to harm that user, or by a rogue mix wishing to associate a valid credential with communication from a user other than the owner of that credential, to conceal the identity of the non-credentialed user.

DP's key difference from the KWF scheme is that the verifier is not centralized; instead, all exit nodes from the anonymity network are entrusted to check signatures for validity before forwarding messages. The Bypass attack can successfully be applied, and becomes trivial if even a single exit node is corrupt, as for the KWF bypass attacks described in Section 3. Other security issues relating to the centralization of the verifier in KWF, such as denial of service or traffic analysis attacks, are not so severe due to this decentralized approach.

8   Conclusions

We find the two proposals for "conditional anonymity" to be a significant departure from the strength and protection assurances in traditional, non-backdoored anonymity systems. The systems studied are ineffective at providing revocation against users wishing to engage in covert communications, and additionally introduce weaknesses that may compromise legitimate users.

From a technical point of view, no practical, deployed, anonymous communication channel fulfils the goals of the KWF or DP schemes, to provide mechanism-independent anonymity revocation. Instead, they allow single insiders, or even eavesdroppers, to leak anonymous messages out of the network, allowing unrevocable communications to take place. Furthermore, the KWF-* mechanisms have the potential to reduce anonymity through the introduction of a single verifier entity that mediates all output messages or streams from the network. The verifier can mount traffic analysis attacks, be subject to denial of service, or censor messages to impact availability or facilitate tracing.

From a deployment as well as a policy point of view, we believe revocation mechanisms to be ill-conceived: it is unclear why any operator or user would choose to use them when alternatives are available, and the proposed schemes systematically fail to ensure any security against the abuse of the revocation interfaces. Ironically, by introducing a strong framework for node collusion to achieve revocation, the amount of trust a given user is likely to place in the system as a whole is reduced. Yet, these issues go beyond the strictly technical focus of this paper.

Acknowledgments

We would like to thank David Chaum, Roger Dingledine, Nick Mathewson, and Steven Murdoch for their input on this subject, and Meredith L. Patterson for feedback on an early draft of this paper. Apu Kapadia spent considerable time and effort providing suggestions that greatly improved the style and essence of this work.

The work of Len Sassaman was supported in part by the Concerted Research Action (GOA) Ambiorics 2005/11 of the Flemish Government, by the IBBT (Flemish Government), by the IAP Programme P6/26 BCRYPT of the Belgian State (Belgian Science Policy), and by the EU within the PRIME Project under contract IST-2002-507591.

References

1. Beimel, A., Dolev, S.: Buses for anonymous message delivery. Journal of Cryptology 16(1), 25–39 (2003)
2. Berthold, O., Federrath, H., Köpsell, S.: Web MIXes: A system for anonymous and unobservable Internet access. In: Federrath, H. (ed.) Designing Privacy Enhancing Technologies. LNCS, vol. 2009, pp. 115–129. Springer, Heidelberg (2001)
3. Borisov, N., Danezis, G., Mittal, P., Tabriz, P.: Denial of service or denial of security? In: Ning, et al. (eds.) [27], pp. 92–102
4. Brands, S., Demuynck, L., De Decker, B.: A practical system for globally revoking the unlinkable pseudonyms of unknown users. In: Pieprzyk, J., Ghodosi, H., Dawson, E. (eds.) ACISP 2007. LNCS, vol. 4586, pp. 400–415. Springer, Heidelberg (2007)
5. Chaum, D.: Untraceable electronic mail, return addresses, and digital pseudonyms. Commun. ACM 24(2), 84–88 (1981)
6. Chaum, D.: The dining cryptographers problem: Unconditional sender and recipient untraceability. Journal of Cryptology 1, 65–75 (1988)
7. Chor, B., Goldreich, O., Kushilevitz, E., Sudan, M.: Private information retrieval. In: Proceedings of the IEEE Symposium on Foundations of Computer Science, pp. 41–50. IEEE Computer Society Press, Los Alamitos (1995)
8. Claessens, J., Díaz, C., Goemans, C., Preneel, B., Vandewalle, J., Dumortier, J.: Revocable anonymous access to the Internet. Journal of Internet Research 13(4), 242–258 (2003)
9. Claessens, J., Díaz, C., Nikova, S., De Win, B., Goemans, C., Loncke, M., Naessens, V., Seys, S., De Decker, B., Dumortier, J., Preneel, B.: Technologies for controlled anonymity. APES deliverable D10, Katholieke Universiteit Leuven (2003)
10. Danezis, G.: The traffic analysis of continuous-time mixes. In: Martin, D., Serjantov, A. (eds.) PET 2004. LNCS, vol. 3424, pp. 35–50. Springer, Heidelberg (2005)
11. Danezis, G., Clulow, J.: Compulsion resistant anonymous communications. In: Barni, M., Herrera-Joancomartí, J., Katzenbeisser, S., Pérez-González, F. (eds.) IH 2005. LNCS, vol. 3727, pp. 11–25. Springer, Heidelberg (2005)
12. Danezis, G., Diaz, C.: A survey of anonymous communication channels. Technical Report MSR-TR-2008-35, Microsoft Research (January 2008)
13. Danezis, G., Dingledine, R., Mathewson, N.: Mixminion: Design of a Type III anonymous remailer protocol. In: IEEE Symposium on Security and Privacy, pp. 2–15. IEEE Computer Society Press, Los Alamitos (2003)
14. Danezis, G., Serjantov, A.: Statistical disclosure or intersection attacks on anonymity systems. In: Fridrich, J. (ed.) IH 2004. LNCS, vol. 3200, pp. 293–308. Springer, Heidelberg (2004)

15. Deibert, R.J., Palfrey, J.G., Rohozinski, R., Zittrain, J. (eds.): Access Denied: The Practice and Policy of Global Internet Filtering. MIT Press, Cambridge (2008)
16. Díaz, C., Preneel, B.: Accountable anonymous communication. In: Security, privacy and trust in modern data management. Springer, Heidelberg (2006)
17. Dingledine, R., Mathewson, N., Syverson, P.F.: Tor: The second-generation onion router. In: USENIX Security Symposium, pp. 303–320. USENIX (2004)
18. Dingledine, R., Shmatikov, V., Syverson, P.: Synchronous batching: From cascades to free routes. In: Martin, D., Serjantov, A. (eds.) PET 2004. LNCS, vol. 3424, pp. 186–206. Springer, Heidelberg (2005)
19. Goldberg, I.: Improving the robustness of private information retrieval. In: IEEE Symposium on Security and Privacy, pp. 131–148. IEEE Computer Society Press, Los Alamitos (2007)
20. Jakobsson, M., Juels, A., Rivest, R.L.: Making mix nets robust for electronic voting by randomized partial checking. In: Boneh, D. (ed.) USENIX Security Symposium, pp. 339–353 (2002)
21. Johnson, P.C., Kapadia, A., Tsang, P.P., Smith, S.W.: Nymble: Anonymous IP-address blocking. In: Borisov, N., Golle, P. (eds.) PET 2007. LNCS, vol. 4776, pp. 113–133. Springer, Heidelberg (2007)
22. Köpsell, S., Hillig, U.: How to achieve blocking resistance for existing systems enabling anonymous web surfing. In: Atluri, V., Syverson, P.F., di Vimercati, S.D.C. (eds.) WPES, pp. 47–58. ACM, New York (2004)
23. Köpsell, S., Wendolsky, R., Federrath, H.: Revocable anonymity. In: Müller, G. (ed.) ETRICS 2006. LNCS, vol. 3995, pp. 206–220. Springer, Heidelberg (2006)
24. Mathewson, N., Dingledine, R.: Practical traffic analysis: Extending and resisting statistical disclosure. In: Martin, D., Serjantov, A. (eds.) PET 2004. LNCS, vol. 3424, pp. 17–34. Springer, Heidelberg (2005)
25. Möller, U., Cottrell, L., Palfrader, P., Sassaman, L.: Mixmaster Protocol — Version 2. IETF Internet Draft (July 2003)
26. Neff, C.A.: A verifiable secret shuffle and its application to e-voting. In: Samarati, P. (ed.) Proceedings of the 8th ACM Conference on Computer and Communications Security (CCS 2001), November 2001, pp. 116–125. ACM Press, New York (2001)
27. Ning, P., De Capitani di Vimercati, S., Syverson, P.F.: Proceedings of the 2007 ACM Conference on Computer and Communications Security, CCS 2007, Alexandria, Virginia, USA, October 28-31, 2007. ACM Press, New York (2007)
28. Patterson, M.L., Sassaman, L.: Subliminal channels in the private information retrieval protocols. In: Proceedings of the 28th Symposium on Information Theory in the Benelux, Enschede, NL. Werkgemeenschap voor Informatie- en Communicatietheorie (2007)
29. Reiter, M.K., Rubin, A.D.: Anonymous web transactions with crowds. Commun. ACM 42(2), 32–38 (1999)
30. Sassaman, L., Cohen, B., Mathewson, N.: The Pynchon Gate: a secure method of pseudonymous mail retrieval. In: Atluri, V., De Capitani di Vimercati, S., Dingledine, R. (eds.) WPES, pp. 1–9. ACM Press, New York (2005)
31. Serjantov, A., Dingledine, R., Syverson, P.F.: From a trickle to a flood: Active attacks on several mix types. In: Petitcolas, F.A.P. (ed.) IH 2002. LNCS, vol. 2578, pp. 36–52. Springer, Heidelberg (2003)

32. Syverson, P., Tsudik, G., Reed, M., Landwehr, C.: Towards an Analysis of Onion Routing Security. In: Federrath, H. (ed.) Designing Privacy Enhancing Technologies. LNCS, vol. 2009, pp. 96–114. Springer, Heidelberg (2001)
33. Tsang, P.P., Au, M.H., Kapadia, A., Smith, S.W.: Blacklistable anonymous credentials: blocking misbehaving users without TTPs. In: Ning, et al. (eds.) [27], pp. 72–81.
34. Wright, M., Adler, M., Levine, B.N., Shields, C.: Defending anonymous communication against passive logging attacks. In: Proceedings of the 2003 IEEE Symposium on Security and Privacy, May 2003, pp. 28–43. IEEE Computer Society Press, Los Alamitos (2003)

Reputation Systems for Anonymous Networks

Elli Androulaki, Seung Geol Choi, Steven M. Bellovin, and Tal Malkin

Department of Computer Science, Columbia University
{elli,sgchoi,smb,tal}@cs.columbia.edu

Abstract. We present a reputation scheme for a pseudonymous peer-to-peer (P2P) system in an anonymous network. Misbehavior is one of the biggest problems in pseudonymous P2P systems, where there is little incentive for proper behavior. In our scheme, using ecash for reputation points, the reputation of each user is closely related to his real identity rather than to his current pseudonym. Thus, our scheme allows an honest user to switch to a new pseudonym keeping his good reputation, while hindering a malicious user from erasing his trail of evil deeds with a new pseudonym.

1 Introduction

Pseudonymous System. Anonymity is a desirable attribute to users (or peers) who participate in peer-to-peer (P2P) system. A peer, representing himself via a pseudonym, is free from the burden of revealing his real identity when carrying out transactions with others. He can make his transactions unlinkable (i.e., hard to tell whether they come from the same peer) by using a different pseudonym in each transaction. Complete anonymity, however, is not desirable for the good of the whole community in the system: an honest peer has no choice but to suffer from repeated misbehaviors (e.g. sending an infected file to others) of a malicious peer, which lead to no consequences in this perfectly pseudonymous world.

Reputation System. We present a reputation system as a reasonable solution to the above problem. In our system, two peers, after carrying out a transaction, evaluate each other by giving (or not) a *reputation point*. Reputation points assigned to each peer sum up to create that peer's reputation value. In addition, reputation values are public, which helps peers to decide whether it is safe or not to interact with a particular peer (more exactly a pseudonym).

Identity Bound Reputation System. We stress that, in our system, the reputation value is bound to each peer. In existing reputation systems [16,18], the reputation value is bound to each pseudonym. Consequently, a new pseudonym of a malicious peer will have a neutral reputation, irrespective of his past evil deeds. Thus, honest peers may still suffer from future misbehavior. On the other side, honest users won't use a new pseudonym, in order to keep the reputation they have accumulated. Thus, they cannot fully enjoy anonymity and unlinkability. Motivated by this discussion, our goal in this paper is to design an identity bound reputation system, combining the advantages of anonymity and reputation.

N. Borisov and I. Goldberg (Eds.): PETS 2008, LNCS 5134, pp. 202–218, 2008.

Our Contribution. First, we formally define security for identity bound reputation systems (Section 3). As far as we are aware, this is the first such security definition. Our definition captures the following informal requirements:

- Each peer has a reputation which he cannot lie about or shed. In particular, though each peer generates as many one time pseudonyms as he needs for his transactions, all of them must share the same reputation. Also, our system is robust against a peer's deliberate attempts to increase his own reputation.
- Reputation are updated and demonstrated in a way that does not compromise anonymity. In particular, the system maintains unlinkability between the identity of a peer and his pseudonyms and unlinkability among pseudonyms of the same peer.

Our second contribution is the construction of a reputation scheme that satisfies the security definition. It is a nontrivial task to realize a secure identity bound reputation scheme, as the requirements of anonymity and reputation maintenance are (seemingly) conflicting. Here, we only briefly give basic ideas for the construction (see Section 2 for high level description of our scheme and Section 5 for the detail). To satisfy the first item, we need a central entity, *Bank*. Bank, aware of the identity of each peer, keeps reputation accounts by the peer, and is considered trusted to perform its functional operations — reputation updates etc. — correctly. Since we do not consider Bank trusted in terms of the anonymity requirements, we need to utilize a two-stage reputation deposit procedure. For the second item, we use the concept of *e-cash*. E-cash is well-suited to our system since it can be spent anonymously, even to Bank. We also use other primitives, such as anonymous credential system and blind signatures.

Organization. In Section 2 we provide a high level description of our scheme. In Section 3 we present our model, including security requirements. The building blocks used by our system are described in Section 4, followed by a detailed description of our system in Section 5. Related work and future directions are discussed in Sections 6 and 7 respectively.

2   System Considerations and High Level Approach

In this section we discuss system considerations and present a high level description of our scheme.

System Considerations and Assumptions. We assume that all communication takes place over an anonymous communication network, e.g., a Mixnet [8] or an Onion Router [24,11]. We further assume that this network is, in fact, secure. While we are not minimizing the difficulty of achieving that — see, for example, [15] or [21] — we regard that problem as out of scope for this paper.

We also assume certain out-of-band properties that are necessary for correspondence to the real world. The most important such assumption is that there is some limit to the number of reputation points any party can hand out per unit time. While we don't specify how this limit is set, we tentatively assume that it costs real money to obtain such points to hand out. This might, for example, be the daily membership fee for participation in the P2P network. Note that the assumption corresponds quite well to the best-known existing reputation system, Ebay. One can only dispense reputation points there after making a purchase; that in turn requires payment of a fee to the auction site. Bhattacharjee and Goel have derived a model for what this fee should be [4]; they call the necessary property "inflation resistance".

A last assumption is unbounded collusion. That is, any number of parties on this network may collude to break anonymity of some other party. We specifically include the bank in this assumption. We assume collusion because in most real environments, it is possible for one party to open multiple accounts on the system. It may cost more money, but it does achieve the goal. Since a bank employee can do the same, we assume that the bank is colluding, too, albeit perhaps in response to a court order. Even if we assume a foolproof system for restricting accounts to one per person, two or more people could communicate via a private back channel, thus effectively creating multiple accounts under control of a single entity.

On the other hand, the bank is trusted to behave honestly in its functional transactions, which involve maintenance of reputation levels and repcoins for each peer (see below). Thus, if the bank is misbehaving (possibly in coalition with other adversarial users), it can compromise the correctness of the system, but not the anonymity. It is possible to distribute the bank functionality among several parties in order to increase fault tolerance and reduce any trust assumptions, but we will not describe this here.

Protocol Overview. Bank keeps the record of each peer's reputation in the *reputation database*. As shown on the left of Figure 1, a peer U (via his pseudonym P_U) can increase the reputation of a pseudonym P_M by giving a *repcoin*,[1] which is basically an e-coin. Bank manages the number of repcoins that each peer has using another database: *repcoin quota database*.

Note that M does not deposit the repcoin using his identity. This is for the sake of maintaining unlinkability between a pseudonym and a peer. If M directly deposited the repcoin, collusion of Bank and U would reveal that M and P_M are linked. In fact, this shows the difficulty of realizing a secure reputation scheme: it is not obtained by using an ecash scheme naively. To preserve unlinkability, we use a level of indirection. When P_M successfully deposits the repcoin, it gets a blind permission from Bank. The blind permission is basically a blind signature, which therefore does not contain any information about P_M. So, M can safely deposit the permission.

We chose to employ an anonymous credential system (see Section 4) to construct the reputation demonstration procedure (on the right side of Figure 1). The anonymous credential enables M, via his pseudonym P_M, to prove his membership in group G_i anonymously. Thus, unlinkability between M and P_M is maintained.

We also note that P_M, instead of revealing its exact reputation value, shows the membership of a group G_i. Demonstration of exact reputation value could allow an attacker who continuously queries for the reputation of many pseudonyms — without even needing to transact with them — to infer whether two pseudonyms correspond to the same user. To make matters worse, with Bank's collaboration, pseudonyms can be linked to a limited number of identities that have the exact same reputation value

---

[1] If M wants to increase of reputation of P_U, they can carry out the same protocol with their roles reversed.

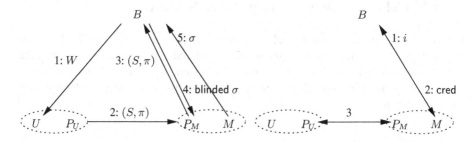

- Reputation granting process (left): (1) U withdraws a wallet W (i.e., repcoins) from the Bank B. (2) U, via P_U, awards (i.e., spends) a repcoin (S, π) to M. (3) M, via P_M, deposits the repcoin (S, π). (4) If the deposit is successful, P_M obtains from B a blind permission σ. Note that σ is blind to B and only visible to M. (5) M deposits σ, and B increases M's reputation point.
- Reputation demonstration process (right): (1) M requests a credential for the group G_i. (2) If M has enough reputation count for G_i, B issues a credential cred to M. (3) By using cred, P_M proves its membership of G_i to P_U .

Fig. 1. Reputation granting and demonstration

with the pseudonym. On the other hand, grouping together identities which belong to the same reputation level, makes small changes in reputation accounts invisible to other pseudonyms. Bank can still see the changes that take place in peers' reputations, but cannot link them to specific pseudonyms any more. The reputation levels (i.e., groups G_i) are defined as a system parameter. Reputation levels are not necessarily required to be disjoint. One example would be that G_i contains peers who has more than 2^i different reputation values.

Punishing Misbehaving Parties. When modeling the security of the system, we aim to achieve our goals (such as anonymity, no lying about reputation level, no over-awarding reputations beyond the allowed limit, etc.) by rendering a break of the security computationally infeasible (modulo some standard cryptographic assumptions). However, some security breaches are impossible to completely prevent. For example, as long as there is no central party involved on-line in each transaction, a user can always award the same reppoint twice to different parties. As another example, if anonymity and unlinkability is to be preserved, a peer with a high reputation level can always give away all his data and secret keys to another peer, allowing the latter to claim and prove the high reputation as his own. In these cases, we build into our model an incentive structure (similar to previous work, e.g., [19]), whereby such security breaches would hurt the offender. In particular, for the first case above, we require that a double awarding of a reppoint would reveal the identity of the offender (which can then lead to consequences outside of our model). For the second case, we require that in order for Alice to empower Bob, who has a lower reputation level, to prove a reputation level as high as Alice's, Alice would have to effectively give Bob her master private key. This information may be quite sensitive, especially if the private key used within the reputation system is the same one used for a public-key infrastructure outside the system.

3 A Model for Anonymous Reputation Systems

In this section, we present our model for anonymous reputation systems. We first enumerate the types of entities and the operations considered in the system, followed by the security definition. The motivation and rationale for our model and choices were discussed in Section 2. We note that some of these definitions were inspired by previous work on other primitives, such as [6,5].

3.1 Participating Entities

The entities in an anonymous reputation system are as follows.

- **Peers.** Peers are the regular users of a P2P network. A peer interacts with other peers via pseudonyms of his choice and can be either a User (buyer) or a Merchant in different transactions. Peers can award reputation points to other peers (through their pseudonyms), and can show their reputation level to other peers.
- **Bank.** Bank manages information with respect to each peer's reputation (where the information is tied to actual identities — public keys — of peers, not to pseudonyms). Specifically, it maintains three databases: the repcoin quota database (denoted D_{quota}), the reputation database (denoted D_{rep}), and the history database (denoted D_{hist}).

  D_{quota} holds the amount of repcoins that each peer is allowed to award to other peers. When a peer withdraws a wallet of repcoins, the amount of his repcoin quota is decreased correspondingly. Bank also replenishes all the peer's account periodically, as per system parameters (for example, every day each peer can award at most 20 repcoins to others; see the discussion in Section 2). D_{rep} contains the amount of reputation points that each peer has earned by receiving repcoins from other peers. In order to prevent peers from double-awarding (awarding two peers with same-serial-numbered repcoins), D_{hist} holds all the repcoins that are deposited.

3.2 Operations

The operations supported in our system are listed below. When an operation is an interactive procedure (or a protocol consisting of multiple procedures) between two entities A and B, we denote it by $\langle O_A, O_B \rangle \leftarrow \text{Pro}(I_C)[A(I_A), B(I_B)]$, where Pro is the name of the procedure (or protocol). O_A (resp. O_B) is the private output of A (resp. B), I_C is the common input of both entities, and I_A (resp. I_B) is the private input of A (resp. B). We also note that depending on the setup, some operations may require additional global parameters (e.g., some common parameters for efficient zero-knowledge proofs, a modulus p, etc). Our system will need these additional parameters only when using underlying schemes that use such parameters, e.g., e-cash systems or anonymous credential systems. To simplify notation, we omit these potential global parameters from the inputs to all the operations.

- $(pk_B, sk_B) \leftarrow \text{Bkeygen}(1^k)$ is the key generation algorithm for Bank.
- $(pk_U, sk_U) \leftarrow \text{Ukeygen}(1^k)$ is the key generation algorithm for peers. We call pk_U the (master) public key of U, and sk_U the master secret key of U.

- $(P, si_P) \leftarrow \mathsf{Pnymgen}(1^k)$ is the pseudonym generation algorithm for peers. The si_P is the secret information used to generate the pseudonym P.
- $\langle W, D'_{\mathsf{quota}} \rangle / \langle \bot, \bot \rangle \leftarrow \mathsf{RepCoinWithdraw}\ (pk_B, pk_U, n)\ [U(sk_U), B(sk_B, D_{\mathsf{quota}})]$. A peer U tries to withdraw n repcoins (in the form of a wallet W) from Bank B. Bank, using D_{quota}, checks if U is eligible for withdrawal. If so, the withdrawal is carried out and D_{quota} is changed accordingly.
- $\langle (W', S, \pi), (S, \pi) \rangle / \langle \bot, \bot \rangle \leftarrow \mathsf{Award}\ (P_U, P_M, pk_B)\ [U(si_{P_U}, W, pk_U, sk_U), M(si_{P_M})]$. A peer U (via P_U), using his wallet W, gives a repcoin (S, π) to M (via P_M). Here S is a serial number and π is the proof of a valid repcoin.
- $\langle \top, (D'_{\mathsf{rep}}, D'_{\mathsf{hist}}) \rangle / \langle \bot, \bot \rangle \leftarrow \mathsf{RepCoinDeposit}\ (pk_B, S, \pi)\ [M(\ P_U, si_{P_U}, pk_U, sk_U\ ), B(\ sk_B, D_{\mathsf{rep}}, D_{\mathsf{hist}}\ )]$. A peer M deposits the repcoin into his reputation account. If the repcoin (S, π) is valid and not double-awarded, then the coin is stored in the history database D_{hist}, and the amount of reputation of pk_M in D_{rep} is increased by one.
- $(pk_U, \Pi_G)/\bot \leftarrow \mathsf{Identify}(S, \pi_1, \pi_2)$. If a repcoin is double-awarded with (S, π_1) and (S, π_2), Bank can find the peer who double-awarded the coin using this operation. Here, Π_G is a proof that pk_U double-awarded the repcoin with the serial number S.
- $\top / \bot \leftarrow \mathsf{VerifyGuilt}(S, \Pi_G, pk_U)$ outputs $\top$ if the peer U (represented by pk_U) indeed double-awarded the coin with the serial number S.
- $\langle C^l_U, \top \rangle / \langle \bot, \bot \rangle \leftarrow \mathsf{RepCredRequest}\ (pk_B, pk_U, l)\ [U(sk_U), B(sk_B, D_{\mathsf{rep}})]$. A peer U requests a credential that will enable U to prove to another peer that he has reputation level l. Bank B refers to D_{rep}, and if U has sufficient reputation it issues a credential C^l_U. (As discussed in Section 2, how exactly the reputation levels are defined is a system parameter).
- $\langle \top, \top \rangle / \langle \bot, \bot \rangle \leftarrow \mathsf{ShowReputation}\ (P_{U_1}, P_{U_2}, pk_B, l)\ [U_1(sk_{U_1}, si_{P_{U_1}}, C^l_{U_1}), U_2(si_{P_{U_2}})]$. A peer U_1 (via P_{U_1}) proves to U_2 (via P_{U_2}) that he has reputation level l.

3.3 Security

In this section we define security for anonymous reputation systems.

Adversarial Model. We will consider two adversarial models, assuming the stronger one for the anonymity-related security properties (unlinkability and exculpability), and the weaker one for the reputation-handling properties (no over-awarding and reputation unforgeability).

For the weaker adversarial model, we assume Bank is *honest-but-curious*, that is, it follows the protocol specification correctly. All other peers may become malicious, and behave in arbitrary ways in the protocol. Adversarial parties may collude with each other, and as long as they are peers, they may decide to share any of their state or secret information with each other, and coordinate their actions; Bank may share the content of its maintained databases (D_{quota}, D_{rep}, and D_{hist}), but *not* Bank's secret keys (thus it is meaningful for Bank to be *honest-but-curious*, even when in coalition with other players).[2]

For the stronger adversarial model, we remove the honest-but-curious restriction on Bank: we assume all parties (including Bank) may be corrupted, collaborating with each other, and behaving arbitrarily.

---

[2] Note that if we allowed Bank to share its secret keys and to behave arbitrarily, it could issue more repcoins than allowed, generate reputation credentials that do not correspond to the correct reputation level, etc.

Correctness

- If an honest peer U_1, who has enough repcoins in his repcoin quota, runs RepCoin-Withdraw with an honest Bank B, then neither will output an error message; if the peer U_1, using the wallet (output of RepCoinWithdraw), runs Award with an honest peer U_2 (via his pseudonym), then U_2 accepts a repcoin (S, π); if the peer U_2 runs RepCoinDeposit with the honest Bank to deposit the repcoin (S, π) then U_2's reputation in Bank will be increased by one.

- If an honest peer U_1 runs RepCredRequest with an honest Bank and a reputation level for which he is eligible, then U_1 gets a valid credential. For a valid credential C_U^l, its owner can always prove his reputation through ShowReputation$(l, C_U^l, \ldots)$ procedure.

Unlinkability

For an adversary A who has corrupted certain parties including Bank, we say that a peer U appears consistent with a pseudonym P to A, if U and P's owner are uncorrupted, and if the levels for which P successfully invoked ShowReputation are a subset of the levels for which U successfully invoked RepCredRequest. We now define the following two unlinkability properties:

Peer-Pseudonym Unlinkability. Consider an adversary who, having corrupted some parties including Bank, is participating in the system for some arbitrary sequence of operations executed by honest and by corrupted parties. Given a pseudonym P that does not belong to a corrupted party, the adversary can learn which peer owns P no better than guessing at random among all non-corrupted peers that appear consistent with P.

Pseudonym-Pseudonym Unlinkability. Consider an adversary who, having corrupted some peers (but not Bank), is participating in the system for some arbitrary sequence of operations executed by honest and corrupted parties. Given two pseudonyms P_1, P_2 that do not belong to corrupted parties, the adversary has no advantage in telling whether P_1, P_2 belong to the same peer or not. Next, consider an adversary who corrupted some peers and Bank as well. Then the above requirement should hold as long as there are *at least two* non-corrupted peers who appear consistent with both P_1 and P_2 (because if there is only one such uncorrupted peer, clearly both pseudonyms belong to the same one).

No Over-Awarding

- No collection of peers should be able to award more repcoins than they withdrew. Suppose that n peers $U_1, \ldots, U_n$ collude together, and that the sum of the amount of repcoins allowed to them is N. Then, the number of different serial numbers of repcoins that can be awarded to other peers is at most N.

- Suppose that one or more colluding peers run the Award protocol with two pseudonyms P_{M_1} and P_{M_2} such that P_{M_1} gets (S, π_1) and P_{M_2} gets (S, π_2). Then, we require that Identify(S, π_1, π_2) outputs a public key pk_U and a proof of guilt Π_G such that VerifyGuilt(pk_U, S, Π_G) accepts.

- Each repcoin that is accepted but not double-awarded in the Award protocol increases exactly one reputation point in the database D_{rep} irrespective of the beneficiary of the repcoin. However, we don't regard it as a breach of security when a peer M_1 received a repcoin but passed it to M_2, who deposited it into his reputation account; in any event, this is just another form of collusion. Another justification is that the peer M_1 sacrifices one reputation point.

Exculpability

This property is to protect the honest peer from any kind of framing attack against him. No coalition of peers, even with Bank, can forge a proof Π_G that VerifyGuilt(pk_U, S, Π_G) accepts where pk_U is an honest peer U's public key who did not double-award a repcoin with the serial number S.

Reputation Unforgeability

- No coalition of peers, where l is the highest reputation level of any one of them, can show a reputation level higher than l for any of their pseudonyms. This implies as a special case that a single peer cannot forge his reputation.
- Consider a peer U with reputation level l, who owns a pseudonym P. Suppose that some coalition of peers has empowered U with the ability to prove that P has reputation level $l' > l$. Let Bad be the set of peers with reputation level at least l' among the coalition (note that by the previous requirement, there must be at least one peer in Bad). Then, it must be that U can learn the master secret key of a peer $U' \in$ Bad.

4   Building Blocks of Our Scheme

Anonymous Credential Systems. In anonymous credential systems — see, for example, [19,6,3] — there are three types of players: *users, organizations, and verifiers.* Users receive credentials, organizations grant and verify the credentials of users, and verifiers verify credentials of the users. Below are the supported procedures.

- $(pk_O, sk_O) \leftarrow$ AC.OKeyGen(1^k). Key generation algorithm for an organization. (pk_O, sk_O) denotes the key pair of the organization O.
- $(pk_U, sk_U) \leftarrow$ AC.UKeyGen(1^k). Key generation algorithm for a user. (pk_U, sk_U) denotes the key par of the user U. Sometimes sk_U is called the master secret key of U.[3]
- $\langle (N, \mathsf{NSecr}_N), (N, \mathsf{NLog}_N) \rangle \leftarrow$ AC.FormNym(pk_O) $[U(sk_U), O(sk_O)]$. Nym[4] generation protocol between U and O, where N is output nym, NSecr_N is secret information with respect to N, and NLog_N is the corresponding log on the organization side.
- $\langle \mathsf{cred}_N, \mathsf{CLog}_{\mathsf{cred}_N} \rangle \leftarrow$ AC.GrantCred(N, pk_O) $[U(pk_U, sk_U, \mathsf{NSecr}_N), O(sk_O, \mathsf{NLog}_N)]$. Credential granting protocol, where cred_N is a credential for the nym N, and $\mathsf{CLog}_{\mathsf{cred}_N}$ is the corresponding log on the organization side.
- $\langle \top, \top \rangle / \langle \bot, \bot \rangle \leftarrow$ AC.VerifyCred(pk_O) $[U(N, \mathsf{cred}_N), V]$. Credential verification protocol.
- $\langle \top, \top \rangle / \langle \bot, \bot \rangle \leftarrow$ AC.VerifyCredOnNym (N, pk_O, pk_{O_1}) $[U(N_1, \mathsf{cred}_{N_1}), O(\mathsf{NLog}_N)]$. In this protocol, U proves to O that N is his valid nym issued by O and that cred_{N_1} on the nym N_1 issued by O_1.

---

[3] Anonymous credential systems do not typically require a specific form for the master public and secret keys, but assume it is inherited from some PKI, where users are motivated to keep their secret key secret. In other variations of anonymous credential systems (with all-or-nothing non-transferability) there is no master public key. Our scheme can be adapted to such systems as well.

[4] Usually, nym and pseudonym are used interchangeably. But to avoid confusion with the term pseudonym in our reputation scheme, we stick to the term nym in anonymous credential systems.

Secure anonymous credential systems satisfy the following conditions (see [19,6,3] for more details): (1) *Unique User for Each Nym.* Even though the identity of a user who owns a nym must remain unknown, the owner should be unique. (2) *Unlinkability of Nyms.* Nyms of a user are not linkable at any time with a probability better than random guessing. (3) *Unforgeability of Credentials.* A credential may not be issued to a user without the organization's cooperation. (4) *Consistency of Credentials.* It is not possible for different users to team up and show some of their credentials to an organization and obtain a credential for one of them that the user alone would not have gotten. (5) *Non-Transferability.* Whenever Alice discloses some information that allows Bob to user her credentials or nyms, she is effectively disclosing her master secret key to him.

E-Cash. An e-cash system consists of three types of players: the *bank*, *users* and *merchants*. Below are the supported procedures (see [5]).

- $(pk_B, sk_B) \leftarrow$ EC.BKeyGen(1^k) is the key generation algorithm for the bank.
- $(pk_U, sk_U) \leftarrow$ EC.UKeyGen(1^k) is the key generation algorithm for users.
- $\langle W, \top \rangle \leftarrow$ EC.Withdraw(pk_B, pk_U, n) $[U(sk_U), B(sk_B)]$. The user U withdraws a wallet W of n coins from the bank.
- $\langle W', (S, \pi) \rangle \leftarrow$ EC.Spend(pk_M, pk_B, n) $[U(W), M(sk_M)]$. The user U spends a coin by giving it to the merchant M. U gets the updated wallet W, and M obtains a coin (S, π) where S is a serial number and π is a proof.
- $\langle \top/\bot, L' \rangle \leftarrow$ EC.Deposit(pk_M, pk_B) $[M(sk_M, S, \pi), B(sk_B, L)]$. M deposits (S, π) into its account in the bank B. L' is the updated list of the spent coins (i.e., (S, π) is added to the list).
- $(pk_U, \Pi_G) \leftarrow$ EC.Identify(S, π_1, π_2). Given two coins with the same serial number, i.e., (S, π_1) and (S, π_2), B finds the identity of the double-spender pk_U and the corresponding proof Π_G.
- $\top/\bot \leftarrow$ EC.VerifyGuilt(S, pk_U, Π_G). It verifies the proof Π_G that the user pk_U is guilty of double-spending coin S.

Secure e-cash scheme satisfies the following condition: (1) *Correctness.* If an honest user runs EC.Withdraw with an honest bank, then neither will output an error message. If an honest user runs EC.Spend with an honest merchant, then the merchant accepts the coin. (2) *Balance.* No collection of users and merchants can ever spend more coins than they withdrew. (3) *Identification of double-spenders.* Suppose the bank B is honest, and M_1 and M_2 are honest merchants who ran the EC.Spend protocol with the adversary whose public key is pk_U. Suppose the outputs of M_1 and M_2 are (S, π_1) and (S, π_2) respectively. This property guarantees that, with high probability, EC.Identify(S, π_1, π_2) outputs a key pk_U and proof Π_G such that EC.VerifyGuilt(S, pk_U, Π_G) accepts. (4) *Anonymity of users.* The bank, even when cooperating with any collection of malicious users and merchants, cannot learn anything about a user's spendings other than what is available from side information from the environment. (5) *Exculpability.* When S is a coin serial number not double-spent by user U with public key pk_U, the probability that EC.VerifyGuilt(S, Π_G, pk_U, n) accepts is negligible.

Blind Signatures. Blind signatures have two types of players: the *bank* and the *users*. A user requests the bank to generate a signature on a message m. Then the bank generates a signature without knowing the message m. Below are the supported procedures (see [14]).

- $(pk_B, sk_B) \leftarrow$ BS.KeyGen(1^k). Key-generation algorithm for the bank B.
- $\langle \top/\bot, \sigma/\bot \rangle \leftarrow$ BS.Sign(pk_B)[$B(sk_B), U(m)$]. Signing protocol.
- $\top/\bot \leftarrow$ BS.Verify(m, σ, pk_B). Verification algorithm.

Secure blind signature scheme satisfies the following conditions: (1) *Unforgeability.* Only the bank who owns the secret key sk_B can generate valid signatures. (2) *Blindness.* The bank B does not learn any information about the message m on which it generates a signature σ.

5   Anonymous Identity-Bound Reputation System

In this section we describe a general scheme based on any implementation of the building blocks. See Appendix A for a specific instantiation of the scheme.

E-cash schemes will be used for the implementation of repcoins, blind signatures will be used in repcoin-withdraw and reputation-update procedures, and anonymous credential systems will be used for the reputation-demonstration procedures. As we shall see, while the first two are used in a relatively straight-forward manner, the last one is used in a more complex way, since the reputation demonstration setting presents a new type of hurdle to overcome if unlinkability is to be achieved even against colluding bank and peers.

Underlying Protocols and Requirements. Our scheme will work with any implementation of these underlying primitives, as long as the master public and secret keys for peers in our system are of the same form as those in the underlying e-cash scheme and anonymous credential system. That is, the key generation algorithms Ukeygen, EC.UKeyGen, and AC.Ukeygen are all the same.[5]

Our scheme will also require a zero knowledge proof of knowledge of both the master secret key corresponding to a master public key, and the secret information of a nym's owner (which is given as an output of the AC.FormNym operation). Thus, when instantiating our scheme with specific primitives, it is useful to choose underlying primitives that admit efficient proofs of this form (as we do in the Appendix A).

Setup. We start with the setup procedure on Bank's side.

- Bank B executes **EC.BKeyGen** procedure of e-cash scheme to create a digital signature key-pair (pk_B, sk_B). This is the key-pair that will be used for creating the repcoins. Bank publishes pk_B.
- B executes **BS.BkeyGen** procedure of blind signatures scheme to create a blind signature key pair to be used in the Reputation Deposit procedure (pk_B^b, sk_B^b). Bank publishes pk_B^b.
- B defines fixed reputation levels l_i, represented by a group G_i. These "reputation" groups — although managed by Bank — play a role similar to the one organizations play in anonymous credential systems. For each one of these groups, Bank runs **AC.OKeyGen** protocol to generate public-secret key pairs (pk_{G_i}, sk_{G_i}). Bank also publishes pk_{G_i}s.

---

[5] As discussed in Section 2, an important part our system setup is the assumption that peers are motivated to keep their master private key secret. For this reason, it is beneficial to have the master public and private keys be part of an external PKI which is used for other purposes (e.g., signing documents) outside our system.

- B does the appropriate setup (if any) for the pseudonym generation. For example, this may involve selecting an appropriate algebraic group G_p.

On the peers' side, each peer U_i invokes **EC.UKeyGen** to create a master public-secret keypair (pk_{U_i}, sk_{U_i}).

Operations. As mentioned, we assume that messages are exchanged through perfectly secure channels. The system operations are realized as follows.

1. Generation of Pseudonyms. Each peer generates his own pseudonyms. There is no particular structure imposed on the pseudonyms, and they need not be certified or registered with Bank (or any other entity). The only requirement is that the pseudonym generation leaves the owner with some secret information (e.g., the random string used for the generation procedure), such that possession of this information proves ownership of the pseudonym. We will also need such a proof to be executed. Thus, in principle, we can simply use a random string r as the secret information and $P = f(r)$ as the pseudonym, where f is some one-way function, with an associated zero-knowledge proof of knowledge of the inverse of P. However, a more efficient solution is to let the pseudonym generation procedure to be a digital signature key generation, keeping the signing key as the secret information and the verification key as the pseudonym. Here, being able to produce valid signatures will prove ownership of the pseudonym, without a need for a zero-knowledge proof.

2. RepCoin Withdrawal. RepCoin Withdrawal takes place between Bank B and a peer U. Both U and B engage in **EC.Withdraw** procedure of a e-cash scheme. For simplicity purposes, we assume that a wallet W of n repcoins has been withdrawn. Since the only properties related to repcoins are anonymity of an honest withdrawer and repudiation of any double spender, the wallet can be like the one suggested in [5], or n separate digital coins withdrawn through any known e-cash scheme.

3. Reputation Award. This procedure is executed between two pseudonyms, one (i.e., P_U) belonging to a peer U and one (i.e., P_M) belonging to a peer M. Both engage in **EC.Spend** protocol of a e-cash scheme. However, this protocol takes place strictly between the two pseudonyms P_U and P_M instead of involving the actual identities U and M. Thus, P_U gives a repcoin to P_M, where no information about identities of the parties involved is revealed.

4. Reputation Update. This protocol is invoked when a peer M wants to increase his reputation based on the repcoins that his pseudonyms have received since the last time he updated his reputation record. As previously discussed, maintaining unlinkability between a pseudonym and its owner is a crucial feature of our system. Towards this end, a single interaction for update (with a merchant presenting himself to Bank either as a peer or as a pseudonym) will not work, as we explain below.

Assume peer M wants to deposit a repcoin he received as P_M from pseudonym P_U of User U. Note that no one except M knows who is the owner of P_M. Given the fact that U knows the exact form of the repcoin he gave to M, if M tried to deposit the repcoin by presenting himself as M to Bank, a collusion of Bank and U would reveal that M is the owner of P_M. Trying to solve this by letting M "rerandomize" the repcoin in some way before depositing it presents problems for enforcing the no over-awarding requirement. On the other hand, if Reputation Update procedure was done by the pseudonym P_M of M, there would be a problem in persuading the Bank to update M's record without revealing that M is the owner of P_M.

Therefore, our Reputation Update protocol has two stages. First, P_M contacts Bank and gets a blind permission from it that shows a repcoin has been deposited and is valid. Second, M deposits that blind permission. In particular, the following procedure takes place:

> **4.1 Obtaining Blind Permission.** Peer M executes EC.Deposit procedure of e-cash scheme using his pseudonym P_M, but here the actual deposit does not happen. Rather, if Bank B accepts the repcoin, M gets from B a blind signature on a random message. That is, P_M sends to B a repcoin that it has received. If B accepts the coin as valid, P_M chooses a random message C and gets a blind signature of C: σ_B^b. We call (C, σ_B^b) a *blind permission*.
>
> **4.2 Deposit of the Blind Permission.** M sends B the permission (C, σ_B^b). Then, B checks if the tuple is fresh and increases the reputation of M.

5. Reputation Demonstration. This protocol is invoked when one peer wants to demonstrate his reputation to another peer, both interacting strictly through their pseudonyms. We will utilize predefined groups G_i corresponding to reputation levels l_i, which are managed by Bank. For a peer U who wants, via P_U, to prove his reputation level l_i to a pseudonym P_V of a peer-verifier V, the protocol proceeds as follows:

- If he has not done it before, U contacts the bank to register in the group G_i that corresponds to the desired reputation level l_i. U interacts with G_i (Bank) by invoking AC.FormNym protocol of a anonymous credential system, in order to generate a nym $N_U^{l_i}$ for U under that group.[6] (U can generate as many nyms as he wants.)
- U contacts G_i, providing its master public pk_U key and a zero knowledge proof of knowledge π that he possesses the corresponding master secret key sk_U. U also presents $N_U^{l_i}$ and a zero-knowledge proof π_N that it has been created correctly and he is the owner.
- G_i checks that U is valid and that his reputation is indeed in that group (or higher), and executes AC.GrantCred to generate a credential $C_N^{l_i}$ for $N_U^{l_i}$.
- U interacts with the verifier P_V under his pseudonym P_U. P_U proves by executing AC.VerifyCred that he possesses a credential from group G_i. Specifically, P_U proves that its owner has registered under a nym to G_i and has acquired — through that nym — a credential of membership.

5.1 Security

The following theorem states the correctness and security of our general scheme. For lack of space, we refer the reader to our technical report [1] for proofs.

---

[6] Recall that there is a big difference between pseudonyms and nyms. As discussed before, Pseudonyms are public-secret key-pairs, used as means to preserve peers' anonymity when involved in transactions. A nym of a peer will be associated with a particular reputation group. Bank, as the manager of the reputation groups, will be able to link the nyms with the peer identities (master public key). In contrast, unlinkability of peers and pseudonyms is maintained, as per our security definitions.

Theorem 1. *If the underlying primitives (anonymous credential system, e-cash system, and blind signatures) are secure, then our scheme satisfies* correctness, peer-pseudonym unlinkability, pseudonym-pseudonym unlinkability, no over-awarding, exculpability, *and* reputation unforgeability.

5.2 Practical Issues

In the absence of a concrete implementation, it is hard to make concrete statements about practical issues. Furthermore, our main result is a framework which can accomodate different algorithms That said, there are at least two areas that deserve further attention, performance and system security.

In general, our protocol is neither real-time nor high-performance. We are not proposing per-packet operations; most of what we do is per-user or per-purchase. As such, real-time performance is not critical; in particular, there are no bottleneck nodes.

A full performance analysis is given in [1]. Here, we note that all of our primitive operations are $O(1)$ in system size. That is, there are no design elements in our scheme whose performance degrades as the size of the system increases. Similarly, no operation takes more than a few messages; all are $O(k + w)$ in message size, where k and w are security parameters. More details for our specific instantiation are given in Appendix A.

In addition to the anonymous peer-to-peer communication necessary for the underlying application, there is now a new communications path: from each party to the bank. Parties who are engaging in our protocol will need to contact the bank. This provides another channel that might be detected by, say, the attacks described in [15]. Indeed, there may exists a sort of "meta-intersection attack" [9]: the peer-to-peer traffic alone may not be suspicious, but it when coupled with conversations with the bank might be sufficient for identification.

A second area for security concern is CPU consumption. Our scheme (see Appendix A) requires public key operations; these are CPU-intensive. An attacker who has identified a candidate participant in real-time might be able to connect to it — we are, after all, talking about peer-to-peer systems — and measure how long its own communications take. The obvious defense is to make sure that any given operation takes constant time; in turn, this likely means preconfiguring each peer node with a maximum number of concurrent connections supported.

6 Related Work

A number of papers have addressed the issue of reputation and privacy.

There are many papers on reputation systems for peer-to-peer networks. Most focus on building distributed reputation systems, rather than worrying about privacy; [12] is typical.

The difficulty of building systems like this is outlined by Dingledine, Mathewson, and Syverson [10]. They present a number of similar systems and show why bolting on reputation is hard.

A typical approach is typified by [26], who incorporate privacy into their scheme. However, their system does not provide unlinkability. It also requires a trusted "observer" module for full functionality.

The work by Kinateder et al. [16,18] is close to ours. The system in [16] differs from ours in two notable ways. First, its reputations are linkable. Indeed, they see this as a virtue, in that recommendations can be weighted depending on the reputation of the recommender. Second, they assume a trusted hardware module (i.e., a TPM chip) on every endpoint. In [18], they describe a more general system based on UniTEC [17]. Reputation statements are signed by a pseudonym's private key. Unlinkability is achieved by switching public keys. Apparently, the UniTEC layer can share reputations between different pseudonyms, but the authors do not explain how this is done. Presumably, this is handled by bookkeeping at that layer. More seriously, although they assert that a trusted module is desirable but not necessary, they do not explain how that could work, and in particular how they can prevent cheating.

Pavlov et al. [22] present a system, based on secret-sharing, which has many of the same properties as ours. However, it depends on locating "witnesses", other parties with knowledge of the target's reputation. In a sufficiently-large community with a low density of interaction, this may be difficult. Furthermore, it does not provide unlinkability; witness testify about a known party's past behavior.

Another work related to ours is Voss [25] and Steinbrecher [23]. In both of the systems, users interact with each other through pseudonyms, and reputation is strongly connected to identities. In fact, in [25] reputation points are implemented as coins, which may have positive or negative value. However, in both cases, Trusted Third Parties[7] are required to ensure unlinkability between identities and pseudonyms.

Approaches other than reputation systems have also been presented to deal with misbehaving users in anonymous or pseudonymous systems. Belenkiy et al. [2] make use of endorsed e-cash to achieve fair and anonymous two-party protocol wherein parties buy or barter blocks of data. Whereas e-cash stands for reputation in our scheme, e-cash stands for actual money in their scheme; a peer uses e-cash to buy data from other peers. Johnson et al. [13] focus on protecting a service in Tor from a malicious user without blocking all the exit Tor nodes. In particular, they present a protocol where misbehaving anonymous users are blacklisted by servers.

7   Future Directions

A few interesting open problems remain.

First, our current scheme uses unit coins for reputation. That is, all reputation credits are worth the same amount. It would be nice to permit variable values; we suspect that this is easy.

More seriously, we do not have negative feedback. There is a vast difference between knowing that a seller has performed well on m transactions and knowing that that seller has performed well on m out of n. The difficulty is forcing the seller to commit to depositing a coin indicating bad behavior; most sellers know when they have done something wrong. In the technical report [1], we developed a partial solution. The scheme does not satisfy the complete unlinkability requirement stipulated in our definition, as Bank knows the number of transactions a peer had interacted in as a seller (modulo this information being leaked, all anonymity requirements are preserved).

---

[7] In [23] TTP appear in the form of designated identity providers.

Finally, we would like to get rid of the bank, which in our scheme is trusted to maintain reputation balances correctly (though not trusted from the privacy perspective). A fully decentralized scheme would eliminate single points of failure, and would be more in keeping with a widespread, anonymous, peer-to-peer network. Note that this would require two significant changes: using a digital cash scheme that does not require a central bank, and devising some other mechanism for inflation resistance.

Acknowledgment

We are grateful to Moti Yung for useful discussions regarding this work. We would like to thank Patrick Tsang, Apu Kapadia, and anonymous referees for helpful comments on the paper.

References

1. Androulaki, E., Choi, S.G., Bellovin, S.M., Malkin, T.: Reputation systems for anonymous networks. Technical Report CUCS-029-07, Computer Science Dept., Columbia University (2007), http://www.cs.columbia.edu/research/publications
2. Belenkiy, M., Chase, M., Erway, C.C., Jannotti, J., Küpçü, A., Lysyanskaya, A., Rachlin, E.: Making p2p accountable without losing privacy. In: WPES, pp. 31–40 (2007)
3. Belenkiy, M., Chase, M., Kohlweiss, M., Lysyanskaya, A.: P-signatures and noninteractive anonymous credentials. In: TCC, pp. 356–374 (2008)
4. Bhattacharjee, R., Goel, A.: Avoiding ballot stuffing in ebay-like reputation systems. In: P2PECON, pp. 133–137 (2005)
5. Camenisch, J., Hohenberger, S., Lysyanskaya, A.: Compact e-cash. In: Cramer, R.J.F. (ed.) EUROCRYPT 2005. LNCS, vol. 3494, pp. 302–321. Springer, Heidelberg (2005)
6. Camenisch, J., Lysyanskaya, A.: An efficient system for non-transferable anonymous credentials with optional anonymity revocation. In: Pfitzmann, B. (ed.) EUROCRYPT 2001. LNCS, vol. 2045, pp. 93–118. Springer, Heidelberg (2001)
7. Camenisch, J., Stadler, M.: Effcient group signature schemes for large groups. In: Kaliski Jr., B.S. (ed.) CRYPTO 1997. LNCS, vol. 1294, pp. 410–424. Springer, Heidelberg (1997)
8. Chaum, D.: Untraceable electronic mail, return addresses, and digital pseudonyms. Commun. ACM 24(2), 84–88 (1981)
9. Danezis, G., Serjantov, A.: Statistical disclosure or intersection attacks on anonymity systems. In: Information Hiding, pp. 293–308 (2004)
10. Dingledine, R., Mathewson, N., Syverson, P.: Reputation in p2p anonymity systems. In: Workshop on Economics of Peer-to-Peer Systems (2003)
11. Dingledine, R., Mathewson, N., Syverson, P.F.: Tor: The second-generation onion router. In: USENIX Security Symposium, pp. 303–320 (2004)
12. Gupta, M., Judge, P., Ammar, M.: A reputation system for peer-to-peer networks. In: NOSSDAV (2003)
13. Johnson, P.C., Kapadia, A., Tsang, P.P., Smith, S.W.: Nymble: Anonymous ip-address blocking. In: Privacy Enhancing Technologies, pp. 113–133 (2007)
14. Juels, A., Luby, M., Ostrovsky, R.: Security of blind digital signatures (extended abstract). In: Kaliski Jr., B.S. (ed.) CRYPTO 1997. LNCS, vol. 1294, pp. 150–164. Springer, Heidelberg (1997)
15. Kesdogan, D., Agrawal, D., Pham, V., Rautenbach, D.: Fundamental limits on the anonymity provided by the mix technique. In: S&P, pp. 86–99 (2006)

16. Kinateder, M., Pearson, S.: A privacy-enhanced peer-to-peer reputation system. In: EC-Web, pp. 206–215 (2003)
17. Kinateder, M., Rothermel, K.: Architecture and algorithms for a distributed reputation system. In: Nixon, P., Terzis, S. (eds.) iTrust 2003. LNCS, vol. 2692, pp. 1–16. Springer, Heidelberg (2003)
18. Kinateder, M., Terdic, R., Rothermel, K.: Strong pseudonymous communication for peer-to-peer reputation systems. In: SAC, pp. 1570–1576 (2005)
19. Lysyanskaya, A., Rivest, R., Sahai, A., Wolf, S.: Pseudonym systems. In: SAC, pp. 184–199 (1999)
20. Okamoto, T.: Provably secure and practical identification schemes and corresponding signature schemes. In: Brickell, E.F. (ed.) CRYPTO 1992. LNCS, vol. 740, pp. 31–53. Springer, Heidelberg (1993)
21. Øverlier, L., Syverson, P.F.: Locating hidden servers. In: S&P, pp. 100–114 (2006)
22. Pavlov, E., Rosenschein, J.S., Topol, Z.: Supporting privacy in decentralized additive reputation systems. In: Jensen, C., Poslad, S., Dimitrakos, T. (eds.) iTrust 2004. LNCS, vol. 2995, pp. 108–119. Springer, Heidelberg (2004)
23. Steinbrecher, S.: Design options for privacy-respecting reputation systems within centralised internet communities. In: SEC, pp. 123–134 (2006)
24. Syverson, P.F., Goldschlag, D.M., Reed, M.G.: Anonymous connections and onion routing. In: IEEE Symposium on Security and Privacy, pp. 44–54 (1997)
25. Voss, M.: Privacy preserving online reputation systems. In: International Information Security Workshops, pp. 245–260 (2004)
26. Voss, M., Heinemann, A., Muhlhauser, M.: A privacy preserving reputation system for mobile information dissemination networks. In: SECURECOMM, pp. 171–181 (2005)

A   An Example of Scheme Instantiation

In this section we give a specific instantiation of our scheme, where we make use of the anonymous credential system by Camenisch and Lysyanskaya [6] (denoted by CL), the e-cash scheme by Camenisch et al. [5] (denoted by CHL), and the blind signature scheme by Okamoto [20] (denoted by Ok). We do so in order to present a concrete and efficient construction (we include the efficiency analysis, relying on that of the underlying primitives, with each of the operations).

Setup(1^k)
Bank B does the setup as follows:

- B executes CHL.BKeygen(1^k) to generate an e-cash key pair (pk_B^{ec}, sk_B^{ec}), and publishes $pk_B^{ec} = (g_{ec}, \hat{g}_{ec}, \tilde{g}_{ec})$;
- B executes Ok.KeyGen(1^k) to generate a blind signature key pair (pk_B^{bs}, sk_B^{bs}) and publishes pk_B^{bs}.
- For each reputation group G_i $(1 \leq i \leq k)$, B executes CL.OKeyGen(1^k) to generate the anonymous credential system key pair $(pk_B^{ac_i}, sk_B^{ac_i})$ for G_i, and publishes $pk_B^{ac_i} = (n_{ac_i}, a_{ac_i}, b_{ac_i}, d_{ac_i}, g_{ac_i}, h_{ac_i})$.
- B creates a cyclic group $G_p = \langle g_p \rangle$ of order $p = \Theta(2^k)$ where the DDH assumption holds. This algebraic group is used for pseudonym generation on the peer's side.

On the peers' side, each peer U executes CHL.UKeyGen(1^k) to obtain (pk_U, sk_U) $= (g_{ec}^{x_U}, x_U)$, and publishes pk_U. Note that x_U will be used as the master secret key of

U in the anonymous credential system (and this discrete-log based key is a reasonable choice for a more general PKI key as well).

Operations

1. Generation of Pseudonyms. Each peer generates his pseudonyms locally using $\mathbb{G}_p$. Specifically, he chooses a random number $r_i \in \mathbb{Z}_p$ and compute $g_p^{r_i}$. The value $g_p^{r_i}$ is considered a pseudonym P_U^i of peer U.

2. RepCoin Withdrawal. A peer U executes CHL.Withdraw with Bank, and obtains a wallet W of 2^w repcoins. This procedure takes $O(1)$ exponentiations and $O(1)$ rounds.

3. Reputation Award. A pseudonym P_U gives a repcoin to P_M by executing CHL. Spend with P_M. This procedure also takes $O(1)$ exponentiations and $O(1)$ rounds.

4. Reputation Update.

4.1 Obtaining Blind Permission. A pseudonym P_M and Bank B participate in CHL.
Deposit protocol, which takes $O(1)$ exponentiations and $O(1)$ rounds. If CHL. Deposit accepts, P_M acquires the blind permission $\sigma_B^{bs} = \mathsf{Ok.Sign}(sk_B^{bs}, r_{perm})$ where r_{perm} is a random message. Obtaining the blind permission takes $O(1)$ exponentiations and $O(1)$ rounds.

4.2 Deposit of the Blind Permission. M (the owner of P_M) sends σ_B^{bs} to B. B checks if the permission $(r_{perm}, \sigma_B^{bs})$ is fresh; if so, it increases M's reputation value. This procedure takes $O(1)$ exponentiations and $O(1)$ rounds.

5. Reputation Demonstration. Suppose that a pseudonym P_U asks P_M to demonstrate its reputation level, and that M (the owner of P_M) wants to show to P_U that it belongs to G_i, i.e., his reputation is at least at level l_i.

- Obtaining a nym under G_i. M contacts Bank B and executes CL.FormNym with respect to G_i[8]. Let $N_M^{l_i}$ be the nym that M obtained from this procedure. Note that $N_M^{l_i}$ is of the form: $g_{ac_i}^{x_U} \cdot h_{ac_i}^{r}$. This takes $O(1)$ exponentiations and $O(1)$ rounds.
- Obtaining a credential for G_i. M contacts B, and he sends B the message $(pk_M, N_M^{l_i})$. Then, M executes with B a zero-knowledge proof of knowledge

$$PK\{(\alpha, \beta) : pk_M = g_{ec}^{\alpha}, N_M^{l_i} = g_{ac_i}^{\alpha} \cdot h_{h_i}^{\beta}\}.^9$$

This takes $O(1)$ exponentiations and $O(1)$ rounds.
  Now, B verifies the proof. If the proof is verified so that M is eligible for a credential of the group G_i, B executes the CL.GrantCred (protocol4) with respect to G_i. Let C_{l_i} be the output credential. This takes $O(1)$ exponentiations and $O(1)$ rounds.
- Showing reputation using the credential. P_M contacts P_U and executes CL. VerifyCred (protocol3) with respect to G_i to prove that owner of P_M has a credential for the group G_i. This takes $O(1)$ exponentiations and $O(1)$ rounds.

---

[8] We use both protocol1 and protocol6 of [6] instead of just protocol1 to ensure the non-transferability of credentials.

[9] This proof can be parsed as "I know the exponent α and β that was used in generating pk_M and $N_M^{l_i}$". See [7,6] for more detail. The proof can be regarded as an authentication procedure.

PAR: Payment for Anonymous Routing

Elli Androulaki[1], Mariana Raykova[1], Shreyas Srivatsan[1],
Angelos Stavrou[2], and Steven M. Bellovin[1]

[1] Columbia University
{elli,mariana,ss3249,smb}@cs.columbia.edu
[2] George Mason University
astavrou@gmu.edu

Abstract. Despite the growth of the Internet and the increasing concern for privacy of online communications, current deployments of anonymization networks depend on a very small set of nodes that volunteer their bandwidth. We believe that the main reason is not disbelief in their ability to protect anonymity, but rather the practical limitations in bandwidth and latency that stem from limited participation. This limited participation, in turn, is due to a lack of incentives to participate. We propose providing economic incentives, which historically have worked very well.

In this paper, we demonstrate a payment scheme that can be used to compensate nodes which provide anonymity in Tor, an existing onion routing, anonymizing network. We show that current anonymous payment schemes are not suitable and introduce a hybrid payment system based on a combination of the Peppercoin Micropayment system and a new type of "one use" electronic cash. Our system claims to maintain users' anonymity, although payment techniques mentioned previously – when adopted individually – provably fail.

1 Introduction

Anonymous networking has been known since 1981 [1]. A more practical scheme, Onion Routing, was first described in 1995 [2]. Currently there is little practical use of network anonymity systems. Some of the problem is undoubtedly sociological: most people do not feel the need to protect their privacy that way; this is one reason that companies such as Zero Knowledge Systems [3, 4] and Digicash [5] failed. Another problem, though, is that strong anonymity against traffic analysis requires cooperation by and implicit trust in many different parties. Any single entity, no matter how trustworthy it appears, can be subverted, whether by technical means, corrupt personnel, or so-called "subpoena attacks". All known solutions require, and in fact enforce, routing through multiple parties. This, though, introduces another problem: economic incentives. In a single-provider anonymity scheme, that problem is conceptually simple: the party desiring privacy pays a privacy provider. This payment can be protected by digital cash [6]. Unfortunately, in a multi-provider Mixnet or onion routing network, the problem is more complex, since each party must be paid. By examining existing digital cash schemes, we show that they do not provide the necessary cost or privacy

N. Borisov and I. Goldberg (Eds.): PETS 2008, LNCS 5134, pp. 219–236, 2008.

properties required to maintain anonymity. For example, in Chaum's original e-cash scheme [6] a double-spender's identity is exposed. This is perfectly acceptable – double-spending is a form of cheating that should be punished – but in the context of an onion routing network, detecting double spending gives an adversary clues to path setup.

To address these problems, we propose a novel hybrid payment scheme by combining features from Micali's micropayment system [7] and a lightweight, blind signature-based e-cash scheme. Our goal is to create incentives for the network participants to act in a cooperative manner based on their personal interests. We show that any solution must be sound in several dimensions. First, it must protect privacy. This is not trivial; witness the many (partial) attacks on various anonymous networking protocols [8, 9]. That said, we do not claim to have fixed those problems. Rather, our aim is avoid introducing any new vulnerabilities that stem from the payments scheme.

Second, we want a system that is in principle deployable. That is, though we assume such things as anonymous payment systems, we do not assume, for example, incorruptible banks. More importantly, we want a system that is compatible with known economic behavior. Therefore, while our system assumes that people are willing to pay for privacy, we want a system where customer payment – the profits of forwarding nodes – are related to privacy desired and effort expended. In essence, there must be a profit motive and the opportunity for market forces to work. To deter exploitation of the payment scheme, we provide mechanisms to detect cheaters: those parties who accept payment but do not provide services.

Third, we do not attempt to achieve absolute financial security. Instead, we are willing to accept small amounts of cheating, by senders or forwarders, as long as the amount is bounded and limited (possibly with some trade-off) by the party who is exposed to loss. Finally, we want a system that is acceptably efficient in practice and does not impose unreasonable resource consumption. To that end, we evaluate the operations of a prototype PAR – which stands for Payment for Anonymous Routing. Our initial performance evaluation indicates that PAR is highly configurable and can operate with acceptable communication and CPU overhead. As opposed to previous work on incentivised anonymity, which used mixnets ([10], [11], [12]), our system guarantees usable efficiency, accountability and maintains anonymity against traffic analysis attacks.

2   System Considerations

We will examine current anonymizing networks and payment schemes and show why current payment schemes, when applied to onion routing schemes, fail to maintain anonymizing network properties, while our hybrid scheme succeeds. Furthermore, we set up the threat model and we identify the individual components and the properties required by a payment scheme to provide the same protection the network anonymity system was designed for.

Anonymizing Network. An anonymizing network is a particular type of peer-to-peer network, in which peers communicate anonymously. Anonymizing

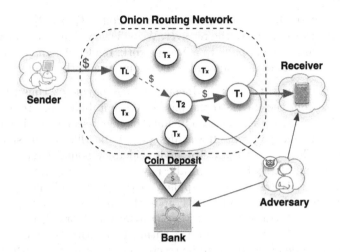

Fig. 1. The PAR architecture combines an onion routing anonymity network (Tor) with a payment scheme. Each node $T_1, T_2, T_3, \cdots, T_L$, where L is the path length, in the path from the sender to the receiver receives payment in coins for its service.

networks aim to offer sender anonymity even against the recipient as well as sender-receiver unlinkability. Neither the recipient nor any other participant should be able to detect the actual sender with a better probability than selecting the sender at random. As a proof of concept, we use Tor [13], the second generation onion routing anonymity network, a well-known and deployed network anonymity system.

Adversarial Model. The participating entities of our system are the Tor relays, the outside users, and a clearance entity, *i.e.* a Bank, where monetary units are deposited/withdrawn. We inherit Tor's local adversary model where users can only observe the traffic going through them and a limited amount of the rest of the network traffic. In addition, we assume that malicious users can manipulate any packet going through them and use this information to compromise anonymity. The Bank, on the other hand is assumed "honest but curious". Therefore, although trusted to be honest in all of its functional operations – cash withdraw and deposit – the Bank can collaborate with any number of users in order to disclose the initiator of a communication or active communication paths. We do not consider covert channels for anonymous communication with routers without paying as a part of our threat model.

System Requirements. Our primary requirement is that the overall system should maintain the anonymity provided by Tor even when the payment deposit information is exposed to a third party including the Bank. Anonymity, however, should not be achieved at the expense of efficiency. Moreover, the payment scheme should meet the requirement necessary for any payment system such as accountability, correctness, and robustness.

Payment Analysis. For our analysis, we classify current payment schemes in two categories: *Identity-bound payments* and *Anonymous payments*.

In Figure 1, the sender provides payment for all nodes $T_1, T_2, T_3, \cdots, T_L$[1] that forward the sender's traffic to the receiver. We will show that both of the current payment schemes, when applied to a Tor network, render the anonymity system vulnerable to attacks that compromise the anonymity of the senders.

Identity-bound Payment Schemes. Identity-bound payments constitute signed endorsements from the payer to the payee. Accountability and robustness are the two main features of this class. The micropayment scheme [7] is an example of an Identity-bound payment. It was designed to be efficient for small, online transactions. When used to pay Tor nodes, identity-bound payments provide immediate accountability because invalid payments from any entity can be easily accounted for. However, when applied in the context of the Tor network, this property has adverse implications: upon clearance, the Bank obtains global knowledge about all transactions in the anonymity network. If the sender uses his own coins to pay the nodes in the path, his identity is exposed to them. Therefore, any node in the path to the receiver can identify him with the help of the Bank. To make things worse, the last node in the path – who may suspect that he is the last node if the receiver is outside Tor – can link the sender to the receiver. A potential way to work around this problem is to distribute payments only to immediate neighbors. With this payment strategy, the sender pays T_L with L coins, T_L pays T_{L-1} with $L-1$ coins etc. This approach makes path tracing much harder and leaks less information but it is far from secure: deposits made by the sender to the first Tor node are still available to the Bank. Counting the coins bound to the sender's identity, the Bank can infer with high confidence the number of packets communicated to the sender and link the sender to the receiver. This analysis indicates that having identity-bound coins reveals too much information, enabling an adversary with access to payment information to break the system's anonymity using simple inference techniques.

Anonymous Payment Schemes. In this scheme, the payment does not carry any identification information of its initial owner. Chaum's Digital cash [6] and the later versions [14, 15, 16] of Tunstall et al. and Camenisch et al. are perfect examples of such anonymous payment schemes. In the general case of digital cash systems, a user withdraws money from a Bank, which he can only spend himself and which when legally spent can never be linked to his identity. Merchants deposit the coins they have received to check whether any of them has been spent more times than its nominal value (double-spending). If the later occurs, the identity of the double-spender is revealed. However, all the anonymous payment schemes demand excessive communication overhead for each transaction because there are a lot of messages that need to be exchanged between the sender and the path nodes.[2] This requirement makes e-cash schemes impractical for our system.

---

[1] In Tor, intermediate communication path nodes are chosen randomly by the communication initiator.

[2] In the compact e-cash payment scheme [16], which is considered efficient a single "spend" procedure in e-cash systems would requires at least two rounds of message exchange between the sender and every node in the path.

An alternative solution would be for all users to withdraw a special kind of anonymous coin from the Bank, which can simply be Bank blind endorsements [17], and use these coins to pay the intermediate Tor nodes. Ideal as it might initially seem, using a completely anonymous payment scheme with Tor has its drawbacks. First of all, there is no immediate accountability, since double-spending in this case will not reveal the double-spender. Thus, to prevent double-spending, any payments received should be immediately checked and deposited in the Bank. Unfortunately, immediate coin deposits could lead to deposit timing attacks exposing Tor's anonymity. More specifically, the timing of deposits by the nodes along a Tor path discloses to the Bank the path as well as an estimated of the number of packets transferred. Accumulating deposits for appropriately long time intervals – sufficiently long that many connections are established, to mitigate timing attacks – would increase the amount of unchecked coins and thus of double-spending. Indeed, since anonymous coins are not traceable beyond the first Tor node, sending valid coins only to the first node is enough to prevent it from been traced. For the rest of the nodes, the cheater uses double-spent coins, exploiting this deposit strategy by transmitting many packets in a short period of time.

Our Contribution: Hybrid Approach. Both of the two aforementioned classes of payment schemes have advantages and disadvantages. Our approach creates a hybrid payment scheme by combining the two payments methods into a single one. In particular, nodes outside the anonymizing network withdraw an initial number of anonymous coins (A-mcoins) from the Bank and use them to pay the first node in the Tor-path (T_L) they have chosen. T_L then uses micropayments[3] to pay T_{L-1}, who also uses micropayments to pay its neighbor. Each time, the amount of money paid decreases according to each node's price. Nodes participating in the Tor network follow the same protocol with the option to use either anonymous or micropayments for the first node in their forwarding path.

In addition, each of the payment coins in the scheme has a corresponding receipt and becomes valid only when it is submitted for deposit together with the receipt. As we will show in the following sections, our payment scheme combines all the desirable properties of the existing payment schemes, but without maintaining any of the problem each one of them causes when used individually and in this way it provides sender-receiver unlinkability along with accountability and efficiency.

3   High-Level Description of PAR Protocol

Here we provide a high-level description of our payment scheme. To help the reader, we start with a brief description of the Tor circuit setup; we then present our payment scheme.

---

[3] Identity-bound payment.

3.1   Tor

Tor is formed by a set of relay nodes (onion routers) that act as traffic indirection points. The region in the dotted lines in Figure 1 depicts a typical communication in Tor. Each onion router maintains a TLS [18] connection to every other onion router. To establish communication, the sender selects a random sequence of Tor relays to form a path to the receiver or what is called a circuit. In Figure 1, the sender selected nodes $T_1, T_2, T_3, \cdots T_L$, where L is the path length. The sender constructs circuits incrementally, by negotiating a symmetric key with each onion router on the path, one hop at a time. Initially, the sender contacts the first path node, T_L, and they both commit in a Diffie Hellman (DH) key agreement procedure. Once this initial circuit has been created, sender uses T_L to extend the circuit to T_{L-1}. In particular, T_L and T_{L-1} establish a circuit – through the TLS channel they share – which T_L relates to the one with the sender. Sender commits anonymously (using T_L as mediator) in a Diffie Hellman (DH) key exchange procedure with T_{L-1}. Repeating this process through the extended tunnel, the sender may add more Tor nodes to the circuit. At the final stage, the last node in the path, T_1, opens a data stream with the receiver and a regular TCP connection is established between the sender and the remote site's IP address. At the end of the circuit setup procedure, every relay in the path shares a secret key with the anonymous path initiator, as well as with each of his path neighbors. The key a path node shares with each of his neighbors is only used for securing their part in the communication path. Each transmitted Tor message along a path, contains an unencrypted header with a circuit ID and a multiply-encrypted payload. At each hop, the corresponding path node decrypts the payload – using the key that node and the sender share – and replaces the circuit ID with the one that corresponds to his circuit with next node in the path.

3.2   PAR

We introduce the hybrid payment scheme from the previous section to the Tor network; again, see Figure 1. In our scheme, payments are conducted between consecutive nodes on the forwarding paths and added inside the transmitted messages using an additional encryption layer. Each forwarding node T_i creates payment coins for its path successor T_{i-1} using sender S's directions and adds these payment coins to the onion message to be forwarded to T_{i-1}. Payment information is provided to each T_i through the secret channel it and the sender share. To avoid exposure as in Tor, T_i further encrypts the resulting message with the key it shares with its successor. To complete the payment transaction and for the coins to become valid, every relay node has to receive the receipts for its payment by its successor. Therefore, each node, other than the last one, upon validating the received message, sends to its predecessor the payment receipt. S controls the payments made along the forwarding path by supplying the receipts for all the coins used.

To avoid cheating, S provides each path node T_i with additional information for it to verify that the payment received from T_{i+1} is indeed valid. Receipts are forwarded to T_{i+1} if and only if the the payments are valid. Since the circuit is used in both directions (*i.e.* to both receive and transmit messages, the last node can either be pre-paid or paid after the delivery of the message by the sender depending on the acceptable bounded risk. In either approach misbehaving nodes will be detected within the first round of sent messages and will be excluded from the forwarding path, which will cause them more loss than the expected gain from fraudulent behavior and they will have no incentive for cheating.

The initial setup stage for Tor circuits will be extended with nodes sharing some hash function that will be used prevent third party manipulations in the payment protocol.

4   A Hybrid Payment Scheme

In this section, we present a detailed description of our payment protocol. However, before proceeding, we first define three properties required to preserve anonymity in an onion routing network:

Sender-Receiver Unlinkability. Let S be a user, who may or may not be a member of the anonymizing network, who sends a message M anonymously[4] to a user R. Then nobody except a global adversary, even with the collaboration of a third party and R, should be able to link sender and receiver or reveal the path between them.

Usable Efficiency. This refers to the fact that the overhead in the packet exchange for the payment scheme and the CPU overload with additional cryptographic operations will be reasonable and will not impede the normal functioning of the system

Accountability. This property ensures that any cheating node trying to forge messages or double-spend coins is caught and expelled from the network.

4.1   Payment Coins

We use two types of payments that consist of two parts: a payment part, which we will call a coin, and a receipt part. A coin becomes valid only when it is accompanied by the corresponding receipt. The receipt is a random number that is bound to the coin by incorporating its hash value in the coin. Thus a random number r serves as a receipt for the coin that contains the hash $H(r)$. Although similar in structure, the two types of payments have different properties and that is why they are named differently: micro-coins (*S-coins*) and anonymous coins (*A-coins*).

S-coins(Signed microcoins). S-coins are generated and used for payments between Tor participants. They are based on the micropayments introduced in

---

[4] Here, "anonymously" means "using the anonymizing network".

[7] but with the addition of receipts. An S-coin is an extension of a microcoin MC :

$$SC_{T_i \to T_j} = sig_{T_i}\{MC, H(r), T_j\}.$$

As in the microcoin case, an S-coin is strongly bound to both the identity of the node T_i, who generates it by signing its content, and the identity of the payee T_j. Finally, it contains the hash of the receipt $H(r)$ that makes the coin valid. The microcoin part of the S-coin MC contains the transaction details τ as well as a sequence number – according to micropayment scheme [7] – without containing any timing information.

S-coins inherit the properties of microcoins. Only a predetermined fraction of them are payable, while no participants in the payment scheme can find out in advance which coins will become payable.

A-coins (Anonymous coins). A-coins use the idea of e-cash ([6]). They are generated by the Bank upon users' requests. Users outside Tor buy a predetermined number of A-coins from the Bank and pay with them for using the anonymizing network. Members of Tor also acquire a number of A-coins and may also use them. All A-coins are of the form

$$AC(r) = sig_B\{r\},$$

where r is a random number generated by the User, and $sig_B\{r\}$ is the blind signature of the Bank of r. A-coins are all payable and subjected to double-spending checks.

4.2   Payment Protocol

Figure 2 presents in detail the messages exchanged in the payment protocol. We further analyze the individual protocol stages.

Initial Set-up. All nodes participating in Tor acquire a public-private signature key pair $(sk_U^s,\ pk_U^s)$ and a public-private encryption key pair $(sk_U^e,\ pk_U^e)$, used to interact with the other members in the network. Bank generates a blind signature key pair $(sk_B^b,\ pk_B^b)$ for signing A-coins. In addition to the hash H already used in Tor for integrity purposes, we establish another collision resistant hash function H_r for the coins' receipts. At the end of the circuit setup procedure in Tor, the sender shares with each node T_i in the path a secret key K_{ST_i} while any two consecutive nodes in a path share a secret key $K_{T_iT_{i+1}}$. In our system, the sender agrees with each path node on a hash function H_{ST_i}. The shared keys are used for communication encryption whereas the hash functions for integrity checks. We use M_k to denote message M encrypted under key K; $sig_U M$ is the signature of user U on M.

Payment Generation. A-coins are generated in cooperation with the Bank. When user U wants to obtain A-coins for payment, he generates a fixed set of

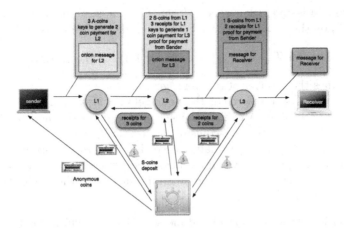

Fig. 2. The intuition behind our payment protocol is that Tor participants use S-coins to avoid exposing the forwarding path; outside senders, by contrast, use A-coins to maintain their anonymity

random numbers $r_1, r_2, \ldots, r_n$, which serve as the receipts for the coins. Then, the user submits to the Bank the hashes $H_r(r_1), H_r(r_2), \ldots, H_r(r_n)$ which in turn signs them and generates coins of the form:

$$AC_i = sig_B(H_r(r_i)).$$

The resulting A-coins can be used for payment to any node in the network.

In the case of S-coins, users can generate them but they have to specify the payee. When user U wants to pay a node T_i with an S-coin, he generates the random number receipt r and its microcoin-like part MC which consists of a number that increases by one per S-coin payed by U to T_i and no timing information at all. The final form of the S-coin is:

$$SC_{U \rightarrow T_i}(r) = sig_U(MC, H_r(r), T_i).$$

Communication Protocol Description. Let S send to R a message M through the path $T_\ell, \ldots, T_1$. The following sequence of payments occurs for the transfer of the message:

- S pays T_ℓ ℓ coins, which may be A-coins or S-coins. Nodes outside Tor can only pay by A-coins while Tor nodes can use either type of coin.
- each node T_{i+1} on the forwarding path pays its successor T_i i S-coins.

The sender S chooses the receipts that will be used by the nodes on the path to generate payments for their successors. It also sends proofs to each of the nodes T_i in the form $H_r(r_1), \ldots, H_r(r_i)$ where $r_1, \ldots, r_i$ will be the receipts for the coins the node will get from its predecessor.

A node T_{i+1} gets the receipt for its payment coins from its successor T_i on the path.

Exchanged Messages. The general form of the message that a node T_{i+1} sends to a node T_i on the forwarding path between sender and receiver is the following:

$$(\quad \{T_i, \quad \text{coins for } T_i, \quad sig_{T_{i+1}}\{H(\text{coins for } T_i)\}, \quad \{M_{S \to T_i}\}_{K_{ST_i}}\}_{K_{T_{i+1}T_i}} \quad)$$

- T_i specifies the receiver of the message
- "coins for T_i" is the payment the node gets for forwarding the packet. The coins here are either A-coins if the sender was an outside node and T_i is the first node in the path, or S-coins of the form $SC_{T_{i+1} \to T_i}$
- $sig_{T_{i+1}}\{H(\text{coins for } T_i)\}$ is mainly needed in the case of A-coins[5] and serves accountability purposes when double-spending has been detected and
- $\{M_{S \to T_i}\}_{K_{ST_i}}$ is the part of the onion message from the sender that has to be read by T_i.

Now consider the last part of the message $M_{S \to T_i}$, which has the following form:

$$(\quad T_{i-1}, \quad T_{i+1} \text{ receipt}, \quad \text{payment guarantee for } T_i,$$

$$\text{values for generation of coins for } T_{i-1}, \quad \{M_{S \to T_{i-1}}\}_{K_{ST_{i-1}}} \quad)$$

- T_{i-1} is the successor of T_i on the path
- the receipts for T_{i+1} are the random numbers that the sender generated encrypted with the key $K_{ST_{i+1}}$; T_i sends them back to its predecessor on the path
- the guarantees that T_i receives for its payment are of the form: $H_{ST_i}(r_1), \ldots, H_{ST_i}(r_j)$, where $r_1, \ldots, r_i$ will be the receipts for the coins he was paid with
- $\{M_{S \to T_{i-1}}\}_{K_{ST_{i-1}}}$ is the part of the onion message from the sender that has to be forwarded to T_{i-1}. In the case when T_i is the last node on the forwarding path, $M_{S \to T_{i-1}}$ is the message to the receiver.

After receiving its message from its predecessor, the node T_i acquires its payment, which is verified using the guarantees received from the sender. Then, it sends the receipts for T_{i+1} to its predecessor. Next, the node uses the values from the sender to generate payment coins for its successor T_{i-1}. It adds the coins to $\{M_{S \to T_{i-1}}\}_{K_{ST_{i-1}}}$, signs the whole resulting message and forwards it to its successor.

Deposit. The deposit of all coins is handled by the Bank, which checks their validity and depositability. The validity of S-coins can be checked immediately by each node which is paid with them while the validity of A-coins is established at the Bank that checks for double-spending. At each deposit time the nodes deposit all coins that they have received during the period. Detailed analysis of the deposit period is provided in a later section. Here, we define the procedure for deposit. Coins are considered for deposit if and only if they are accompanied by

---

[5] It can be eliminated in the case of S-coins.

the corresponding receipt. The valid coins will be handled in two different ways: The deposit of S-coins is, in essence, a deposit of the underlying microcoins. This means that only a fraction of them will become depositable [7]. All A-coins are depositable at their nominal value.

4.3 Discussion

We preserve Tor's anonymity by allowing each node on the path to know only its predecessor and its successor. To this end, we harness the layered structure of the message passed by the sender to the forwarding path and the fact that payments are made between consecutive nodes. However, the sender still has control of the payments made along the path by sending the receipts used for their generation. A node that attempts to cheat can be easily identified by its successor. Since the successor holds the receipts for the cheater's payment there is no incentive for the cheater to either mangle or drop the message. Finally, Tor encryption guarantees both the confidentiality and integrity of all transmitted messages.

5 Security Analysis

There has been a wealth of research related to attacks against onion routing systems including Tor. Our goal is to ensure that PAR does not introduce new types of attacks, especially ones that can target either the anonymity or the robustness of an onion routing system. In addition, we prove the security properties of PAR using the augmented Tor threat model introduced earlier.

Sender-Receiver Unlinkability and Deposit Rate
We provide a formal model of information leakage of the payment scheme that can expose anonymity when combined with known attacks against anonymity networks. Although two differentiable types of payments are used in PAR this does not bring any higher risk than currently exists in Tor for the identity of the senders, which can be recognized as such if they use A-coins. The reason for this is that only nodes outside the system are required to pay the first node in their forwarding path with A-coins and currently lists of the relay nodes in Tor are publicly available and therefore outside nodes using the anonymizing system can be also recognized by the first relay that they use.

We will consider attacks that have access to the deposit information in addition to corrupted nodes. In our payment scheme, the Bank can be considered a global adversary since it observes the deposits of coins made at all nodes. That is why in the analysis of possible attacks we will speak in terms of whether the Bank can disclose any of the anonymization that occurs in Tor's forwarding paths, with or without cooperation from malicious nodes.

The most serious type of attack for an anonymization network is one that manages to link senders and receivers communicating over the network. Since the senders using PAR pay with anonymous coins if they are outside nodes, the Bank cannot identify the start of the path that they choose to use. If the sender is a Tor node that forwards other traffic as well, the payments for all of its own and forwarded traffic are indistinguishable; hence the Bank cannot trace the traffic originating at the node just by observing deposits. The receivers are also unidentifiable by the Bank, since there is no monetary transaction between the last node and the receiver.

We have shown that the Bank by itself cannot link sender and receiver. Now we must consider the question whether an adversary observing the deposits can obtain partial information about a forwarding path by discovering three consecutive inside nodes in the path, i.e., being able to guess to where a node forwards packets received from a particular predecessor. Consecutive nodes in a path can be inferred from the signed coins deposits, but the only thing that this means is that there is at least one path that has that pair; nothing more is learned about which connection this path serves.

For the purposes our analysis let $cp^{T,\tilde{T},i}_{<T_\ell,...,T_1>}$ be the packets transferred on a connection path such that $T = T_i$ and $\tilde{T} = T_{i-1}$. We denote the packets on all connection paths that have $\tilde{T}$ as a successor of T by

$$C(T,\tilde{T}) = \{cp^{T,\tilde{T},i}_{<T_{i_l},...,T_{i_1}>} | 1 < i \leq \ell\}.$$

Then the number of coins that a node $\tilde{T}$ will receive from T will be

$$G(T,\tilde{T}) = \sum_{\forall cp^{T,\tilde{T},i}_{<T_\ell,...,T_1>} \in C(T,\tilde{T})} i * c^{T,\tilde{T},i}_{<T_\ell,...,T_1>}.$$

If we denote the number of anonymous coins that a node T deposits with $G_{ac}(T)$, we can calculate the number of packets forwarded by T (assuming that a node is paid with one coin for each packet forwarded):

$$\sum_{T'} G(T',T) + G_{ac}(T) - \sum_{T''} G(T,T'').$$

In order to hide the exact number of packets that it has forwarded, a node can deposit some of its own anonymous coins; thus the above expression will no longer be a correct estimate. Not knowing the rate of packet transfer nor the number of connections in which two nodes are consecutive, an adversary cannot receive enough information just from the deposits of coins to determine three consecutive nodes in a path.

Let us now assume that there is a malicious node that colludes with the Bank in order to reveal more about a path. The malicious node can disclose his predecessor and his successor on a particular connection path, as well as his position in that path. Let $T = T_i$ be such a malicious node in the path $T_\ell, ..., T_1$. Now the adversary can find out who are the nodes T_{i+1} and T_{i-1} and the number of packets k that T_i forwarded on that connection. The only thing that it can infer about the identities of T_{i+2} and T_{i-2} is that if

$$(i - 1) * k > G(T_{i-1}, \tilde{T}) \tag{1}$$

then the node $\tilde{T}$ cannot be a successor of T_{i-1} and similarly if

$$(i + 1) * k > G(\tilde{T}, T_{i+1}) \qquad (2)$$

$\tilde{T}$ cannot be a predecessor of T_{i+1}. This is true only if we assume that the connections among different nodes have the same forwarding rate. Thus the chance of the adversary finding out anything more about the path than what it would have found out from a malicious node in Tor without any payments is very small.

In the discussion above we have made an implicit assumption that the deposits of coins occur at certain intervals during which enough connections have been established. The statement "enough connections" means that there are no cases where only one node deposits another node's signed coins and it is clearly its successor in any connection. Also, we minimize the probability of Eq. 1 or Eq. 2 being true.

Deposit Rate. Now we give an estimate of what we consider "enough" connections and packets transferred during a deposit period. The situation in which an adversary may eliminate a link between two Tor nodes as being part of the path transferring the packets on a particular connection is when the payments made for that link are not enough for the packets that were expected to be sent on the connection. To avoid such situation, we want the expected payments made for packets forwarded along a link between any nodes during a deposit period to exceed the expected payment for the packets forwarded on a single connection.

Let us assume that there are N packets sent across a network consisting of n nodes over C connections during a deposit interval. Let L be the average length of the forwarding path. Then since the probability of a node being in any position on the path is $\frac{1}{n}$, the expected payment that a node will get per packet sent over PAR will be

$$\frac{1}{n}(1 + \ldots + L) = \frac{L * (L + 1)}{2n}$$

Now considering that every node will forward on average $\frac{N}{n}$ packets, a node will be paid $\frac{N*L*(L+1)}{2n^2}$, which distributed across the $n-1$ edges going out of it yields $\frac{N*L*(L+1)}{2n^2*(n-1)}$ payment per edge. At the same time the average payment made for the packets on a connection is $\frac{N*L*(L+1)}{2C}$.

We observe that for

$$\frac{N * L * (L + 1)}{2n^2 * (n - 1)} > \frac{N * L * (L + 1)}{2C}$$

to hold, we need $O(n^3)$ connections across the whole network or an average of $O(n^2)$ connections per node. We stress that with so many connections, an adversary would not be able to eliminate even a single possible path route for a given connection. If we now consider the situation when the adversary can narrow the possible successors of a particular node down to some number n_c, there are still n_c^ℓ possible paths for the connection. However in this case we would want

$$\frac{N * L * (L + 1)}{2n^2 * n_c} > \frac{N * L * (L + 1)}{2C}$$

and we will need a total of $O(n^2)$ connections across the network or $O(n)$ per node.

In previous discussion we mentioned that each node may deposit some of its own anonymous coins to provide more anonymity of the traffic it is forwarding. We now point out that by having each node deposit anonymous coins we will additionally disguise the entry points for outside traffic being forwarded in the network. Since the ratio of anonymous and signed coins in the payment scheme is $\frac{2}{L-1}$, to preserve this ratio across all nodes each node should add its own anonymous coins to maintain the same deposit ratio.

Usable Efficiency. The efficiency of our payment scheme is comparable to that of micropayments [7, 19]: the majority of the payment coins in our system are signed coins based on microcoins with the additions of receipts. These are much more efficient than ecash [6], which requires zero knowledge proofs. (Even our anonymous coins are lightweight blind signatures.)

Accountability. The accountability property requires that the identity of a node that behaves maliciously – double-spending, forging attempts, message manipulation, etc. – will be revealed along with a proof of his guilt.

No node can tamper with the forwarded onion message since it is protected with layers of encryption that can be opened only in the corresponding order. Thus any attempt for forgery will be exposed by its successor. In addition, no double spending is possible for S-coin payments. Each of the coins is a signature by the spender; furthermore, it specifies the receiver and the payment details.

Double spending for anonymous coins is possible and can only be detected at deposit procedure. However, messages containing A-coins, contain also signed hashes of the coins, which serve as proof of A-coins' origin if a double-spending has occurred. Thus, the nodes paid with the same coin have an proof for the misbehavior.

There is an issue of whether maintaining logs of coin related message exchanges is necessary after coins' deposit for satisfying accountability in our system. Indeed, keeping some A-coin/S-coin related logs is required to detect malicious actions by the spender/payee; In particular Bank is required to keep a log of the serial numbers of the A-coins that have been deposited so far and as well as the biggest serial number of S-coins each pair of peers has exchanged. The A-coins exchanges are required to be maintained for detecting the double-spender but only for the time of one deposit period.

Thus far, we have showed that our payment scheme abides by its design principles. We now prove that it still satisfies properties common for any viable payment scheme.

Correctness. When all participants act honestly and follow the protocol, our payment scheme fulfills its goals: all packets are delivered, the nodes on the forwarding path are paid, and the anonymity of the sender and receiver is maintained. If all nodes properly forward the onion message that is initiated by the sender it is guaranteed to reach its receiver because each forwarding node knows where exactly to send it. According to the payment scheme, each node receives exactly one coin more than it has to pay its successor per packet. Thus all nodes are paid equally for their service. We have already shown that payments observed by the Bank are not enough to compromise the anonymity of the identities of sender and receiver.

Robustness. Robustness refers to the probability that the path chosen by the sender will be secure in the presence of malicious parties in the network. Let us assume that the fraction of malicious nodes is α. Then the probability that there is no malicious node on a path of length l is $(1 - \alpha)^l$. The computed probability, however, is important for the case when we assume that a malicious mode on the path prevents the traffic, i.e. it drops or misdirects it. This also holds in Tor with no payments. Now we restrict our attention to malicious nodes only in the context of the payment system, i.e. nodes that may expose the connections going through them and the corresponding payments for them. Based on our analysis showing that a node acting in this malicious way can disclose its predecessor and successor in the forwarding path, at least half of the nodes on a path will have to be malicious in order to expose the identities of sender and receiver. Thus the probability of preserving the anonymity of sender and receiver over a path of length l is $(1 - \alpha)^{l/2}$.

Monetary Unforgeability. No coin forgery is possible in the payment scheme since both types of coins are protected with signatures. Signed coins contain personal signatures of the payer; anonymous coins contain the Bank's signatures.

6   System Performance Evaluation

In this section, we quantify the computational overhead added to Tor by our payment scheme. We execute the `openssl speed` command 1000 times and compute the average estimated running time of blind and digital signatures (RSA), and symmetric key encryption and hashes (SHA1). We will focus on the overhead imposed on the communication initiator S as well as on a random path node T_i.

We define c_h to be the cost of a hash function, c_e the cost of a symmetric encryption procedure, and $c_s(c_{bs})$ and $c_{vs}(c_{bvs})$ the (blind) signature and (blind) signature verification cost. For 1024 byte messages hashed with SHA1, $c_h = 0.0045$ milliseconds. For CBC DES encryption[6] in blocks of 256 bytes and RSA signature and verification in blocks of 1024 bytes the estimated running times are $c_e = 0.020$, $c_s = 3.361$, and $c_{sv} = 0.142$ milliseconds. Assume a path of length L. For each payment round, S has to generate L receipts for the required A-mcoins and have them blindly signed by the Bank, and symmetrically encrypt the A-mcoins' receipts with $K_{ST_{L-1}}$. In addition, S should calculate the content

---

[6] We used DES for our tests, precisely because it is slower than AES; we wished to set a lower bound on performance.

of S-mcoins that each path node T_i will pay its successor T_{i-1}, and encrypt the receipts with $K_{ST_{i-1}}$ key. Thus the overall computational cost for S for each payment round would be:

$$Cost_S = L * (c_{bs} + c_h + c_e) + \frac{L * (L - 1)}{2} * (c_h + c_e)$$

For the usual case of $L = 4$, $Cost_S$ averages to 14.24 milliseconds overall, or to 1.4 milliseconds per coin to be paid.

On the other hand, each node T_i in the path, should create $i - 1$ for T_{i-1}'s S-mcoins and verify the validity of S-mcoins it received by T_{i+1} (signature verification and receipt):

$$Cost_{T_i} = i * (c_{vs} + c_h) + (i - 1) * c_s$$

In this case T_i will have to spend 0.045 milliseconds for each coin it gets payed and 3.36 milliseconds for each coin it pays.

The performance impact of our scheme is dominated by two factors: the path length and the number of packets per payment. However, the two have very different properties. The number of packets per payment, N, represents the tradeoff between performance and risk. By setting N high, the total cost of our scheme is minimized, since the expense is amortized over a large number of transmissions. However, N also represents how willing nodes are to transmit packets without assurance of payment. If N is too high, a cheater can send a fair amount of data before being caught. Minimizing that risk requires setting N low, and hence increasing the cost.

7   Related Work

Previous research on applying payments in anonymizing networks was focused on mixnets: Franz, et al [10], Figueiredo et al. [11] and Reiter et al. [12] all use a blind signature type of electronic cash to induce mixes to operate honestly. The approach of Franz et al. divides electronic payment and messages into small chunks and allows mixes and users to do the exchange step-by-step, which made the resulting system extremely inefficient. Furthermore, the receiver is required to participate in the payment procedure, which is undesirable: the receiver may not know or care about Tor. Figueiredo provided a completely anonymous payment system for mixnets, but without any accountability and robustness. Reiter et al. proposed a fair exchange protocol for connection-based and message-based mixnets. However, their protocol assumes that mixes would work properly to receive their payment after they commit to their service. They do not provide any guarantee that participants will indeed get paid beyond the fact that the initiator will have no reason for not paying them. Furthermore, computationally expensive offline zero knowledge computations are required in the case of a message-based mixnet protocol [20], which renders the system inefficient and thus currently non-deployable.

8   Conclusions

Current anonymity networks appear to lack wide participation due to their volunteer nature. We posit that by providing economic incentives, we can help incentivize users to both participate and to use anonymity networks to protect their communications. Unfortunately, current payment schemes cannot be used to enable payments in Tor. To address this, we introduce a novel hybrid scheme and prove that it is possible to add a secure payment scheme to an onion-based anonymity network. Our approach combines features of existing payment schemes in an innovative way, achieving provable sender-receiver unlinkability, accountability and efficiency at the same time.

Furthermore, we relate the anonymity of the overall architecture to the amount of traffic that has been forwarded through the network and the number of Tor relays. To avoid exposure, we provide initial lower-bound on the minimum payment deposit time required. Additionally – and similar to Tor – it appears that longer paths have a higher risk of including malicious nodes that may try to expose sender and receiver. On the other hand, shorter paths are more robust, incurring lower communication and computation overhead. These two limitations, namely the path length and the presence of malicious nodes, are also part of the underlying Tor network and reasonable parameters for the scheme can minimize their effect. Finally, a preliminary evaluation of our scheme indicates that PAR does not incur prohibitive communication and computational costs that could prevent its practical deployment.

Acknowledgment

We are grateful to Steven Murdoch and the referees for useful remarks and suggestions regarding this work.

References

1. Chaum, D.L.: Untraceable Electronic Mail, Return Addresses, and Digital Psuedonyms. Communications of the ACM (1981)
2. Goldschlag, D.M., Reed, M.G., Syverson, P.F.: Hiding routing information. In: Anderson, R. (ed.) IH 1996. LNCS, vol. 1174, pp. 137–150. Springer, Heidelberg (1996)
3. Back, A., Goldberg, I., Shostack, A.: Freedom systems 2.1 security issues and analysis. White paper, Zero Knowledge Systems, Inc. (May 2001)
4. Boucher, P., Shostack, A., Goldberg, I.: Freedom systems 2.0 architecture. Zero Knowledge Systems, Inc. (December 2000)
5. Chaum, D.: Achieving Electronic Privacy. Scientific American, 96–101 (August 1992)
6. Chaum, D., Fiat, A., Naor, M.: Untraceable electronic cash. In: Goldwasser, S. (ed.) CRYPTO 1988. LNCS, vol. 403. Springer, Heidelberg (1990)
7. Micali, S., Rivest, R.L.: Micropayments revisited. In: CT-RSA, pp. 149–163 (2002)

8. Øverlier, L., Syverson, P.: Locating hidden servers. In: Proceedings of the IEEE Symposium on Security and Privacy (2006)
9. Kesdogan, D., Agrawal, D., Pham, V., Rautenbach, D.: Fundamental limits on the anonymity provided by the mix technique. In: Proceedings of the IEEE Symposium on Security and Privacy (2006)
10. Franz, E., Jerichow, A., Wicke, G.: A payment scheme for mixes providing anonymity. In: Lamersdorf, W., Merz, M. (eds.) TREC 1998. LNCS, vol. 1402, pp. 94–108. Springer, Heidelberg (1998)
11. Figueiredo, D.R., Shapiro, J.K., Towsley, D.: Using payments to promote cooperation in anonymity protocols (2003)
12. Reiter, M.K., Wang, X., Wright, M.: Building reliable mix networks with fair exchange. In: ACNS, pp. 378–392 (2005)
13. Dingledine, R., Mathewson, N., Syverson, P.: Tor: The second-generation onion router. In: Proceedings of the 13th USENIX Security Symposium (August 2004)
14. Tunstall, J.: Electronic currency. In: Proceedings of the IFIP WG 11.6 International Conference (October 1989)
15. Hayes, B.: Anonymous one-time signatures and flexible untracable electronic cash. In: AusCrypt 1990: A Workshop on Cryptology, Secure Communication and Computer Security (January 1990)
16. Camenisch, J., Hohenberger, S., Lysyanskaya, A.: Compact e-cash. In: Cramer, R.J.F. (ed.) EUROCRYPT 2005. LNCS, vol. 3494, pp. 302–321. Springer, Heidelberg (2005)
17. Okamoto, T.: Efficient blind and partially blind signatures without random oracles. In: Halevi, S., Rabin, T. (eds.) TCC 2006. LNCS, vol. 3876, pp. 80–99. Springer, Heidelberg (2006)
18. Dierks, T., Allen, C.: The TLS protocol version 1.0. RFC 2246 (January 1999)
19. Rivest, R.: Peppercoin micropayments. In: Juels, A. (ed.) FC 2004. LNCS, vol. 3110, pp. 2–8. Springer, Heidelberg (2004)
20. Clarke, I., Sandberg, O., Wiley, B., Hong, T.W.: Freenet: A Distributed Anonymous Information Storage and Retrieval System. In: International Workshop on Design Issues in Anonymity and Unobservability (2001)

Author Index